AF371828

Origami Symphony No. 2

Trio of Sharks & Playful Prehistoric Mammals

Books by John Montroll
www.johnmontroll.com
Instagram: @montrollorigami

Origami Symphonies

Origami Symphony No. 1: The Elephant's Trumpet Call
Origami Symphony No. 2: Trio of Sharks & Playful Prehistoric Mammals
Origami Symphony No. 3: Duet of Majestic Dragons & Dinosaurs
Origami Symphony No. 4: Capturing Vibrant Coral Reef Fish
Origami Symphony No. 5: Woodwinds, Horns, and a Moose
Origami Symphony No. 6: Striped Snakes Changing Scales

General Origami

Origami Fold-by-Fold
DC Super Heroes Origami
Origami Worldwide
Teach Yourself Origami: Second Revised Edition
Christmas Origami: Second Edition
Storytime Origami
Origami Inside-Out: Third Edition

Animal Origami

Dogs in Origami
Perfect Pets Origami
Dragons and Other Fantastic Creatures in Origami
Bugs in Origami
Horses in Origami
Origami Birds
Origami Gone Wild
Dinosaur Origami
Origami Dinosaurs for Beginners
Prehistoric Origami: Dinosaurs and other Creatures: Third Edition
Mythological Creatures and the Chinese Zodiac Origami
Origami Sea Life: Third Edition
Bringing Origami to Life: Second Edition
Origami Sculptures: Fourth Edition
African Animals in Origami: Third Edition
North American Animals in Origami: Third Edition
Origami for the Enthusiast: Second Edition

Geometric Origami

Origami Stars
Galaxy of Origami Stars: Second Edition
Origami and Math: Simple to Complex: Second Edition
Origami & Geometry
3D Origami Platonic Solids & More: Second Edition
3D Origami Diamonds
3D Origami Antidiamonds
3D Origami Pyramids
A Plethora of Polyhedra in Origami: Third Edition
Classic Polyhedra Origami
A Constellation of Origami Polyhedra
Origami Polyhedra Design

Dollar Bill Origami

Dollar Origami Treasures: Second Edition
Dollar Bill Animals in Origami: Second Revised Edition
Dollar Bill Origami
Easy Dollar Bill Origami

Simple Origami

Fun and Simple Origami: 101 Easy-to-Fold Projects: Second Edition
Origami Twelve Days of Christmas: And Santa, Too!
Super Simple Origami
Easy Dollar Bill Origami
Easy Origami 2
Easy Origami Animals
Easy Origami Polar Animals
Easy Origami Ocean Animals
Easy Origami Woodland Animals
Easy Origami Jungle Animals
Meditative Origami

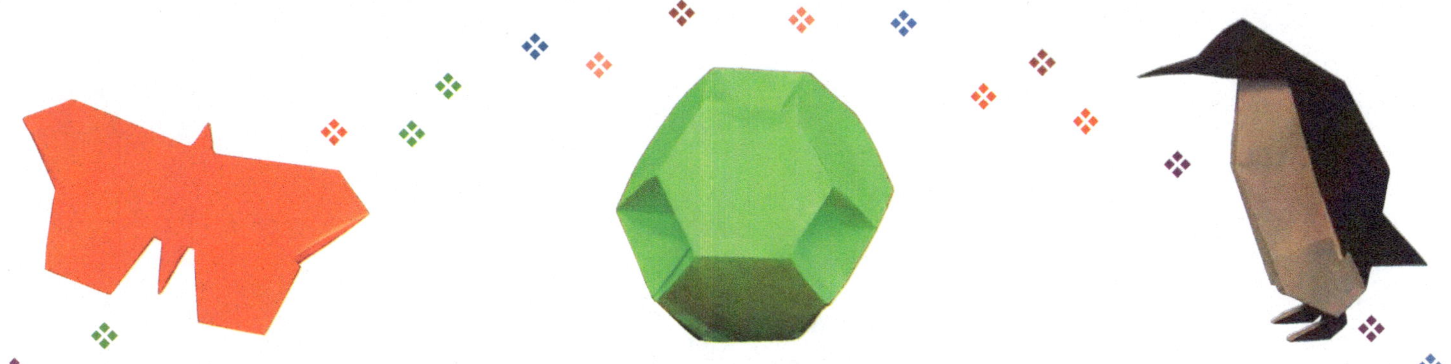

Origami Symphony No. 2

Trio of Sharks & Playful Prehistoric Mammals

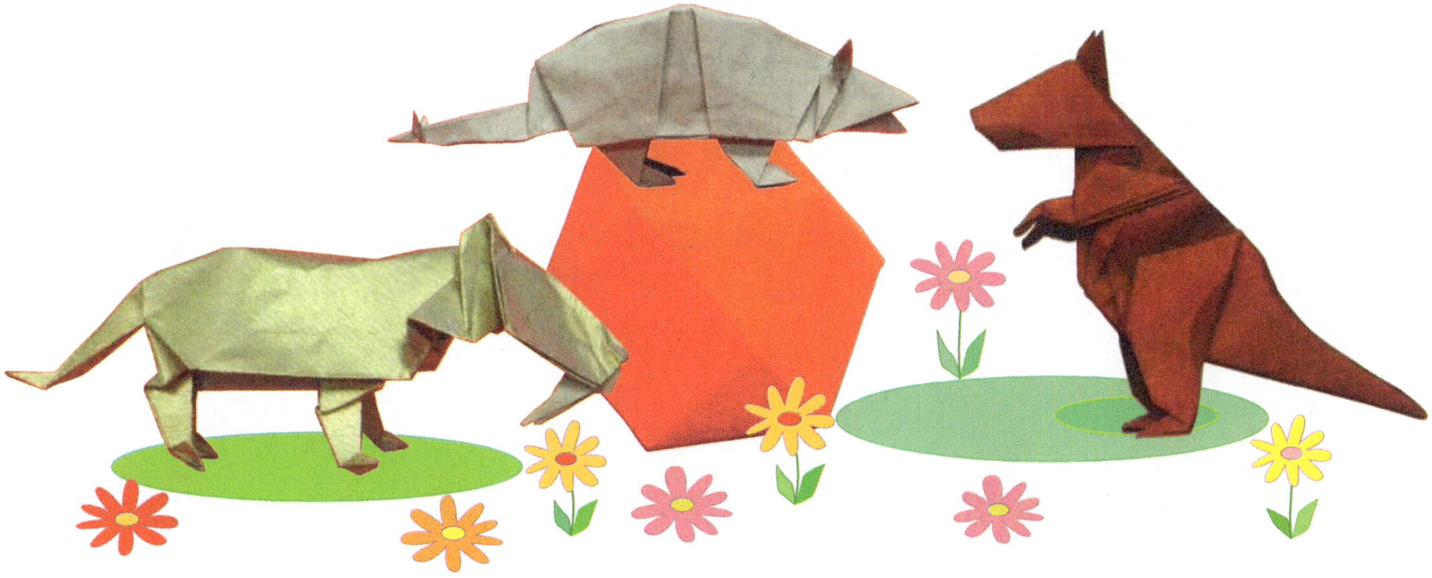

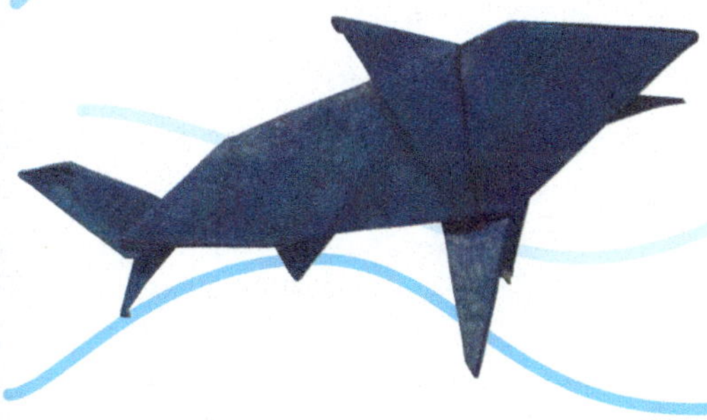

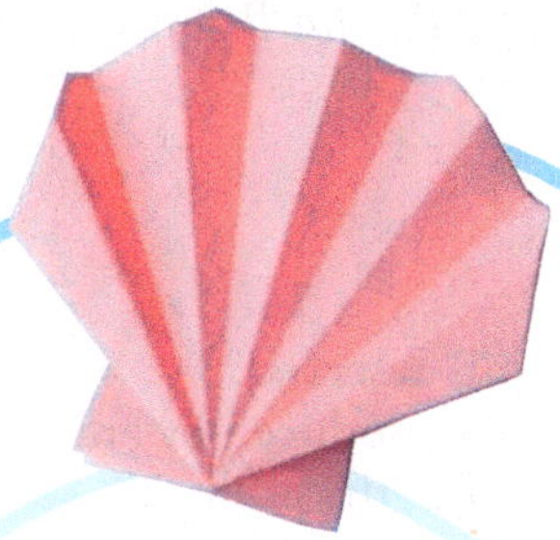

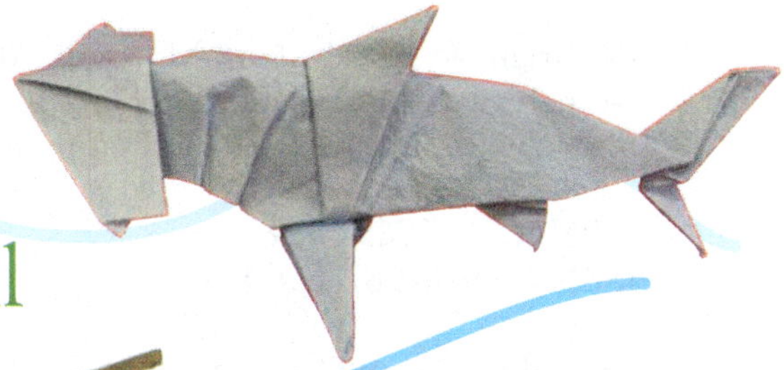

John Montroll

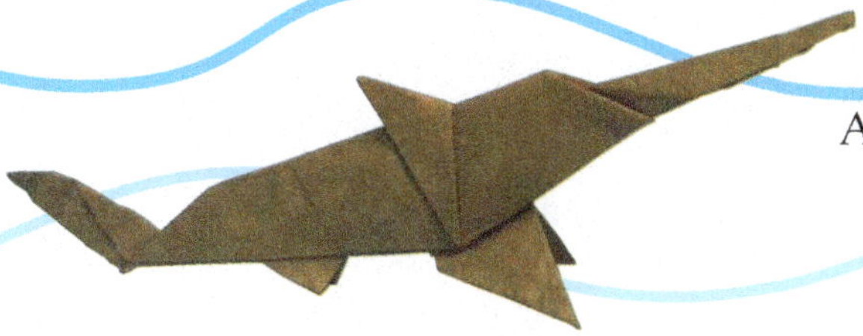

Antroll Publishing Company

Origami Symphony No. 2: *Trio of Sharks & Playful Prehistoric Mammals*

Copyright © 2019 by John Montroll. All rights reserved.
No part of this publication may be copied or reproduced by any
means without the express written permission of the author.

ISBN-10: 1-877656-48-8
ISBN-13: 978-1-877656-48-4

Antroll Publishing Company

Introduction

Welcome to the world premier of the Second Origami Symphony! Just as in a musical symphony, an origami symphony is an elaborate composition that usually has four movements of various themes and styles that flow together. As the musical symphony brought music to new heights, I wish to do the same for origami.

The four movements of this symphony show a wide range of styles, subjects, and levels of difficulty. The symphony opens with the first movement, Allegro Agitato, Sharks in the Sea. With a simple Sailboat and a colorful Ocean Liner, we journey into the sea to watch Flyingfish, Dolphins, Orcas, and Sharks. After the scary Sharks, we relax with the peaceful creatures from the second movement, Andante, Dulce. These playful creatures are depicted as intermediate level designs, and includes a Dove, Butterfly, Unicorn, Sheep, Panda, and Koala Bear. The models become more complex in the third movement, Minuet of Dimpled Polyhedra with a Trio of Archimedean Solids. The fourth movement ends the symphony with the March of the Prehistoric Mammals. A playful Megatherium, Glyptodon, Woolly Mammoth and more come to life as we remember them.

Each of the 38 models of this symphony are folded from a single uncut square. All can be folded from standard origami paper. Many models use my special techniques that keep them relatively simple for the complexity of their shape. This gives the models a life-like quality. The diversity of styles throughout the symphony highlight the richness of origami.

The diagrams are drawn in the internationally approved Randlett-Yoshizawa style. You can use any kind of square paper for these models, but the best results will be achieved with standard origami paper, which is colored on one side and white on the other (in the diagrams in this book, the shading represents the colored side). Large sheets, such as nine inches squared, are easier to use than small ones.

Origami supplies can be found in arts and craft shops, or at Dover Publications online: www.doverpublications.com. You can also visit OrigamiUSA at www.origamiusa.org for origami supplies and other related information including an extensive list of local, national, and international origami groups.

Please follow me on Instagram @montrollorigami to see posts of my origami.

I thank Ian Patzman-Rivard and John Paul Libanati for the photography. I thank my editor, Charley Montroll. I also thank the many folders who continued to encourage me to develop the presentation of origami through an origami symphony.

I hope you enjoy this playful origami symphony.

John Montroll
www.johnmontroll.com

Contents

★ Simple
★★ Intermediate
★★★ Complex

First Movement
Allegro Agitato: Sharks in the Sea

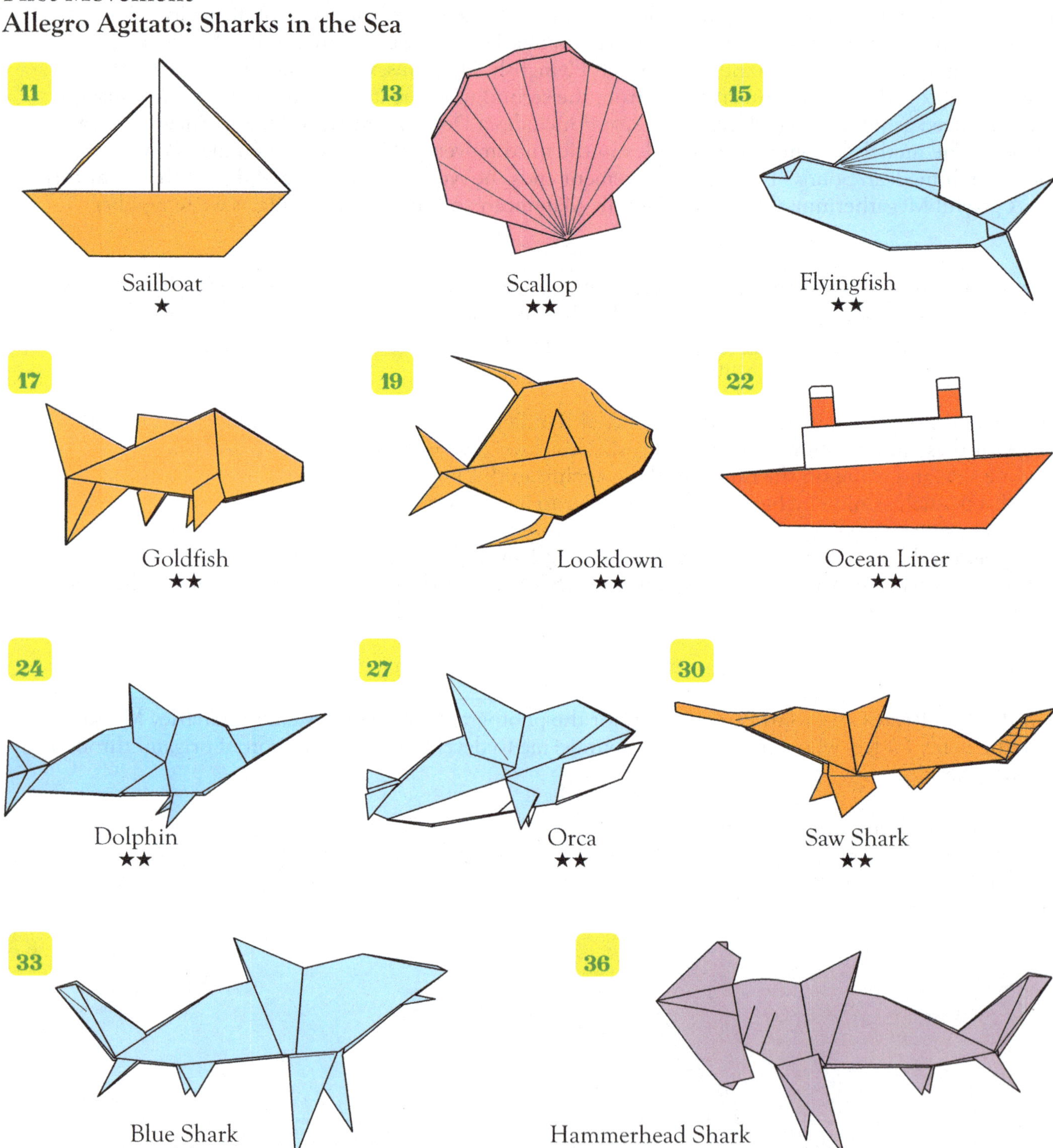

11 Sailboat ★

13 Scallop ★★

15 Flyingfish ★★

17 Goldfish ★★

19 Lookdown ★★

22 Ocean Liner ★★

24 Dolphin ★★

27 Orca ★★

30 Saw Shark ★★

33 Blue Shark ★★

36 Hammerhead Shark ★★

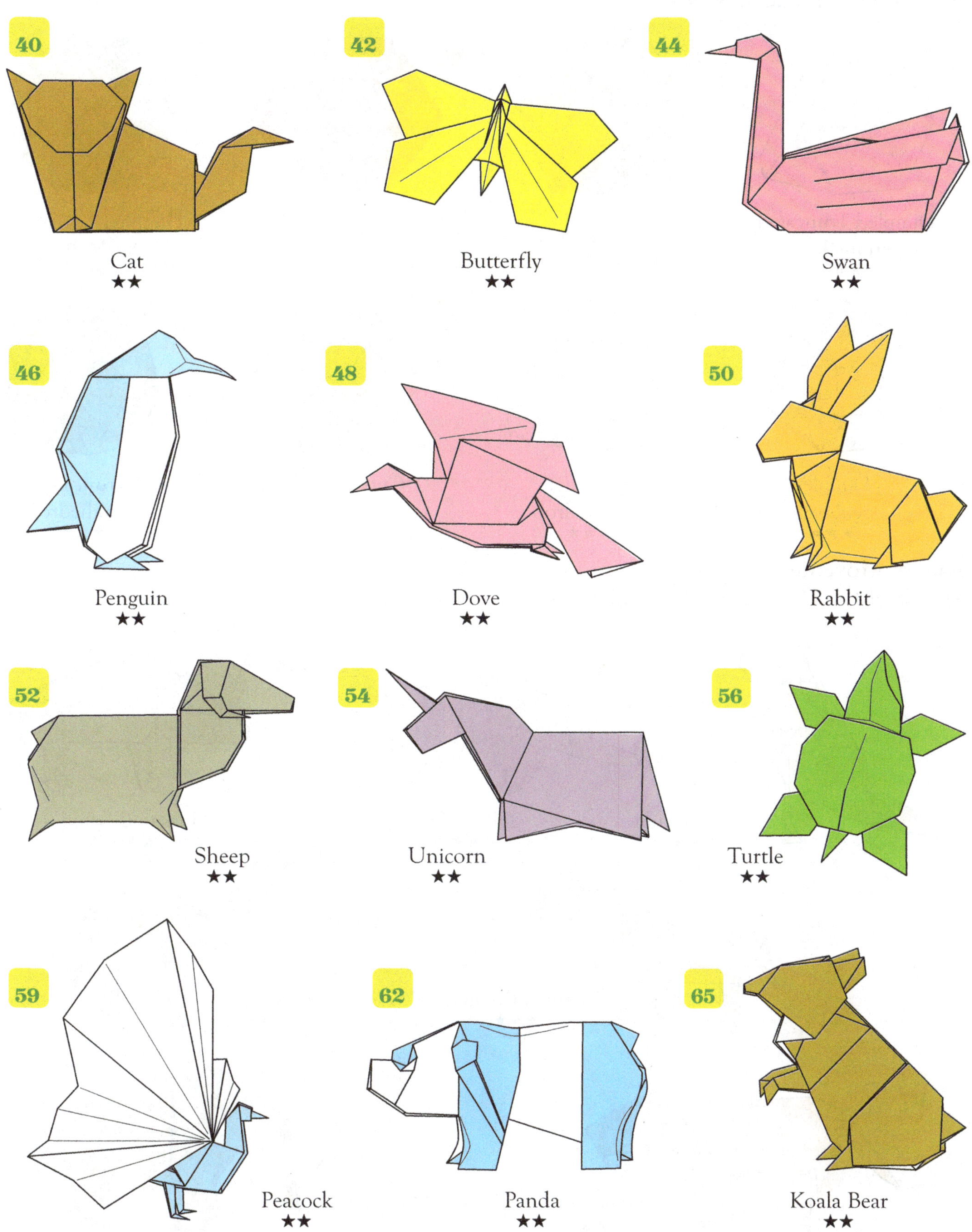

Third Movement
Minuet of Dimpled Polyhedra with a Trio of Archimedean Solids

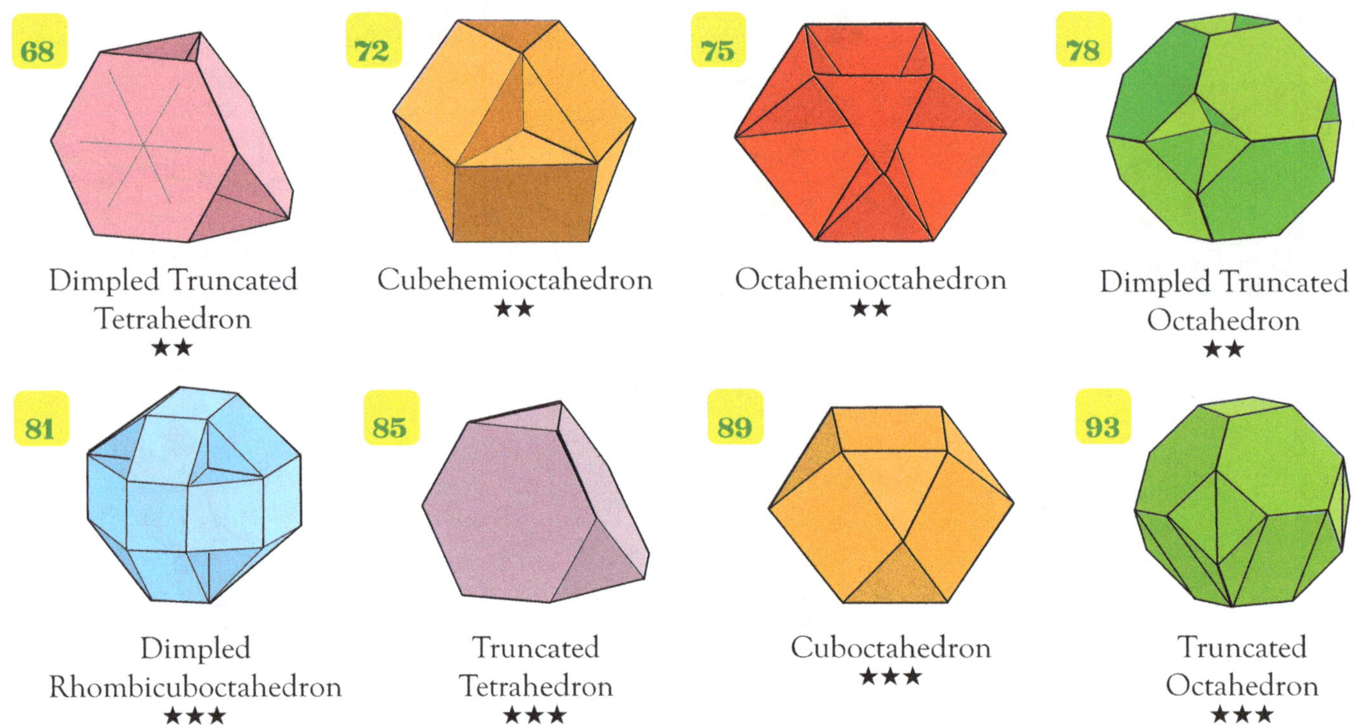

68
Dimpled Truncated Tetrahedron
★★

72
Cubehemioctahedron
★★

75
Octahemioctahedron
★★

78
Dimpled Truncated Octahedron
★★

81
Dimpled Rhombicuboctahedron
★★★

85
Truncated Tetrahedron
★★★

89
Cuboctahedron
★★★

93
Truncated Octahedron
★★★

Fourth Movement
March of the Prehistoric Mammals

98 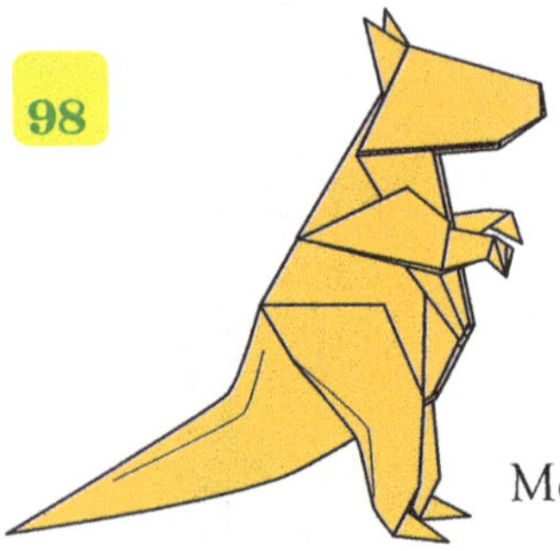
Megatherium
★★★

101 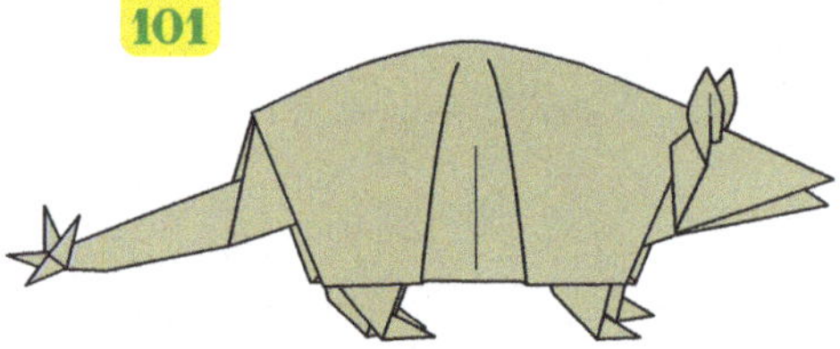
Glyptodon
★★

104 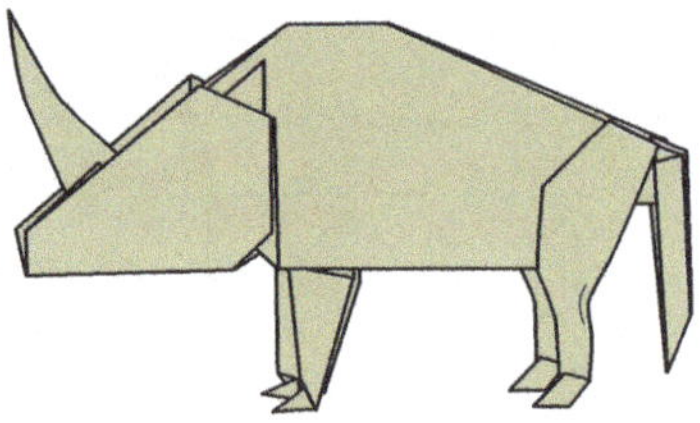
Elasmotherium
★★★

108 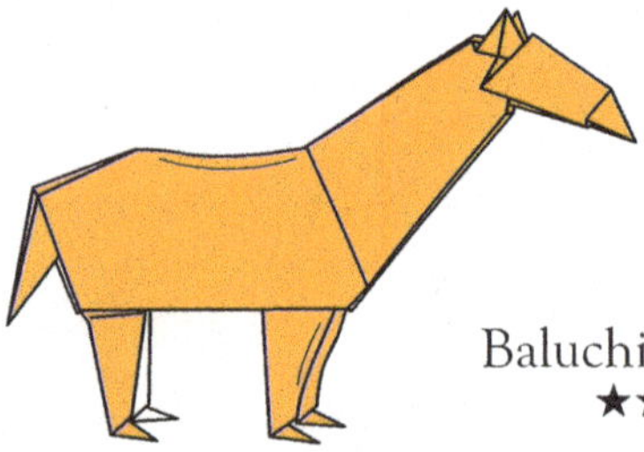
Baluchitherium
★★★

112 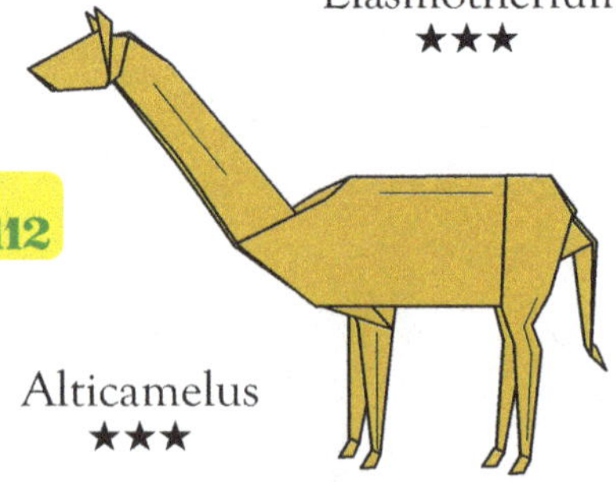
Alticamelus
★★★

117 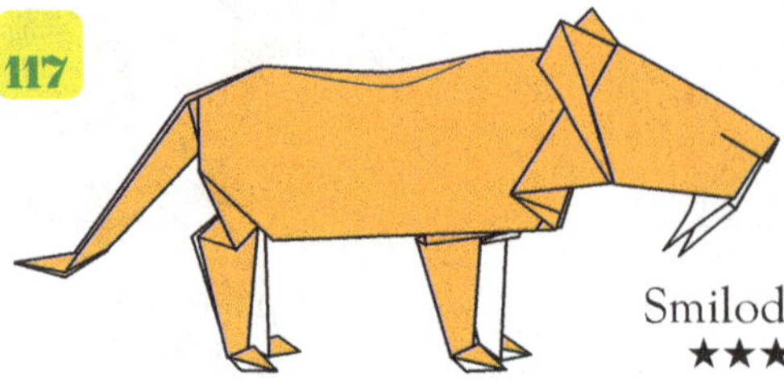
Smilodon
★★★

122 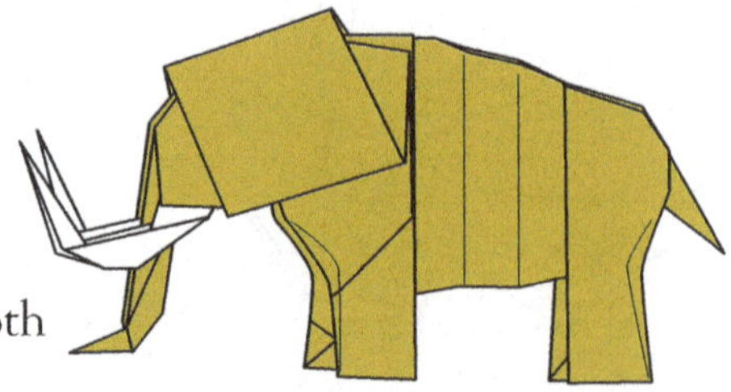
Woolly Mammoth
★★★

Symbols

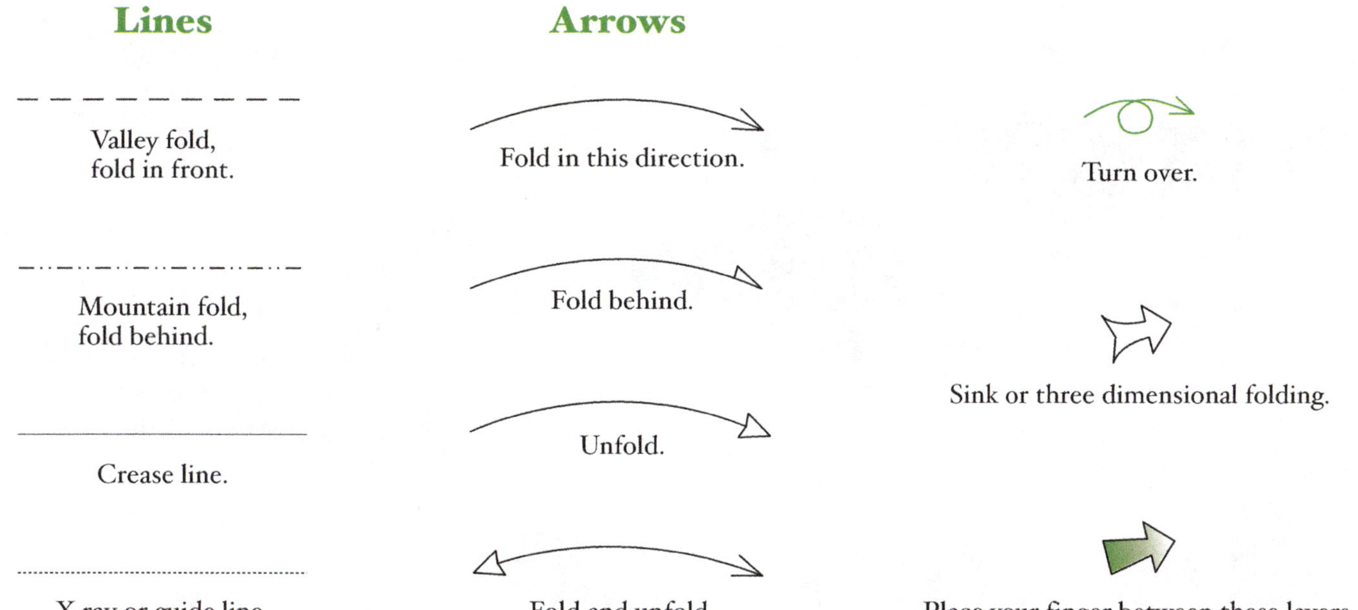

Origami, Music, and Creativity

Origami can be anything we want it to be. If it involves paperfolding, we call it origami. Whether simple, complex, depicting any theme or subject, number of sheets used for a model, use of cuts, or anything else, it is up to the individual folder to enjoy what works for them.

Music can also be anything we want. As long as it involves sound waves, hopefully with some structure, we call it music.

From ancient times, humans recognized that music altered our mind, changed our mood, and carried a level of enjoyment that could not otherwise be experienced. At the time, we knew nothing of the intricacies of the brain, that music releases endorphins, giving us what can best be described as a high.

As music developed, great minds came up with a method of naming notes, rhythmic ideas, along with the development of musical instruments, and further musical ideas. This enabled people from that time period, using the known framework, to compose works and carry music further.

Prior to 1000 AD, there was no notation for writing music on paper, at least not in a useful sense, nor was there any thought to do so. Musicians knew the works and taught their pupils by having them follow their hand signals and verbal commands, to perhaps sing the next note higher, hold it for this long...

When a Benedictine monk, Guido of Arezzo, around the year of 1025 AD, had ambitions to work on a code of musical notation so music can be written on paper, the music community was horrified as it would take away their jobs. It took Pope John XIX to recognize the value of Guido's work, and he instructed the Roman clergy to use this new system, which brought it to general use. Through the centuries, much was improved upon this system.

It is fair to say that anyone involved in music has their own way to enjoy and contribute to it. A few have the gift of composing music. These composers have spent an untold amount of time to compose and produce music that would not have otherwise existed, and we are all grateful for their work. Others have designed and crafted musical instruments. Because of all of them, musicians that specialize in a particular instrument or voice have great works to practice and perform. Teachers are involved with teaching how to read music, how to play an instrument, and how to make it sound musical. The audience is also part of the musical experience.

We origami folk see the magic in simply folding paper to create a wide range of subjects. We delight in the mystery and puzzle of design, dexterity in the folding process, and artistry in the finished look. While the development of origami is behind the music curve, it is catching up, and in the past few decades has made huge strides. As in the music story above where I mentioned composers, performers, teachers, and the audience, along with someone inventing musical notation, all of this applies to origami. Any and all participants have their own creative side that allows the art to continue and develop, and be enjoyed by larger populations.

Origami Symphony No. 2

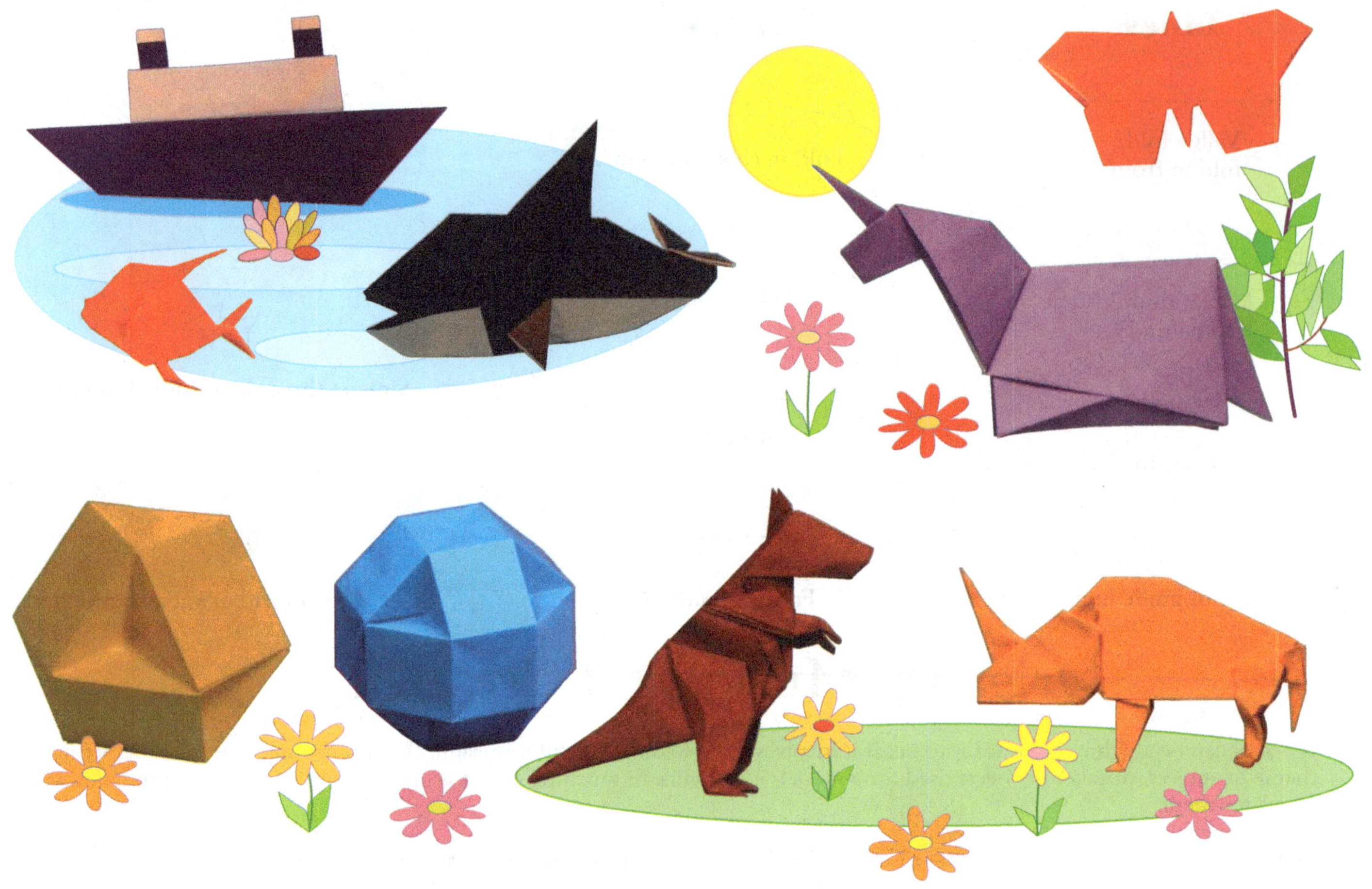

Playful creatures come to life in this origami symphony. Flyingfish, jumping Dolphins, marching Penguins, climbing Koala Bears, and even a Woolly Mammoth join in the symphony. Danger also lurks at every corner, from Sharks to Smilodon, the Saber-Tooth Tiger. Dimpled Polyhedra reflect all sides.

Origami Symphony No. 2 opens in the sea, exploring fascinating sea creatures from a simple Sailboat. Scallops and Flyingfish greet us along with playful Goldfish and a Lookdown. After the Sailboat ride, we take to the ocean on a colorful Ocean Liner. Dolphins dance around us and a black and white Orca appears. The first movement ends after a close encounter with three Sharks.

After the scary Sharks, we relax with the moderately simple peaceful creatures from the second movement. Butterflies and Doves fill the sky. Rabbits, Sheep, and a Unicorn are depicted with simple folds. A black and white simple Panda and Koala Bear join us to close the movement.

The third movement is a Minuet of Dimpled Polyhedra with a trio of Archimedean Solids. Several of the Dimpled Polyhedra are variations of Platonic Solids, with sunken corners, yet complex enough to require intricate folding methods. These challenging models add complexity and variety to origami.

The symphony ends with the fourth movement of our favorite Prehistoric Mammals. This includes a Megatherium (the prehistoric Giant Ground Sloth), Glyptodon (from the Armadillo family), Elasmotherium (furry form of the Rhinoceros), a Woolly Mammoth, and more. While possibly playful, we see these large animals as scary creatures which are fun to fold and display.

Throughout the symphony, playful, peaceful, and dangerous creatures keep the balance. Intricate geometric shapes add to the diversity. Colorful scenes from the four movements show the spirit of origami.

First Movement

Allegro Agitato: Sharks in the Sea

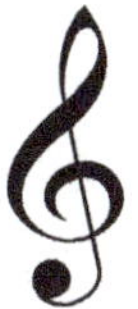

The seas and oceans are filled with magnificent creatures. Let's explore them by Sailboat and Ocean Liner. On our journey, we will spy upon a Scallop, Flyingfish, Lookdown, Dolpfin, Orca, and three hungry sharks. Models range in skill level from simple to intermediate.

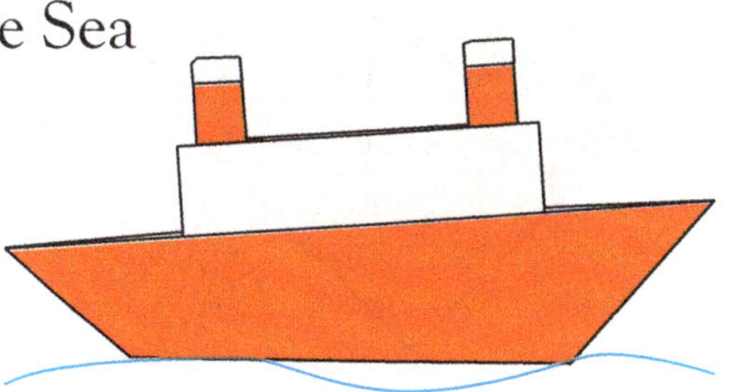

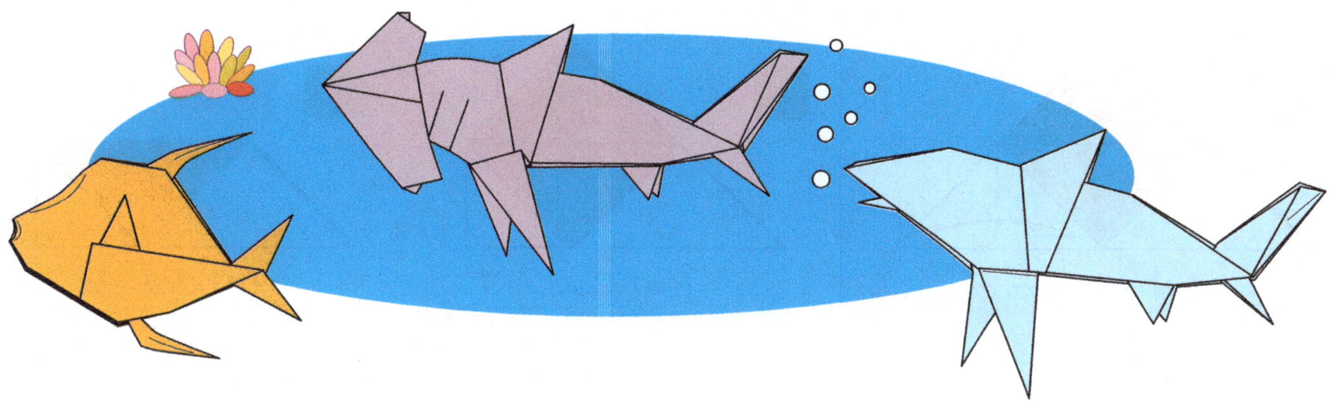

Sailboat

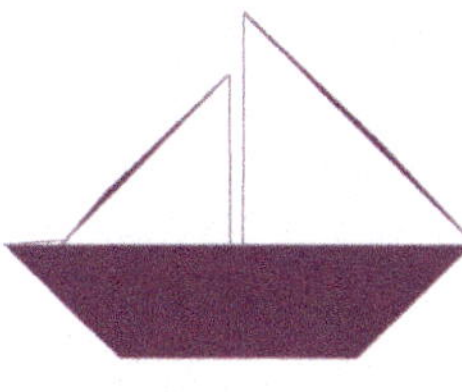

Let's sail into the seas to begin our journey. This Sailboat design was inspired by simplifying a traditional version.

From the earliest days of human civilization, people have sought ways to get from one place to another, either close by or far away. Walking could take them to the next village, but boats could take them much further. Sailboats provided a way to use the wind itself as a means of travel, and this opened up world exploration in a way walking never could.

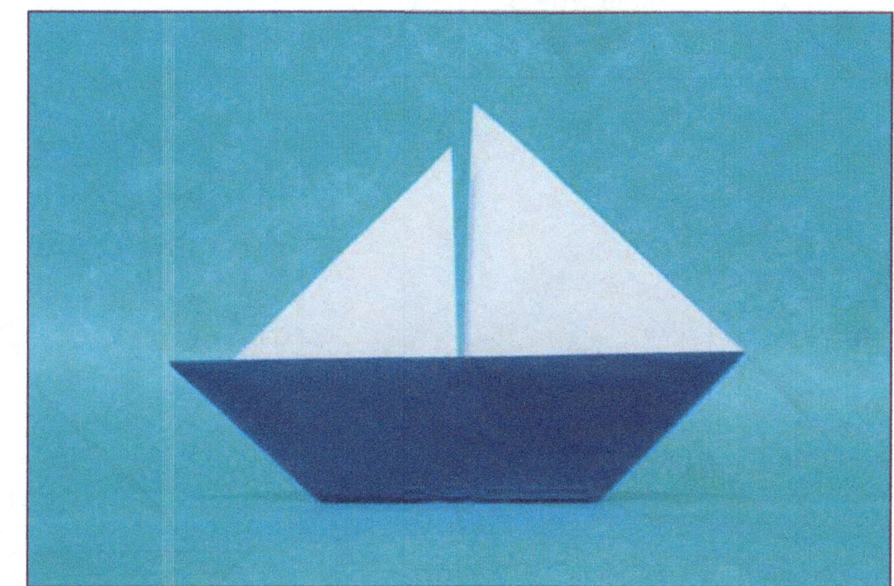

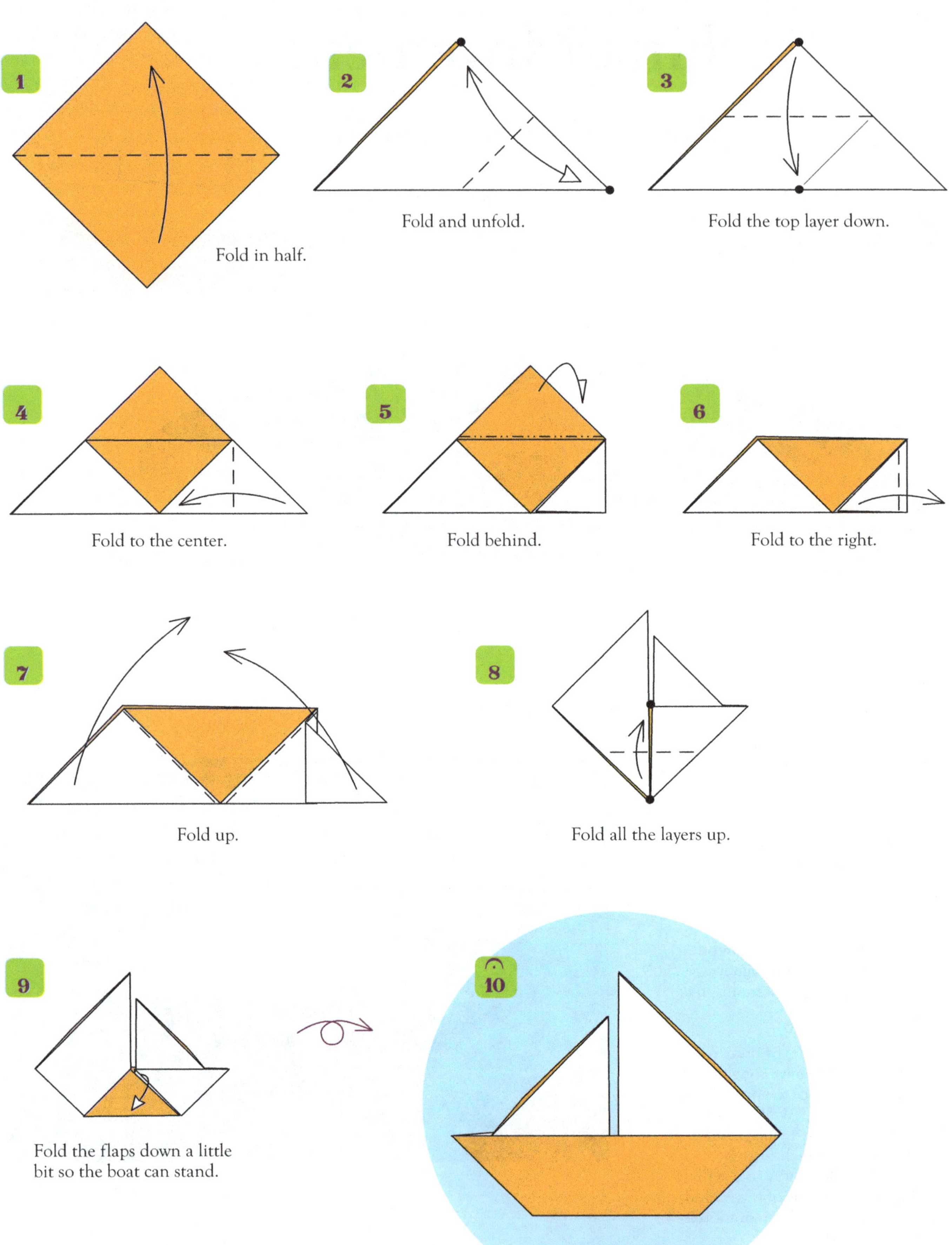

1 Fold in half.

2 Fold and unfold.

3 Fold the top layer down.

4 Fold to the center.

5 Fold behind.

6 Fold to the right.

7 Fold up.

8 Fold all the layers up.

9 Fold the flaps down a little bit so the boat can stand.

10 Sailboat

Scallop

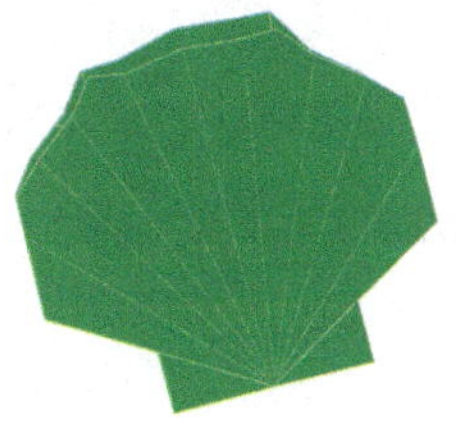

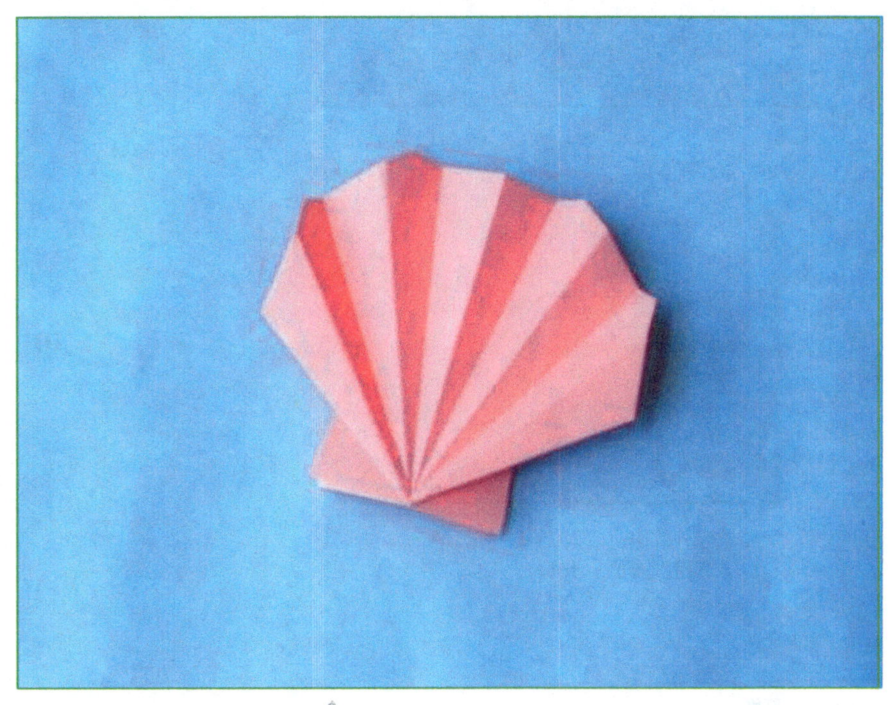

With its many eyes and wavy shape, the Scallop uses its own form of propulsion to travel the oceans. Opening and closing its shell propels the Scallop where it needs to go, and its hard shell and strong closing muscle keep it safe from predators.

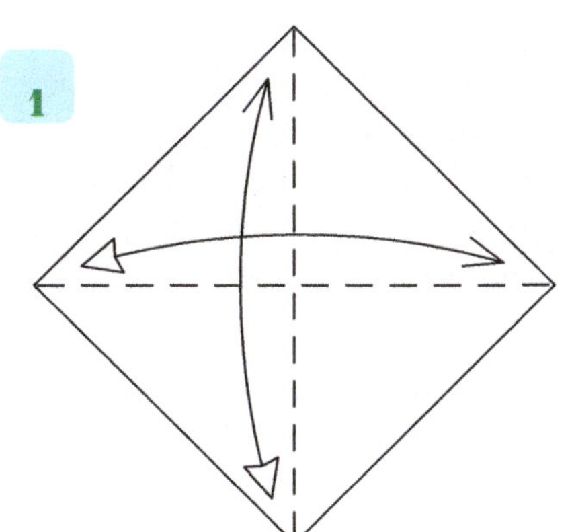

Fold and unfold.

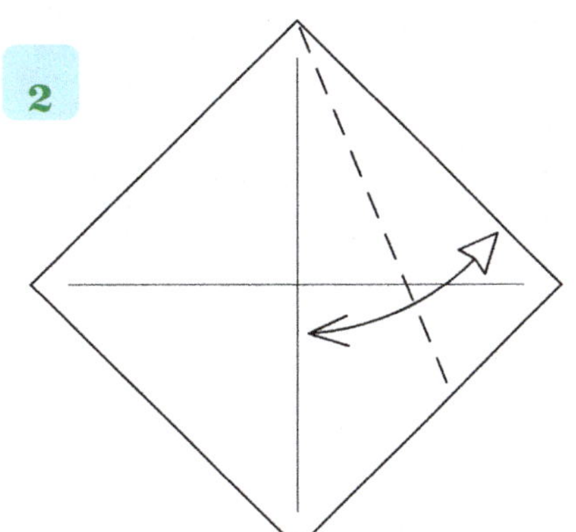

Fold to the center and unfold.

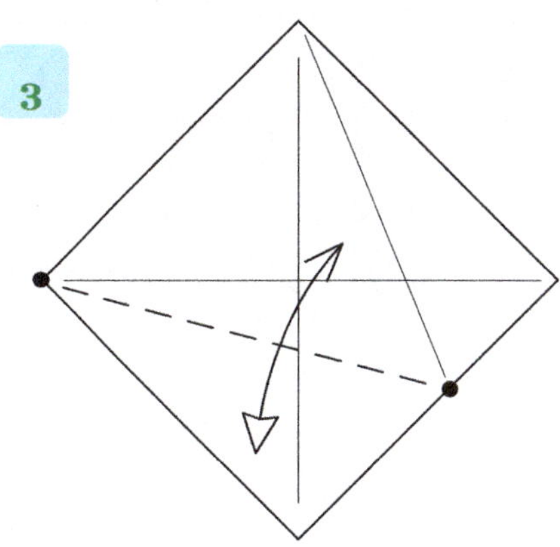

Fold and unfold.

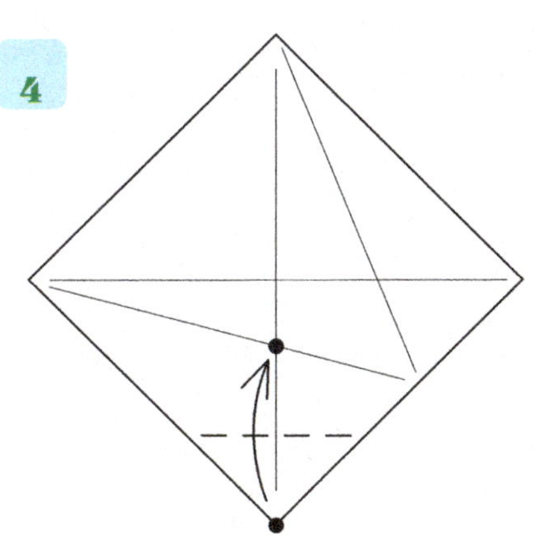

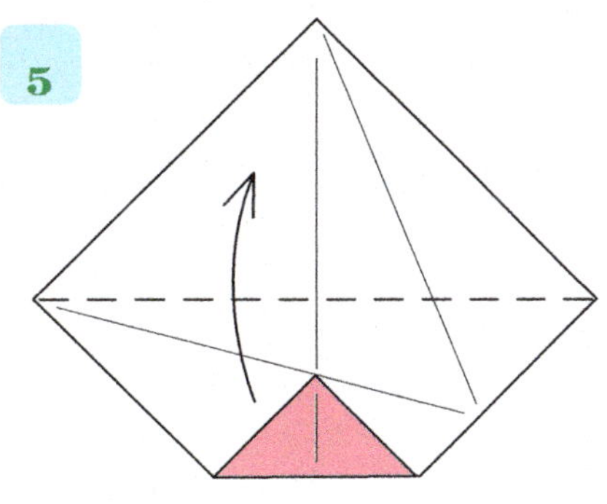

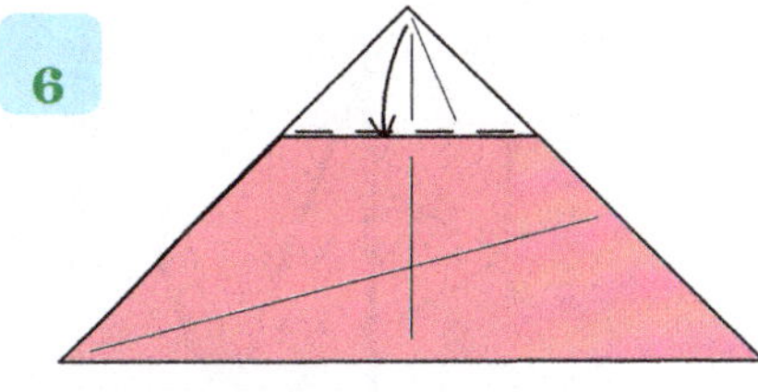

Fold inside.

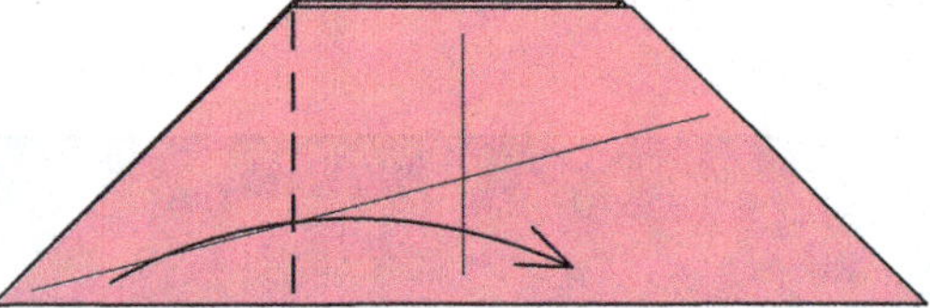

7

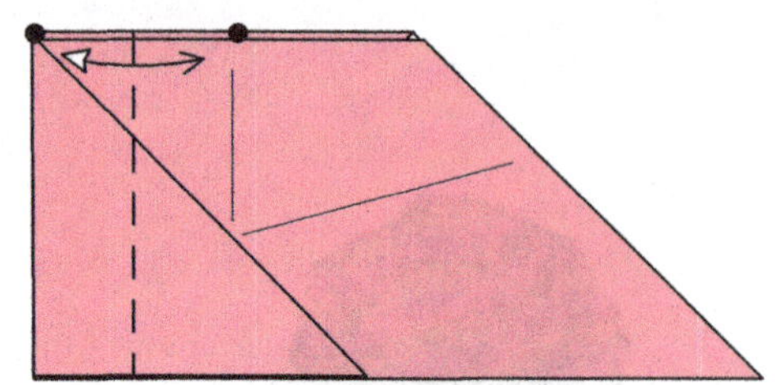

8

Fold and unfold.

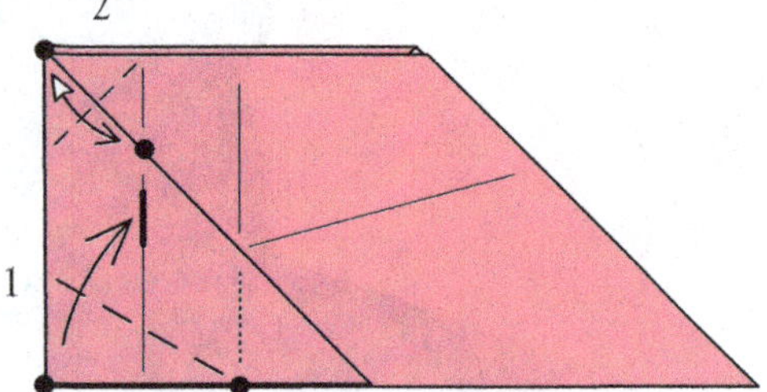

9

1. Bring the corner to the line.
2. Fold and unfold.

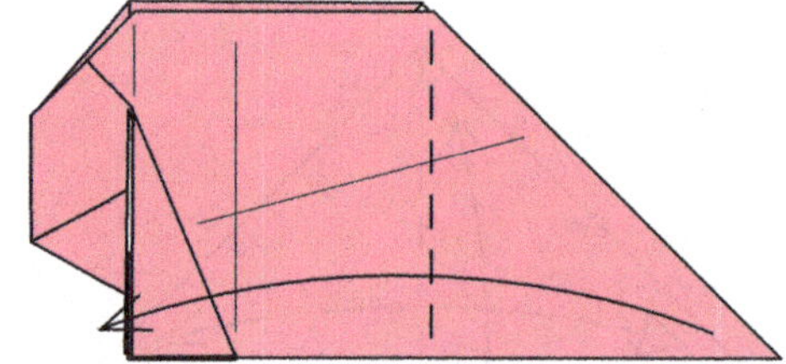

10

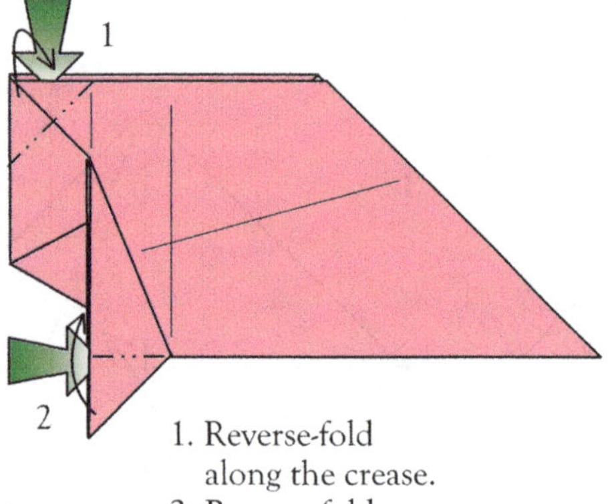

11

1. Reverse-fold along the crease.
2. Reverse-fold.

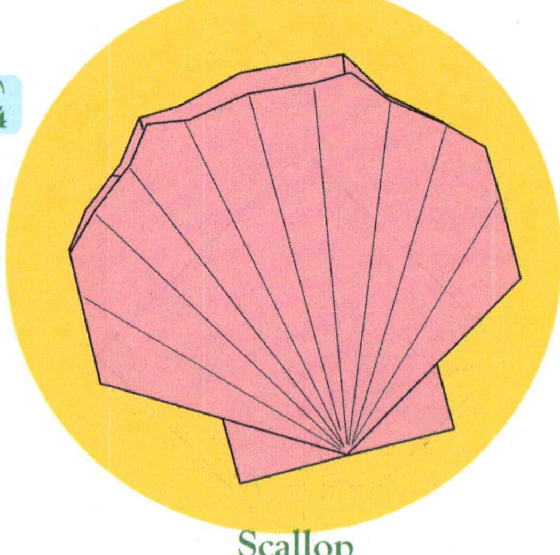

12

Repeat steps 7–11 on the right.

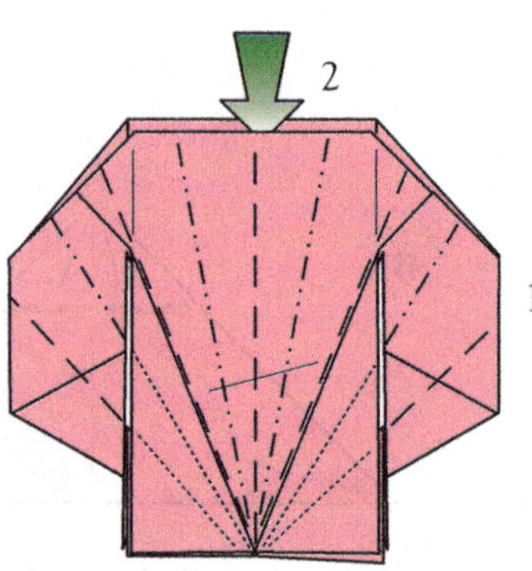

13

1. Pleat-fold all the layers.
2. Open the shell a little bit.

14

Scallop

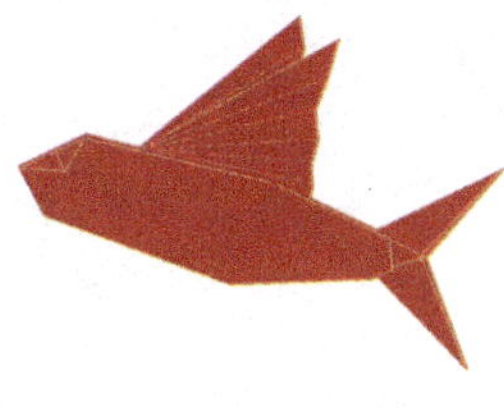

Flyingfish

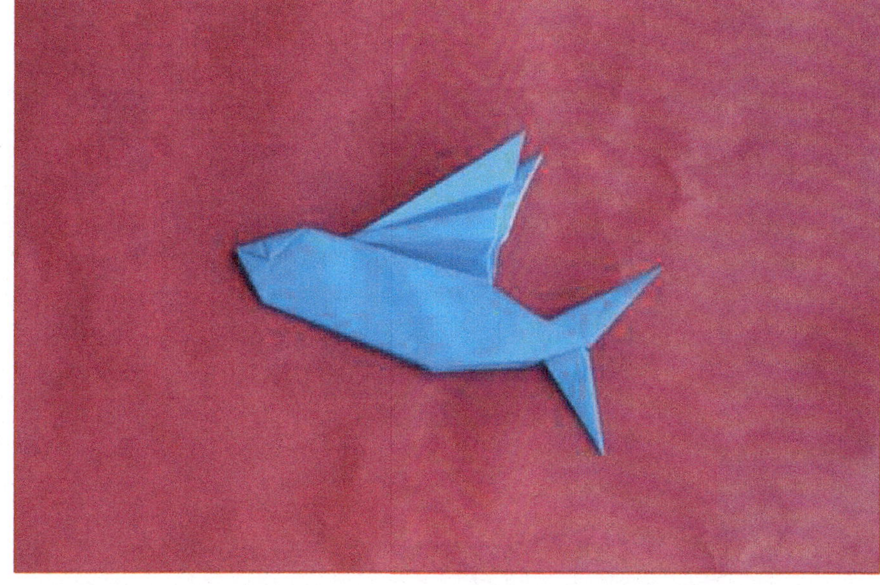

These fascinating fish have large extending fins that serve as wings, allowing the Flyingfish to take long gliding jumps out of the water. Seeing a school of Flyingfish taking to the air is an amazing sight to see over the glistening water.

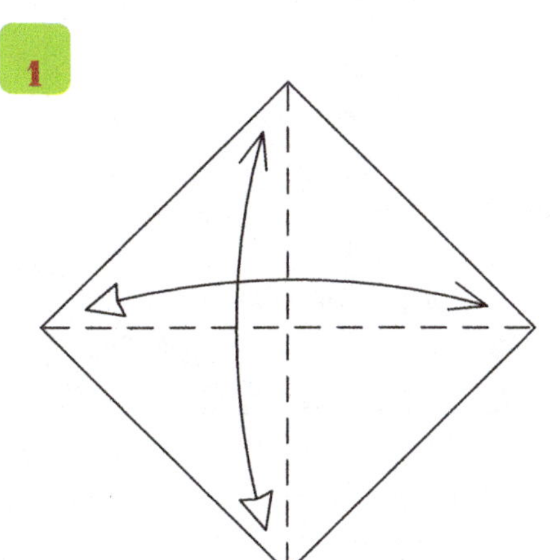

Fold and unfold.

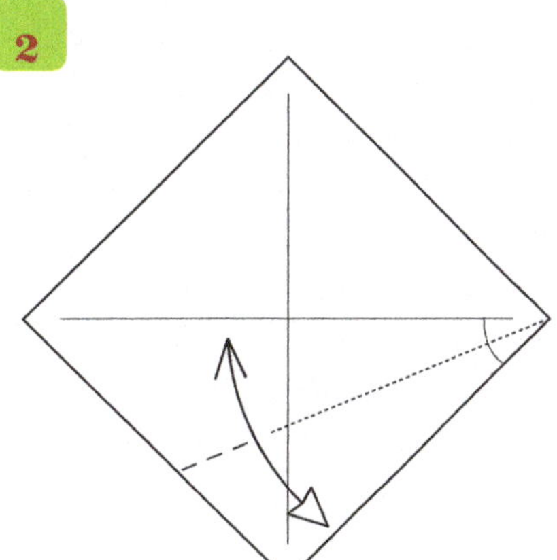

Fold to the center and unfold. Fold on the left.

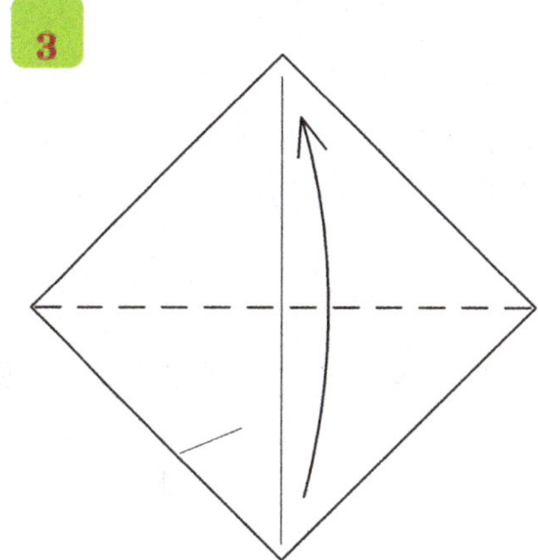

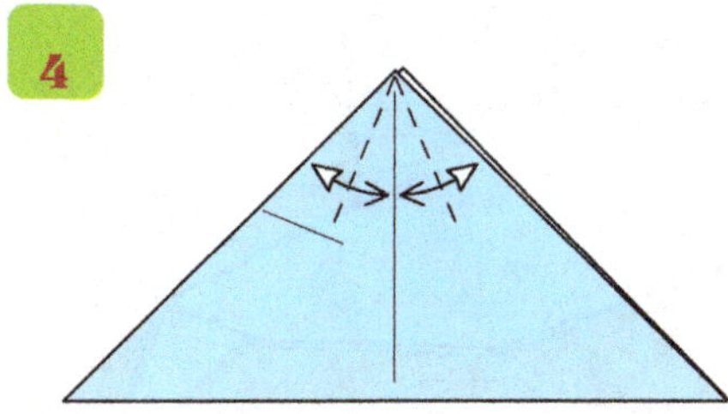

Fold and unfold all the layers.

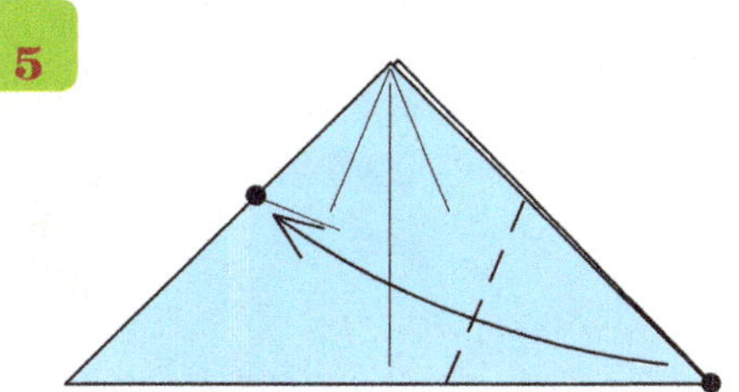

The dots will meet.

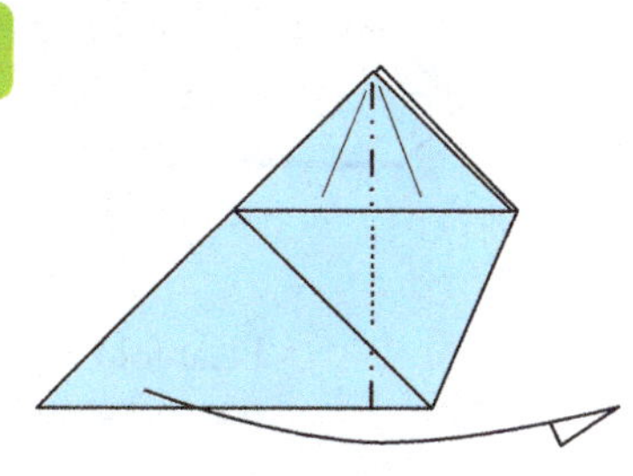

Fold along the crease and rotate 90°.

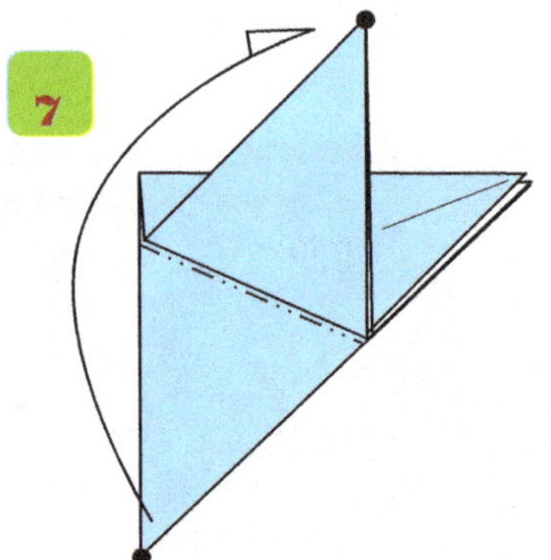

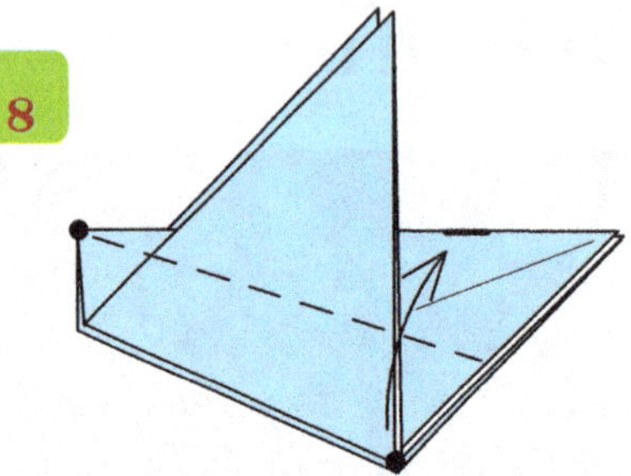

Fold up so the lower dot meets
the top edge. Repeat behind.

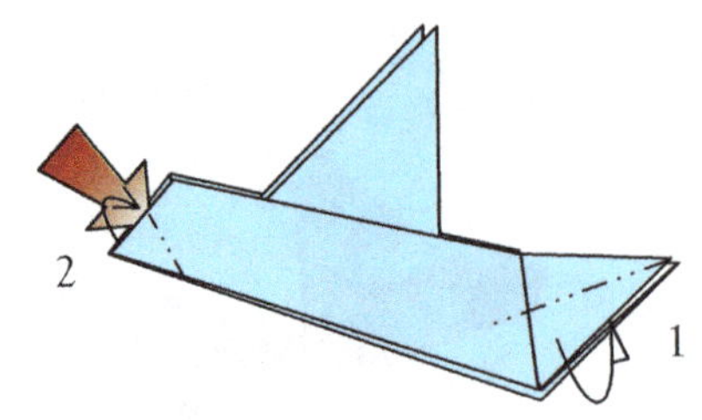

1. Fold the top layer inside,
   repeat behind.
2. Reverse-fold.

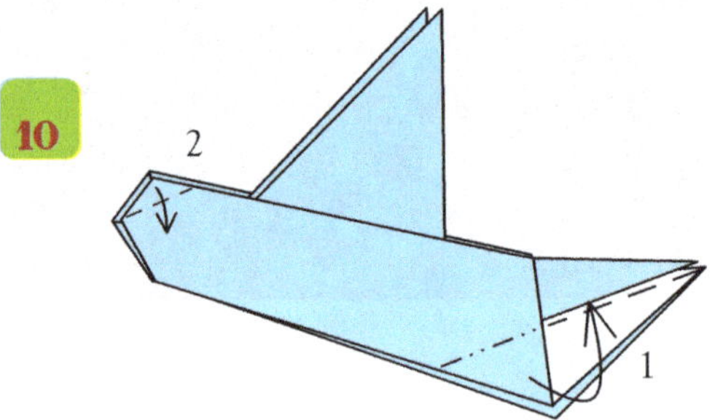

1. Reverse-fold and tuck inside.
2. Valley-fold.
Repeat behind.

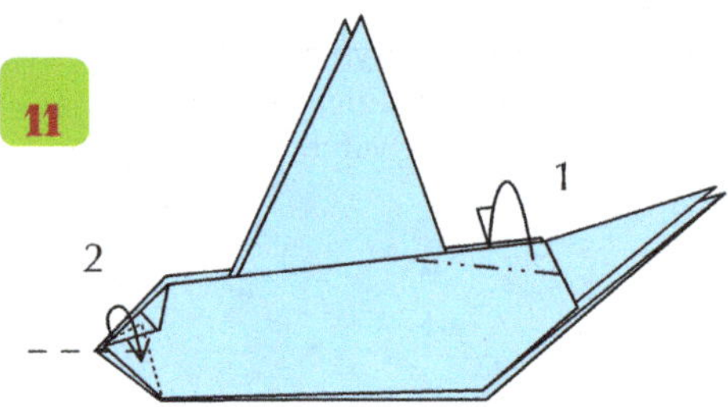

1. Fold inside, repeat behind.
2. Fold the inner layer down.

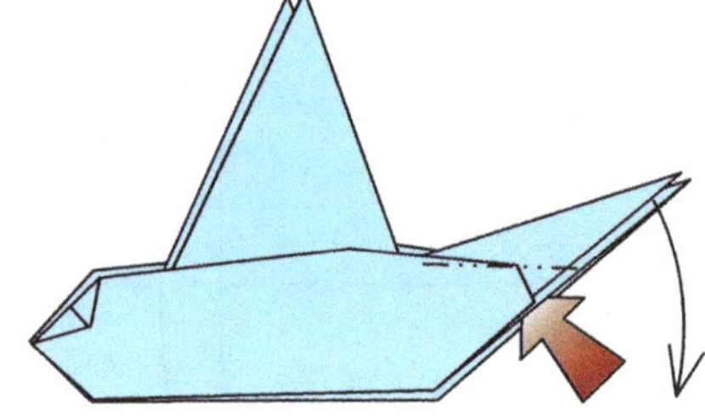

Reverse-fold two flaps.

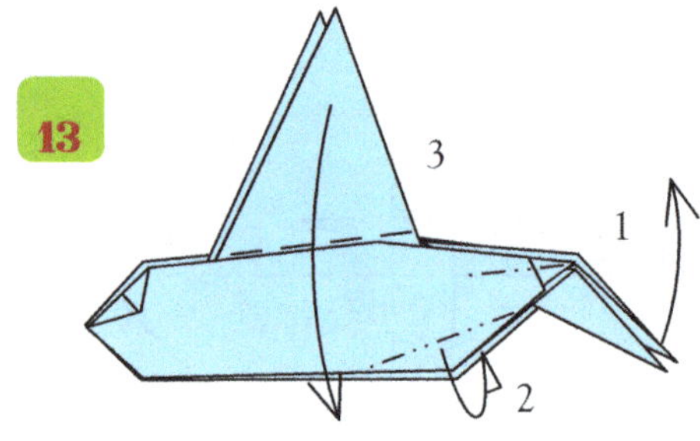

1. Reverse-fold.
2. Fold inside, repeat behind.
3. Fold down, repeat behind.

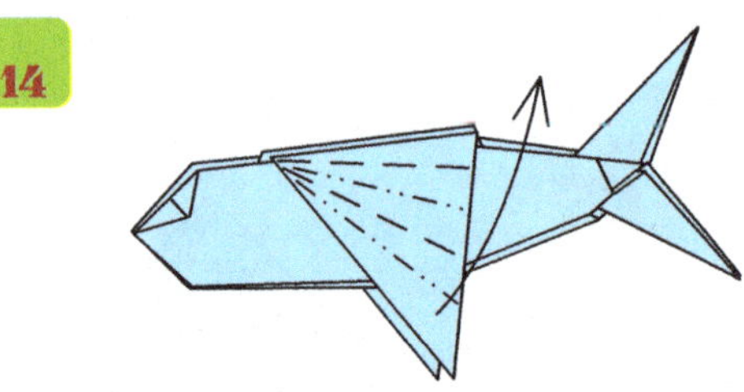

Pleat-fold and
repeat behind.

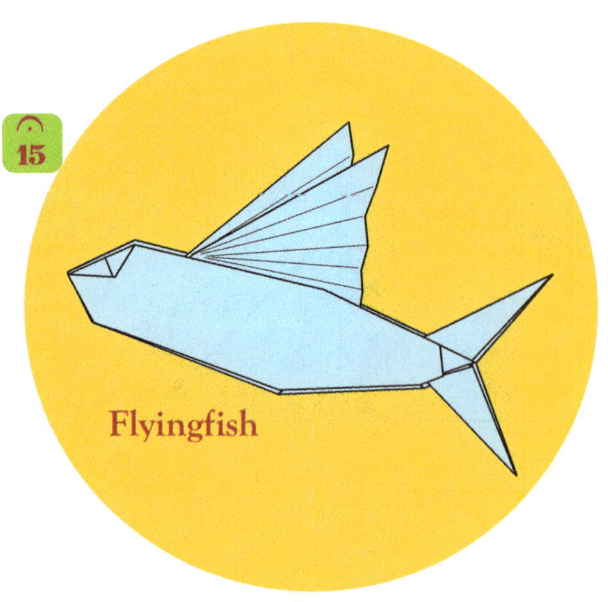

Flyingfish

Goldfish

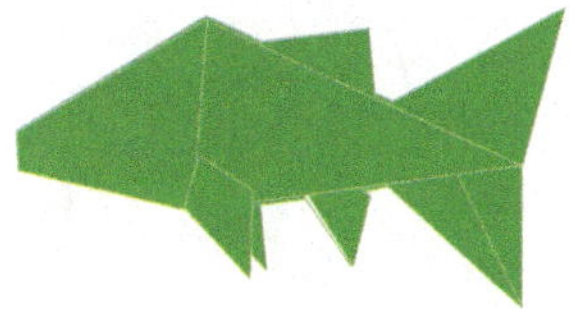

The Goldfish, actually a member of the Carp family, has been a first pet for millions of families. Easy to take care of and fun to watch and feed, these fish have been mainstays in home aquariums and garden ponds for centuries, beginning with their being kept and bred as pets in Ancient China. While limited to a rather small size in fishbowls, Goldfish in the wild can grow bigger and bigger throughout their lives, and some have grown to over 12 inches in length with a weight of several pounds.

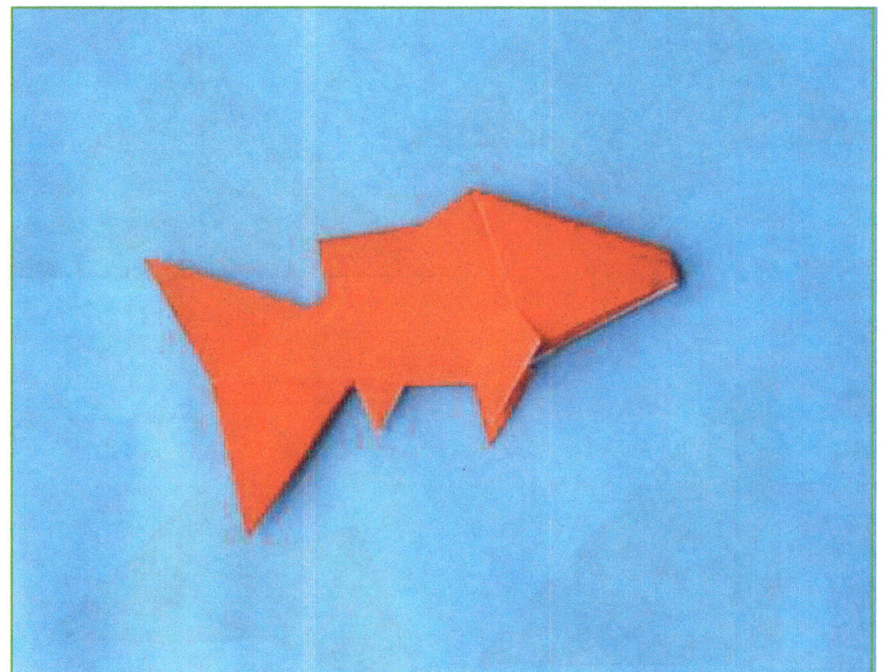

1

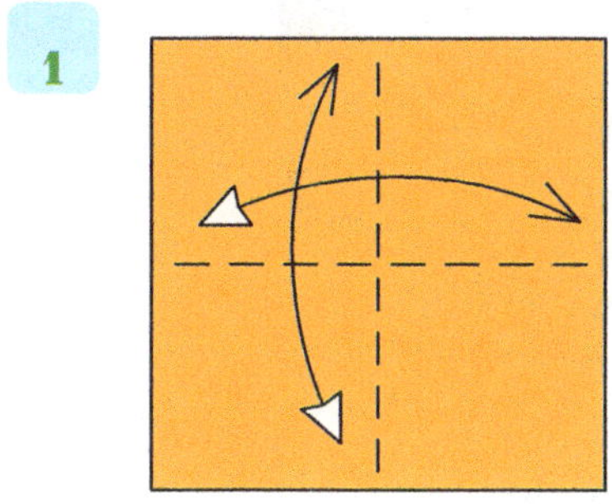

Fold and unfold.

2

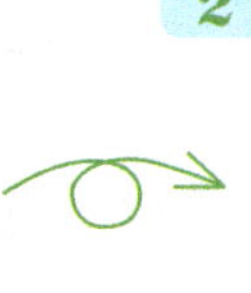

Fold and unfold.

3

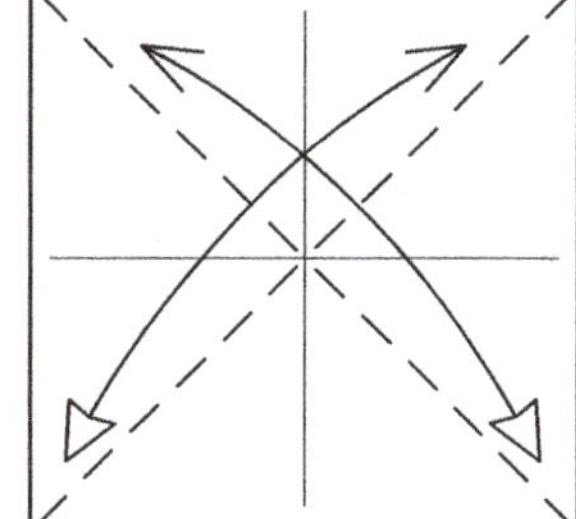

Fold along the creases.

4

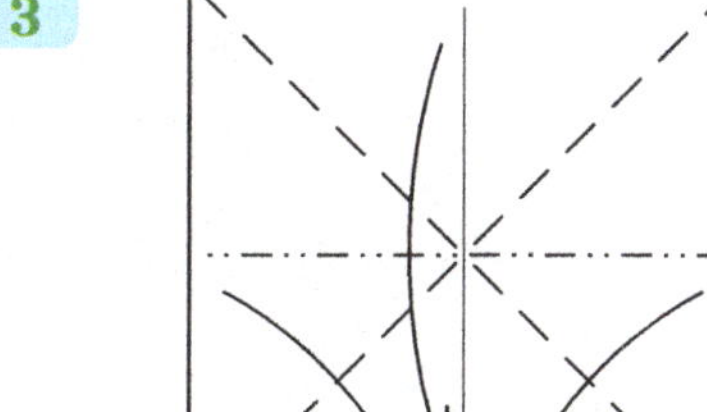

Fold the top flap.

5

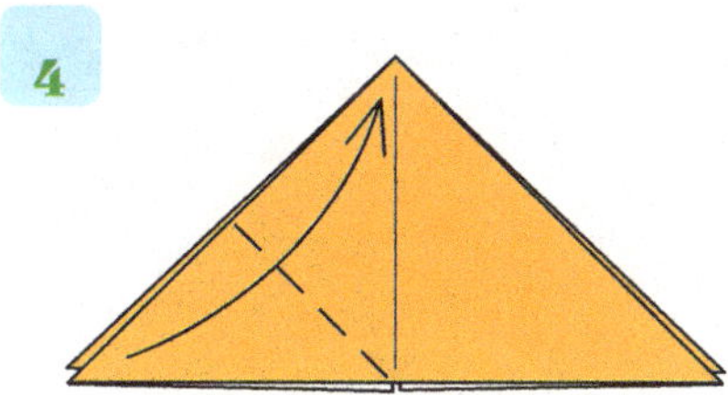

Fold and unfold
through all the layers.

6

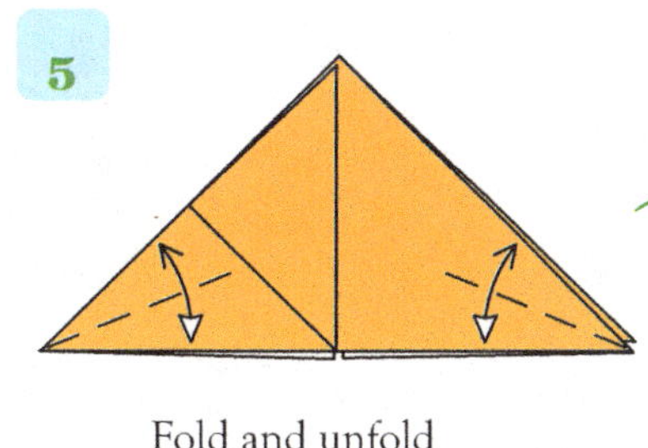

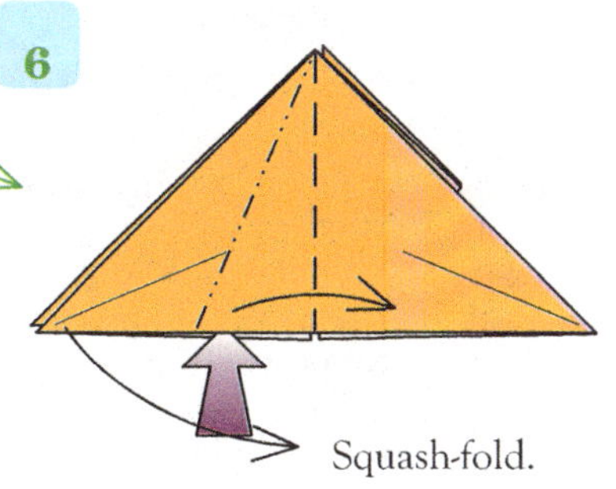

Squash-fold.

7

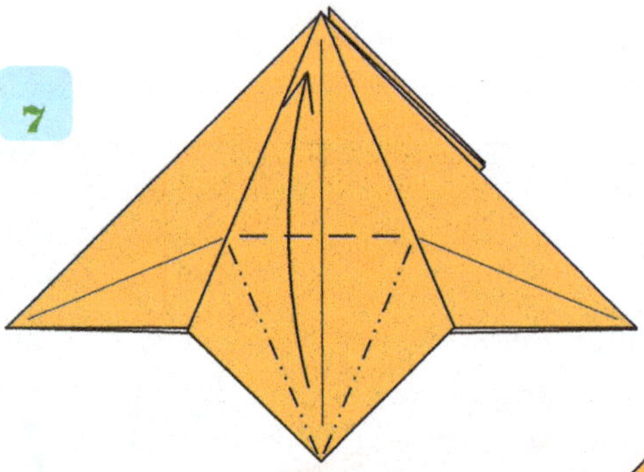

Petal-fold.

8

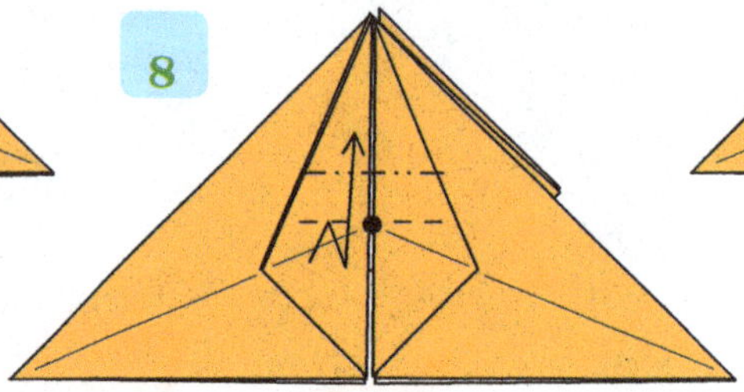

Pleat-fold.

9

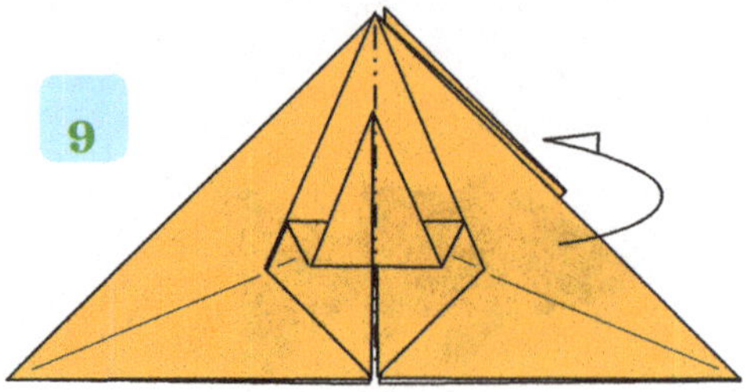

Fold in half and rotate 90°.

10

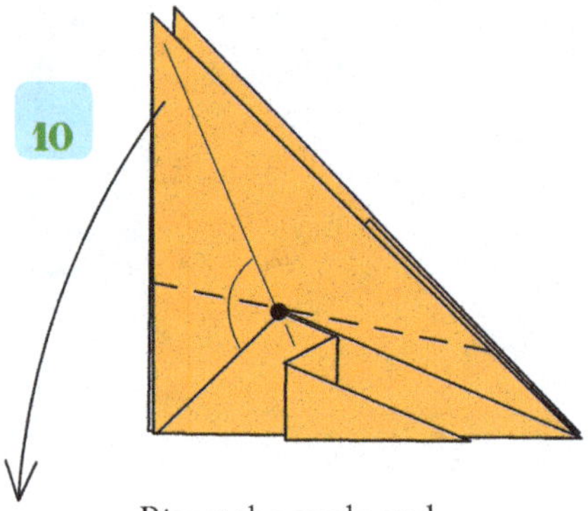

Bisect the angle and
repeat behind.

11

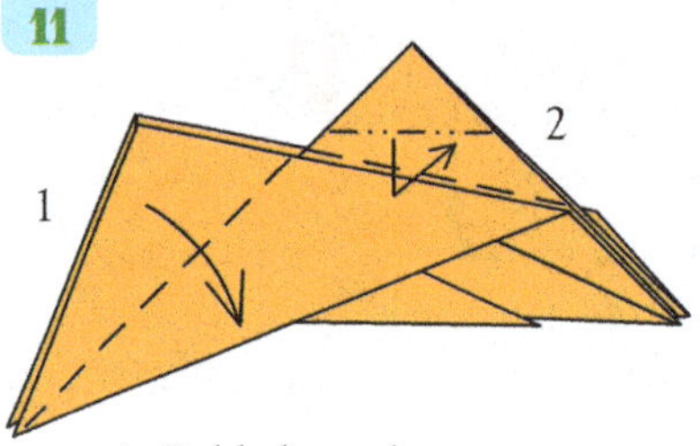

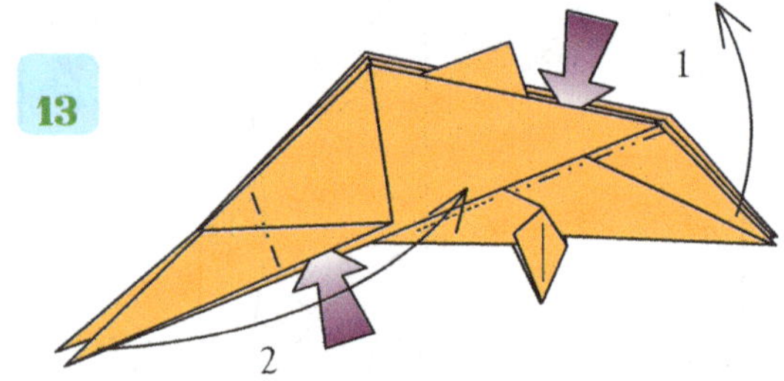

1. Fold along the crease,
   repeat behind.
2. Pleat-fold.

12

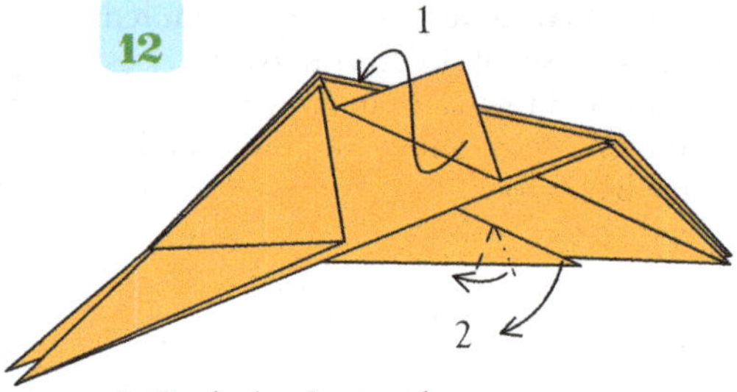

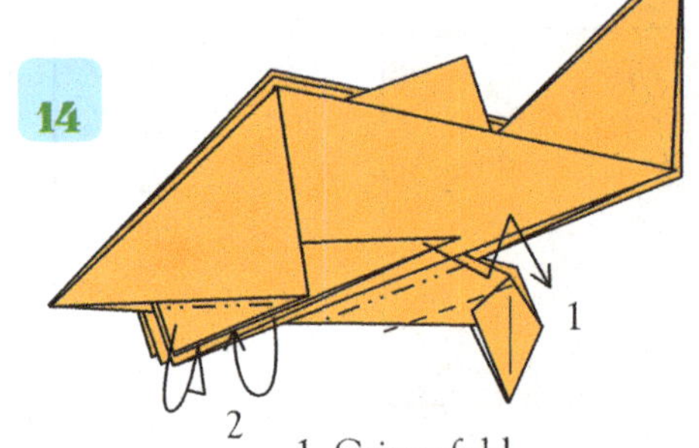

1. Tuck the fin inside.
2. Outside-reverse-fold and spread.

13

1. Reverse-fold.
2. Reverse-fold,
   repeat behind.

14

1. Crimp-fold.
2. Fold two flaps inside,
   repeat behind.

15

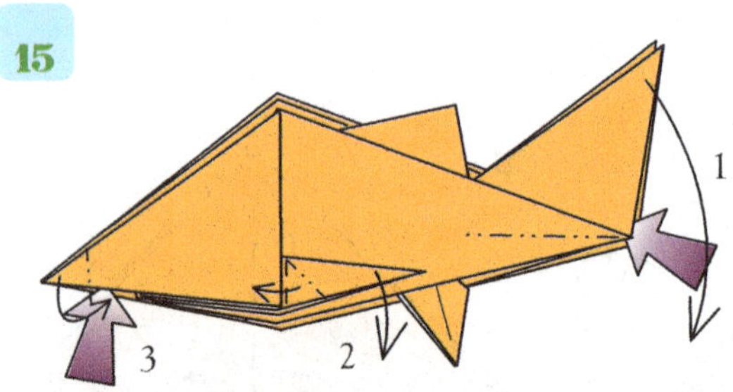

1. Reverse-fold.
2. Squash-fold, repeat behind.
3. Reverse-fold.

16

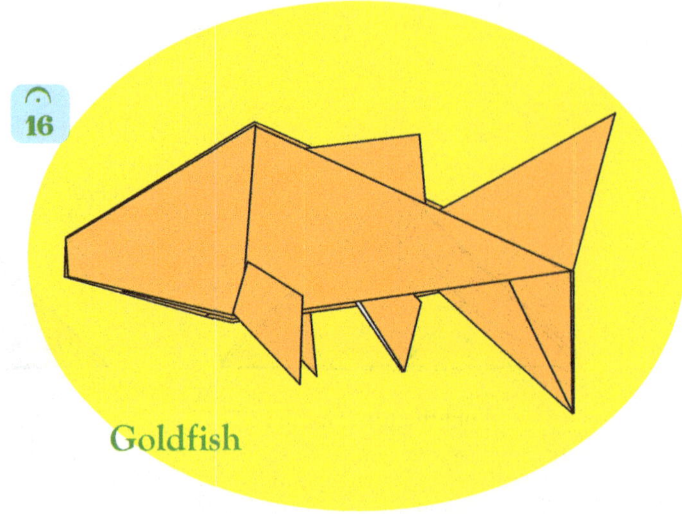

Goldfish

Lookdown

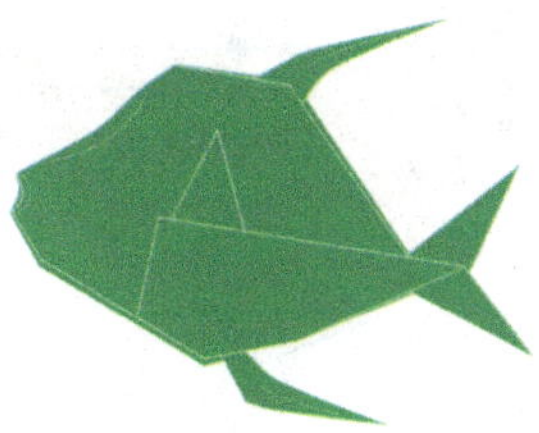

The Lookdown is a curious fish with a unique body shape and eye placement that makes it appear to always be looking down. From the side, they appear rather lumpy, but when seen head-on, they are very thin.

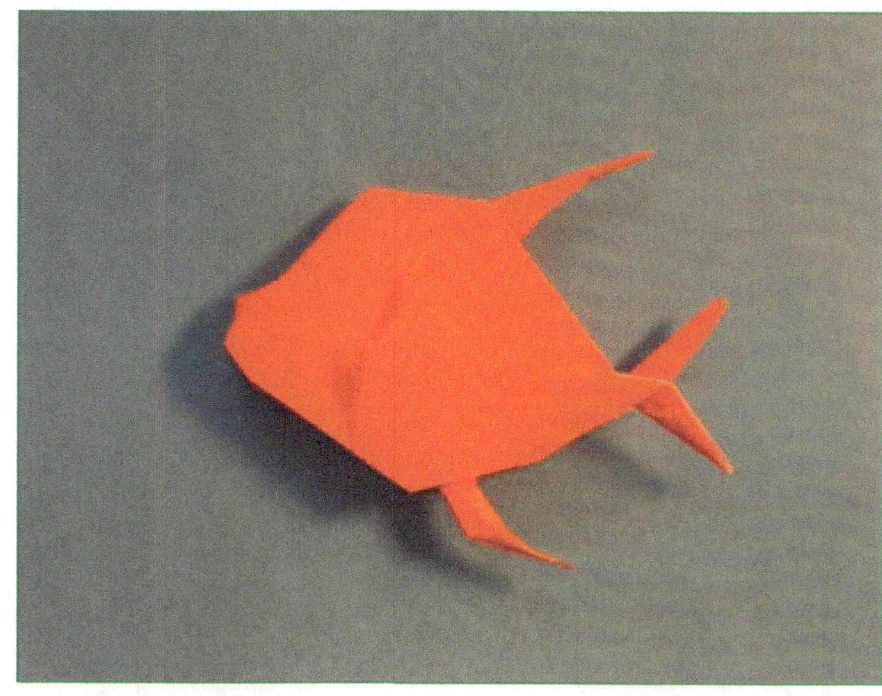

1

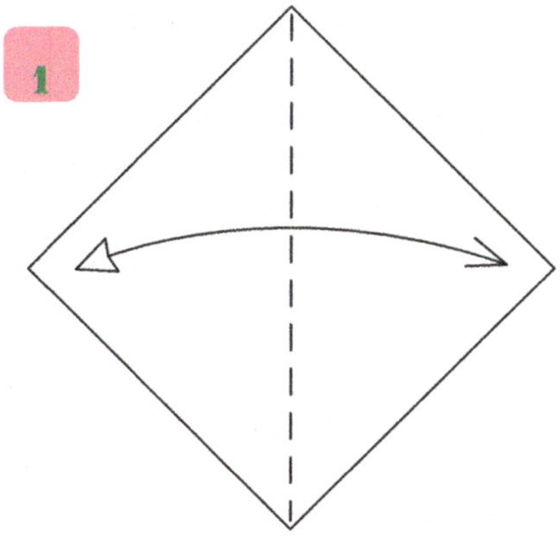

Fold and unfold.

2

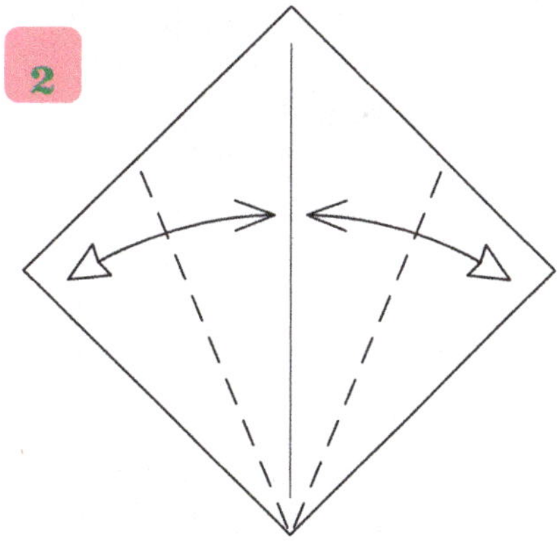

Fold and unfold.

3

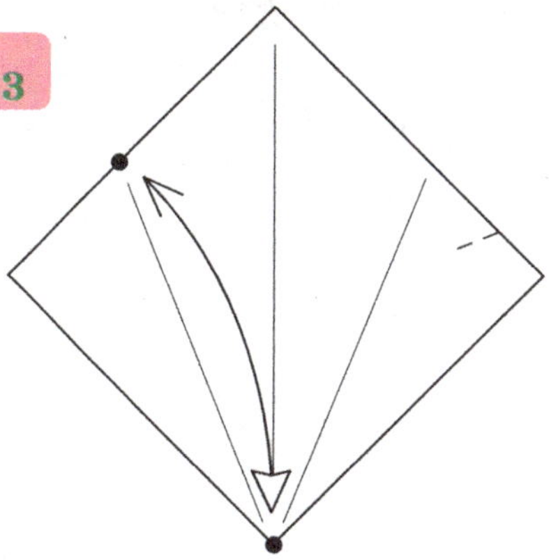

Fold and unfold on the right.

4

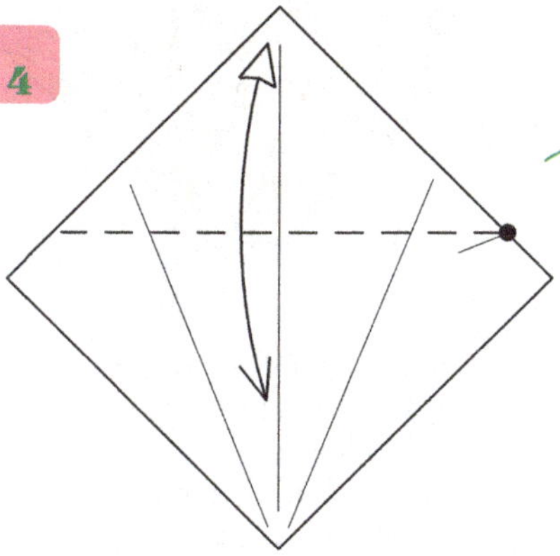

Fold and unfold.

5

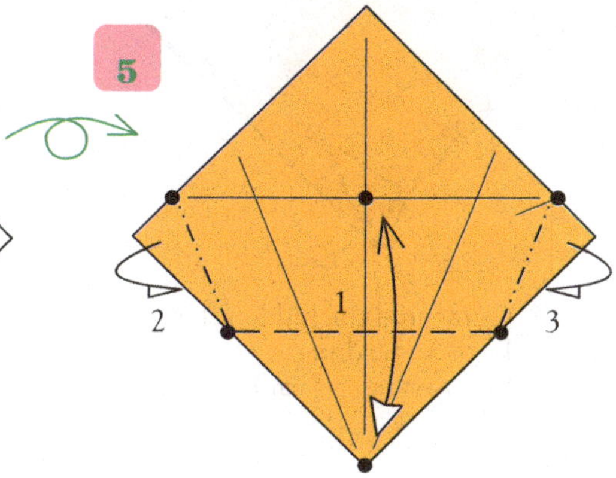

Fold and unfold at 1.

6

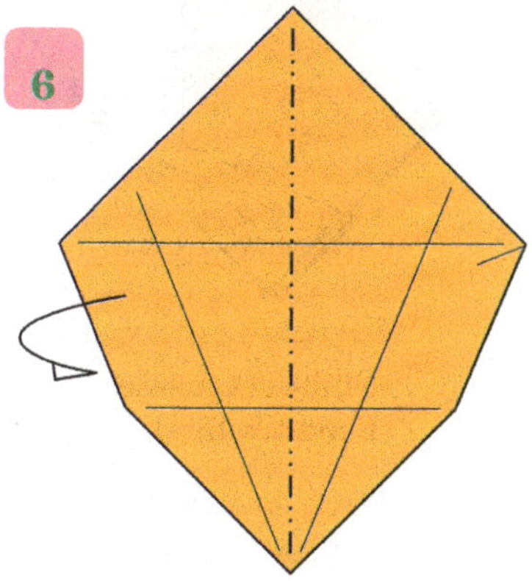

Rotate 90°.

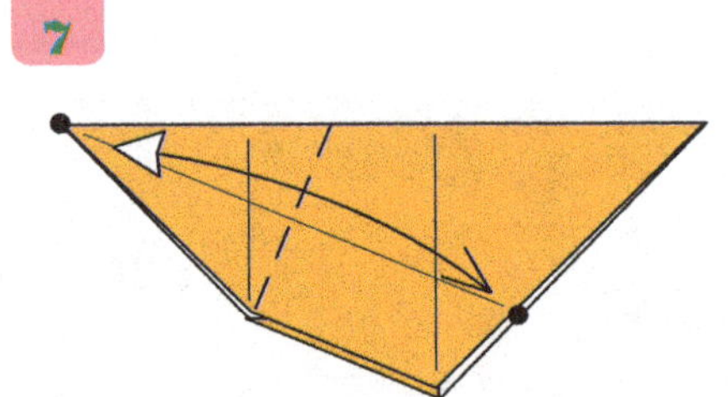

Fold and unfold.

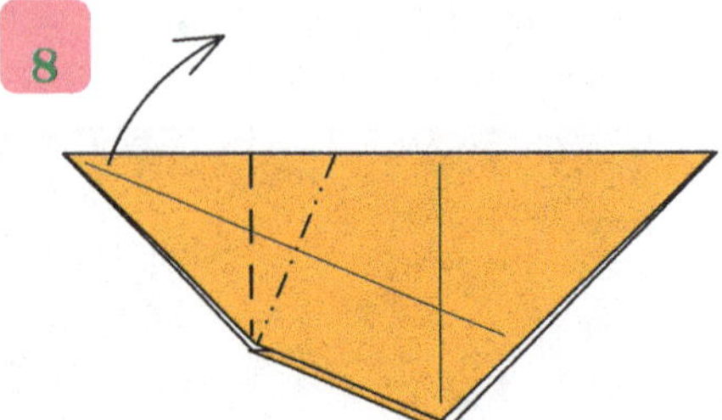

Crimp-fold.

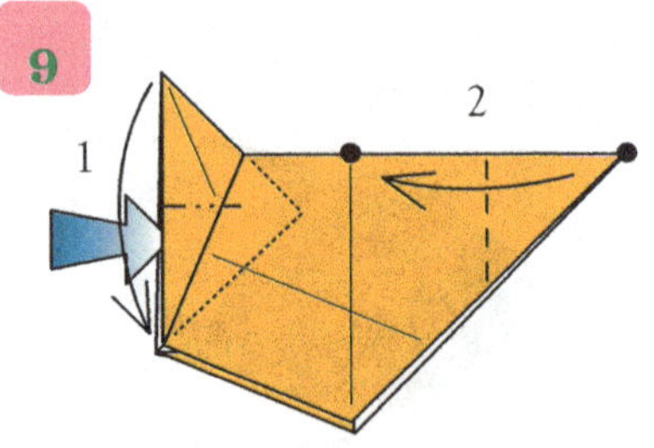

1. Valley-fold.
2. Fold and unfold.

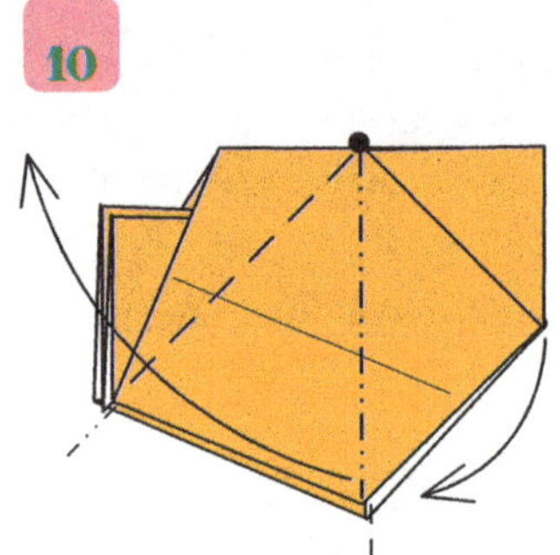

Crimp-fold. Rotate
the dot to the left.

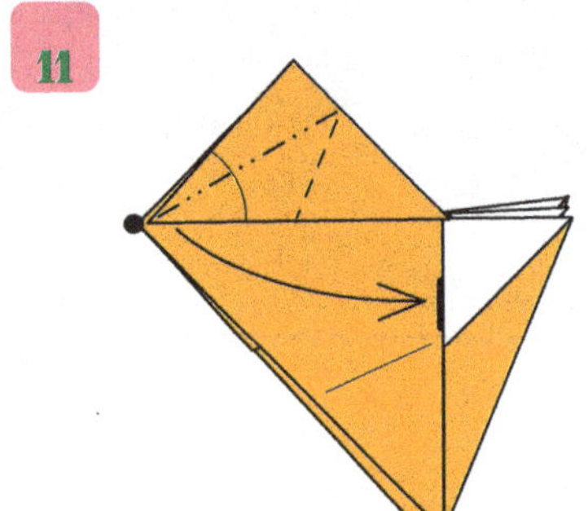

Squash-fold at
an angle of 1/3.

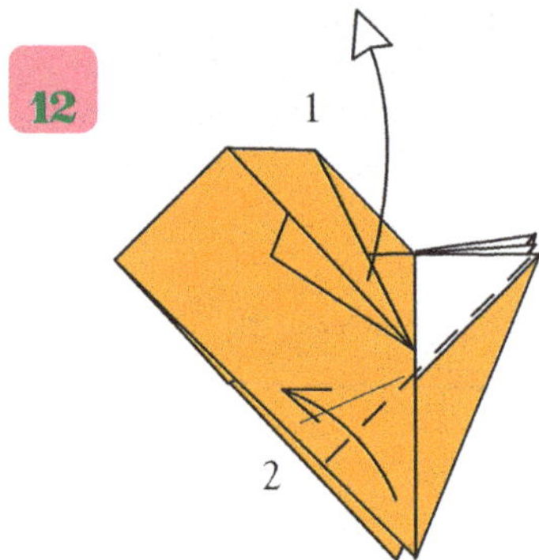

1. Unfold.
2. Repeat behind.

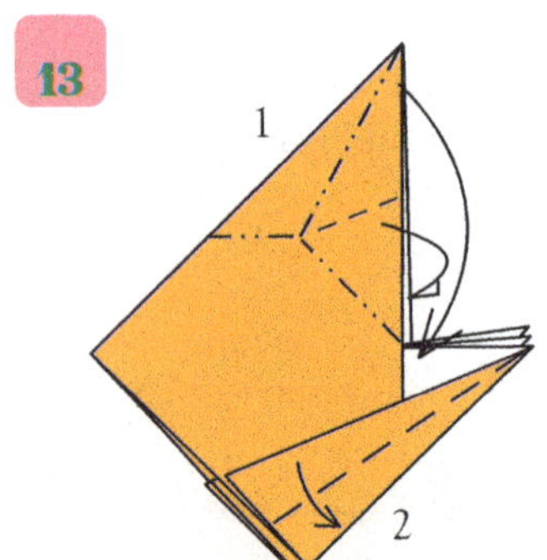

1. Double-rabbit-ear.
2. Repeat behind.

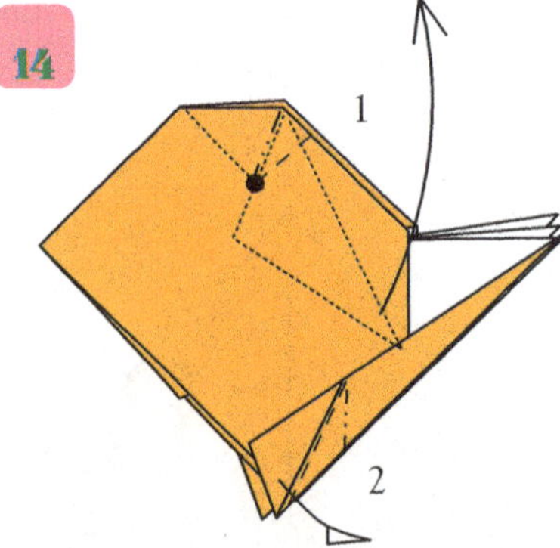

1. Crimp-fold the hidden flap.
   Pivot at the dot.
2. Reverse-fold, repeat behind.

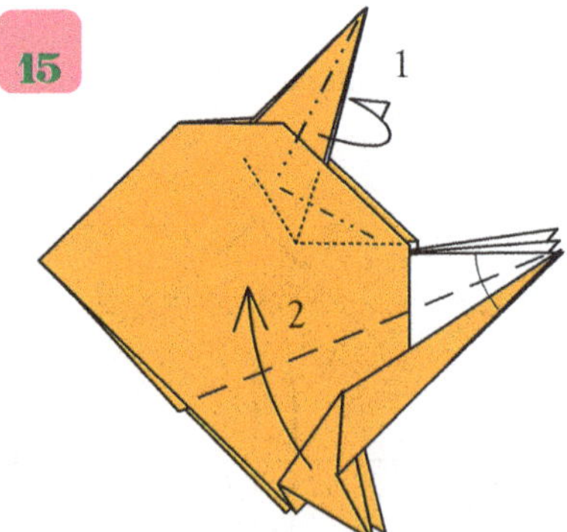

1. Squash-fold to thin the fin.
   Repeat behind. There is a
   hidden flap, one of the
   squash folds can cover it.
2. Repeat behind.

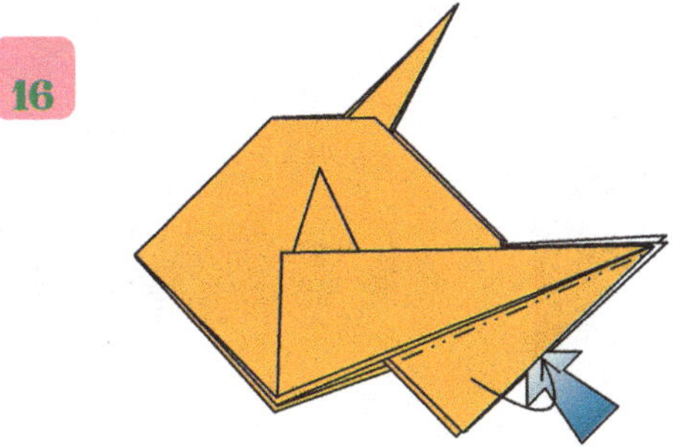

Reverse-fold and
repeat behind.

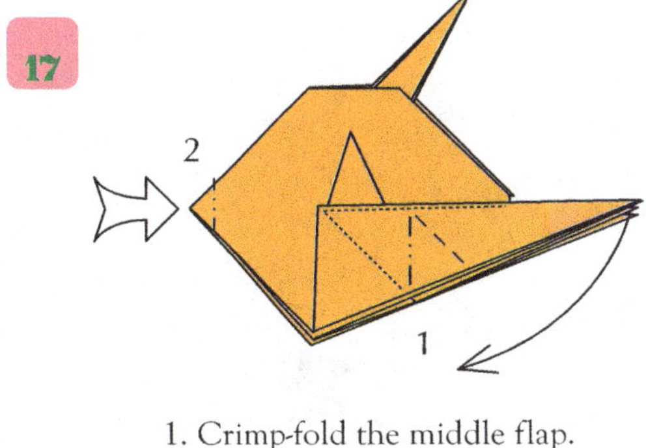

1. Crimp-fold the middle flap.
2. Spread to sink.

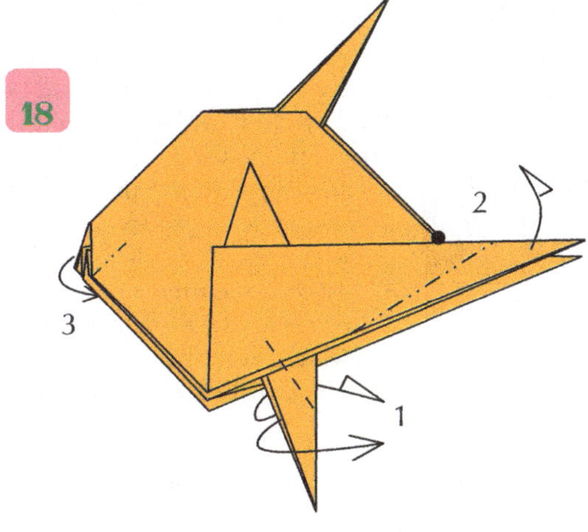

1. Outside-reverse-fold.
2. Mountain-fold the tail
   so it meets the dot,
   repeat behind.
3. Make a small reverse fold,
   repeat behind.

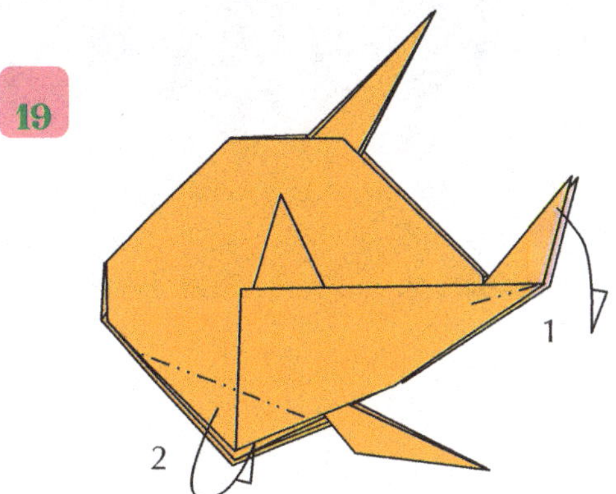

1. Mountain-fold.
2. Fold inside, repeat behind.

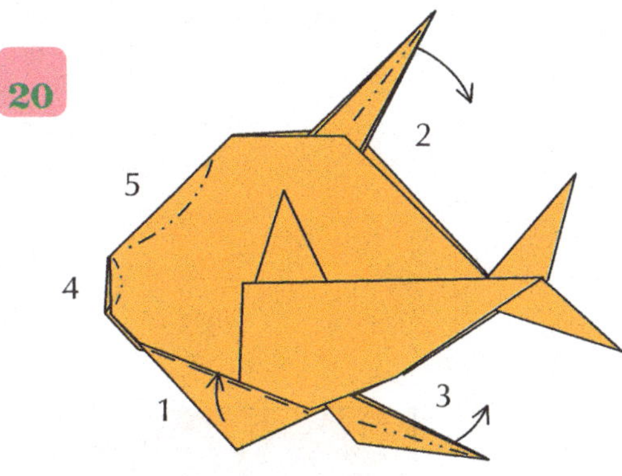

1. Fold inside.
2. Thin and curl the fin.
3. Thin and curl the fin.
4. Shape the mouth.
5. Shape the face.

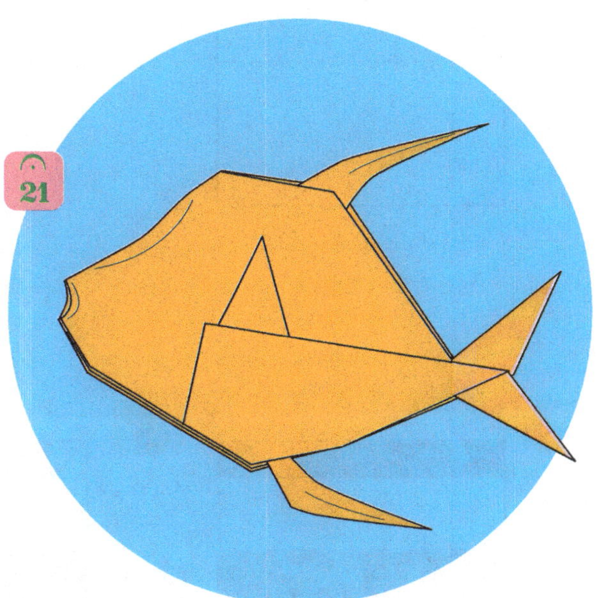

Lookdown

Ocean Liner

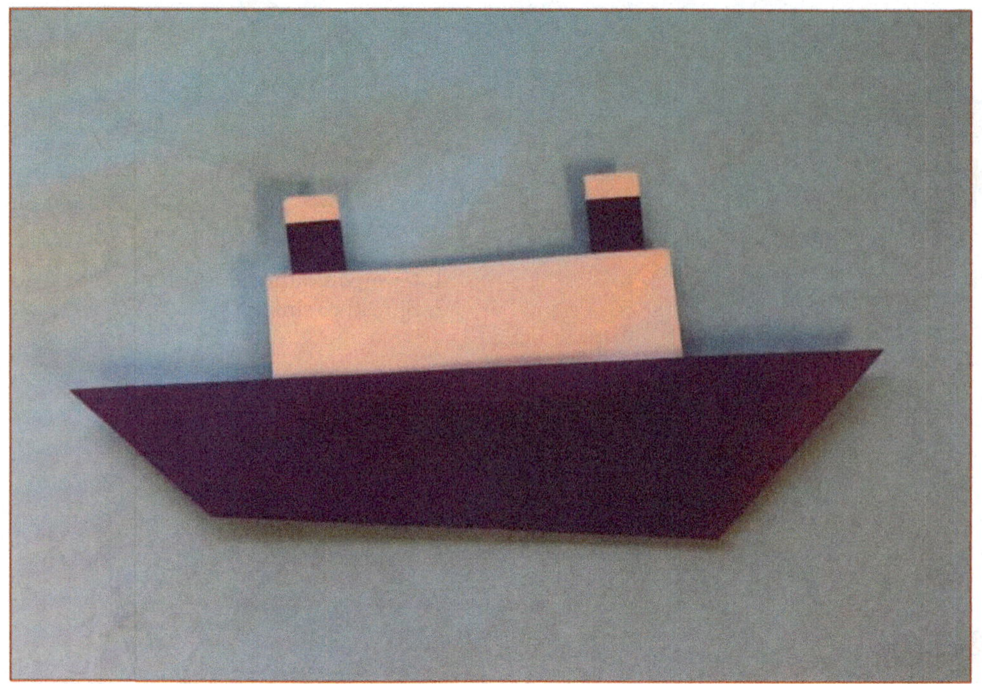

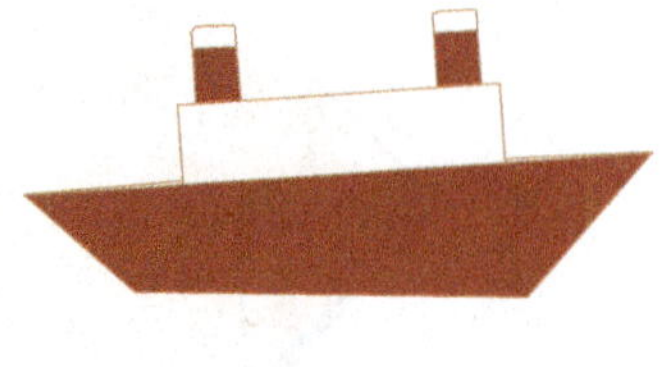

The sailboat took us only so far. Let's explore the oceans in an Ocean Liner and travel much further.

After centuries of sailboats, rowboats, and other water craft, the industrial age brought the advent of machine-powered boats that didn't have to rely on human or wind power. Using coal, steam, and eventually gas and diesel fuel, these large ships can carry thousands of people across the world at one time and provide a luxurious way to take a vacation with the sea, open sky, and exotic ports of call as their backdrop.

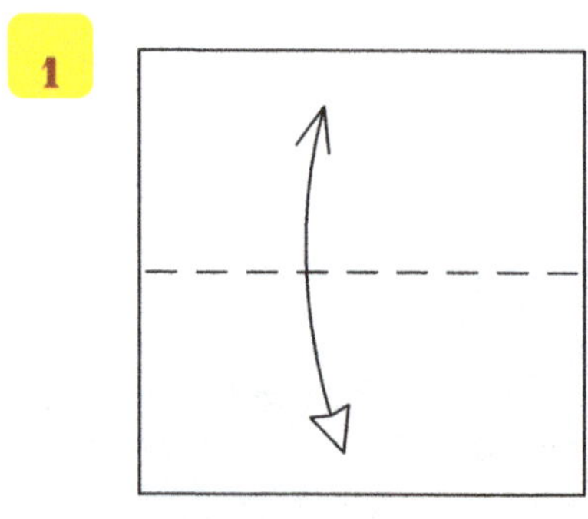

Fold and unfold.

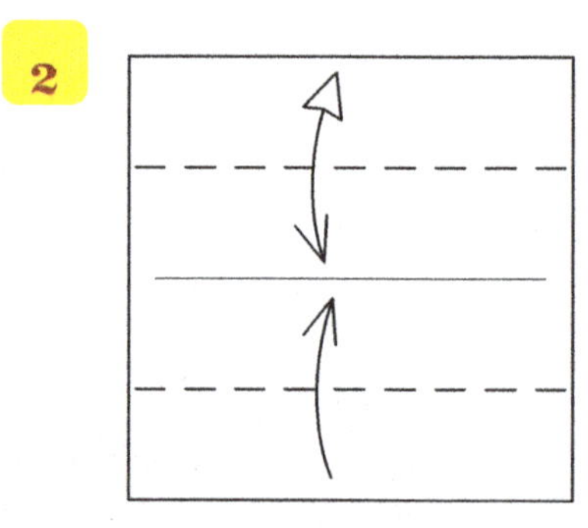

Fold and unfold
on the top.

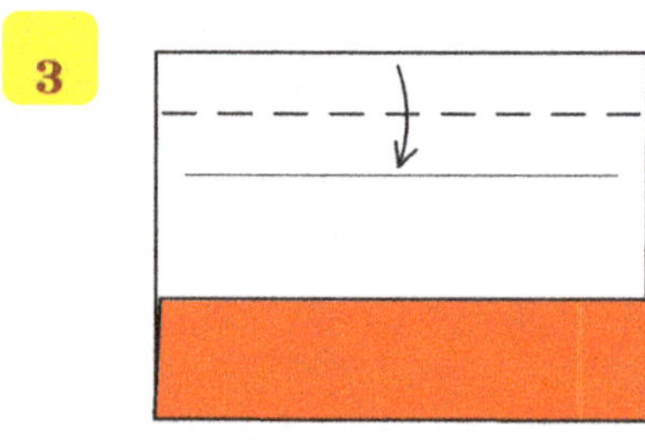

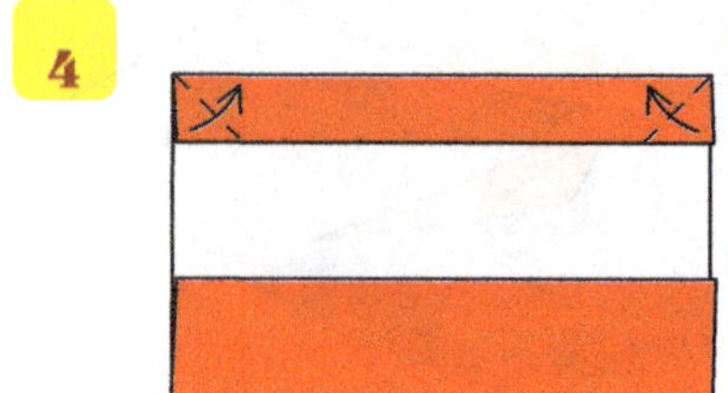

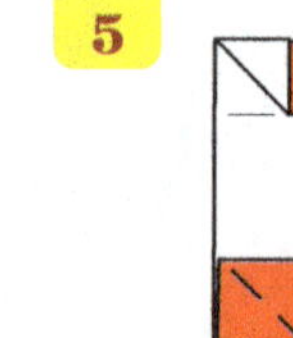

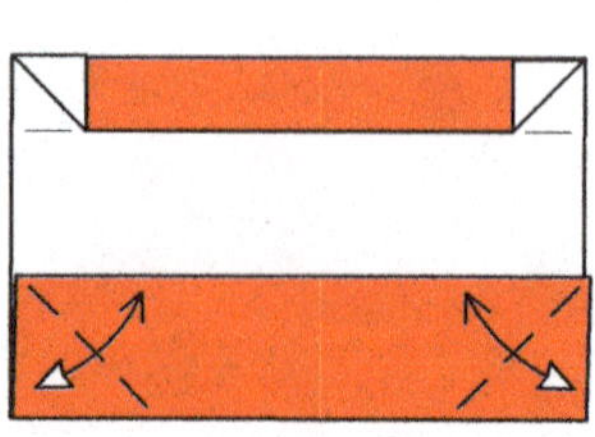

Fold and unfold.

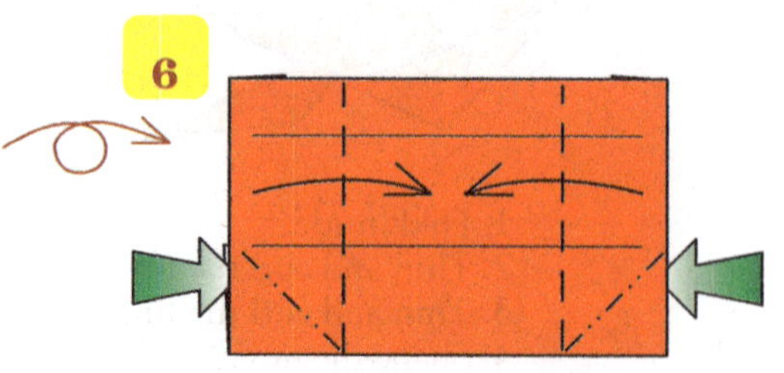

Make squash folds.

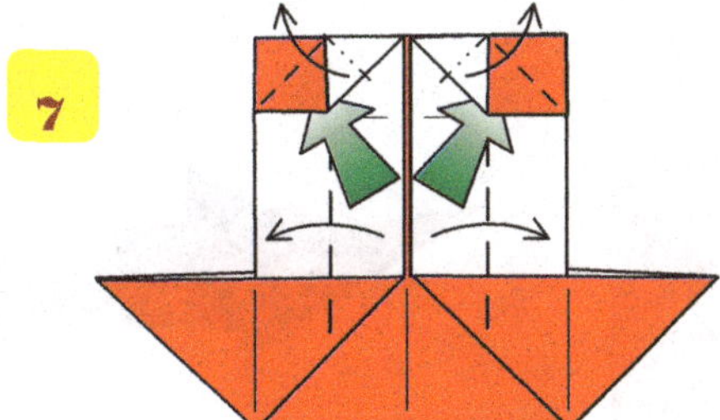

7

Make squash folds.

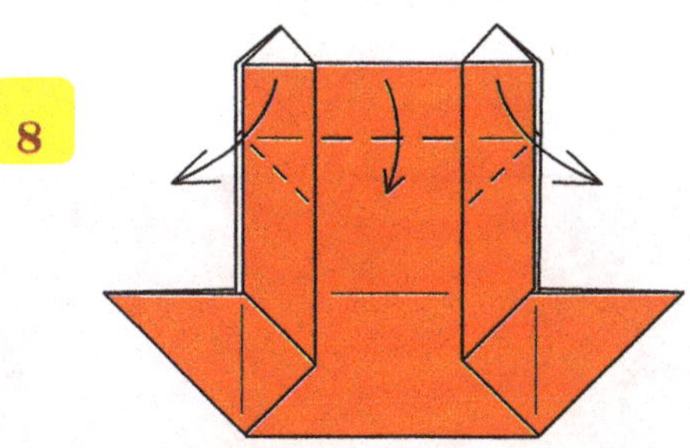

8

Petal-fold.

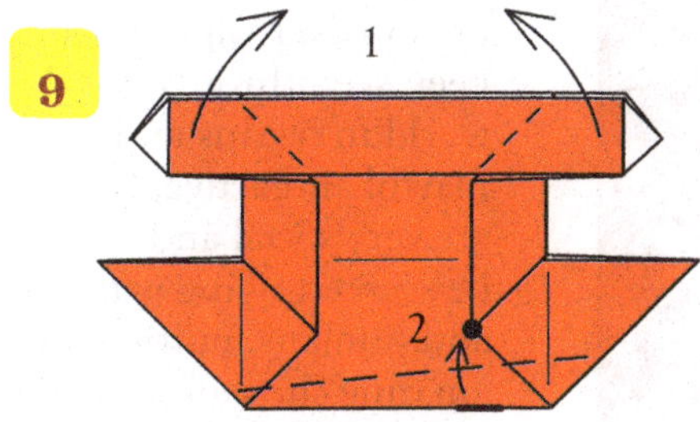

9

1. Fold up.
2. Bring the edge to the dot.

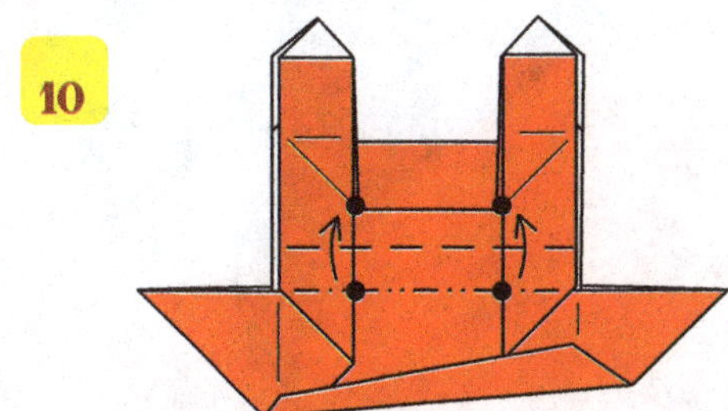

10

Pleat-fold.

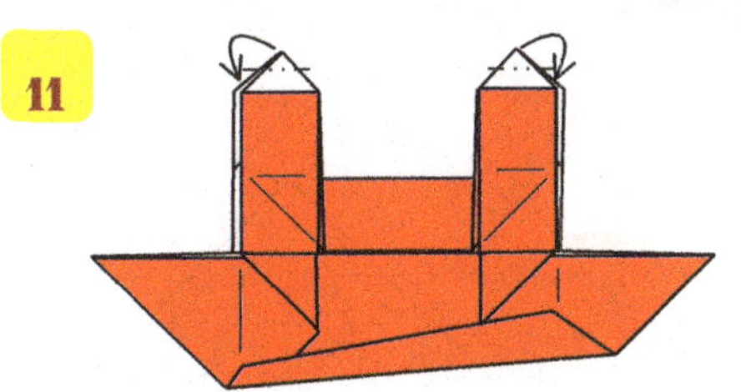

11

Make reverse folds.

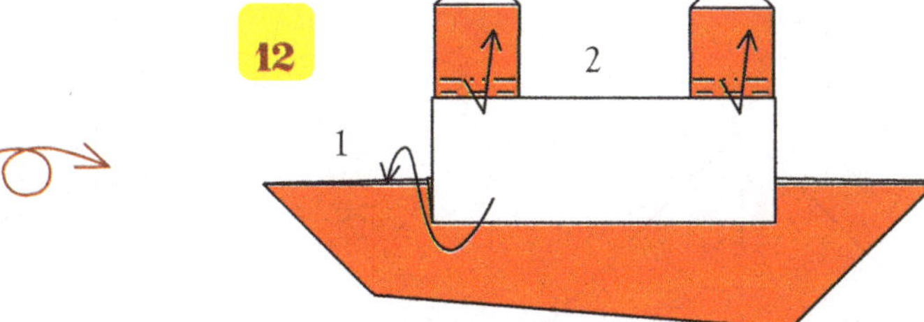

12

1. Tuck inside.
2. Make pleat folds.

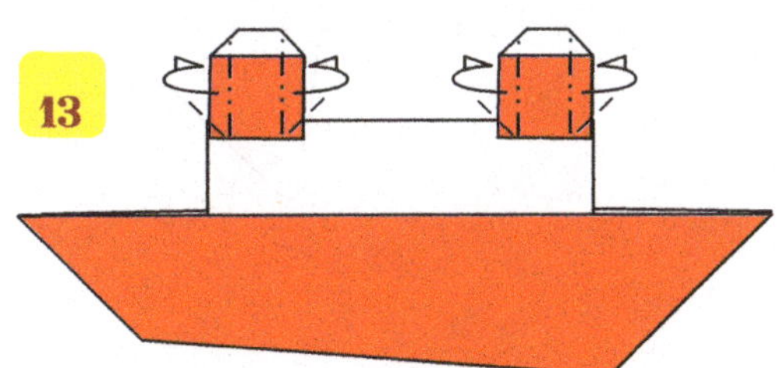

13

Make small reverse folds
to thin the smoke stacks.

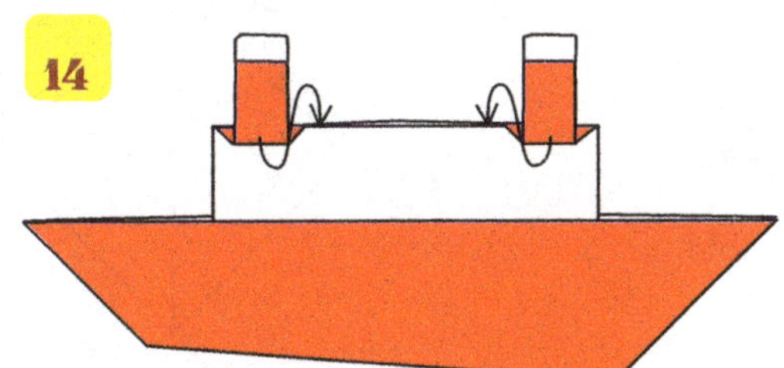

14

Tuck inside and rotate.

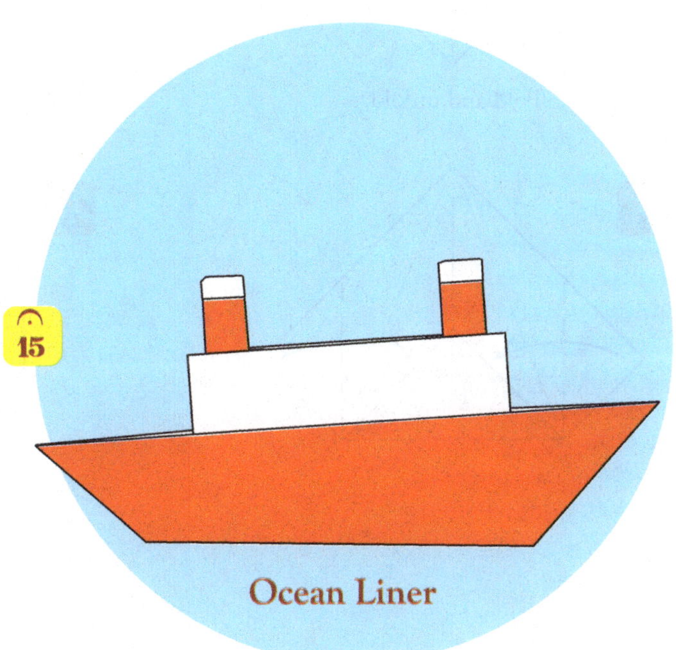

15

Ocean Liner

Dolphin

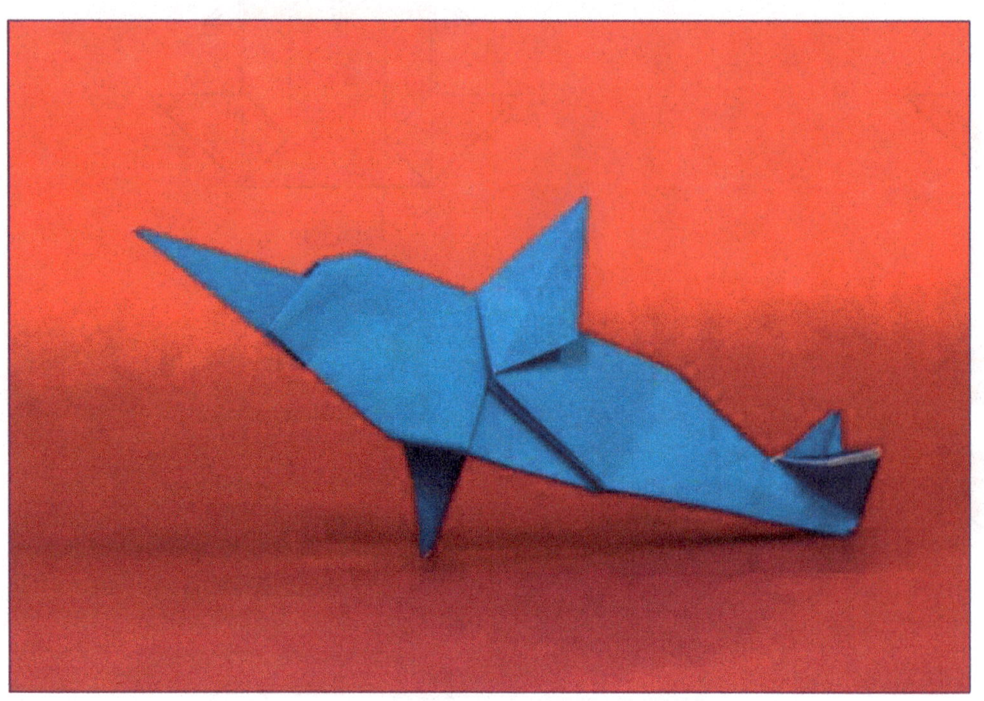

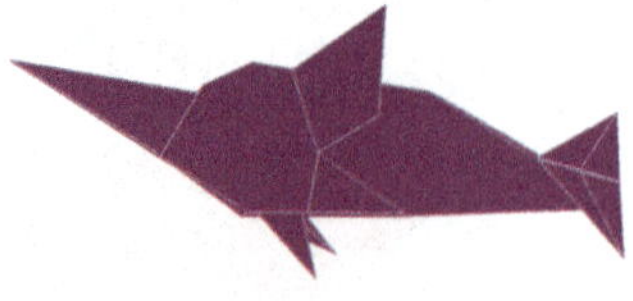

Very intelligent aquatic mammals, Dolphins can been seen throughout the world in oceans and lakes. Playful and active, Dolphins are very social and can often be seen engaging with boats and humans, putting on an amazing show of jumping and gliding speedily through the water.

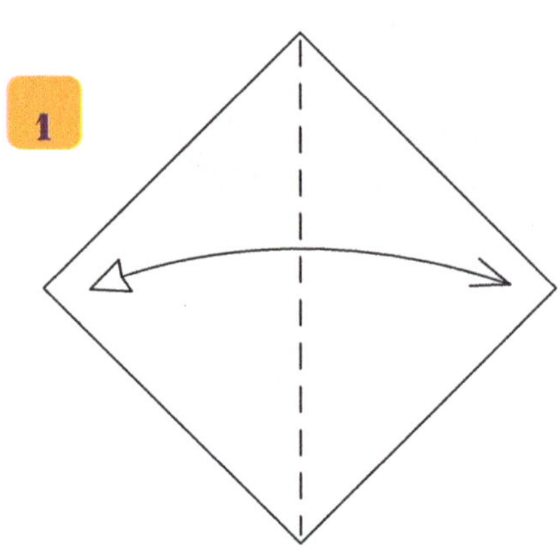

1 Fold and unfold.

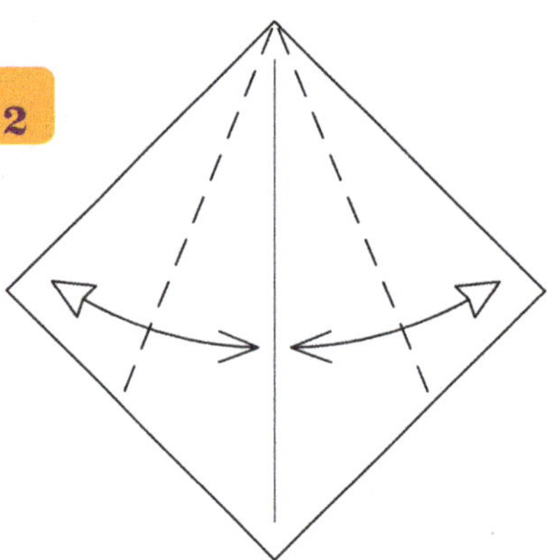

2 Fold and unfold.

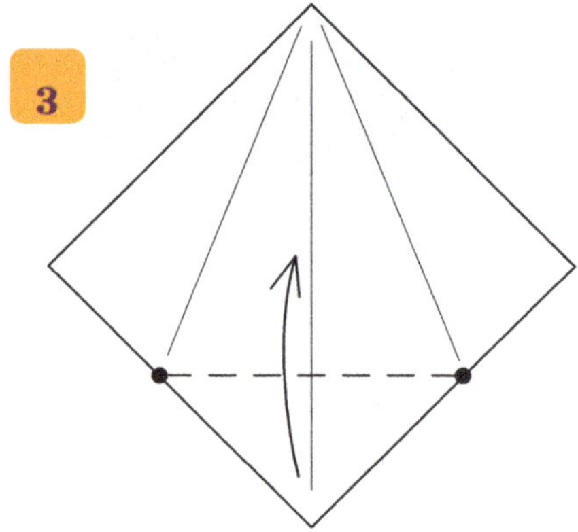

3

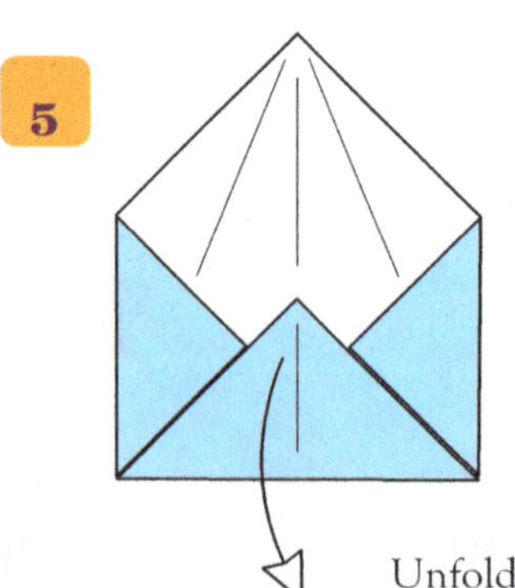

4

5 Unfold.

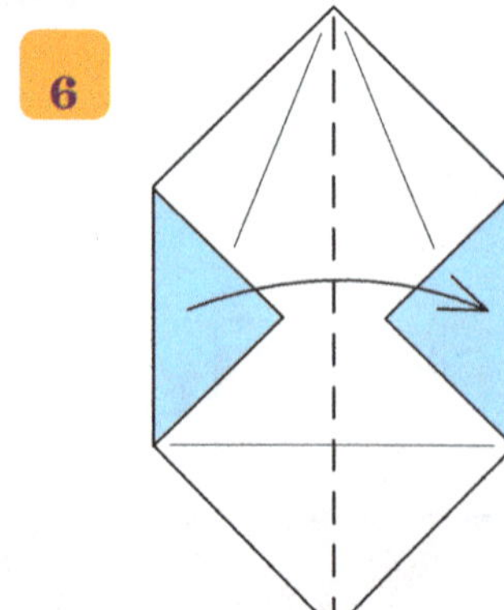

6 Fold in half and rotate 90°.

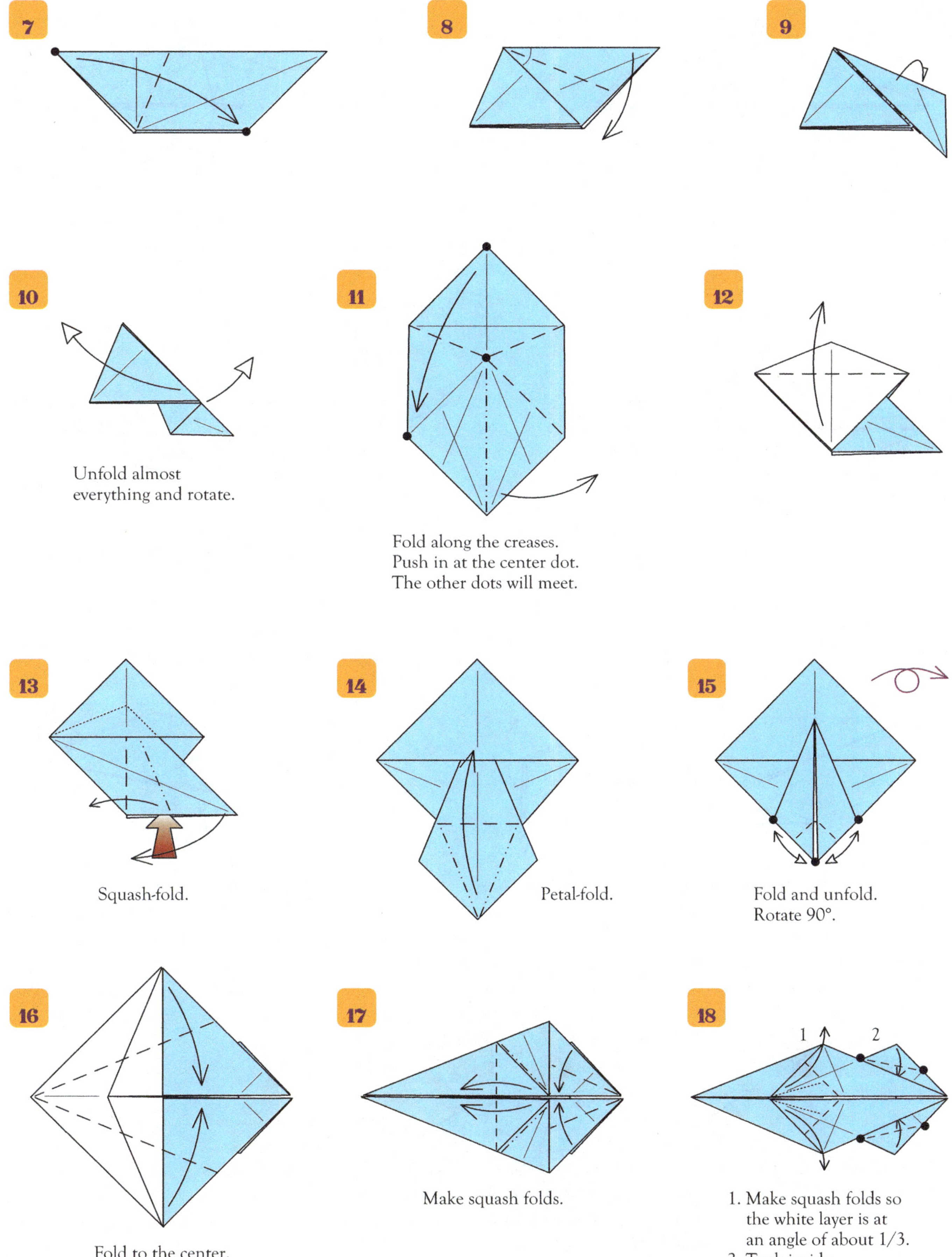

Unfold almost
everything and rotate.

Fold along the creases.
Push in at the center dot.
The other dots will meet.

Squash-fold.

Petal-fold.

Fold and unfold.
Rotate 90°.

Fold to the center.

Make squash folds.

1. Make squash folds so
   the white layer is at
   an angle of about 1/3.
2. Tuck inside.

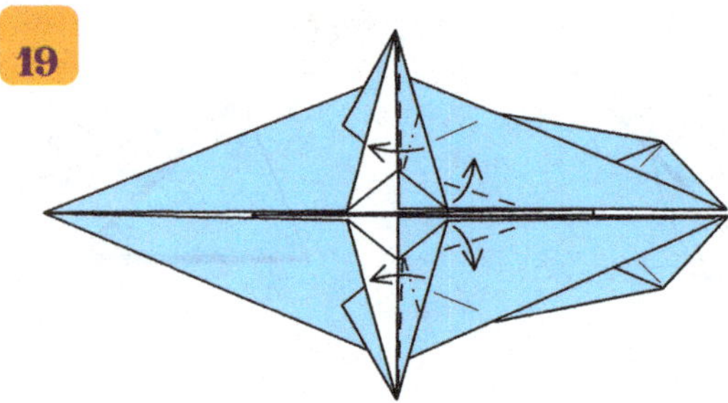

Make squash folds.

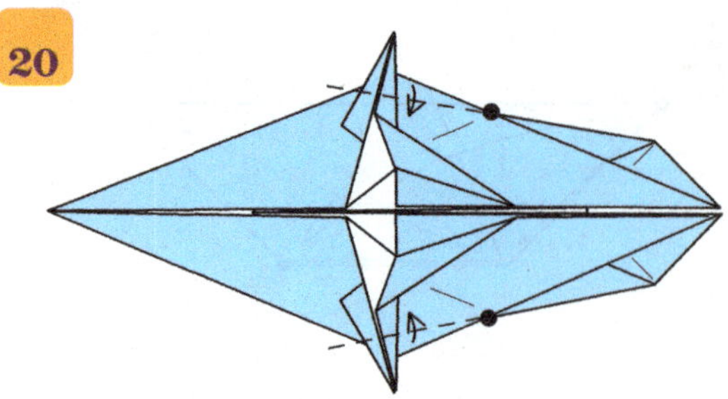

Fold behind the fin.

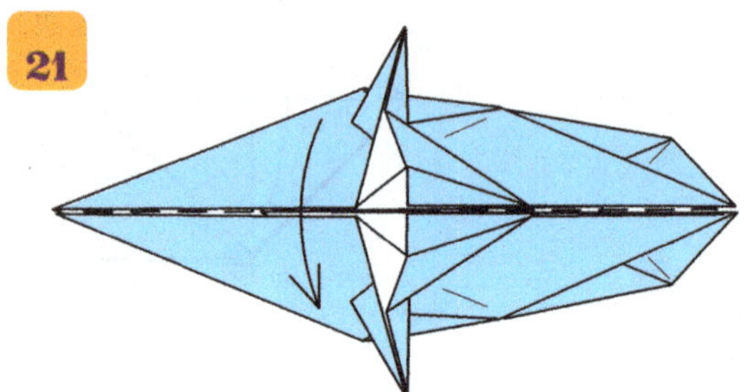

Fold in half.

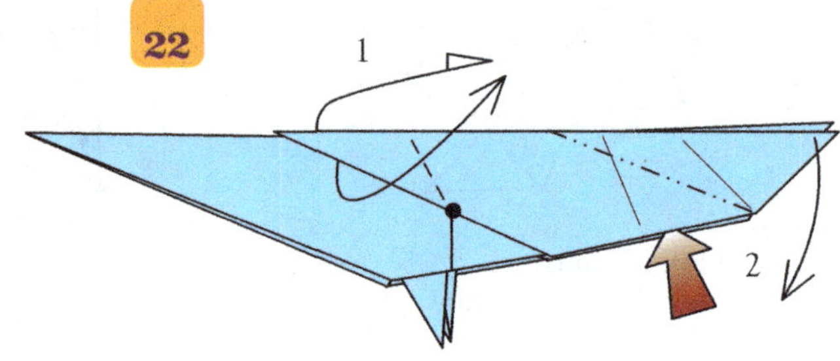

1. Outside-reverse-fold.
2. Reverse-fold.

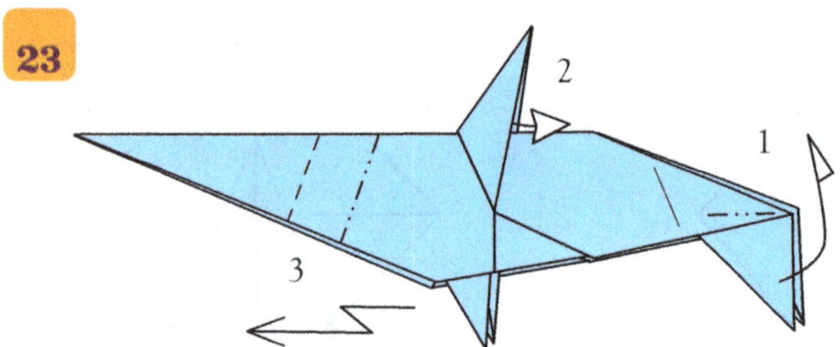

1. Fold along the crease,
   repeat behind.
2. Pull out, repeat behind.
3. Crimp-fold.

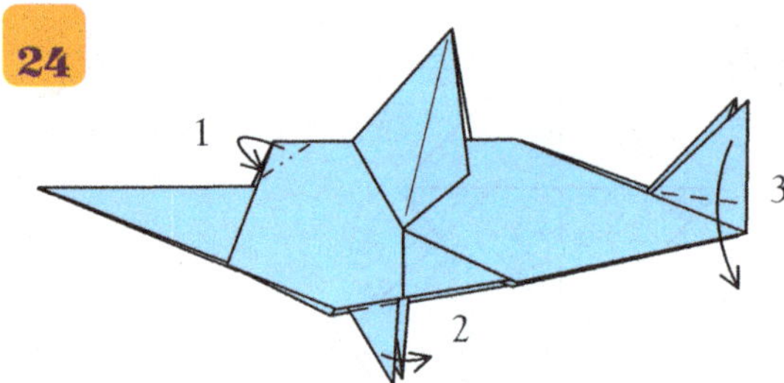

1. Reverse-fold.
2. Shape the fin, repeat behind.
3. Shape the tail, repeat behind.

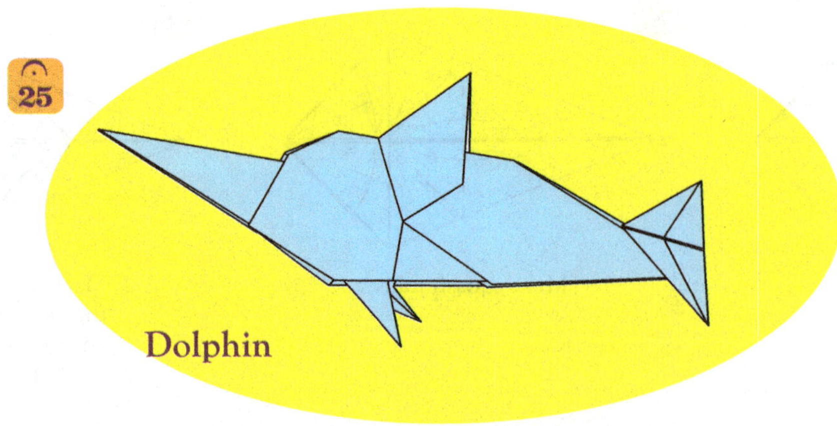

Dolphin

Orca

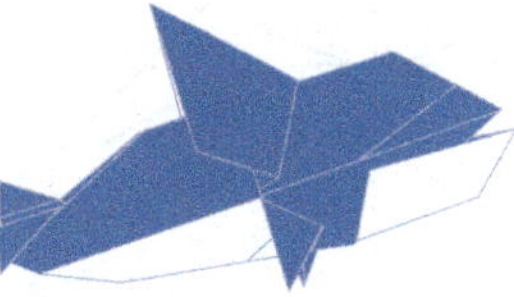

Orcas bear a very distinctive black and white coloring that makes them instantly identifiable. While they can be fierce when protecting their young or seeking food, the highly intelligent Orca can also be playful and gentle.

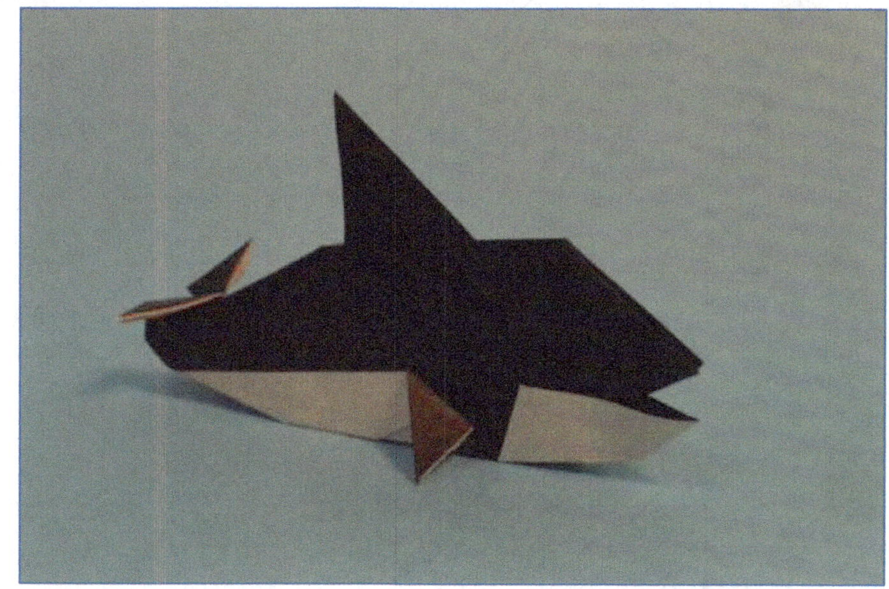

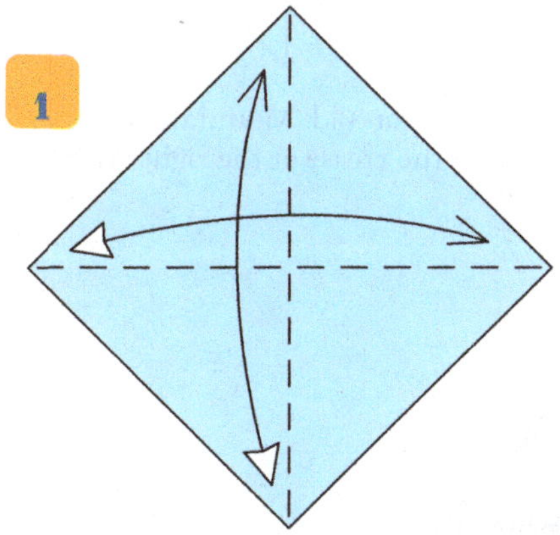

1

Fold and unfold.

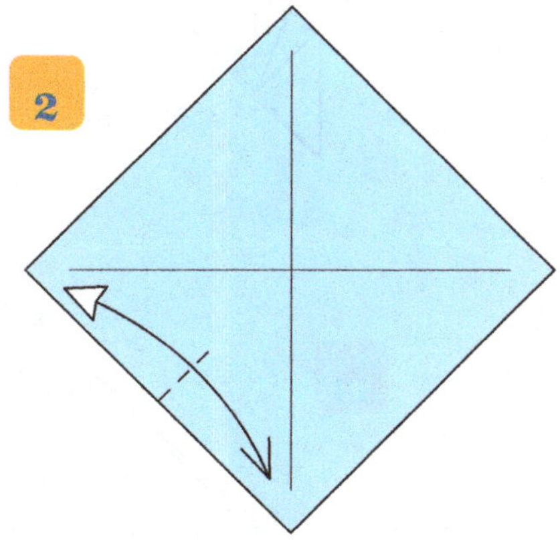

2

Fold and unfold
on the edge.

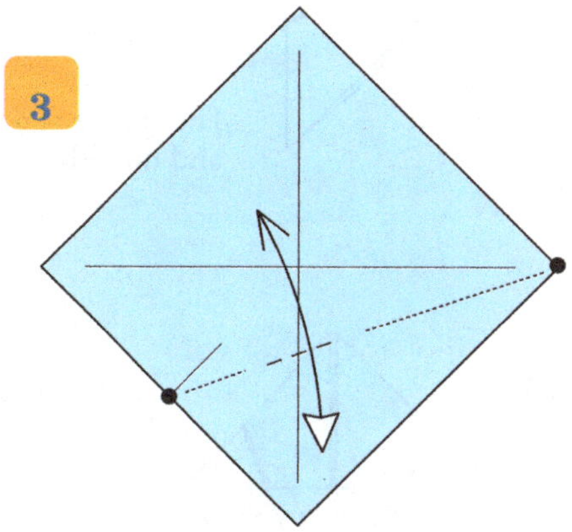

3

Fold and unfold
on the diagonal.

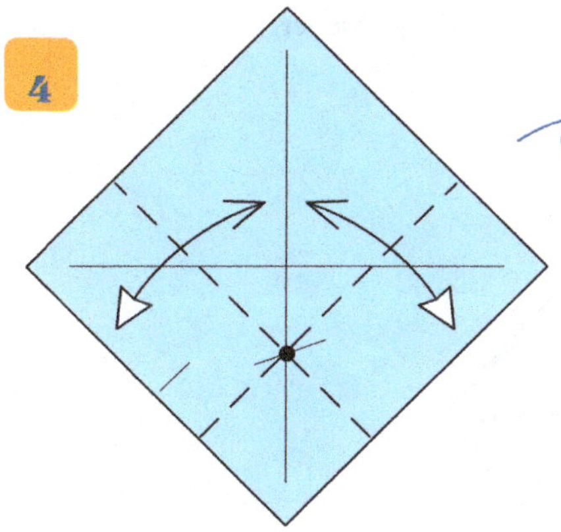

4

Fold and unfold.

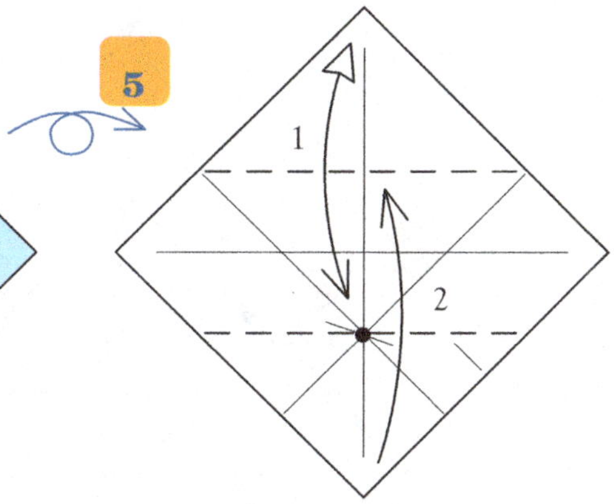

5

1. Fold and unfold.
2. Fold up.

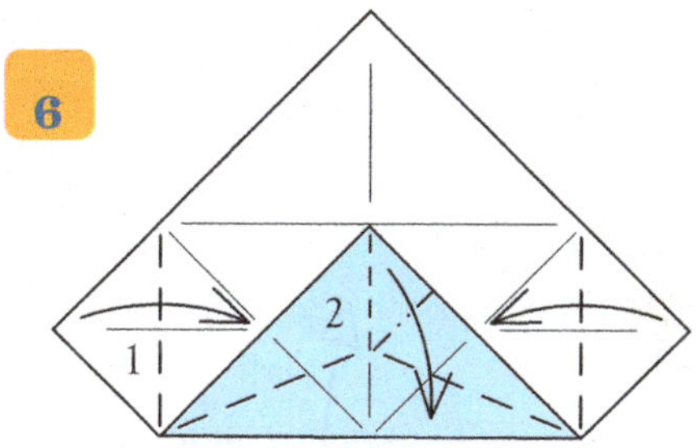

6

1. Fold on the left and right.
2. Rabbit-ear.

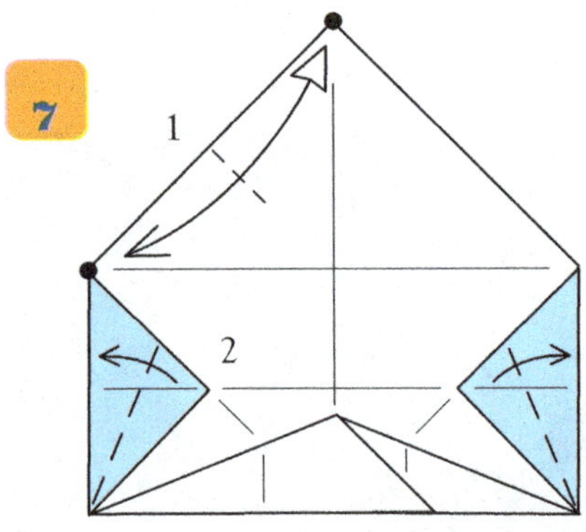

1. Fold and unfold.
2. Fold on the left and right.

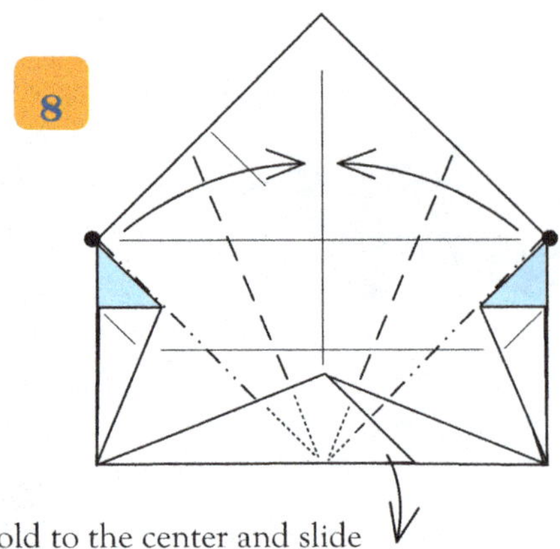

Fold to the center and slide
the bottom corner down.

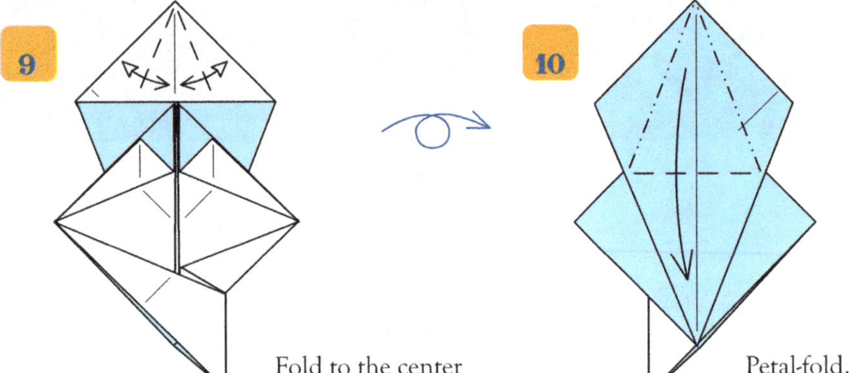

Fold to the center
and unfold.

Petal-fold.

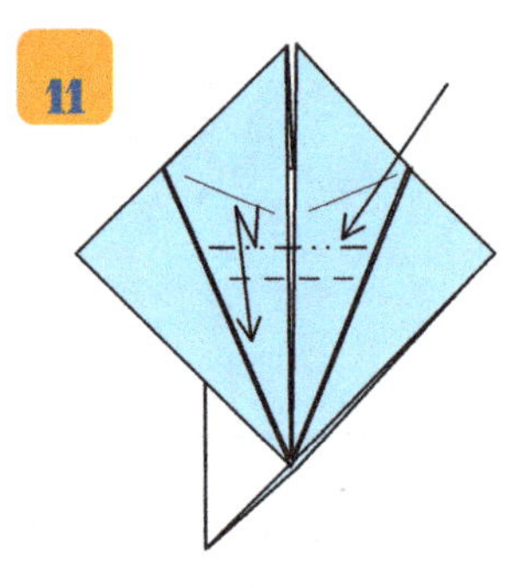

Pleat-fold. Mountain-fold along
the crease at the right arrow.

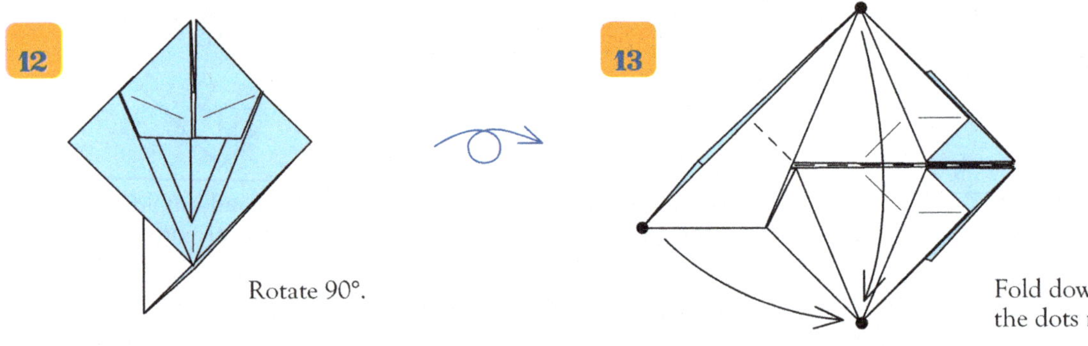

Rotate 90°.

Fold down so
the dots meet.

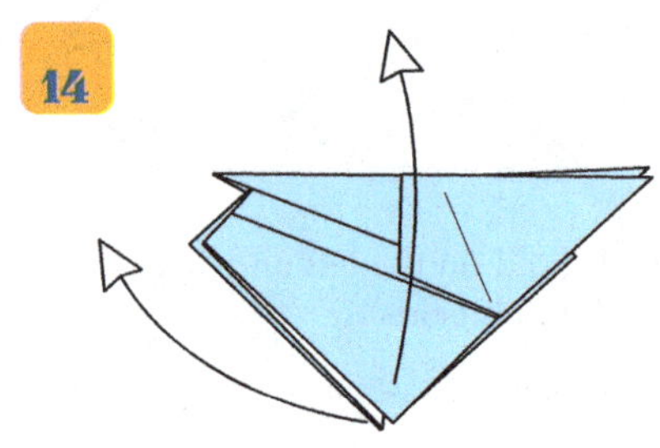

Unfold back to step 13.

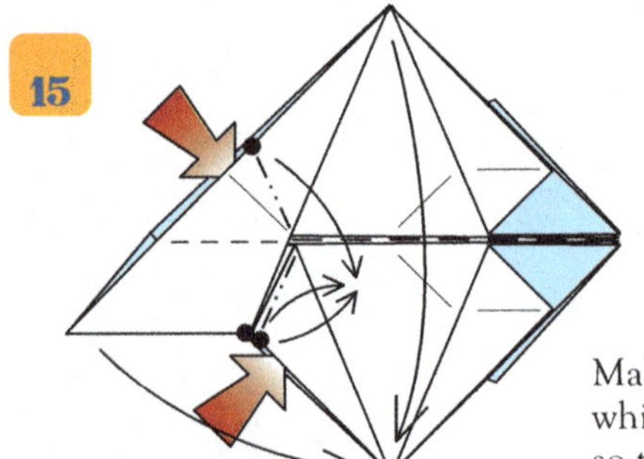

Make squash folds
while folding down
so the dots meet.

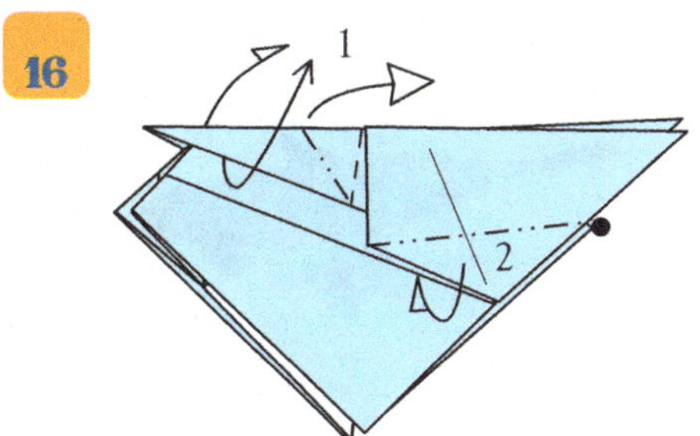

1. Outside-reverse-fold and spread.
2. Fold behind, repeat behind.

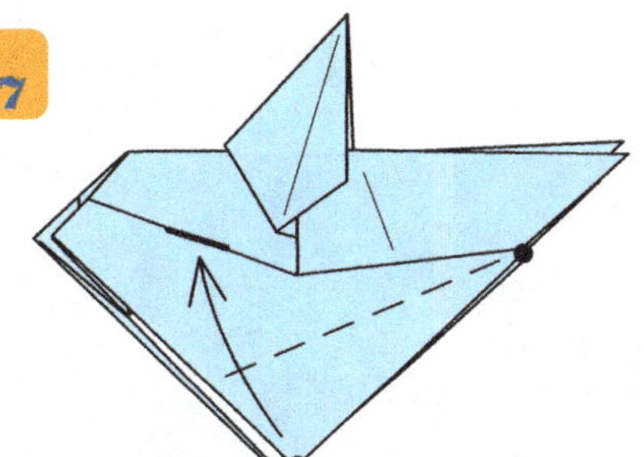

Bring the dot to the
line. Repeat behind.

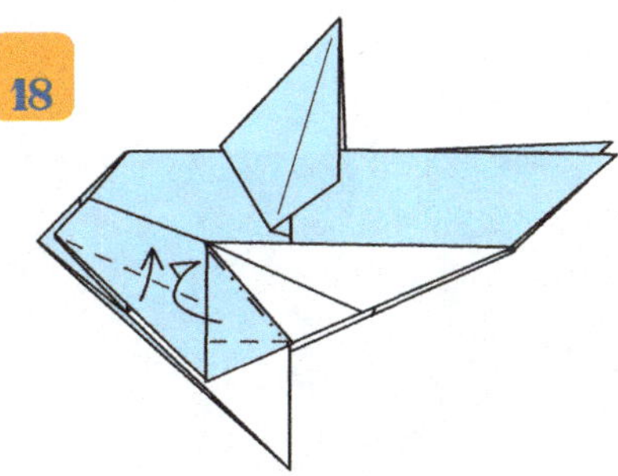

Reverse-fold and
repeat behind.

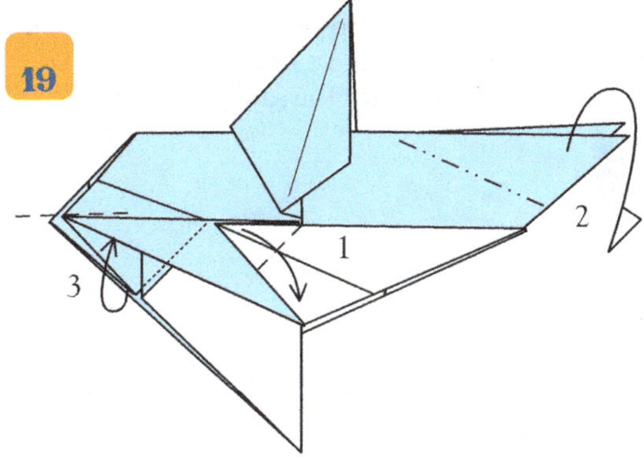

1. Fold down, repeat behind.
2. Reverse-fold.
3. Fold the layers together to
   tuck inside.

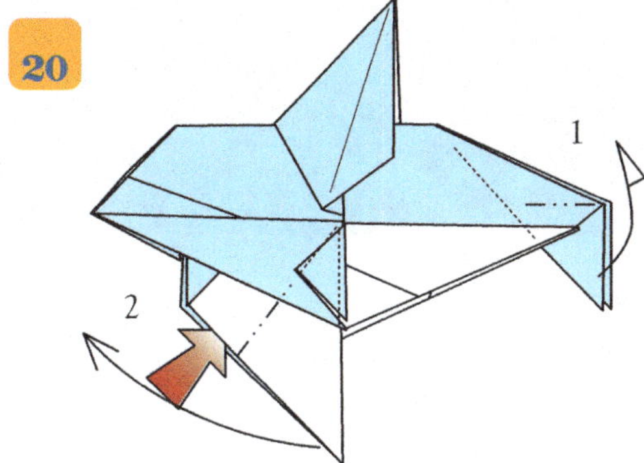

1. Fold up, repeat behind.
2. Reverse-fold.

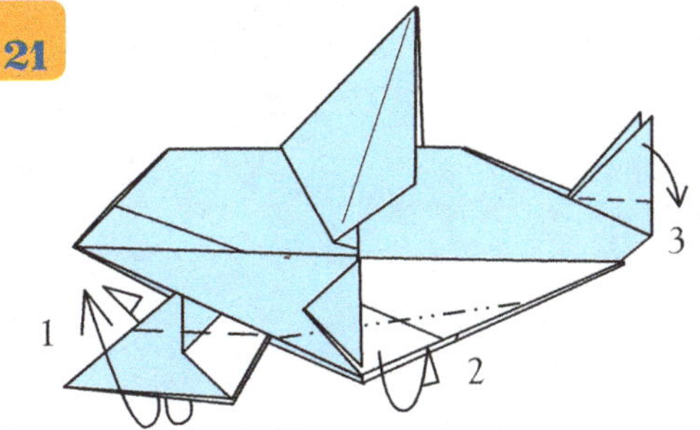

1. Outside-reverse-fold.
2. Fold inside, repeat behind.
3. Fold out, repeat behind.
   The tail is 3D.

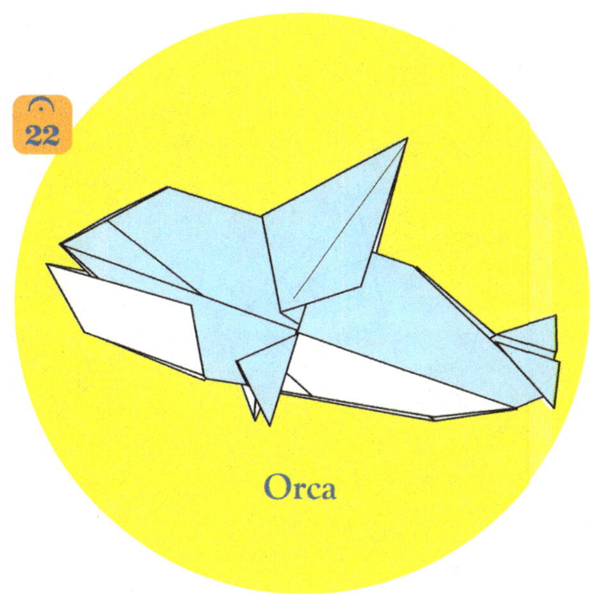

Orca

Saw Shark

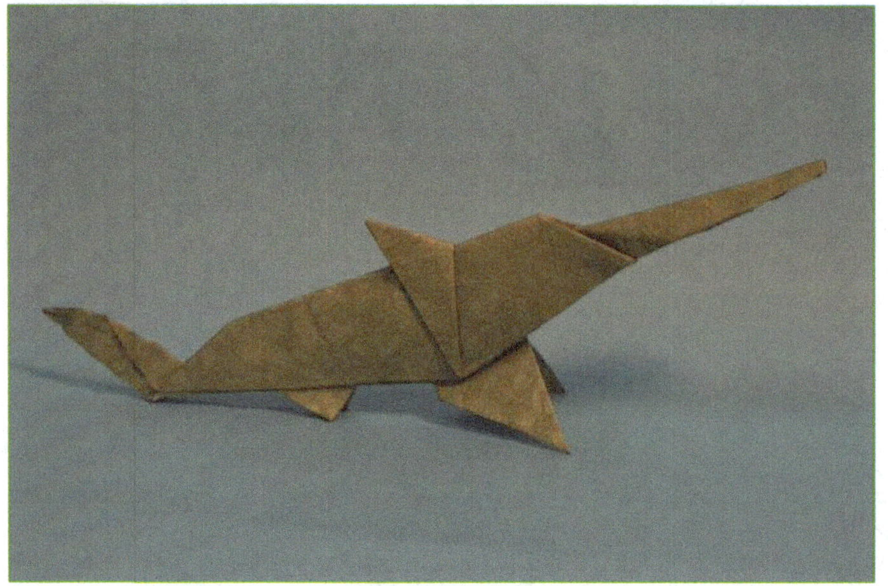

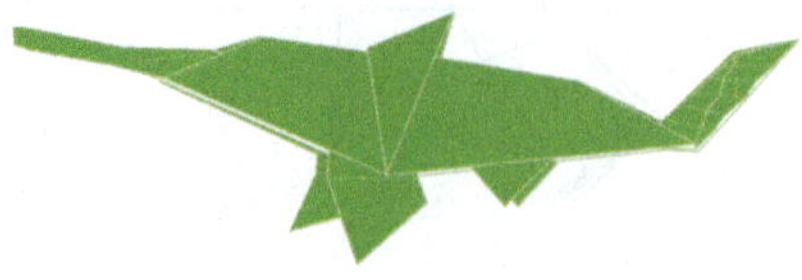

Saw Sharks bear a long saw-shaped snout that is used to slash their prey and provide them with protection from other aquatic predators. They also have special receptors in their saws that allow them to detect prey that is hidden underneath the sandy ocean floor.

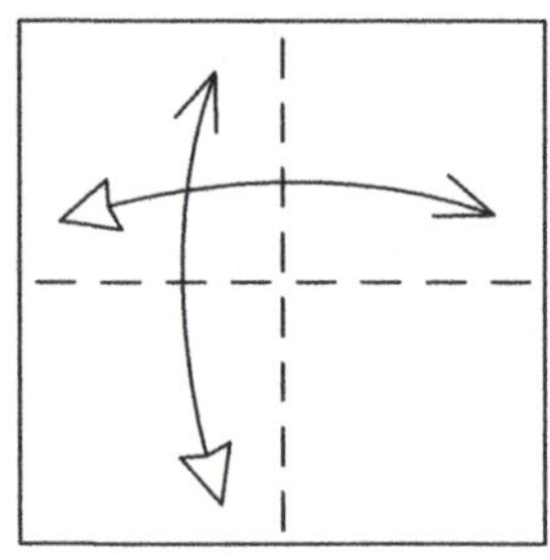

Fold and unfold. Rotate.

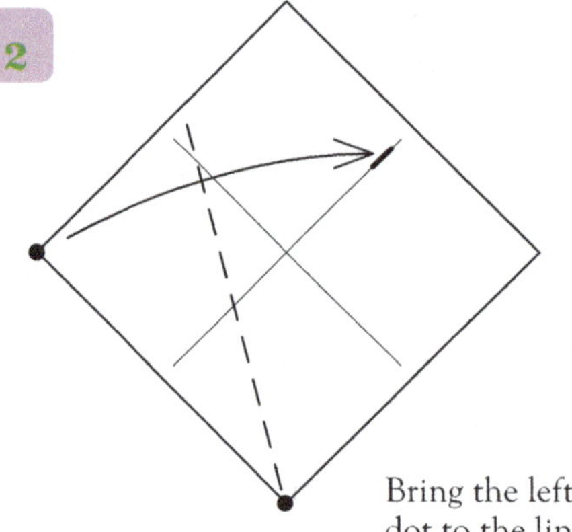

Bring the left dot to the line.

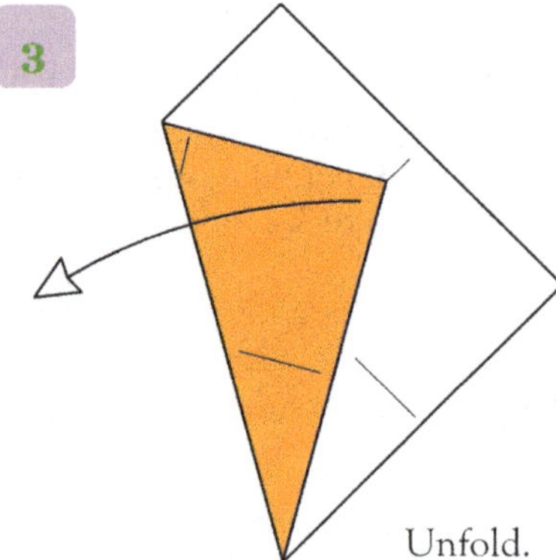

Unfold.

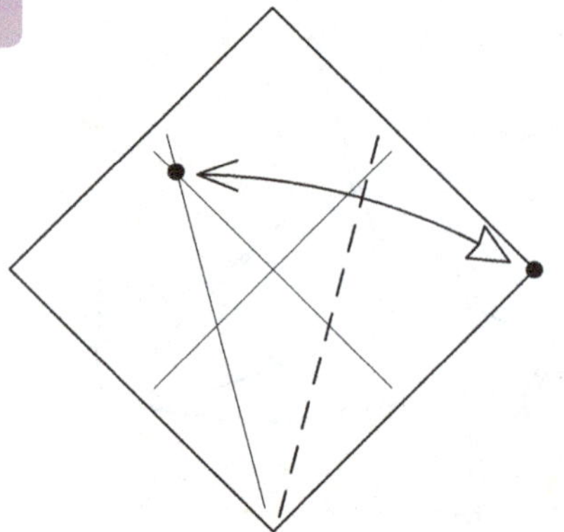

Fold and unfold. Rotate 180°.

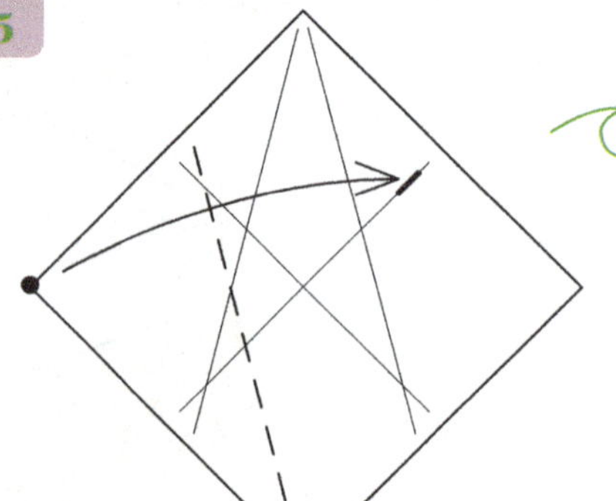

Repeat steps 2–4.

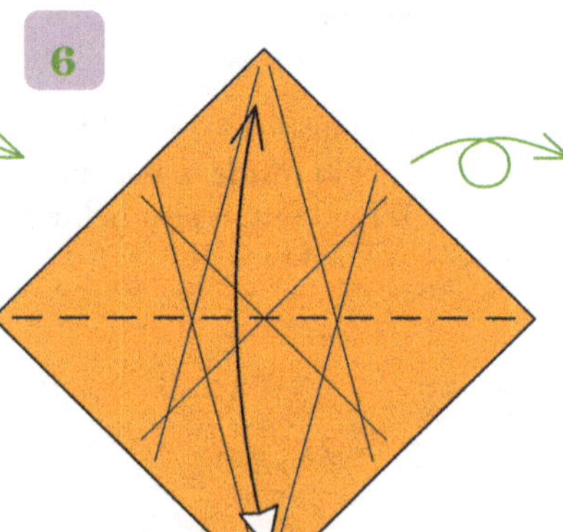

Fold and unfold.

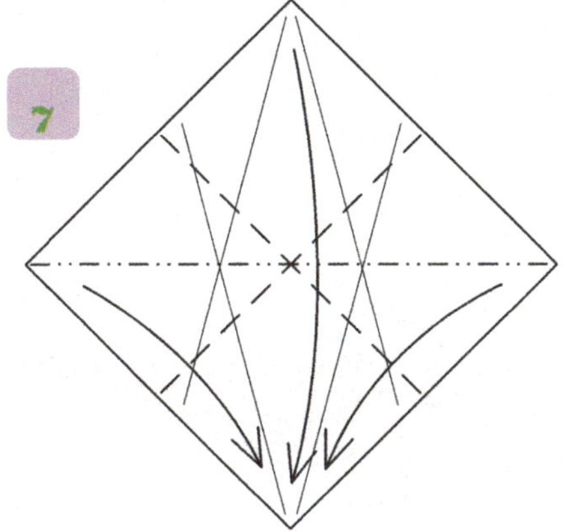

Fold along the creases.

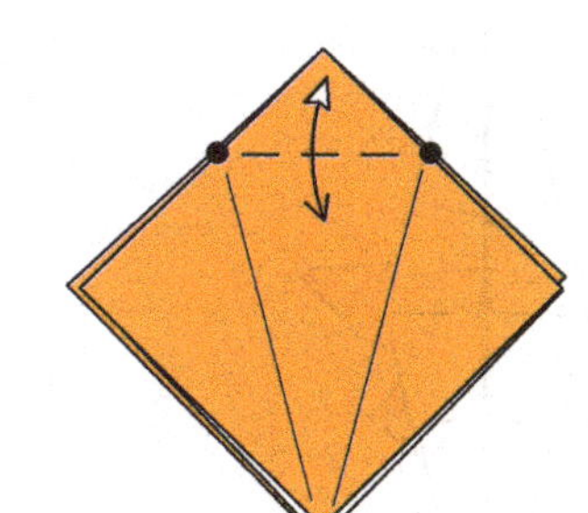

Fold and unfold.

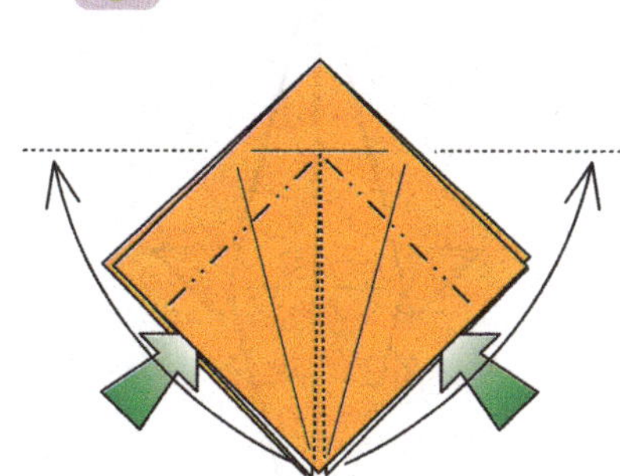

Make reverse folds.

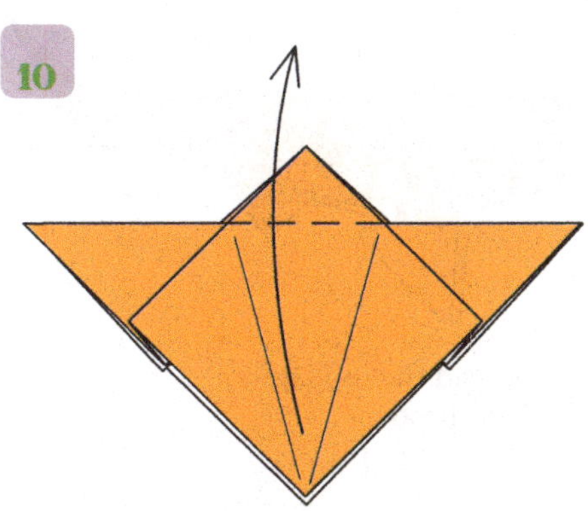

It is easier to do steps
9 and 10 as one step.

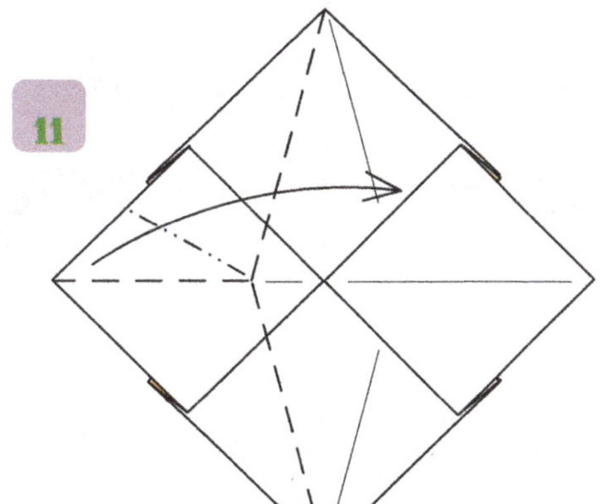

Rabbit-ear along
some of the creases.

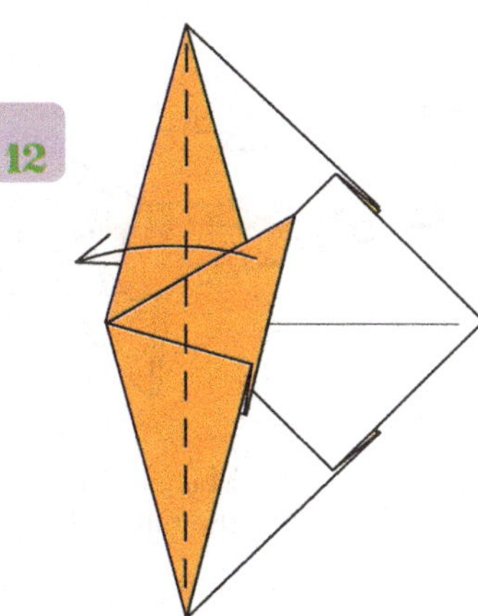

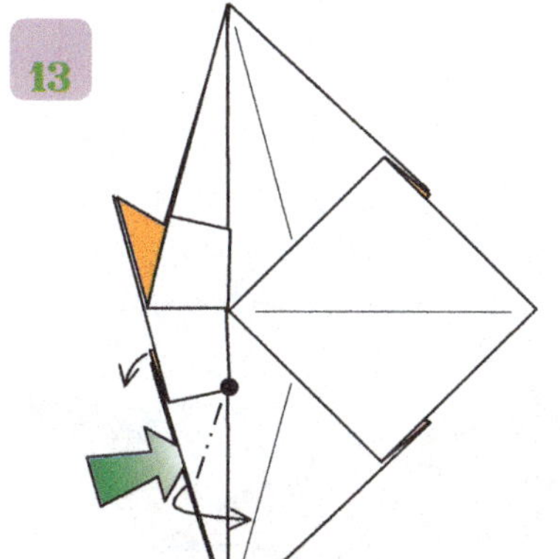

Pivot at the dot.

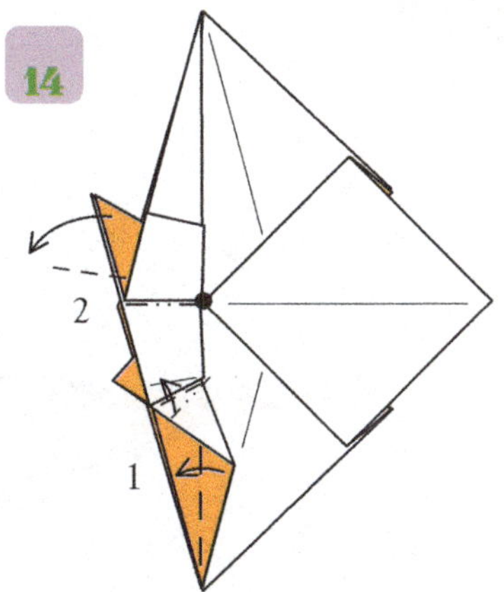

1. Squash-fold.
2. Pivot at the dot.

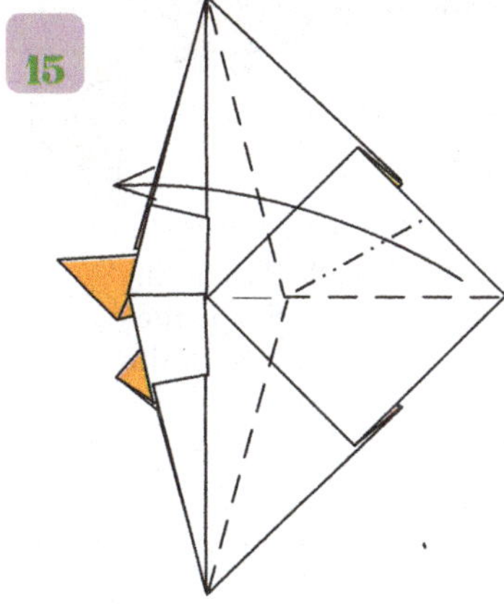

Repeat steps 11–14
on the right.

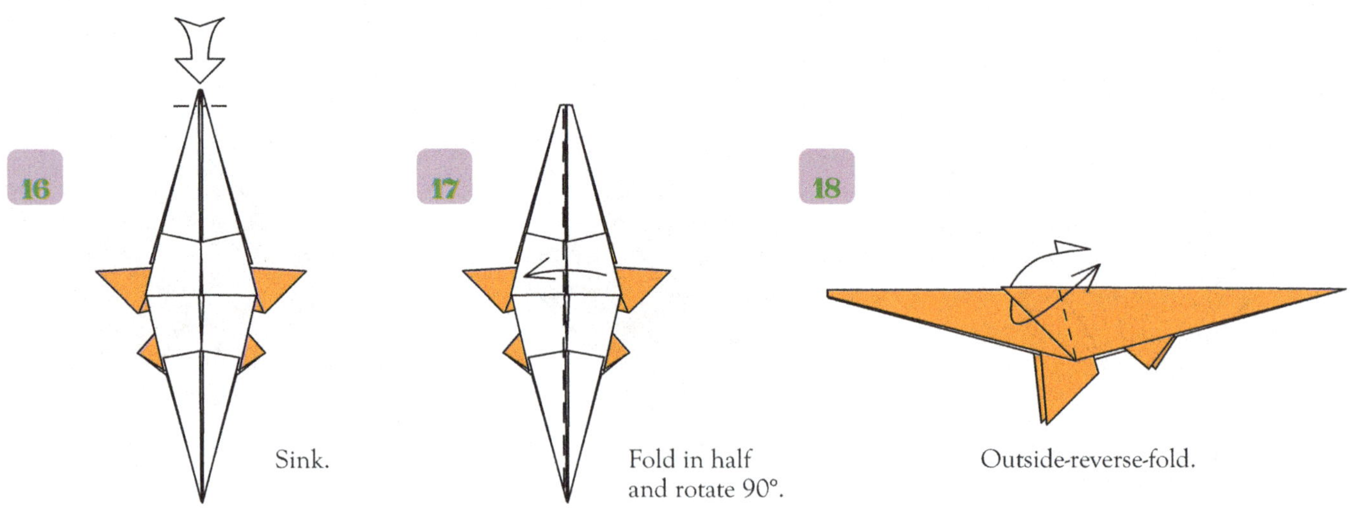

16

Sink.

17

Fold in half
and rotate 90°.

18

Outside-reverse-fold.

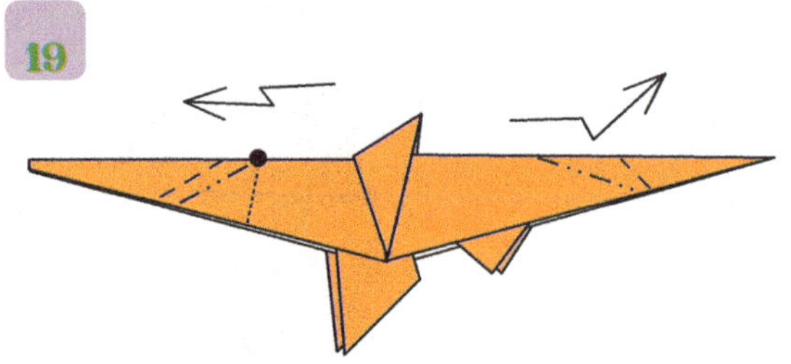

19

Make crimp folds at
the tail and head.

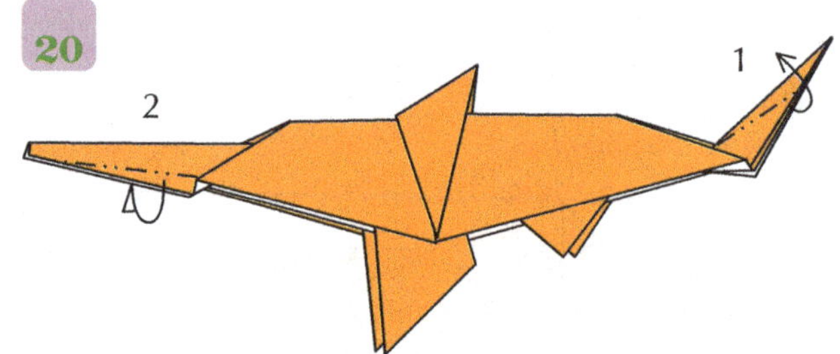

20

2

1

1. Spread the top layer.
2. Fold inside.
Repeat behind.

21

3

1

2

1. Pleat-fold.
2. Shape the fin, repeat behind.
3. Flatten the head.

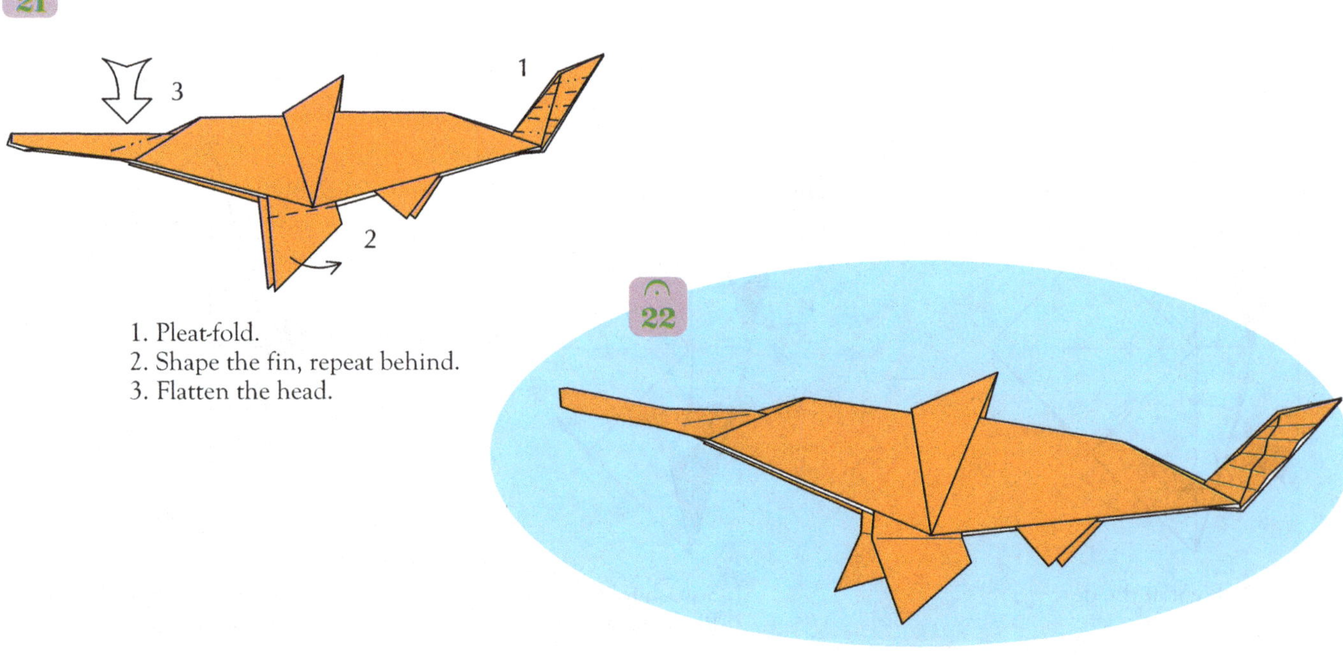

22

Saw Shark

Blue Shark

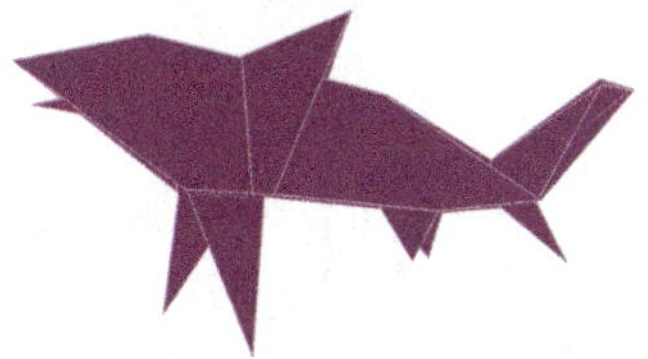

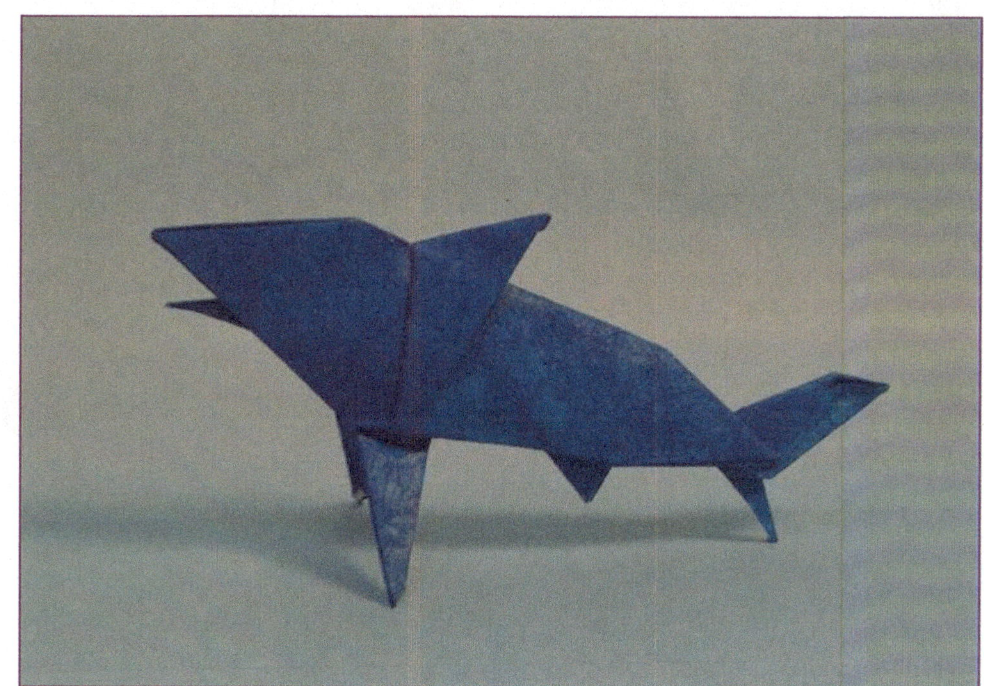

Blue Sharks can be found throughout the oceans of the world, preferring cooler waters. Fast swimmers, they have a varied appetite that includes such prey as squid, octopus and other invertebrates as well as crustaceans such as lobsters.

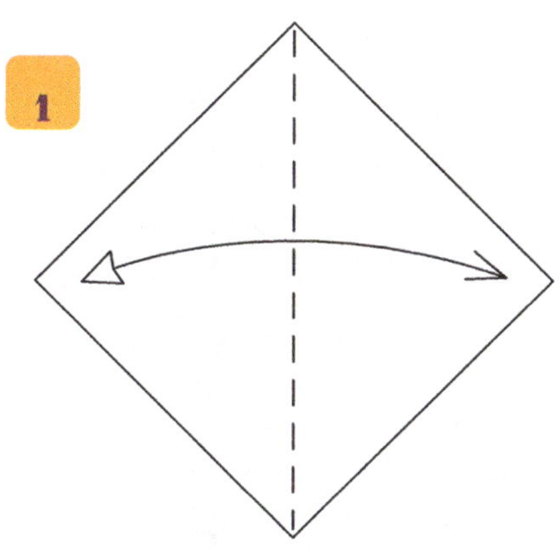

1

Fold and unfold.

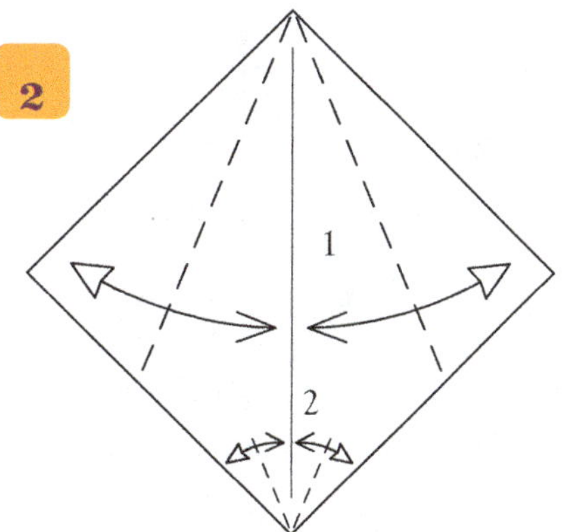

2

Fold and unfold.

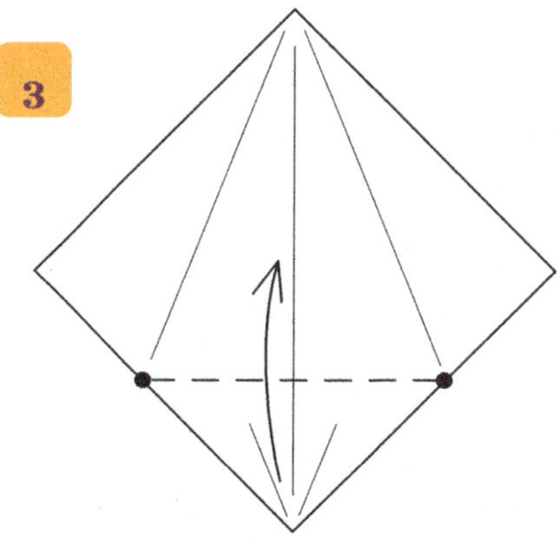

3

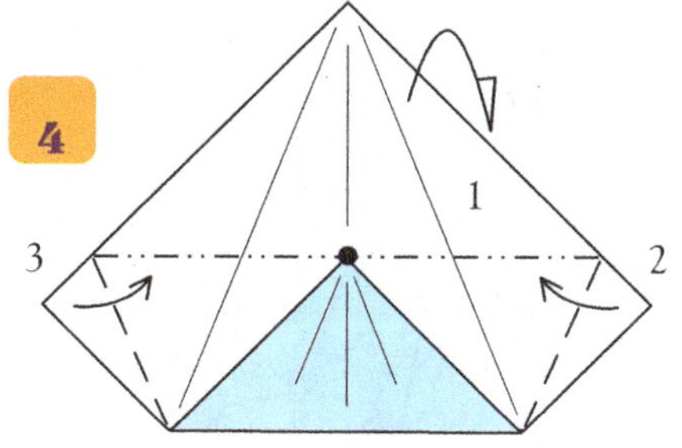

4

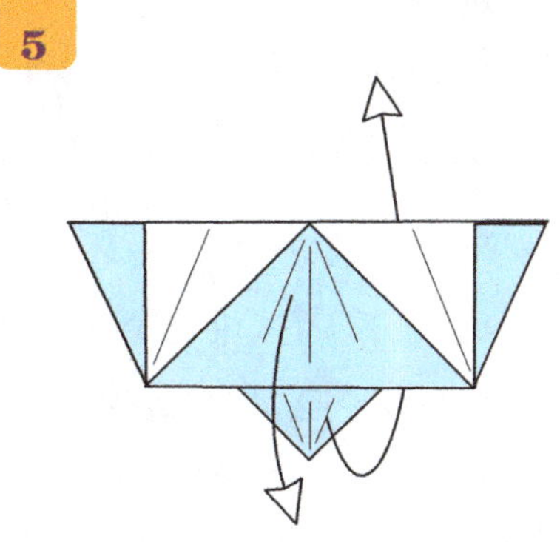

5

Unfold.

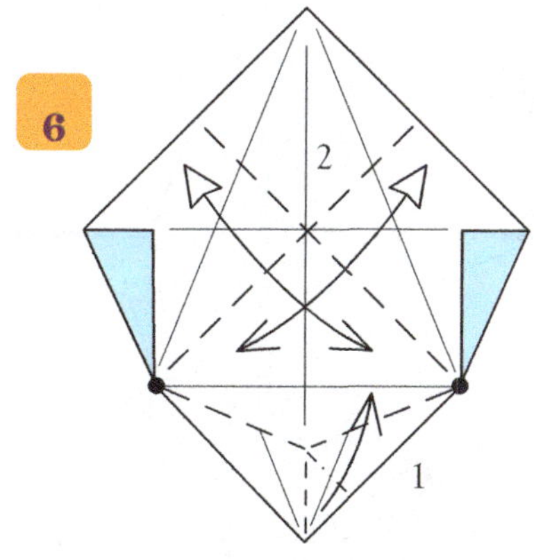

6

1. Rabbit-ear.
2. Fold and unfold.

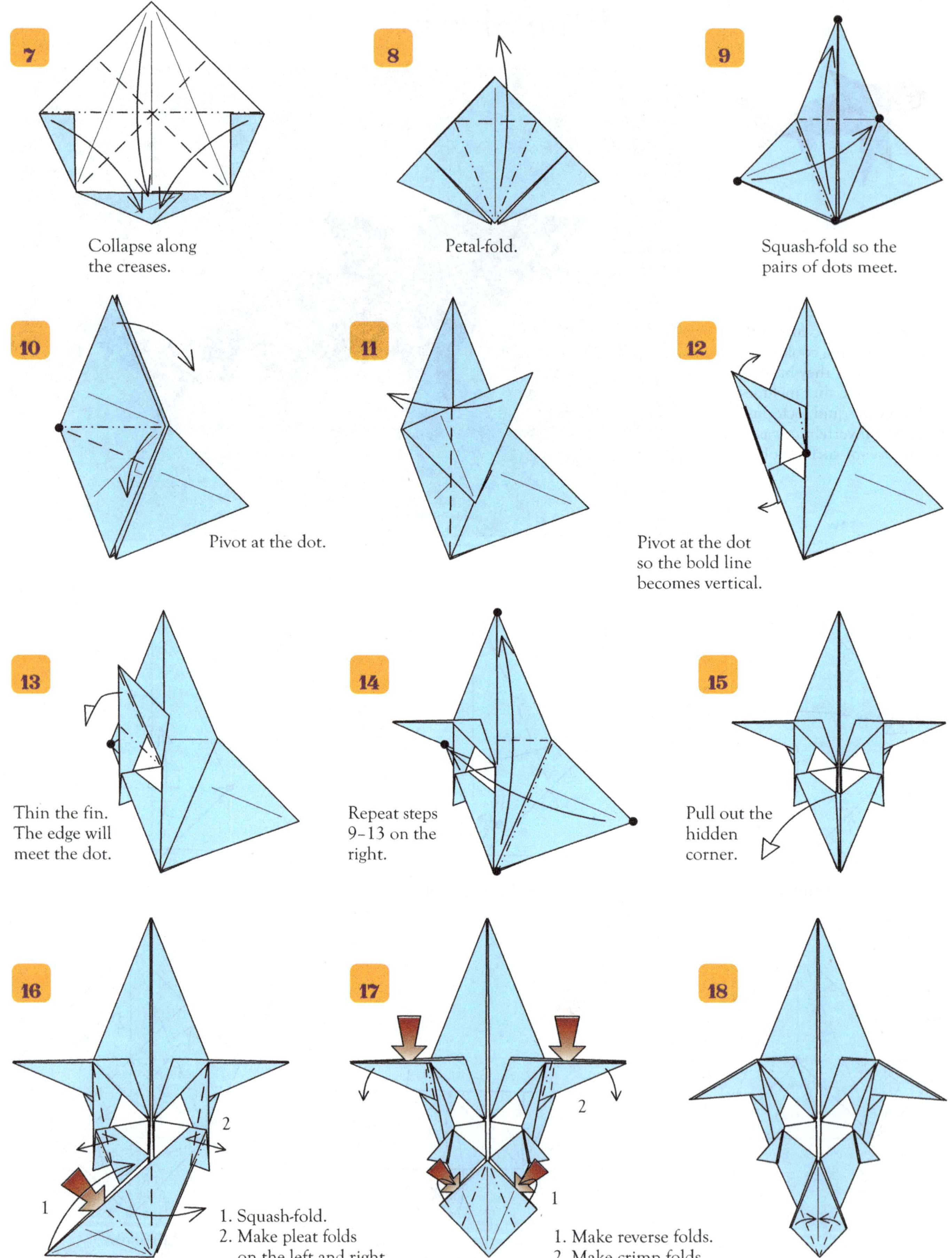

7 Collapse along the creases.

8 Petal-fold.

9 Squash-fold so the pairs of dots meet.

10 Pivot at the dot.

11

12 Pivot at the dot so the bold line becomes vertical.

13 Thin the fin. The edge will meet the dot.

14 Repeat steps 9–13 on the right.

15 Pull out the hidden corner.

16
1. Squash-fold.
2. Make pleat folds on the left and right.

17
1. Make reverse folds.
2. Make crimp folds.

18

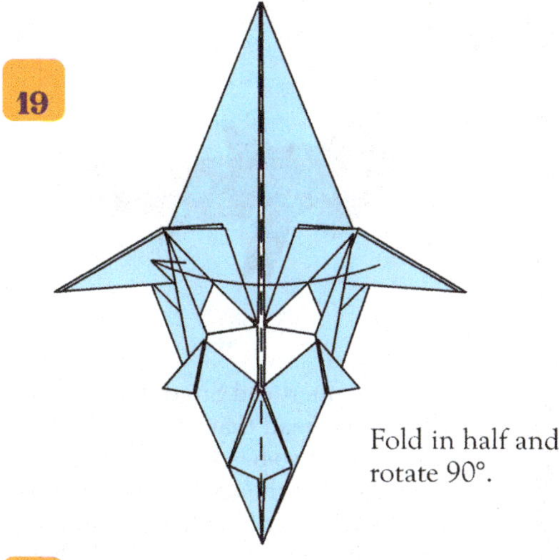

Fold in half and
rotate 90°.

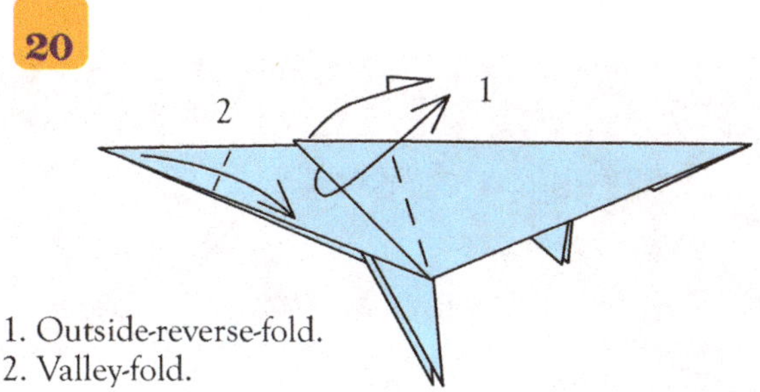

1. Outside-reverse-fold.
2. Valley-fold.

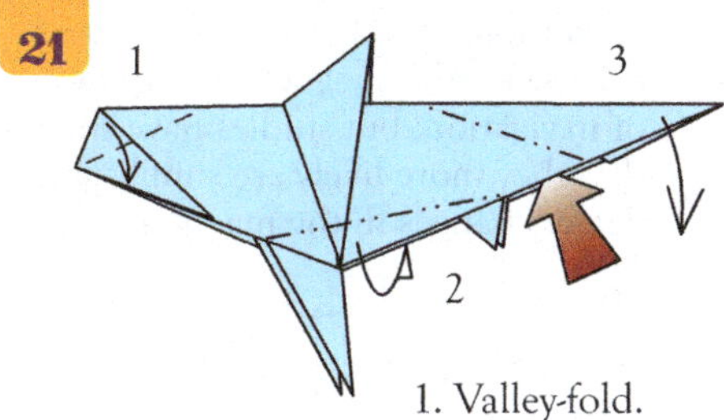

1. Valley-fold.
2. Fold inside, repeat behind.
3. Reverse-fold.

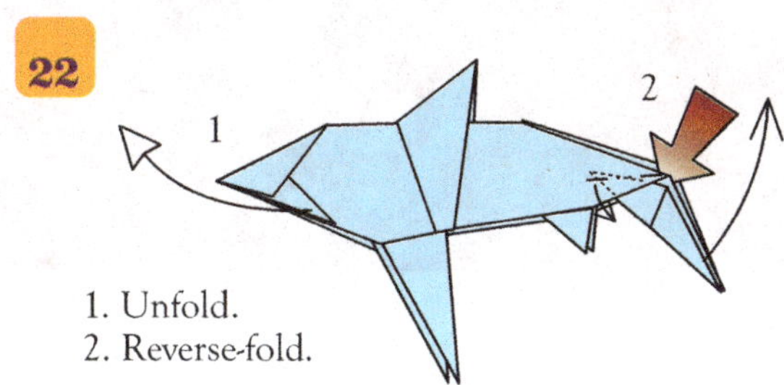

1. Unfold.
2. Reverse-fold.

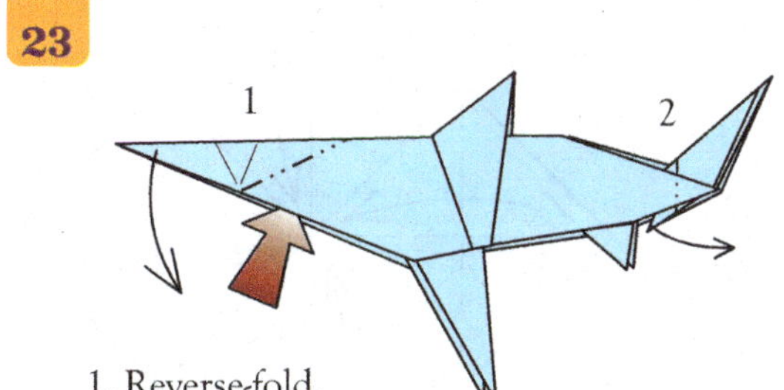

1. Reverse-fold.
2. Reverse-fold.

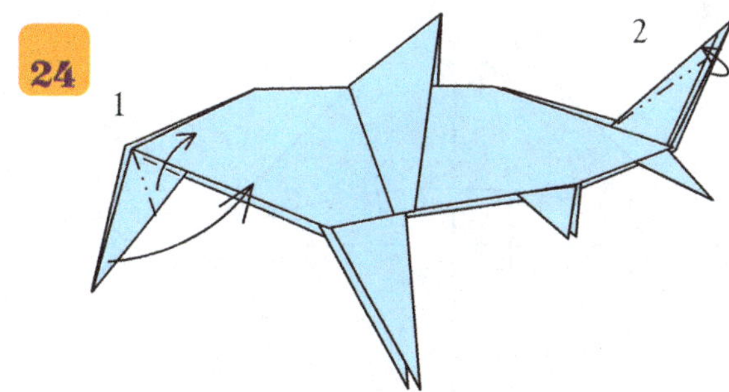

1. Pleat-fold along the creases.
2. Spread two layers, repeat behind.

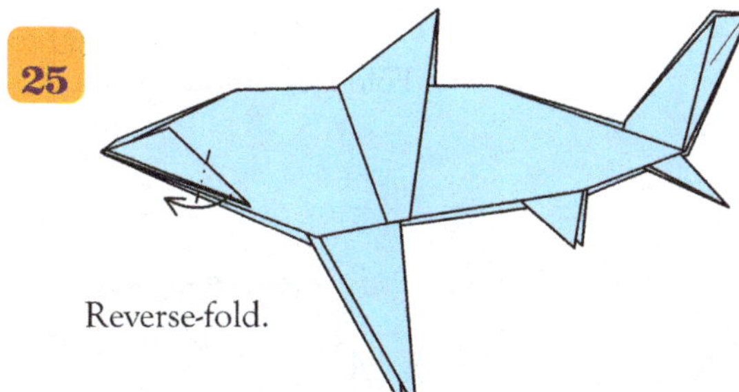

Reverse-fold.

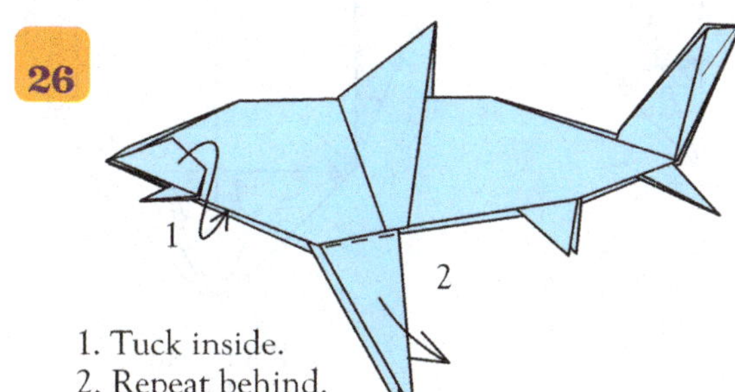

1. Tuck inside.
2. Repeat behind.

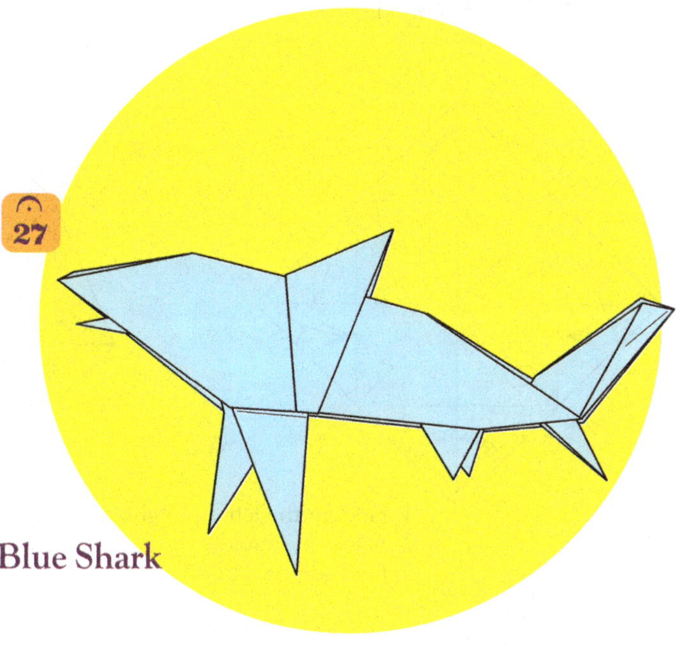

Blue Shark

Hammerhead Shark

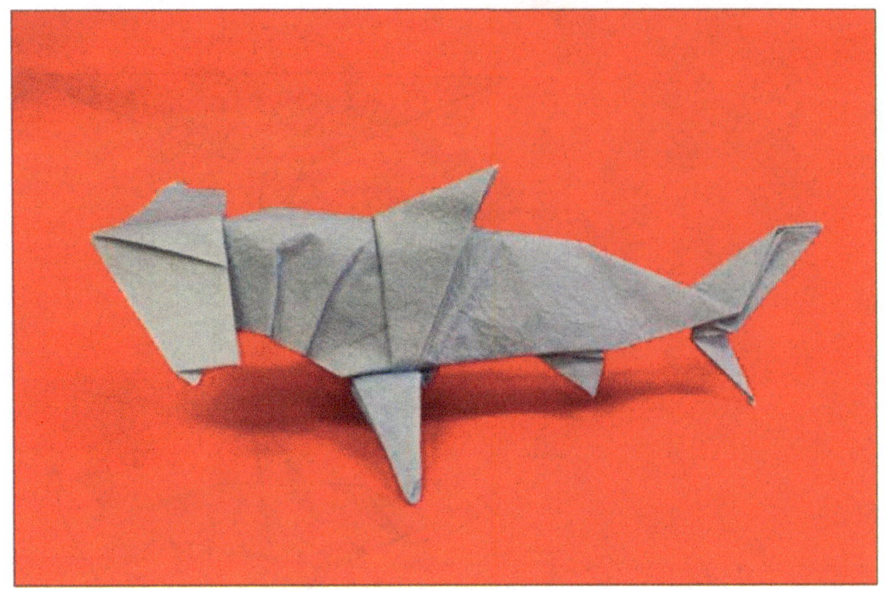

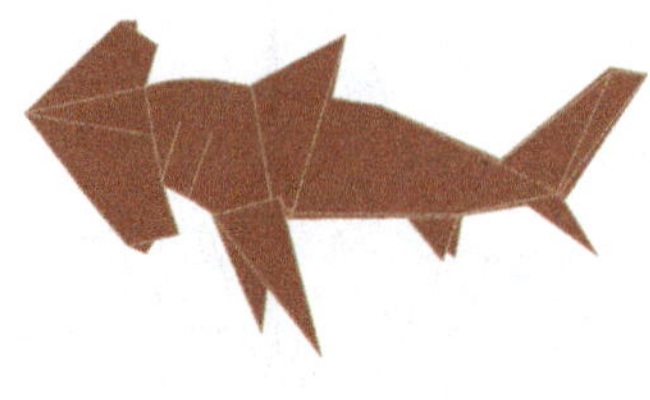

The Hammerhead Shark has a distinctive head that actually does resemble a two-headed hammer. Its eyes are located at the ends of each hammer's head, making it look like a swimming letter "T". Hammerhead Sharks have been thought to be able to detect and use the Earth's magnetic field as a means of navigation, but studies have shown that they more likely are simply able to detect changes in the magnetic field.

1

Fold and unfold.

2

Fold and unfold.

3

Fold and unfold.

4

1. Fold on the left and right.
2. Fold and unfold.
3. Fold and unfold.

5

1. Fold on the left and right.
2. Fold down.

6

1. Rabbit-ear.
2. Fold behind.

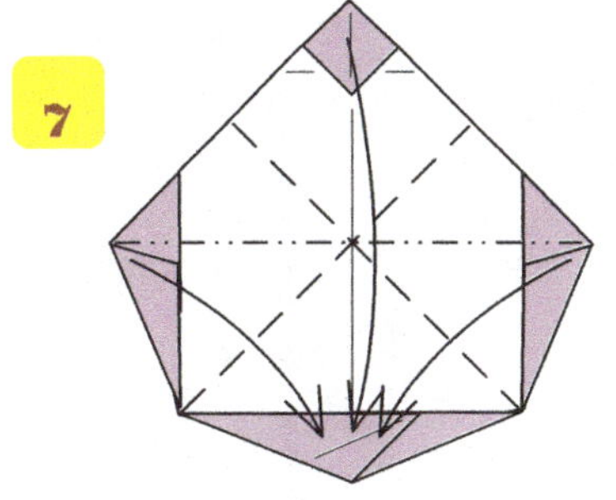

7 Collapse along the creases.

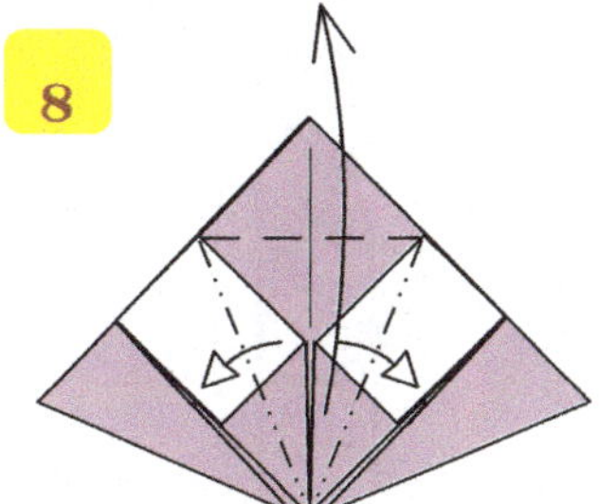

8 Petal-fold and swing out from behind.

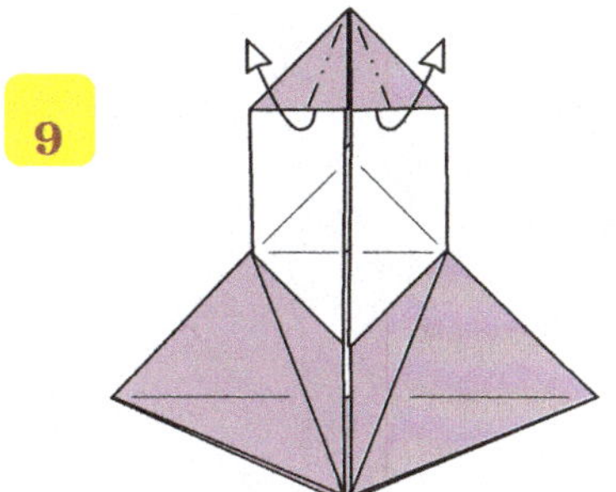

9 Unlock the paper.

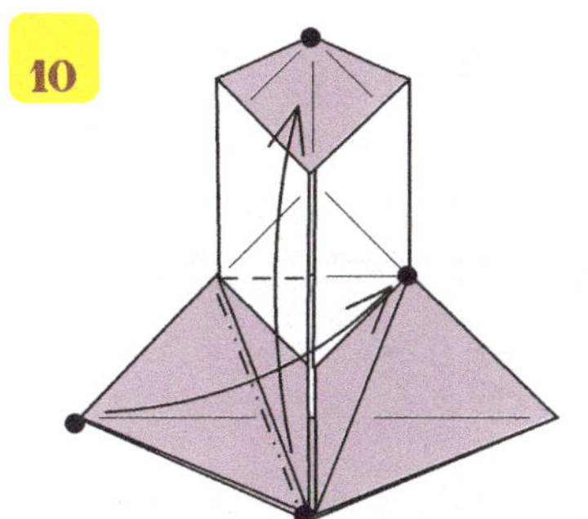

10 Squash-fold so the pairs of dots meet.

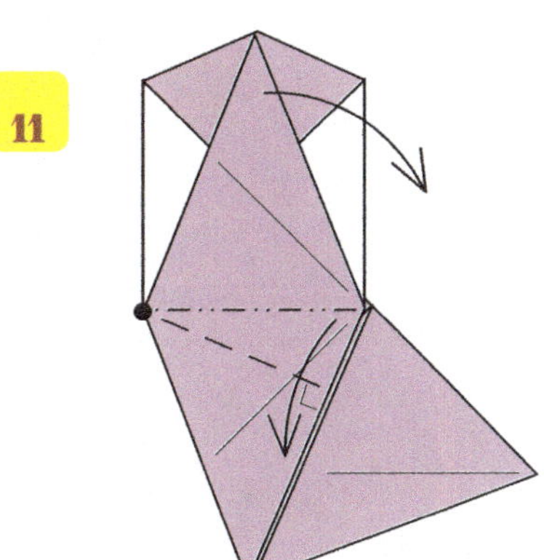

11 Pivot at the dot.

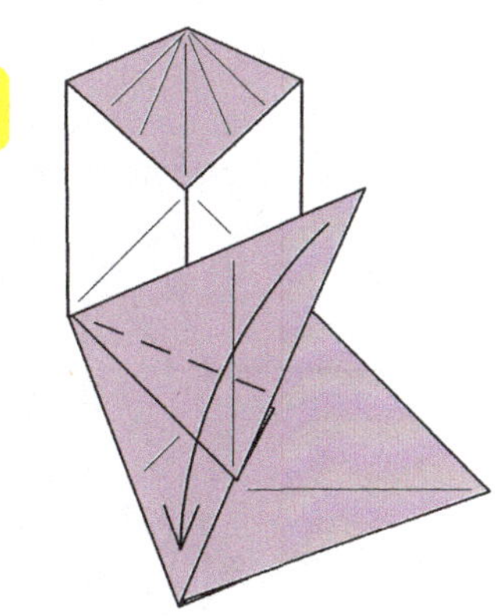

12

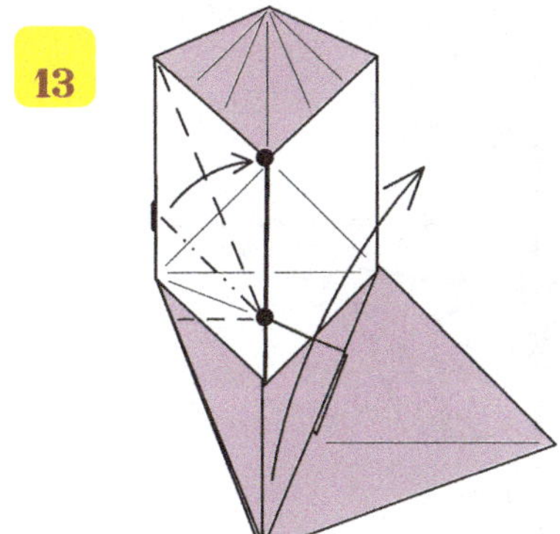

13

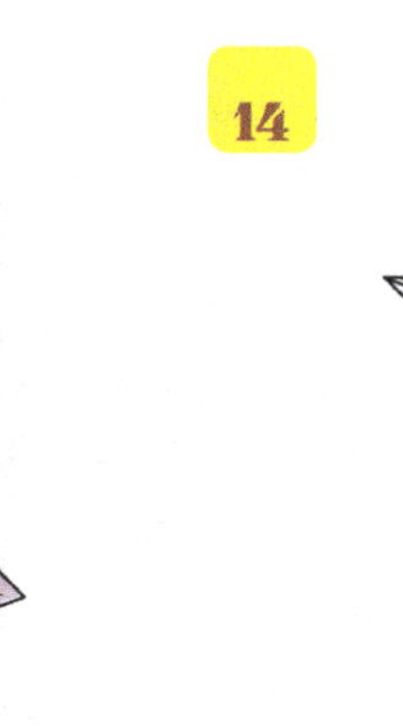

14

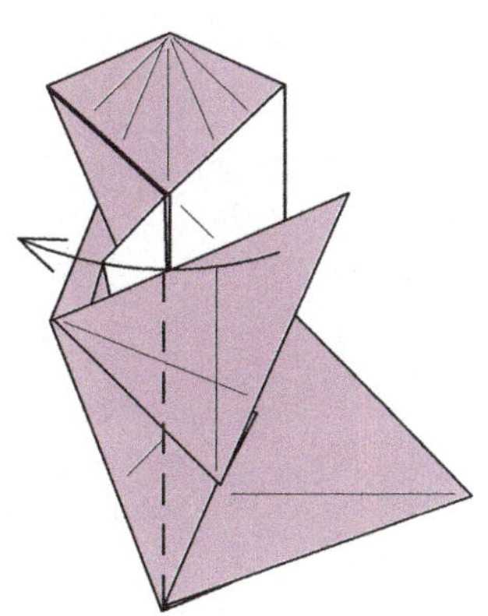

15 Pivot at the dot so the bold line becomes vertical.

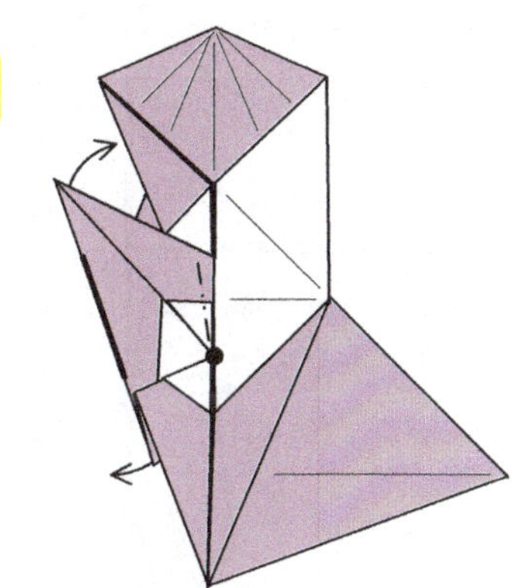

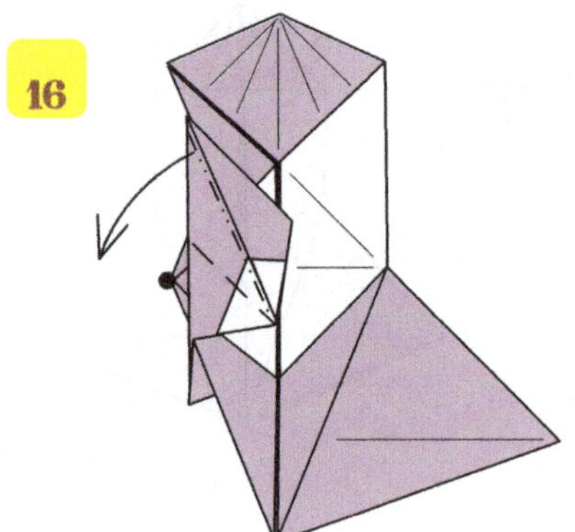

Squash-fold the fin. The
edge will meet the dot.

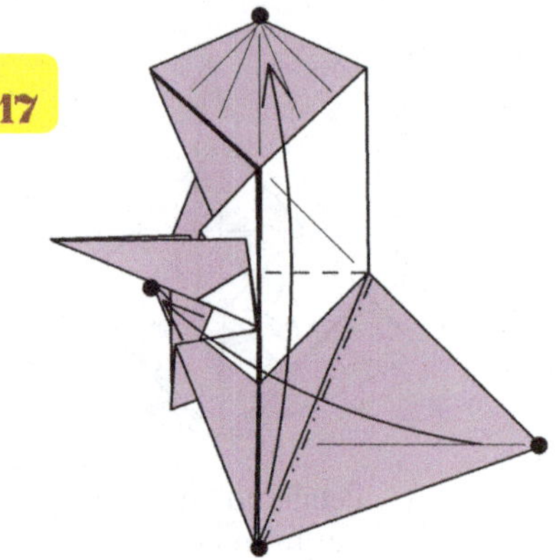

Repeat steps 10–16
on the right.

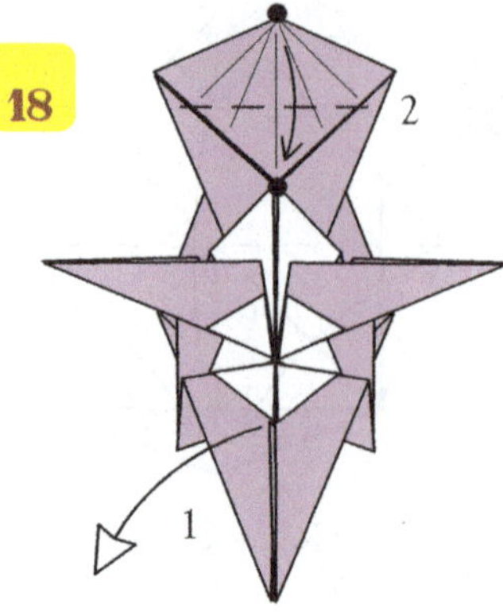

1. Pull out the hidden corner.
2. The dots will meet.

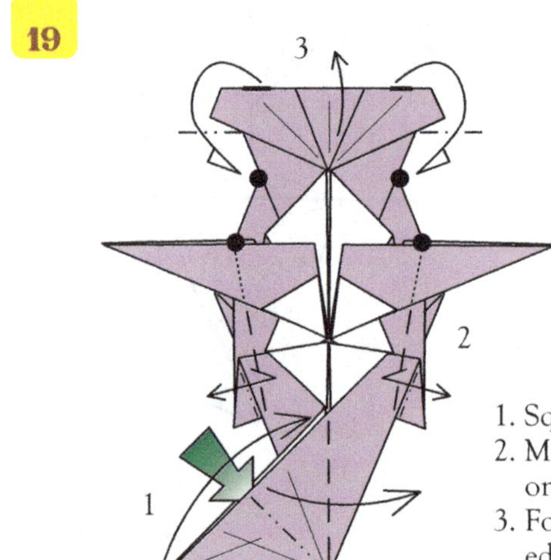

1. Squash-fold.
2. Make pleat folds
   on the left and right.
3. Fold behind so the
   edge meets the dots.
   Swing the head up.

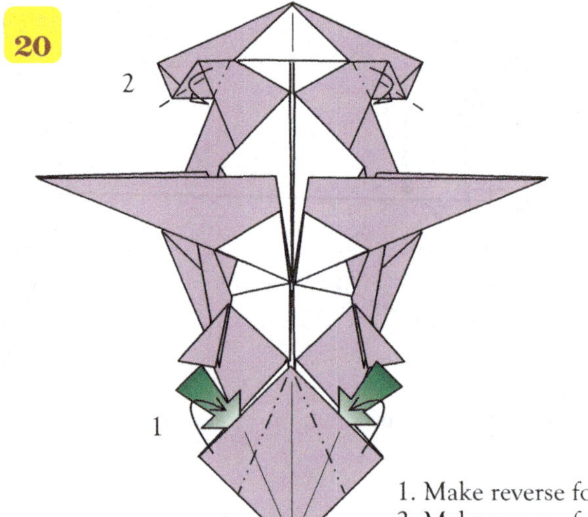

1. Make reverse folds.
2. Make reverse folds.

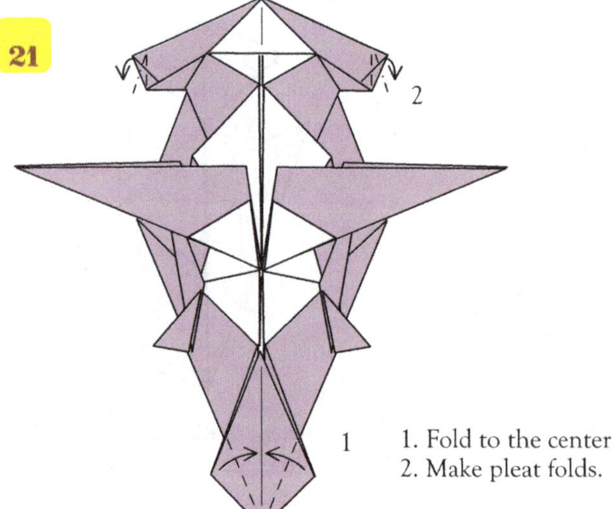

1. Fold to the center.
2. Make pleat folds.

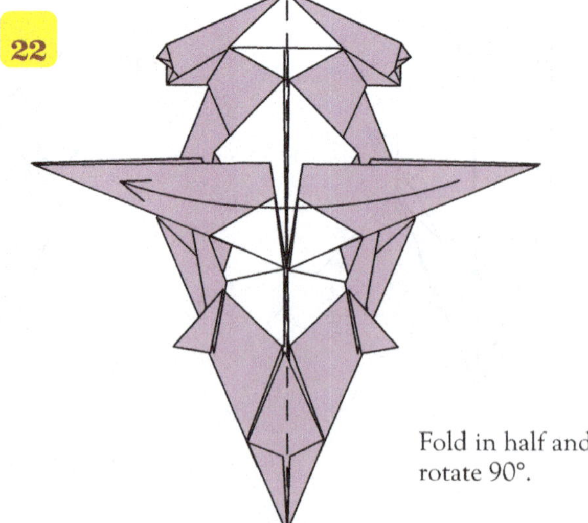

Fold in half and
rotate 90°.

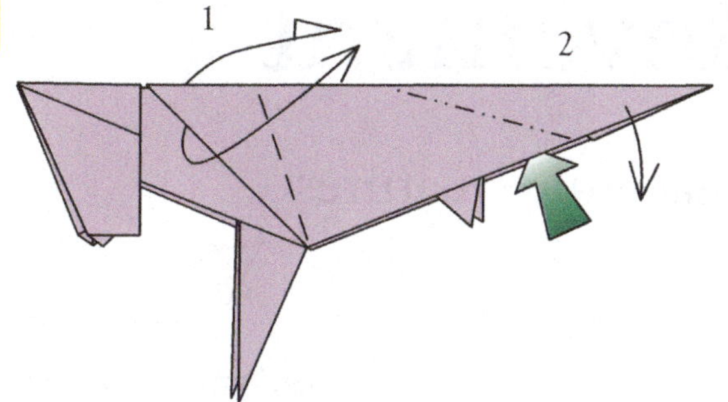

1. Outside-reverse-fold.
2. Reverse-fold.

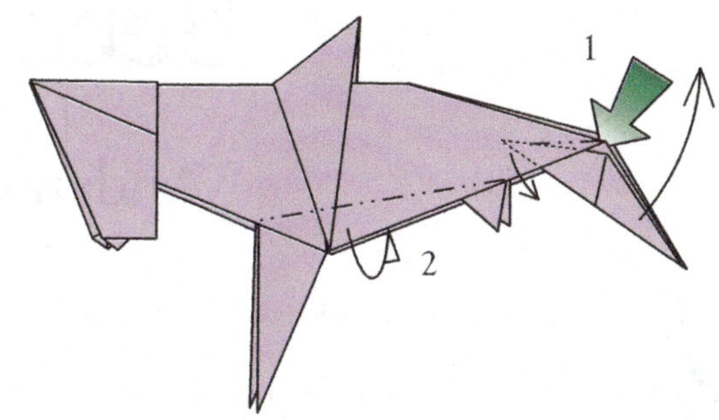

1. Reverse-fold.
2. Fold inside, repeat behind.

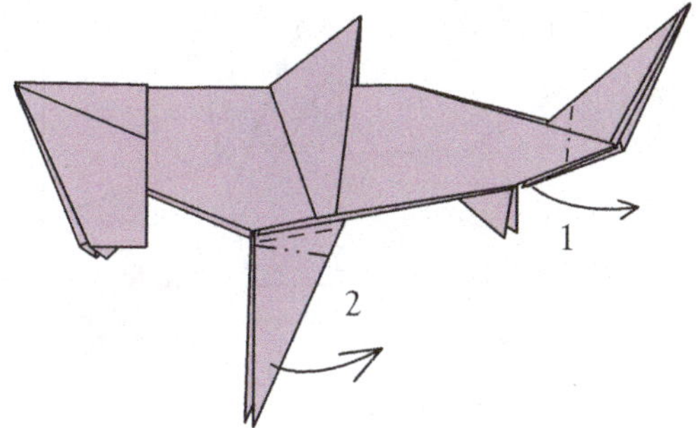

1. Reverse-fold.
2. Pleat-fold, repeat behind.

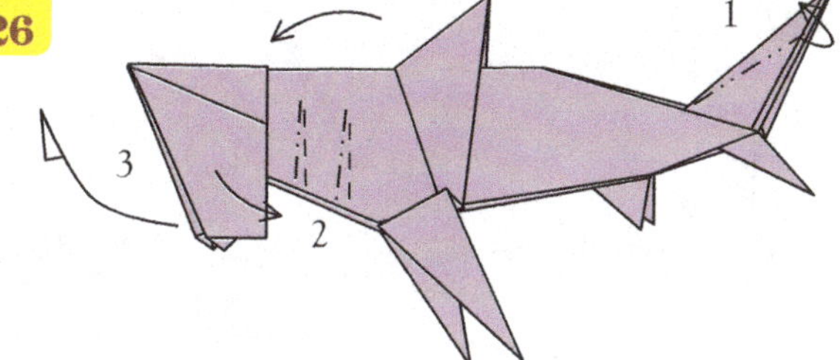

1. Spread two layers, repeat behind.
2. Shape the neck with two thin crimp folds.
3. Spread and flatten the head.

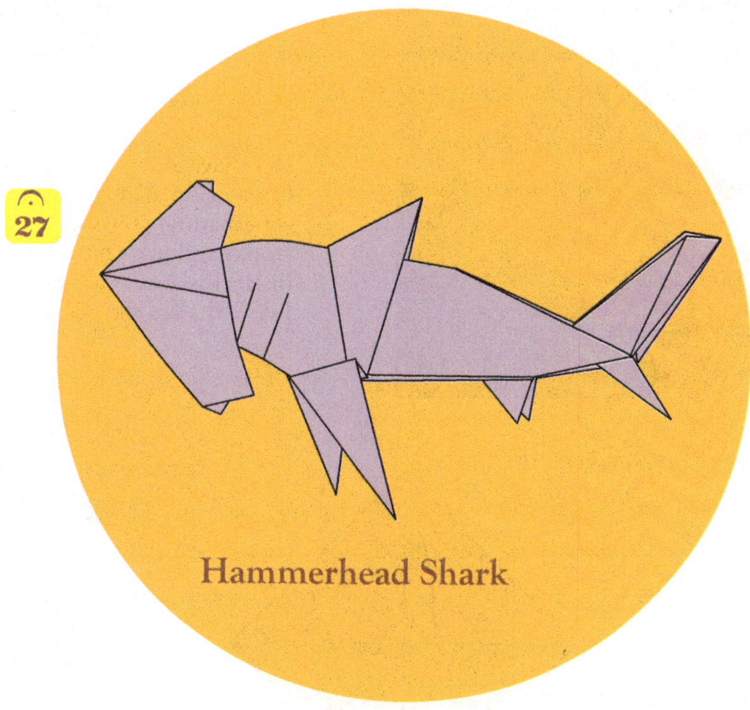

Hammerhead Shark

Second Movement

Andante: Dulce, Peaceful Creatures

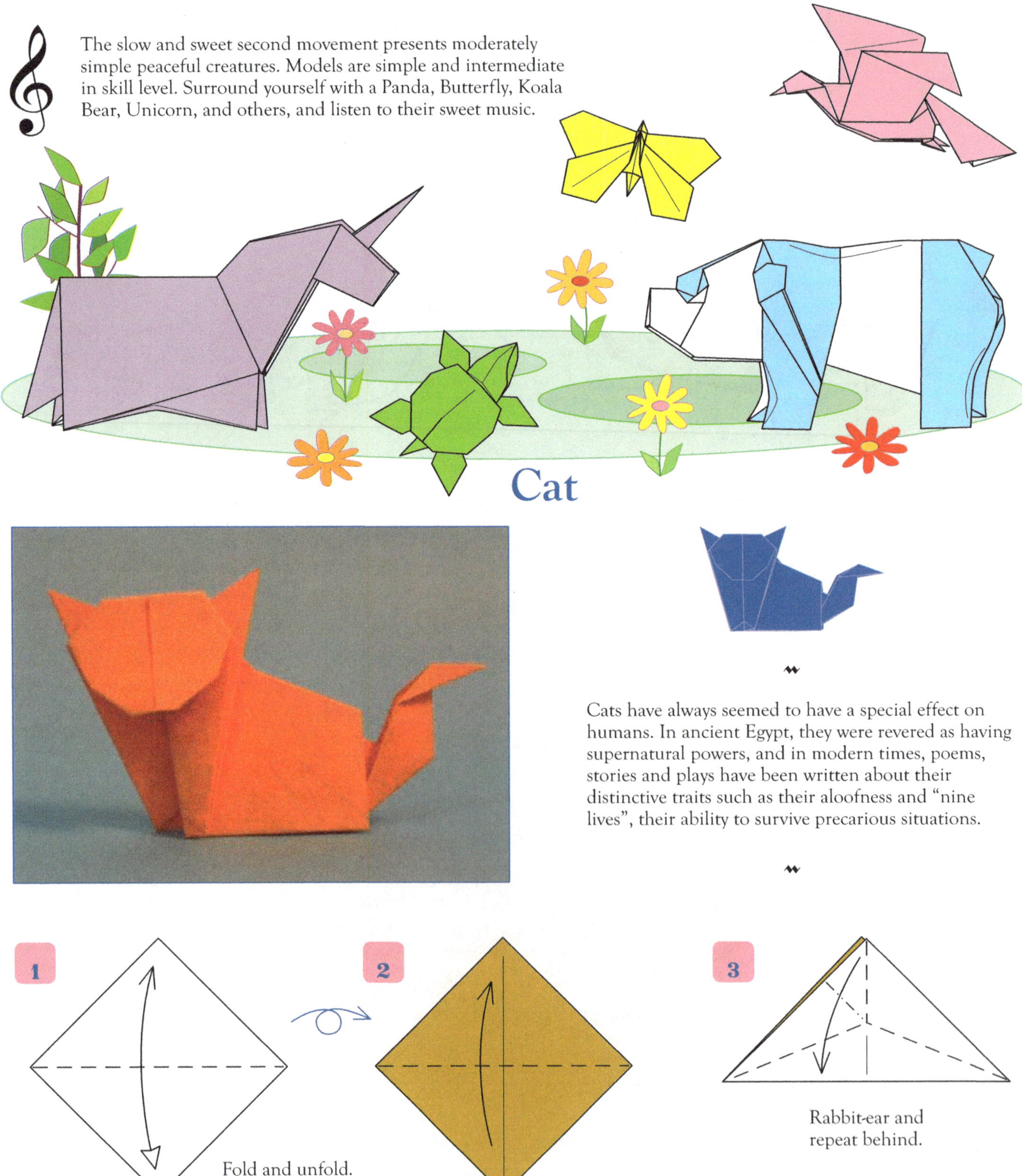

The slow and sweet second movement presents moderately simple peaceful creatures. Models are simple and intermediate in skill level. Surround yourself with a Panda, Butterfly, Koala Bear, Unicorn, and others, and listen to their sweet music.

Cat

Cats have always seemed to have a special effect on humans. In ancient Egypt, they were revered as having supernatural powers, and in modern times, poems, stories and plays have been written about their distinctive traits such as their aloofness and "nine lives", their ability to survive precarious situations.

1

Fold and unfold.
Rotate 90°.

2

3

Rabbit-ear and
repeat behind.

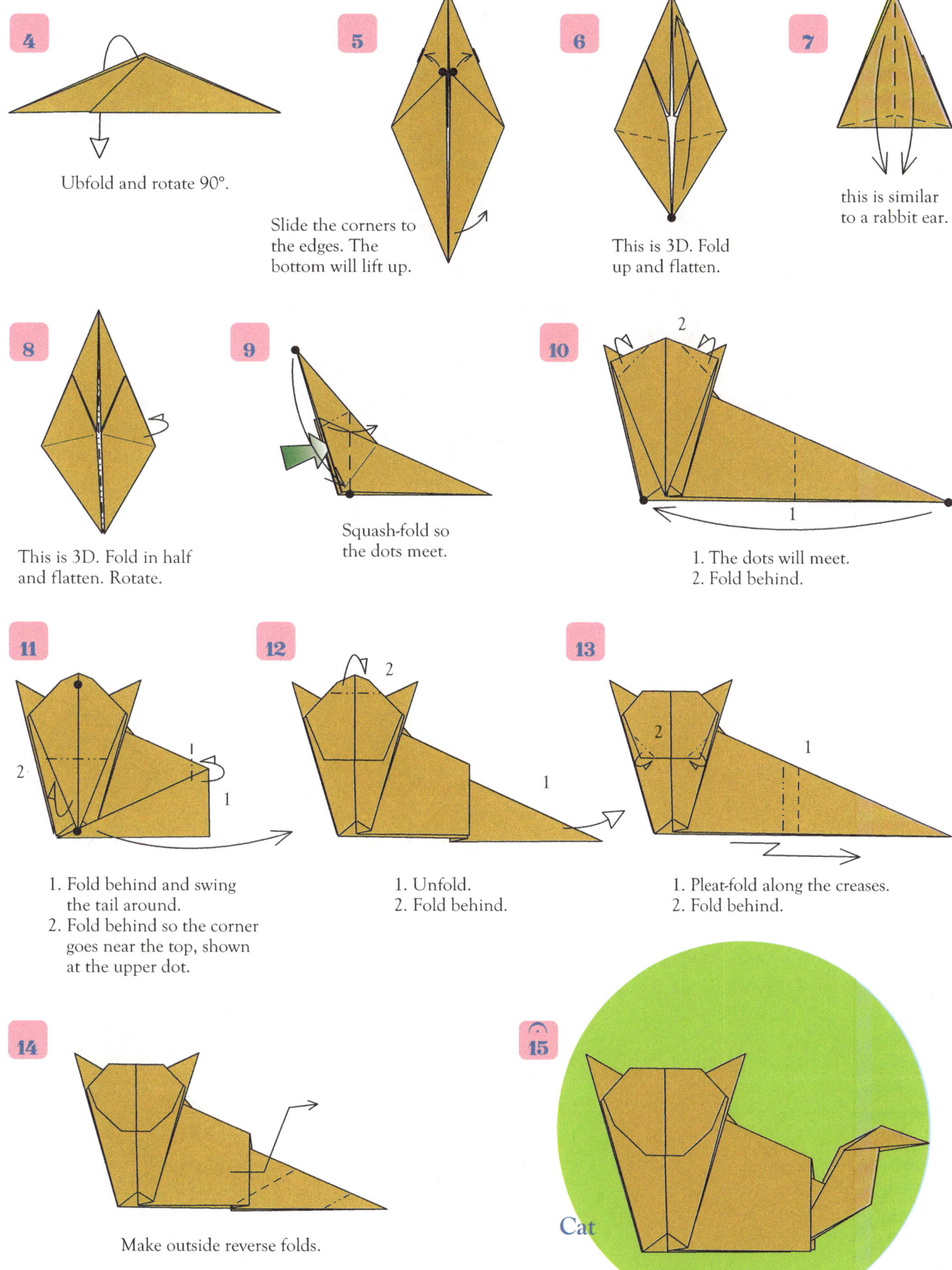

4 Ubfold and rotate 90°.

5 Slide the corners to the edges. The bottom will lift up.

6 This is 3D. Fold up and flatten.

7 this is similar to a rabbit ear.

8 This is 3D. Fold in half and flatten. Rotate.

9 Squash-fold so the dots meet.

10
1. The dots will meet.
2. Fold behind.

11
1. Fold behind and swing the tail around.
2. Fold behind so the corner goes near the top, shown at the upper dot.

12
1. Unfold.
2. Fold behind.

13
1. Pleat-fold along the creases.
2. Fold behind.

14 Make outside reverse folds.

15 Cat

Butterfly

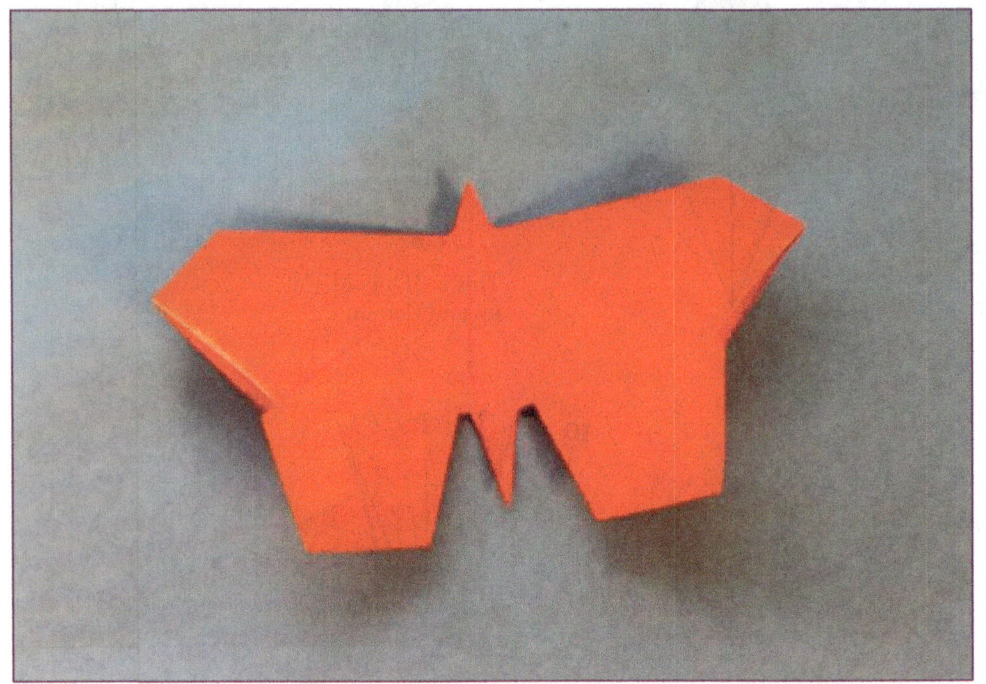

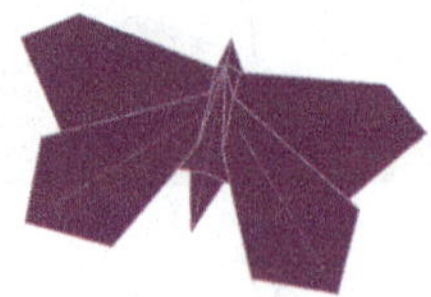

The Butterfly has long been seen as a symbol of change, due to its journey from caterpillar to cocoon to the finally emerging winged beautiful insect we are all familiar with.

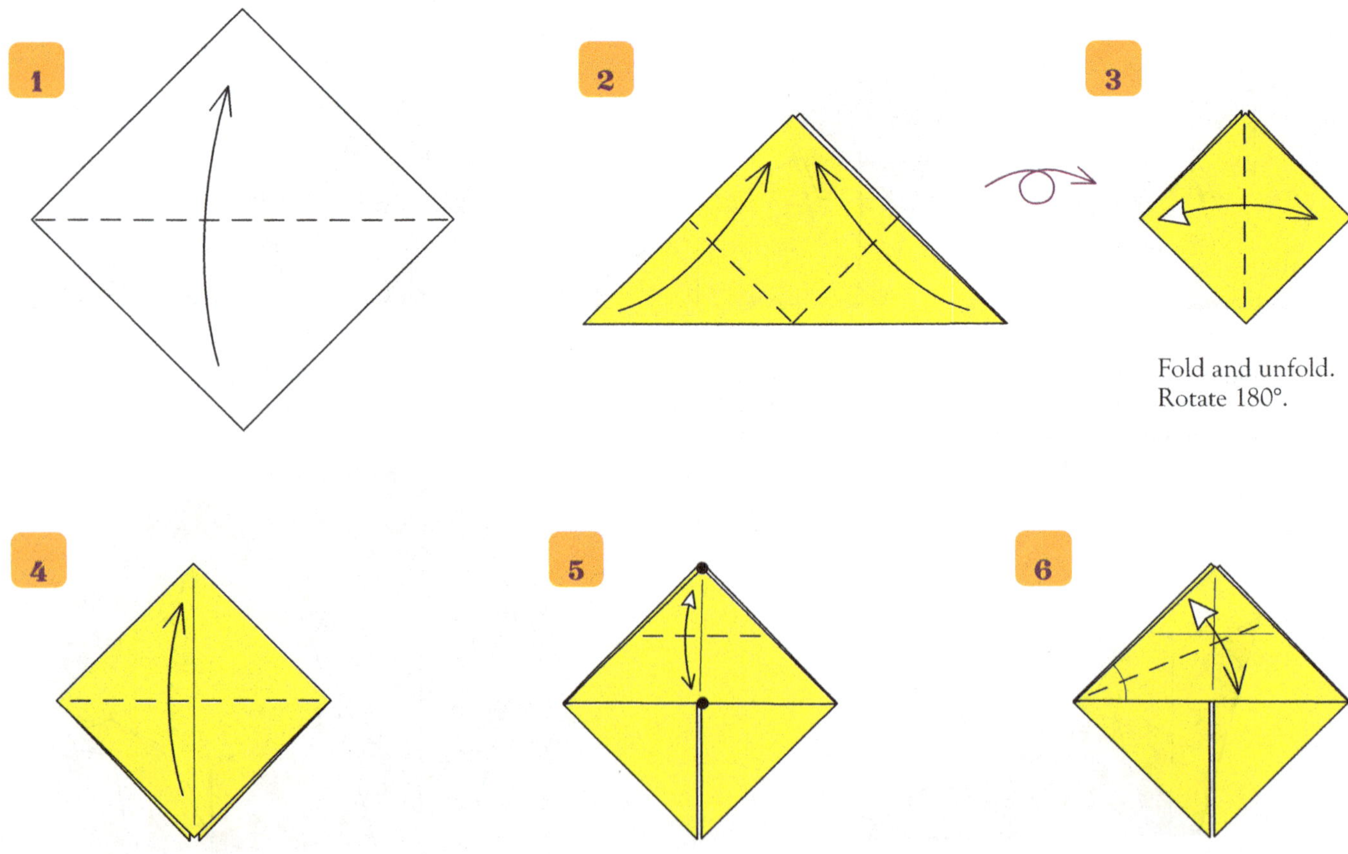

Fold and unfold. Rotate 180°.

Fold two layers up.

Fold and unfold the top two layers.

Fold and unfold the top two layers.

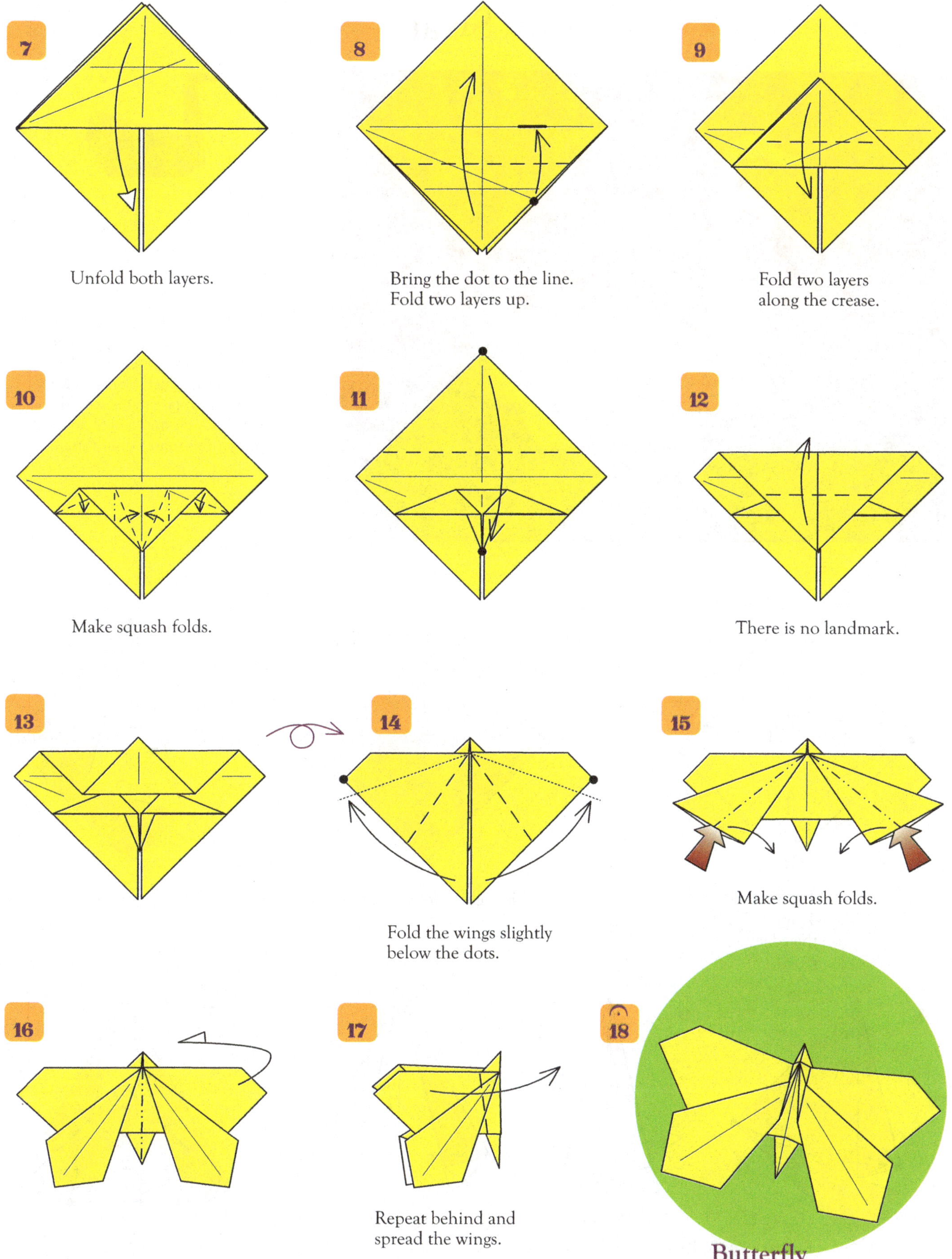

7 Unfold both layers.

8 Bring the dot to the line. Fold two layers up.

9 Fold two layers along the crease.

10 Make squash folds.

11

12 There is no landmark.

13

14 Fold the wings slightly below the dots.

15 Make squash folds.

16

17 Repeat behind and spread the wings.

18

Butterfly

Swan

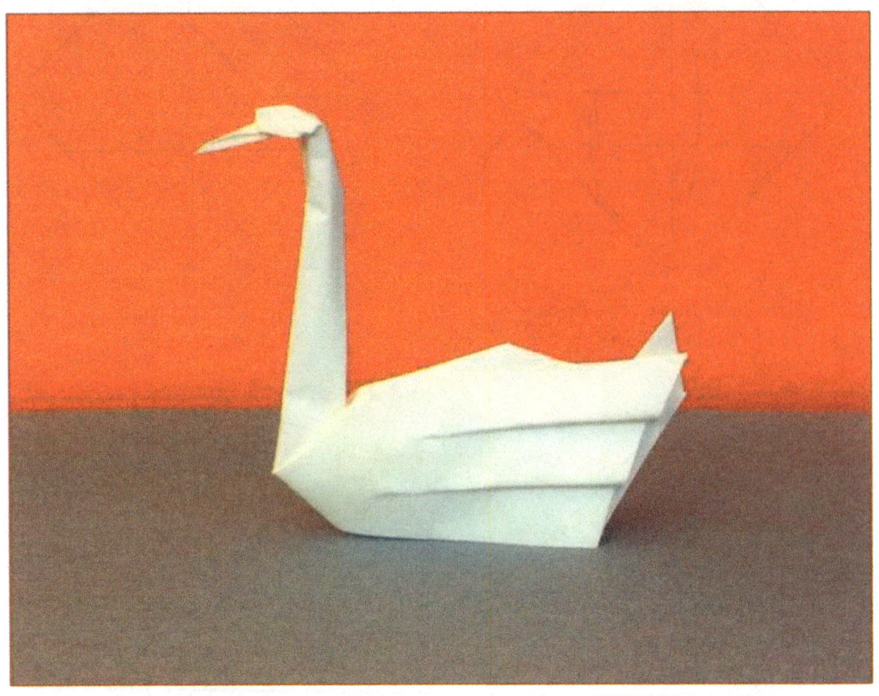

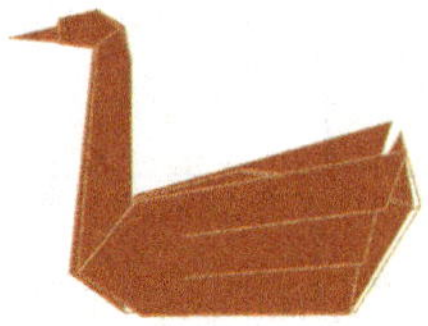

These beautiful birds typify elegance and beauty with their long necks and graceful glides through the water. So-called Mute Swans do in fact make sounds, such as snorts and hisses, when calling their mates or children.

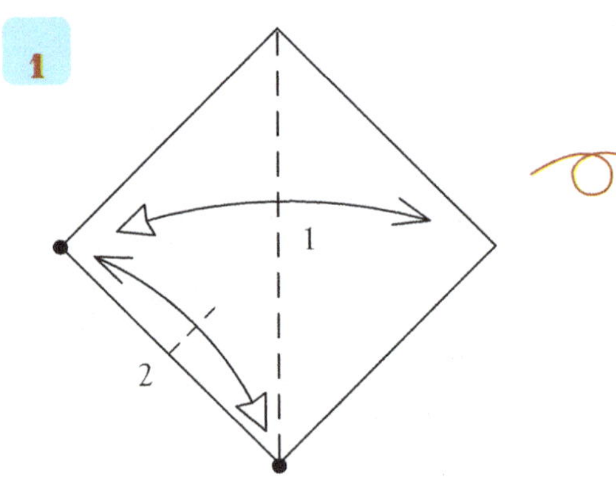

1. Fold and unfold.
2. Fold and unfold on the edge.

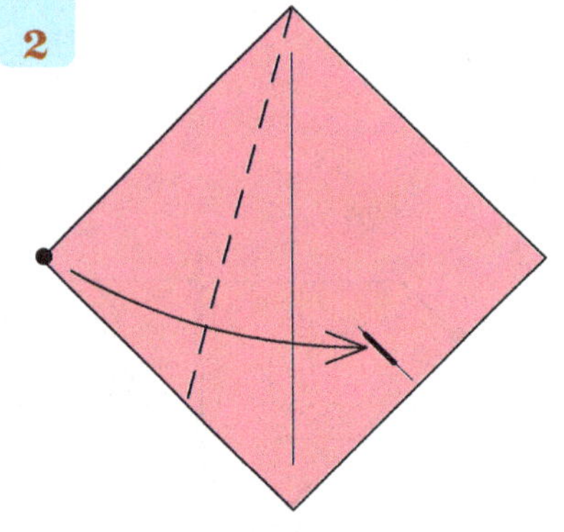

Bring the dot to the line.

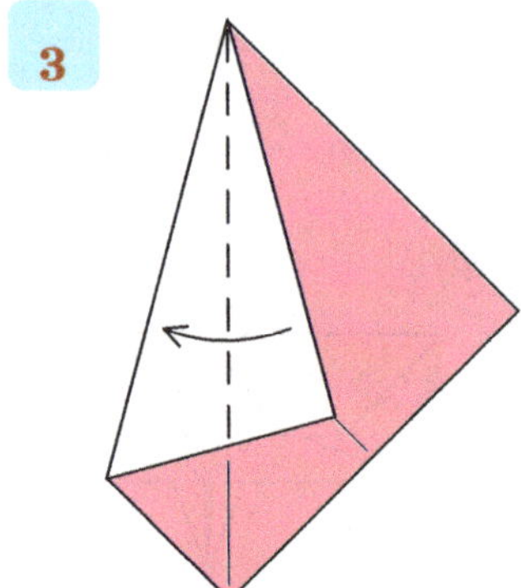

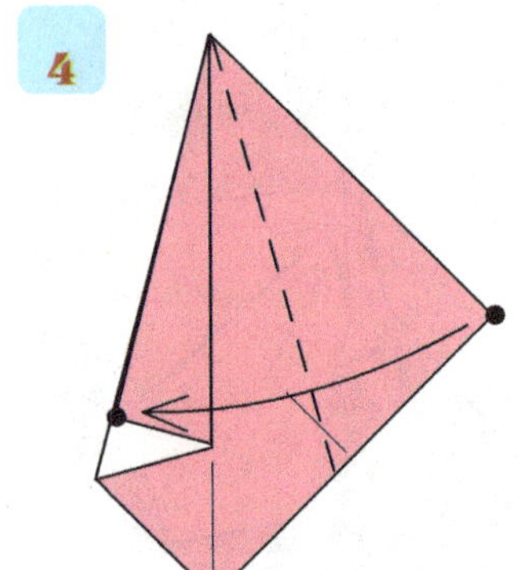

Repeat steps 2–3 on the right.

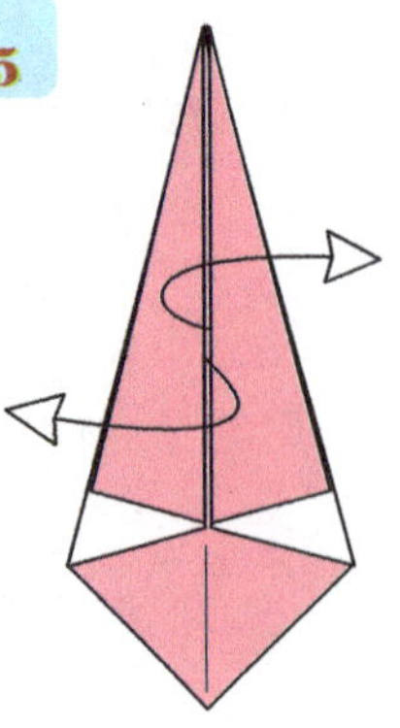

Unfold.

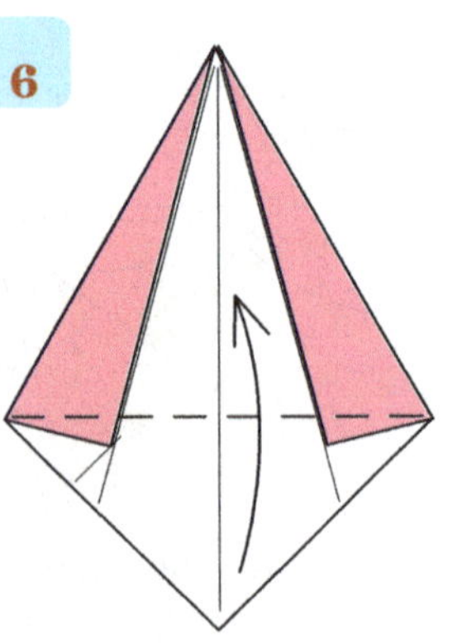

Bring the edges to the dots.

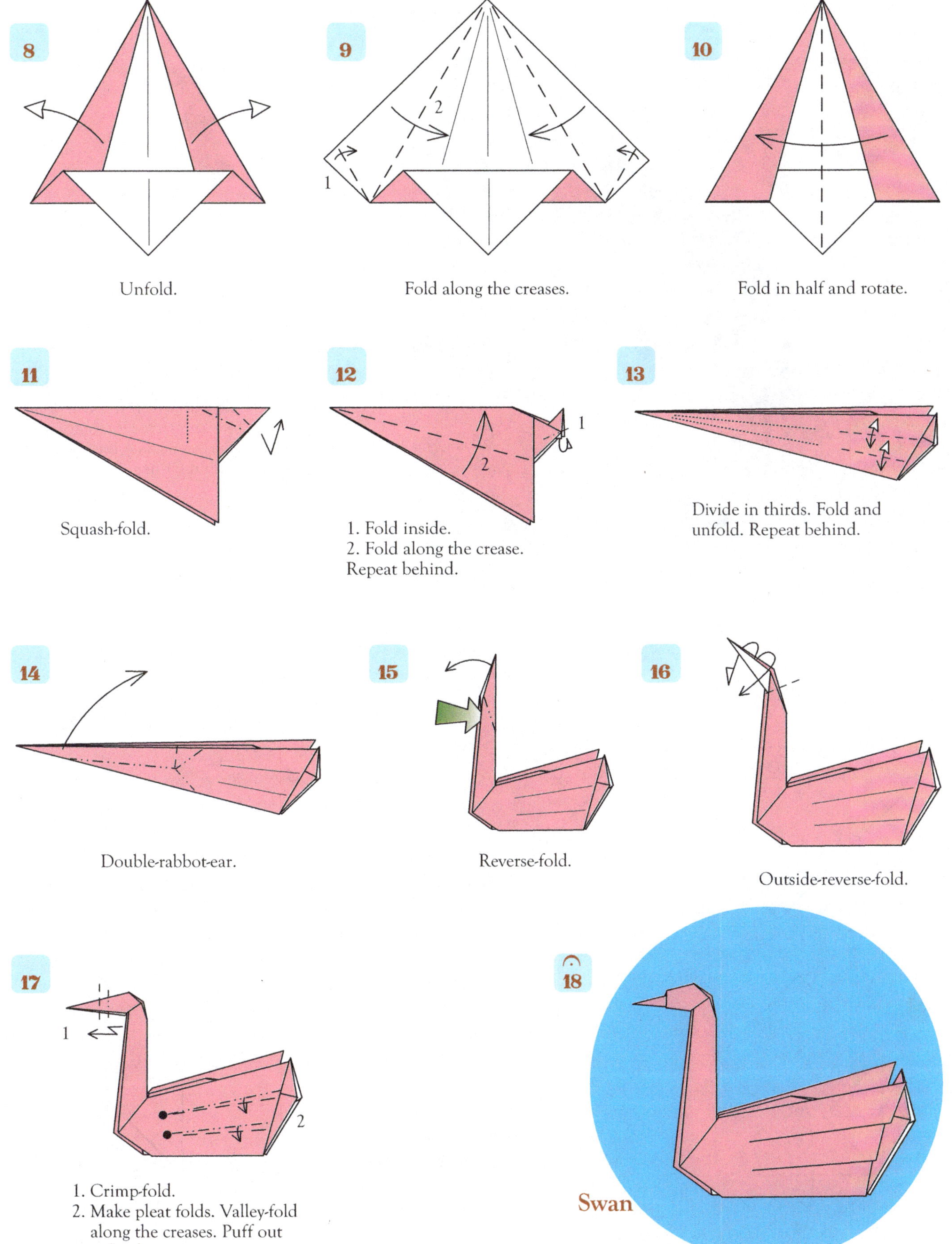

8 Unfold.

9 Fold along the creases.

10 Fold in half and rotate.

11 Squash-fold.

12
1. Fold inside.
2. Fold along the crease.
Repeat behind.

13 Divide in thirds. Fold and unfold. Repeat behind.

14 Double-rabbit-ear.

15 Reverse-fold.

16 Outside-reverse-fold.

17
1. Crimp-fold.
2. Make pleat folds. Valley-fold along the creases. Puff out at the dots.

18 Swan

Penguin

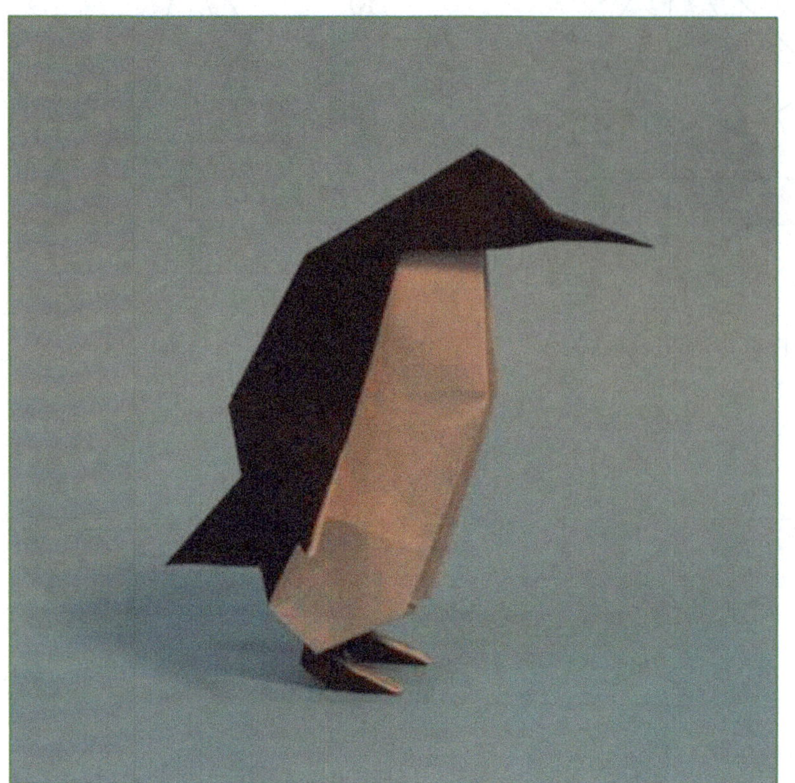

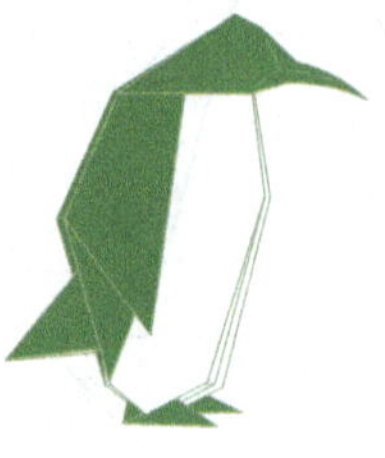

Sometimes elegant and sometimes comical, Penguins have their own permanent tuxedos and tend to walk with a distinctive waddle. Penguins are also known for the gentle way they care for their young, and Emperor Penguins stay with their mates throughout their whole lives.

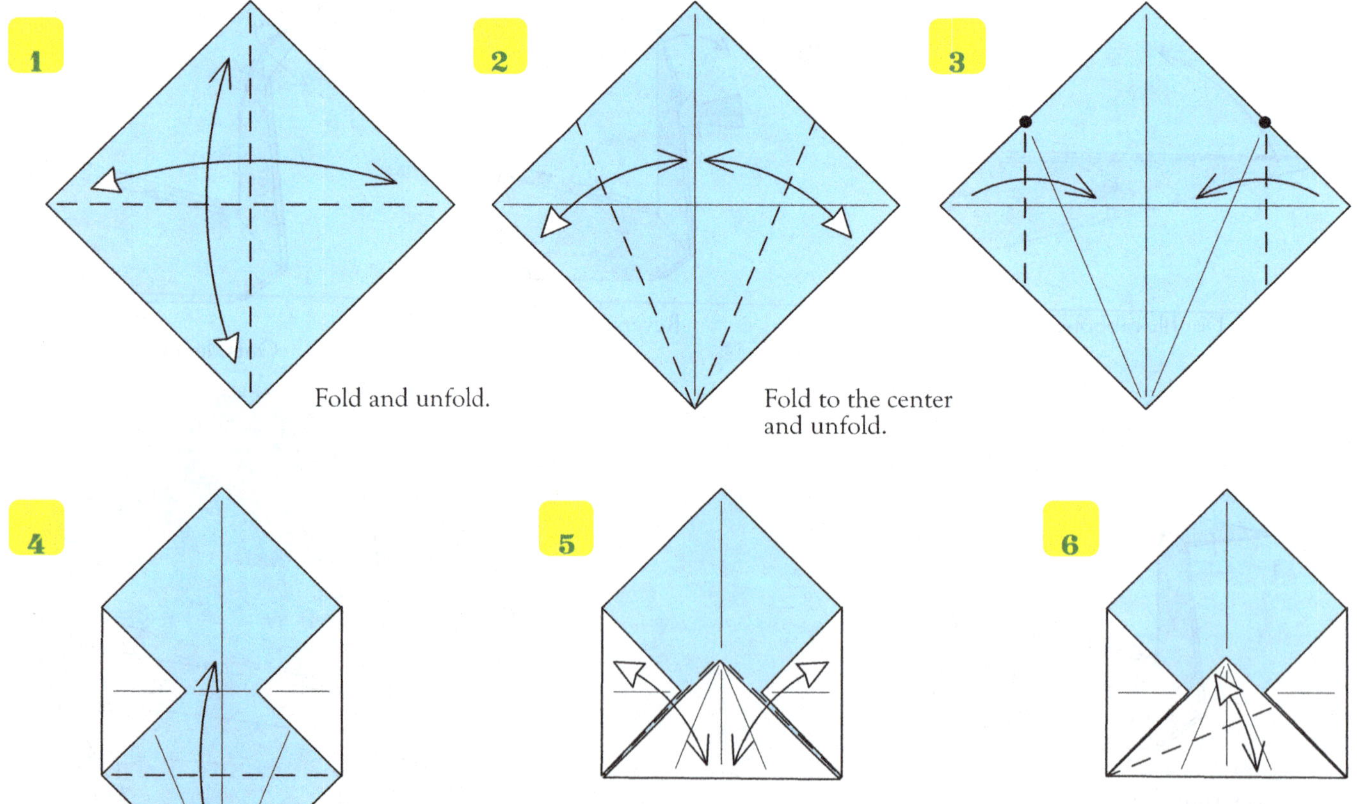

1 Fold and unfold.

2 Fold to the center and unfold.

3

4

5 Fold and unfold.

6 Fold and unfold.

7

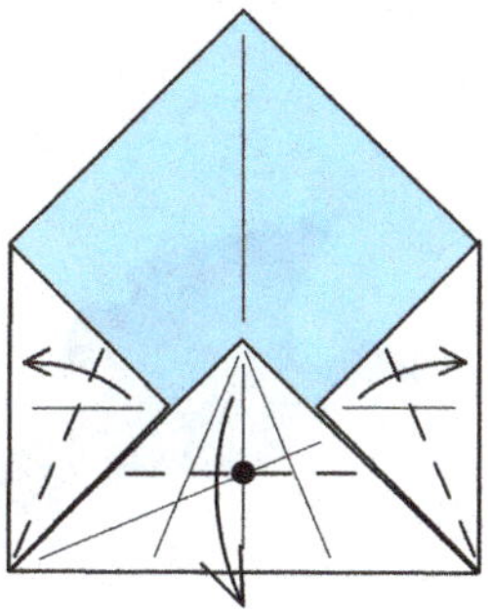

8

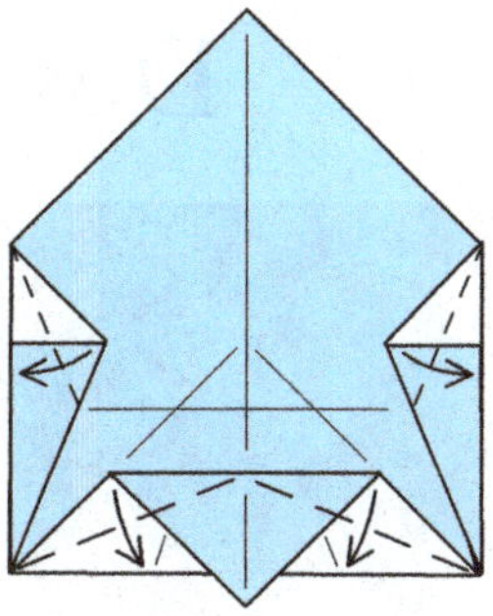

9

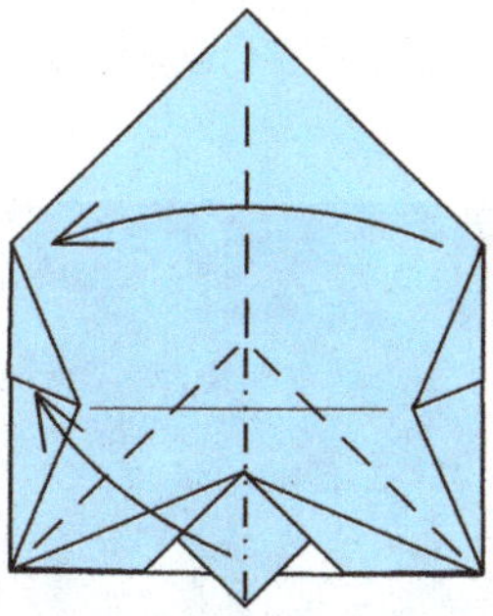

Fold along the creases.

10

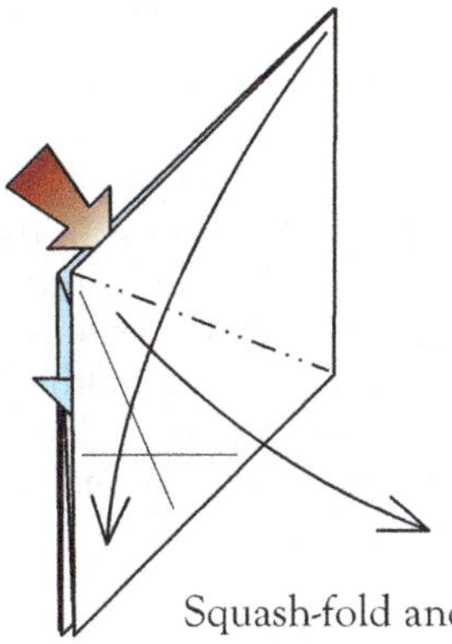

Squash-fold and rotate.

11

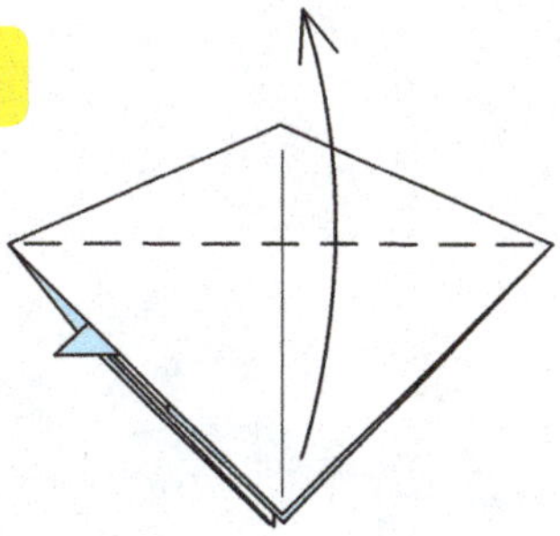

12

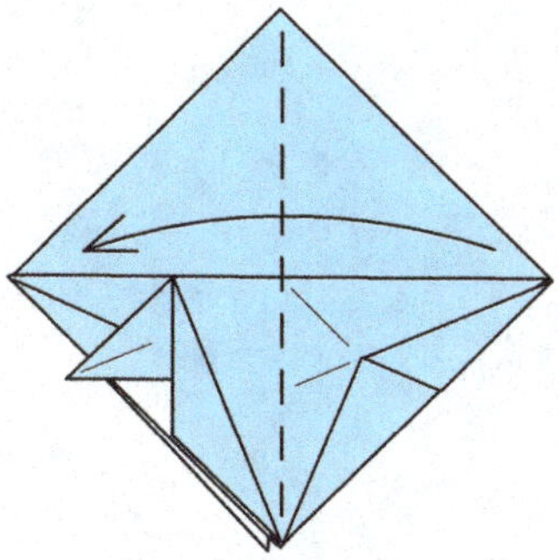

13

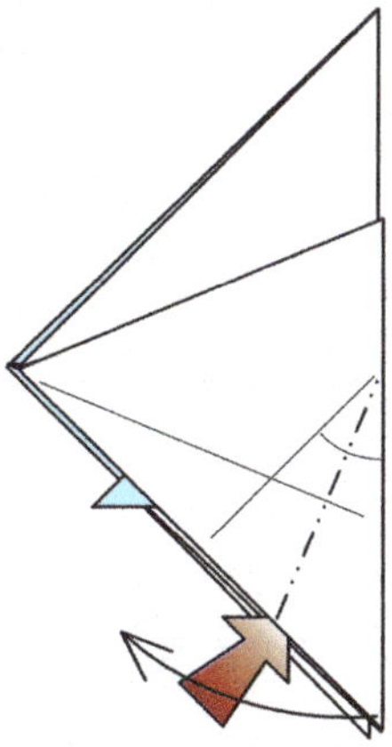

Reverse-fold and repeat behind.

14

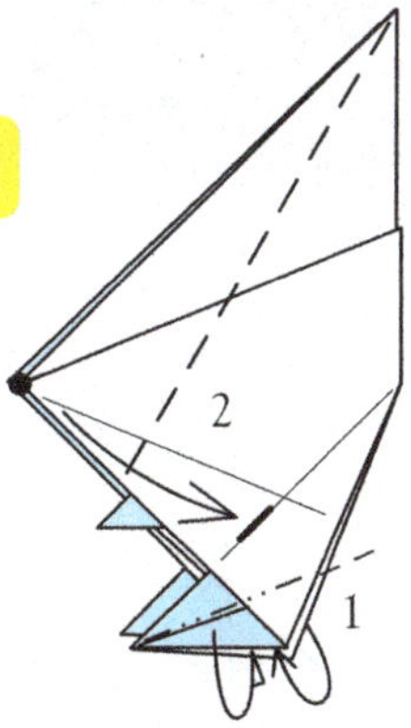

1. Fold inside on the front and back, repeat behind.
2. Bring the dot to the line, repeat behind.

15

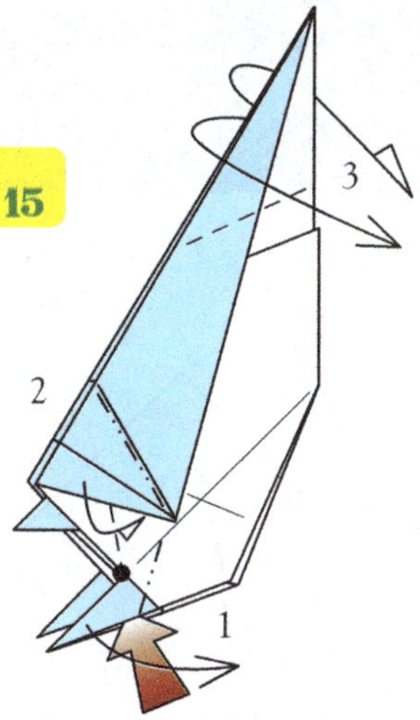

1. Reverse-fold, repeat behind.
2. Reverse-fold, repeat behind.
3. Outside-reverse-fold.

16

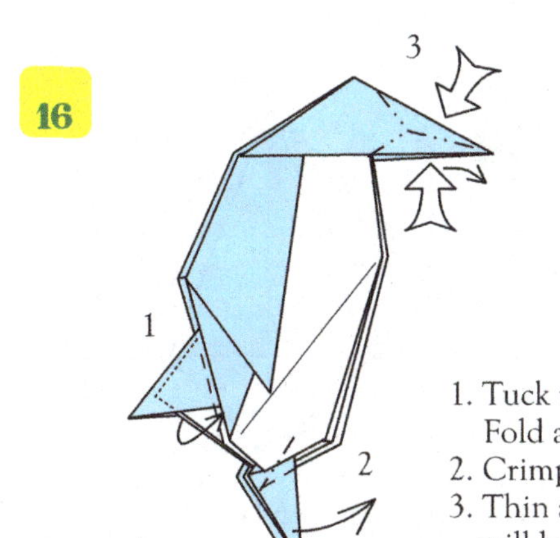

1. Tuck the white paper inside. Fold all the layers together.
2. Crimp-fold, repeat behind.
3. Thin and shape the beak. It will be 3D.

17

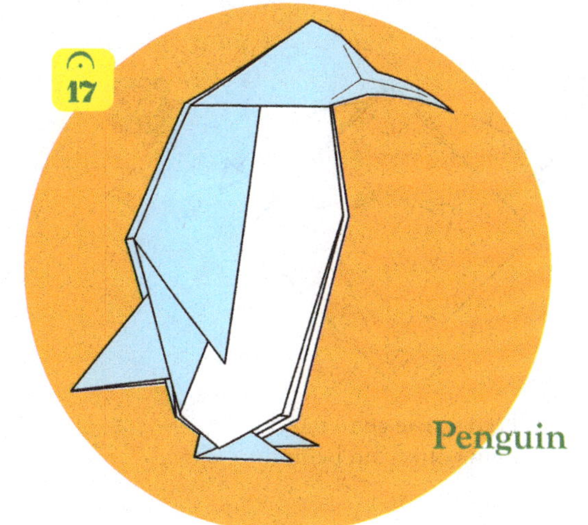

Penguin

Dove

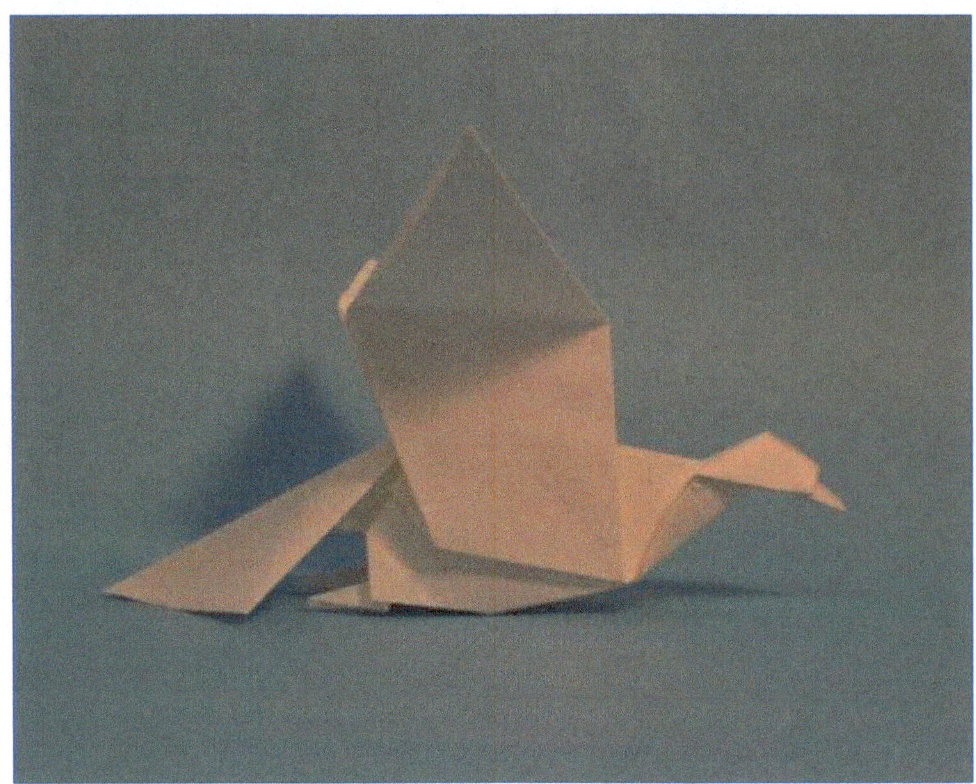

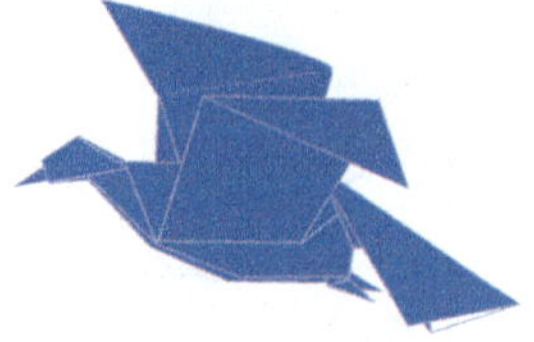

Many varieties of Doves can be seen soaring through the skies around the world, and the White Dove has long been used as a symbol of peace. Other Doves include Mourning Doves and Blue Ground Dove.

1

2

Fold and unfold.

3

Fold to the center.

4

Fold to the center and swing out from behind.

5

Rotate 180°.

6

Fold the top layer inside.

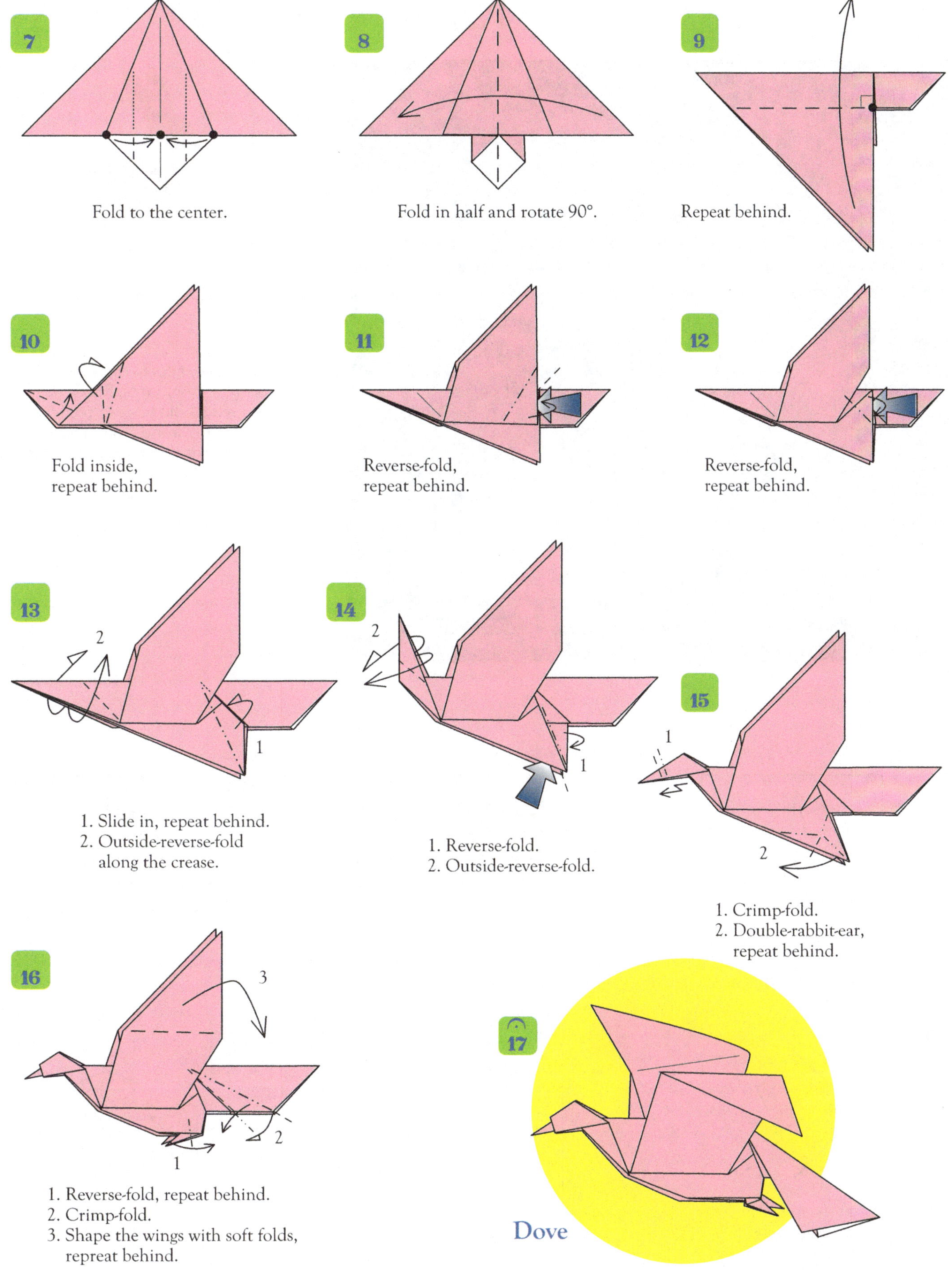

7 Fold to the center.

8 Fold in half and rotate 90°.

9 Repeat behind.

10 Fold inside, repeat behind.

11 Reverse-fold, repeat behind.

12 Reverse-fold, repeat behind.

13
1. Slide in, repeat behind.
2. Outside-reverse-fold along the crease.

14
1. Reverse-fold.
2. Outside-reverse-fold.

15
1. Crimp-fold.
2. Double-rabbit-ear, repeat behind.

16
1. Reverse-fold, repeat behind.
2. Crimp-fold.
3. Shape the wings with soft folds, repreat behind.

17

Dove

Rabbit

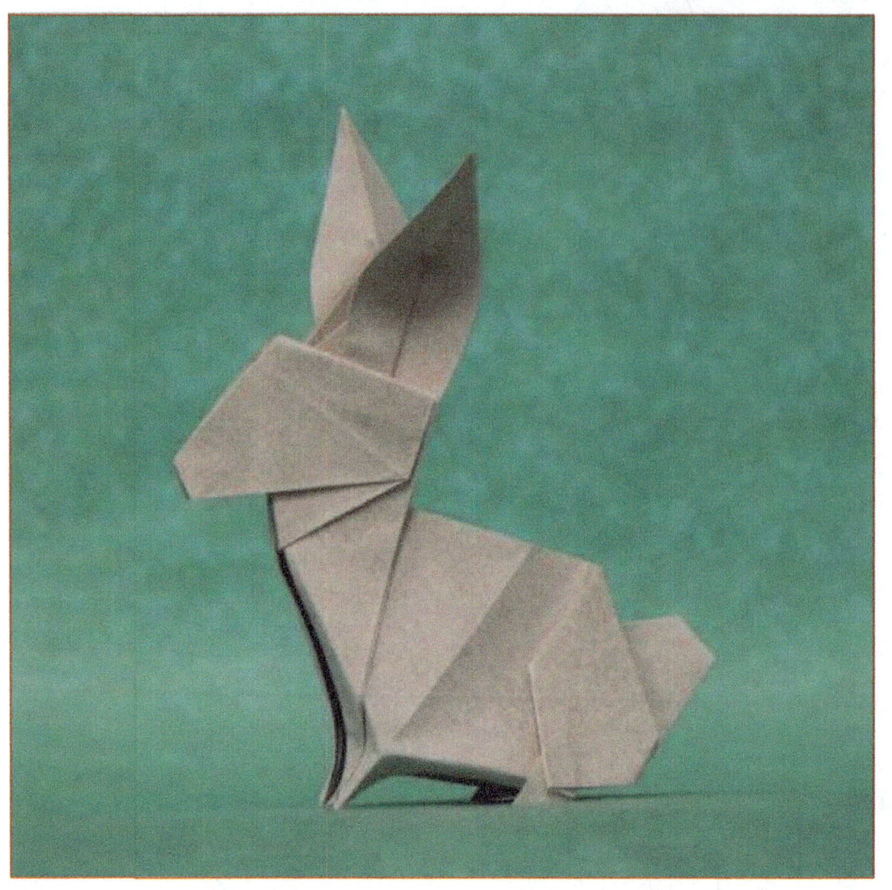

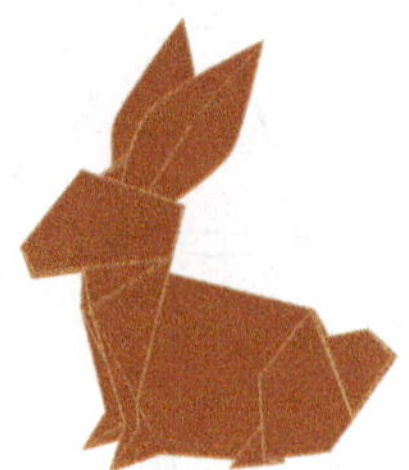

From fairy tales to cartoons to many peoples' front yards, Rabbits have secured a solid place in popular culture the world around. Often depicted as clever and sometimes troublesome, these furry creatures make wonderful pets.

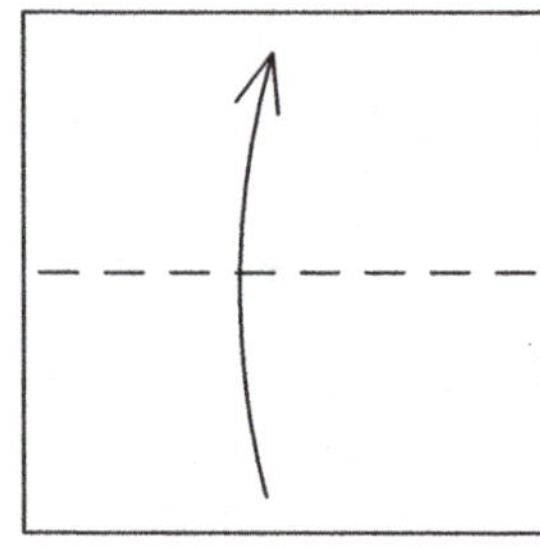

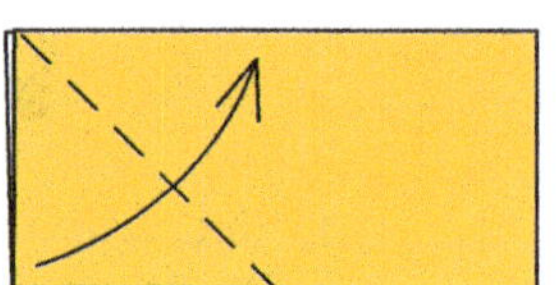

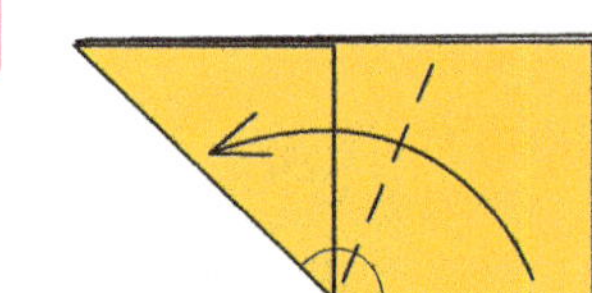

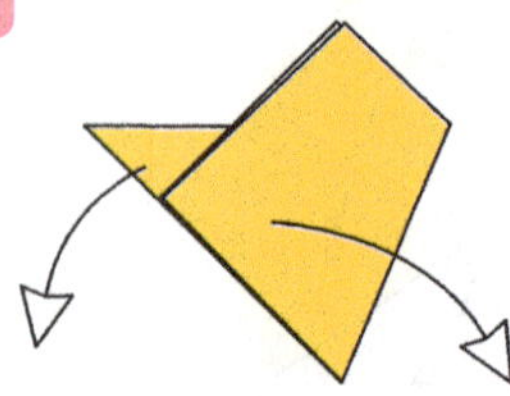

Unfold everything and rotate.

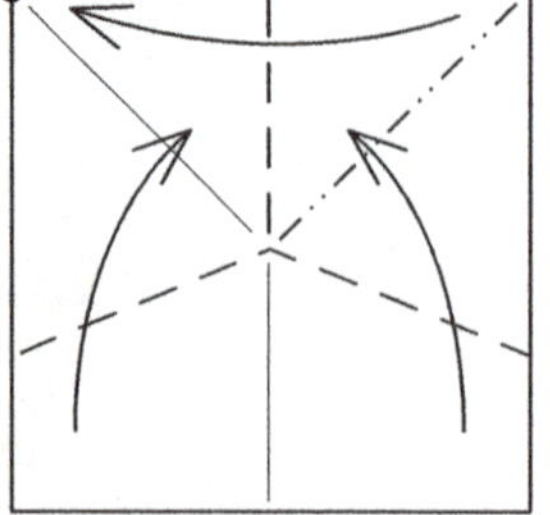

Fold along the creases. Rotate the dot to the bottom.

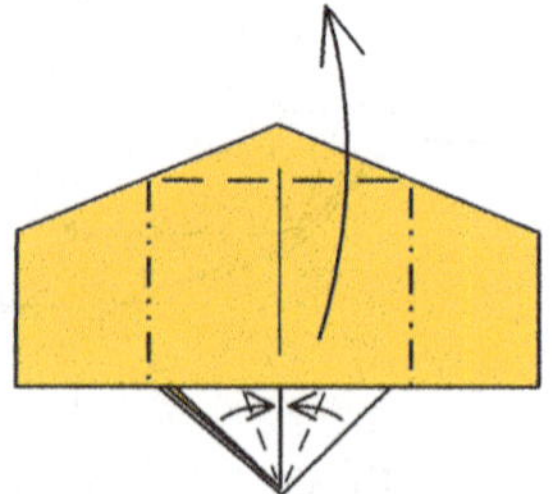

Petal-fold.

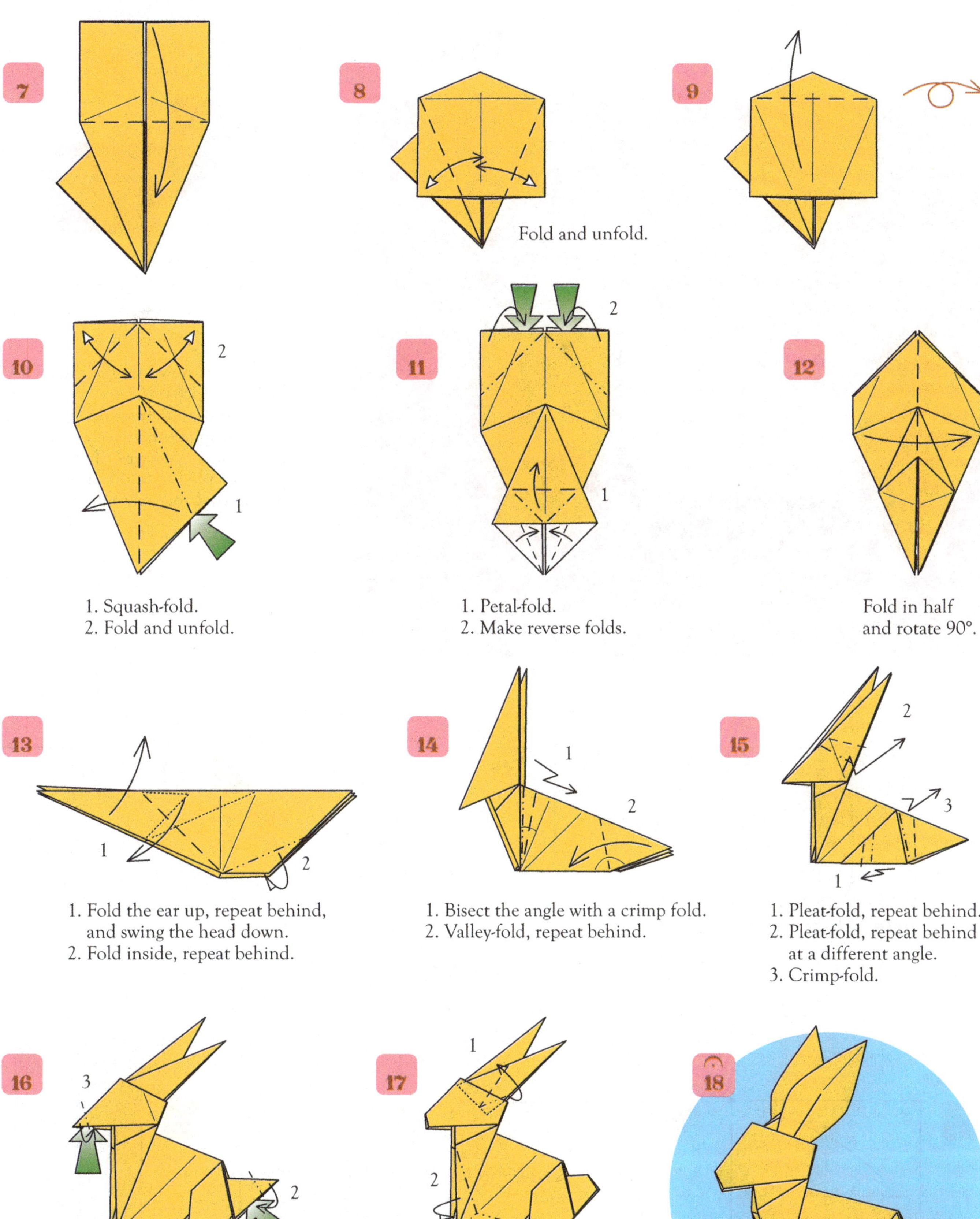

7

8

Fold and unfold.

9

10

1. Squash-fold.
2. Fold and unfold.

11

1. Petal-fold.
2. Make reverse folds.

12

Fold in half
and rotate 90°.

13

1. Fold the ear up, repeat behind,
   and swing the head down.
2. Fold inside, repeat behind.

14

1. Bisect the angle with a crimp fold.
2. Valley-fold, repeat behind.

15

1. Pleat-fold, repeat behind.
2. Pleat-fold, repeat behind
   at a different angle.
3. Crimp-fold.

16

1. Reverse-fold,
   repeat behind.
2. Reverse-fold.
3. Reverse-fold.

17

1. Squash-fold to make the ear 3D.
2. Make a 3D rabbit ear.
Repeat behind.

18

Rabbit

Sheep

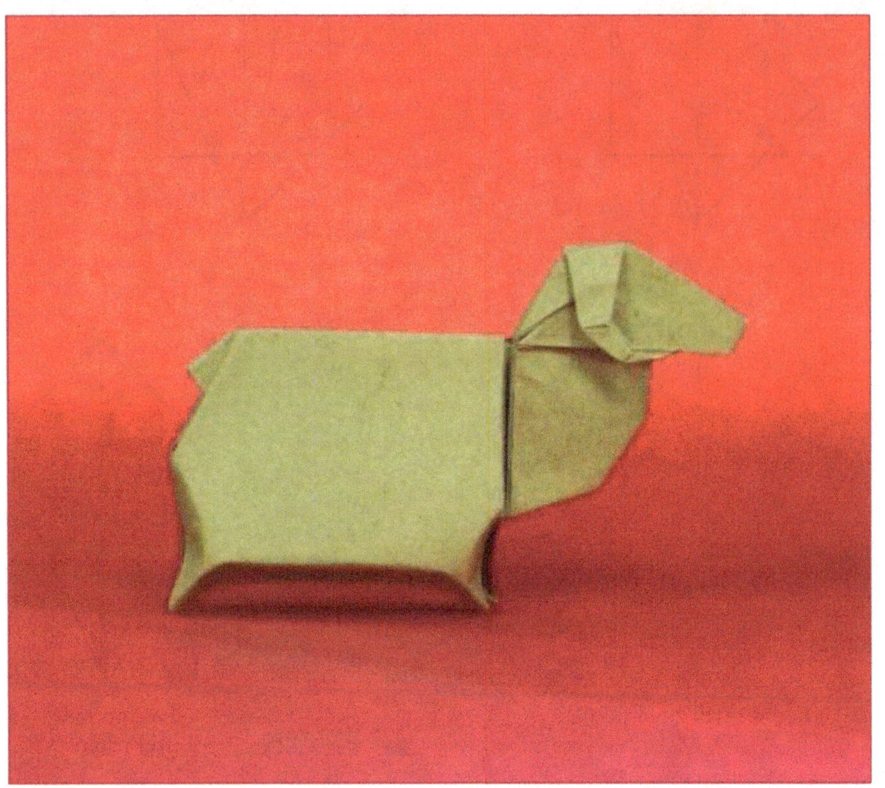

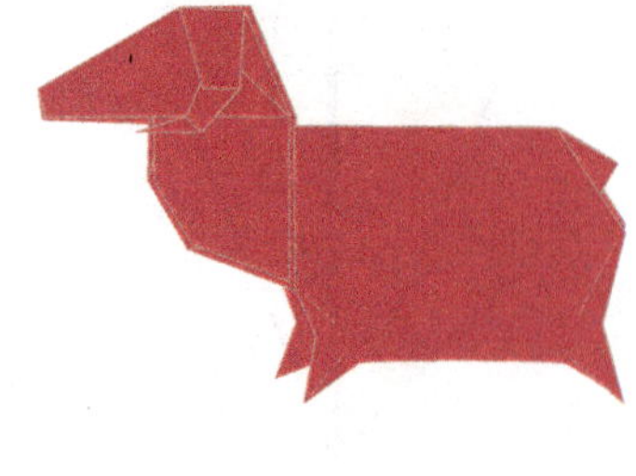

Sheep are known for their tendency to follow each other and are generally docile unless frightened or surprised. A staple in farming communities and mountainous villages, Sheep provide families and the world with their warm wool and rich milk.

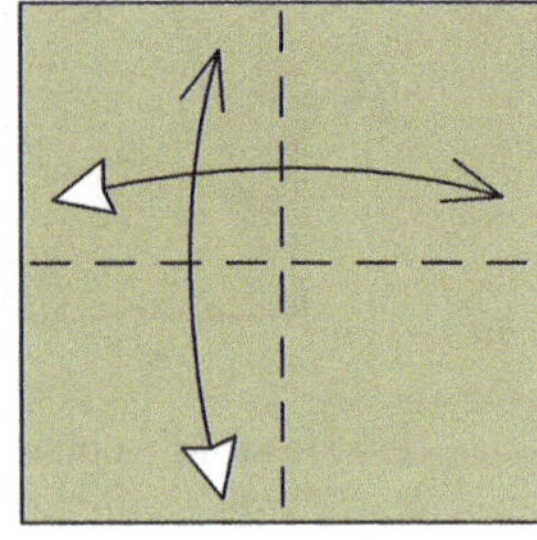

Fold and unfold.

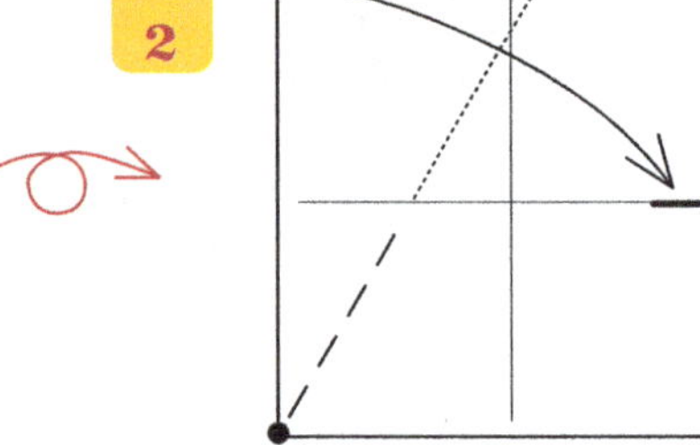

Bring the dot to the line.
Crease on the bottom half.

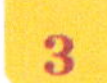
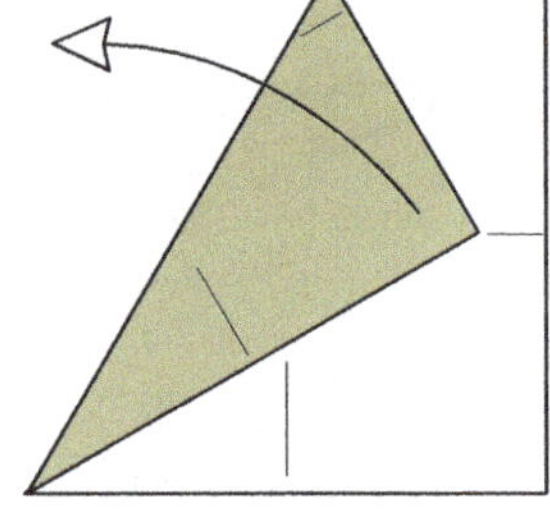

Unfold.

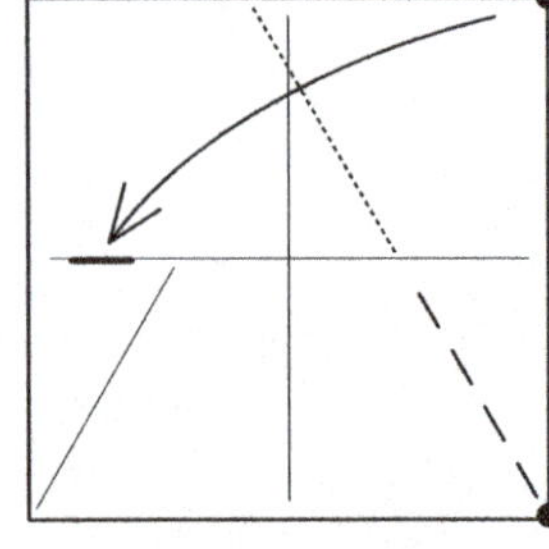

Repeat steps 2–3
on the right.

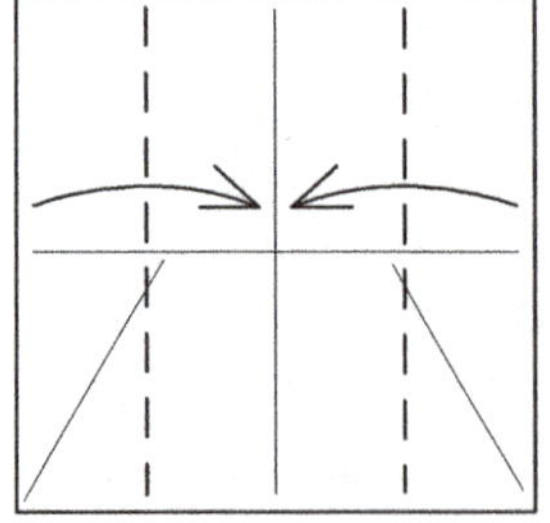

Fold to the center.

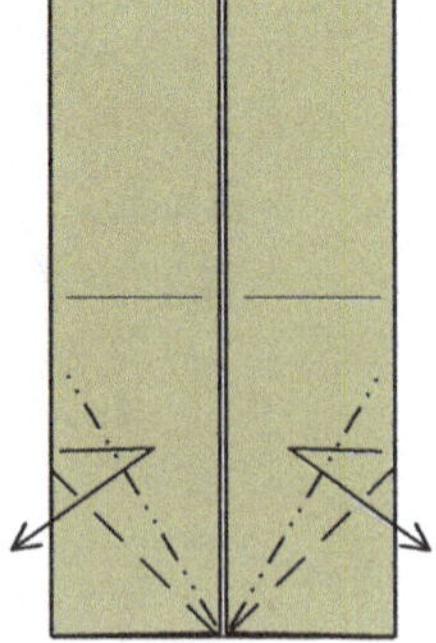

Fold to the center
and unfold.

Make crimp folds
along the creases.

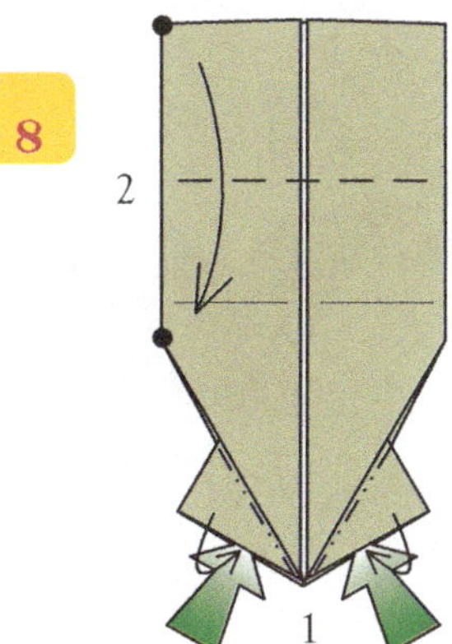

1. Make reverse folds.
2. Valley-fold.

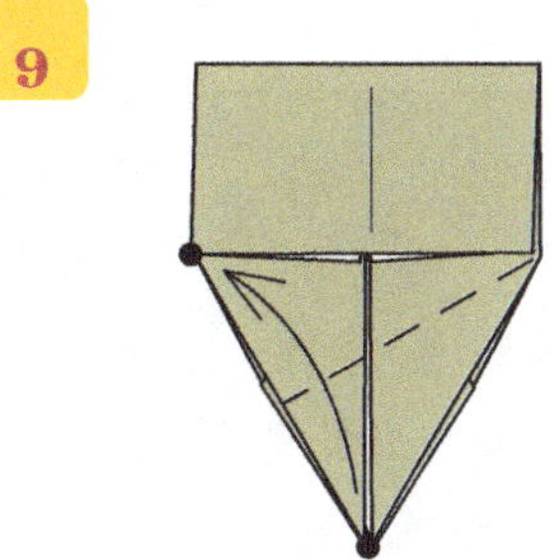

Fold in half
and rotate 90°.

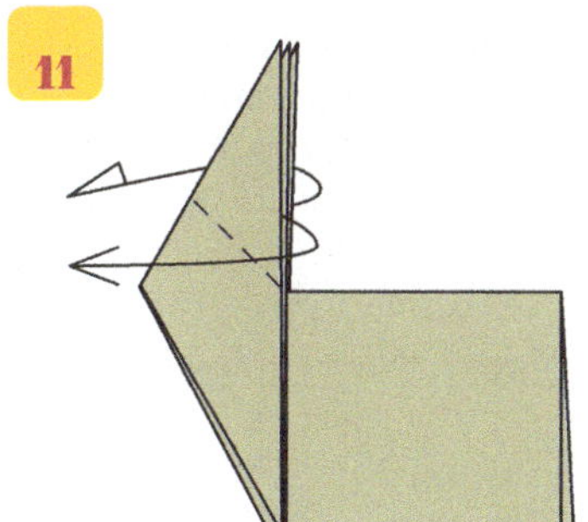

Outside-reverse-fold.

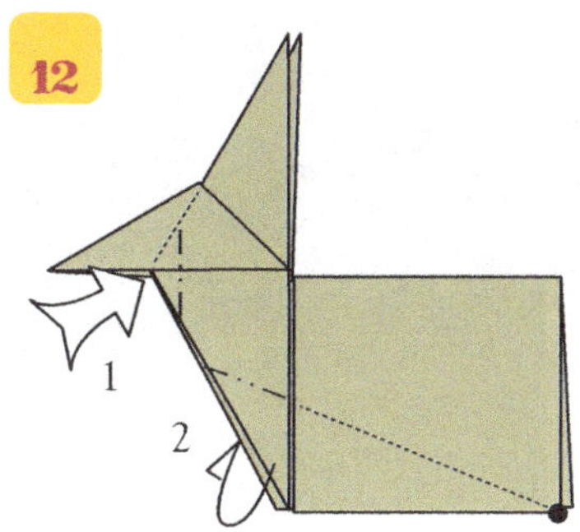

1. Sink.
2. Fold inside,
   repeat behind.

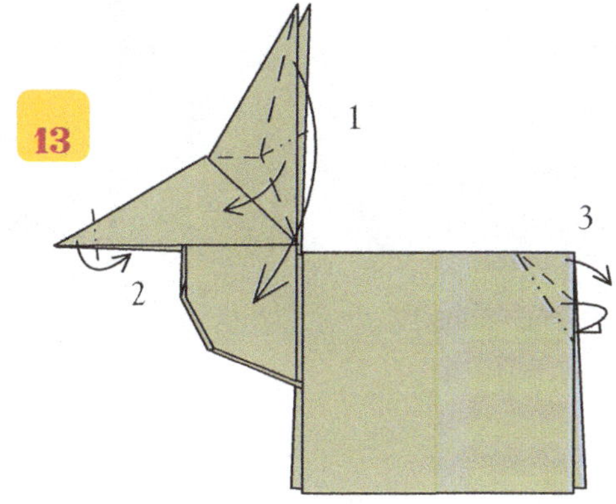

1. Rabbit-ear the horns,
   repeat behind.
2. Reverse-fold.
3. Crimp-fold.

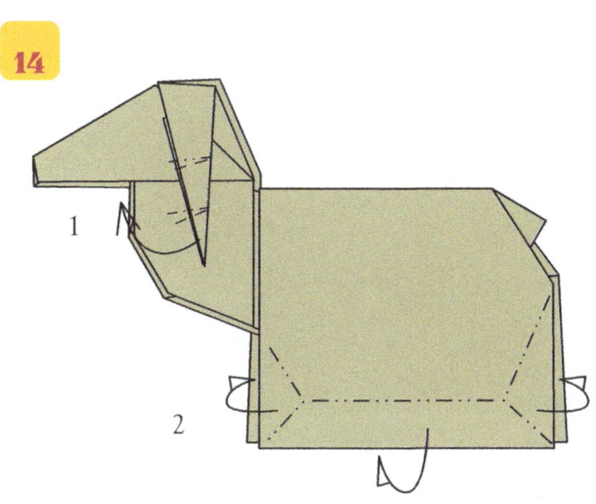

1. Shape the horns with crimp folds.
2. Shape the legs and body so the
   sheep will be 3D.
Repeat behind.

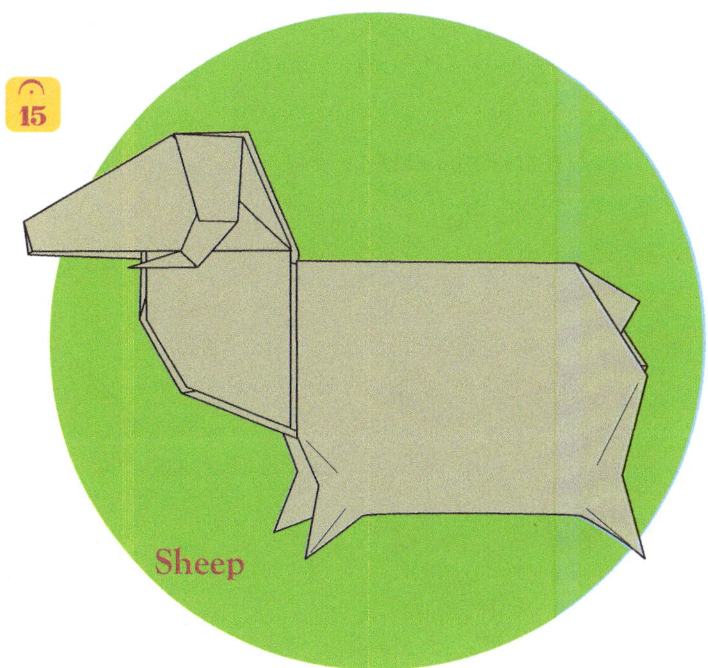

Sheep

Unicorn

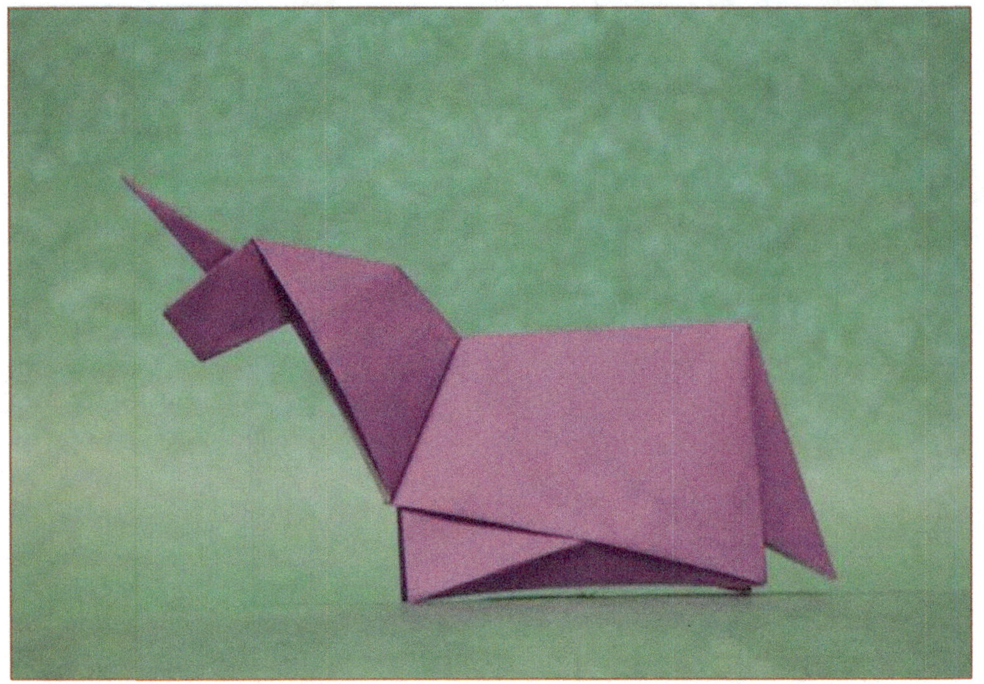

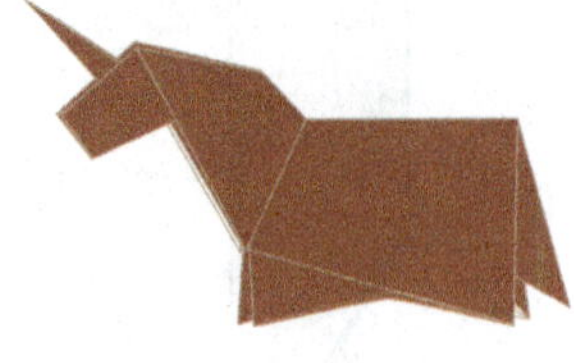

This mythical beast, a horse with a single horn protruding from its forehead, is popular with all ages, and children can be seen sporting hats that make them look like Unicorns. Unicorns are also a symbol of purity and are often shown alongside rainbows to symbolize happiness.

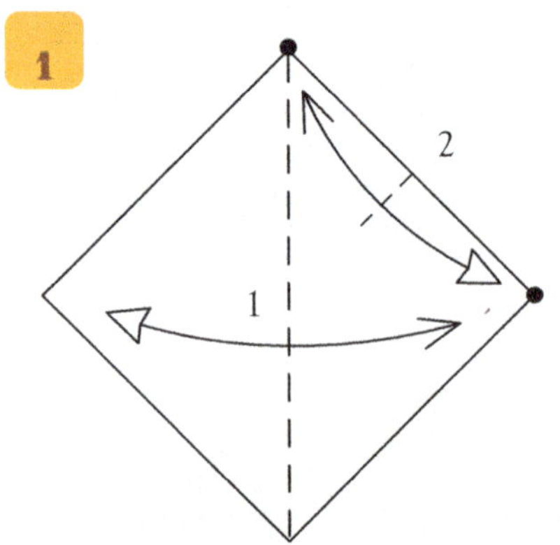

1. Fold and unfold.
2. Fold and unfold on the edge.

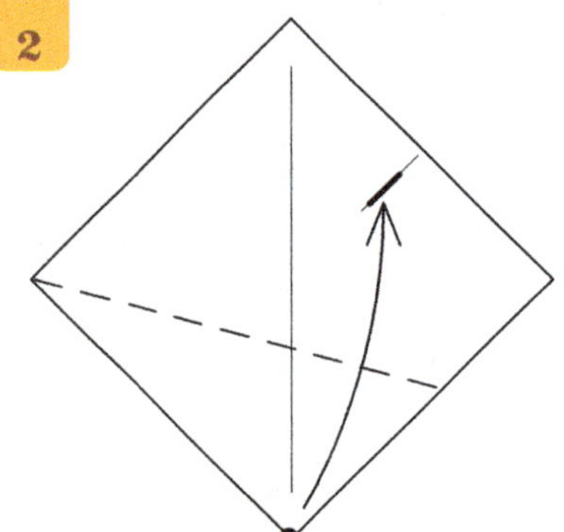

Bring the dot to the line.

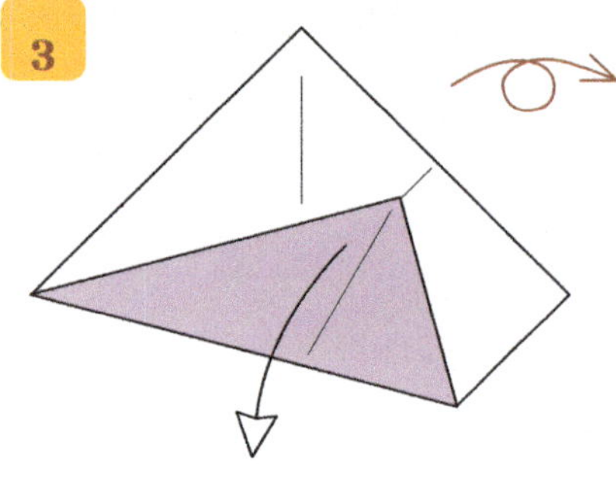

Unfold.

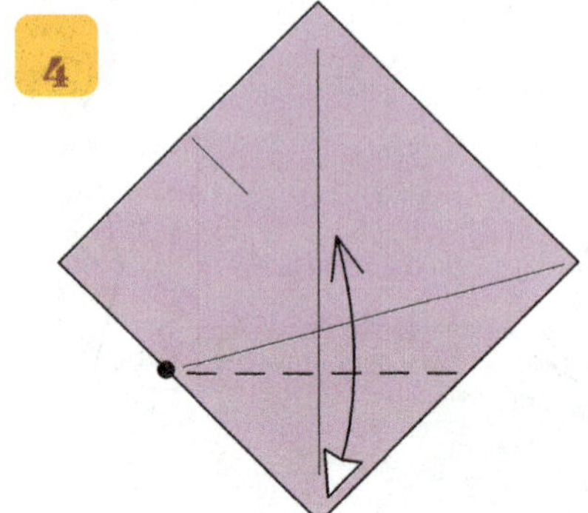

Fold and unfold.

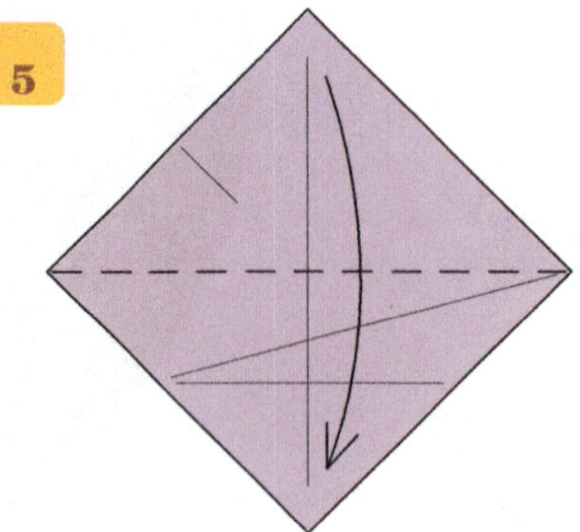

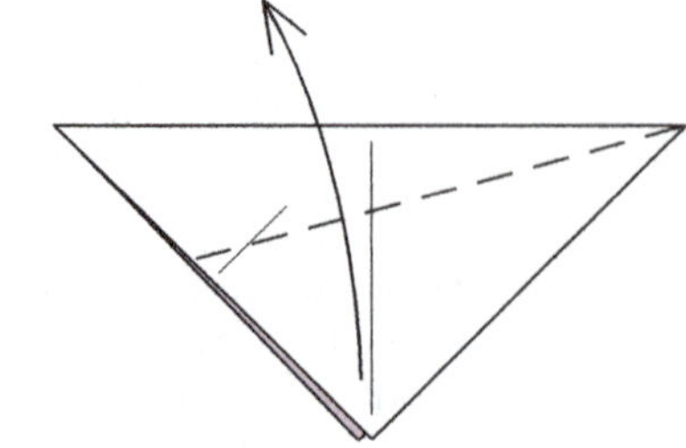

Fold along a hidden crease.

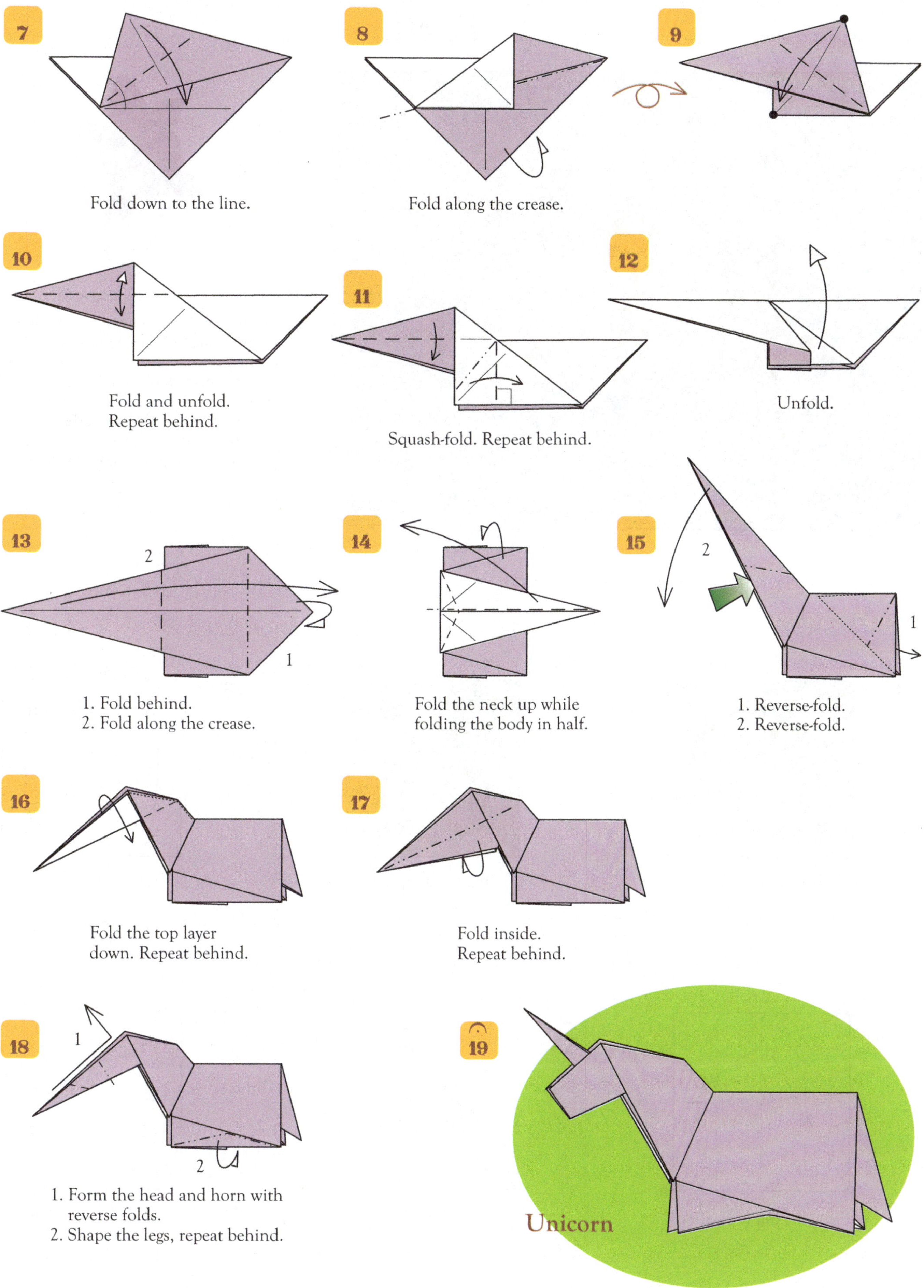

7 Fold down to the line.

8 Fold along the crease.

9

10 Fold and unfold. Repeat behind.

11 Squash-fold. Repeat behind.

12 Unfold.

13
1. Fold behind.
2. Fold along the crease.

14 Fold the neck up while folding the body in half.

15
1. Reverse-fold.
2. Reverse-fold.

16 Fold the top layer down. Repeat behind.

17 Fold inside. Repeat behind.

18
1. Form the head and horn with reverse folds.
2. Shape the legs, repeat behind.

19

Unicorn

Turtle

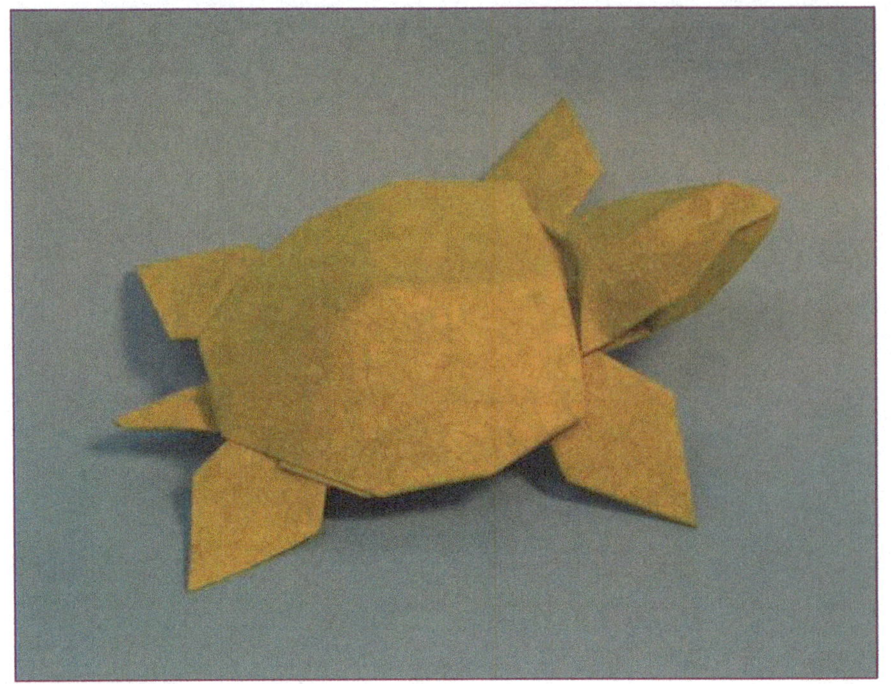

Carrying their homes on their backs, Turtles are believed to be one of the longest-living creatures on Earth, some with a lifespan of over 150 years. From the tiny Stinkpot Common Musk Turtle to the huge Leatherback Sea Turtle, these shelled reptiles are have fascinated humans for millennia.

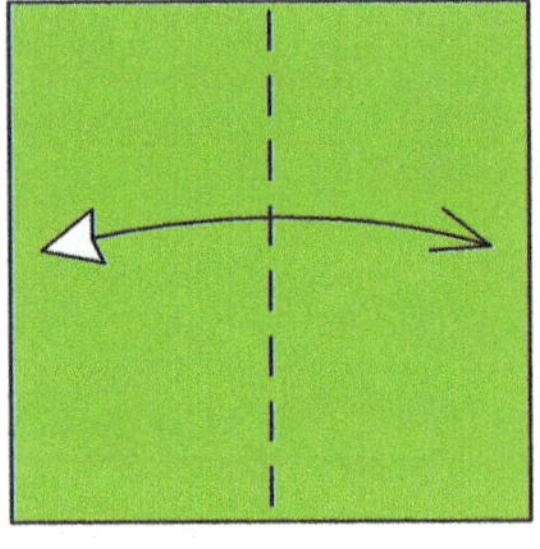

1

Fold and unfold.

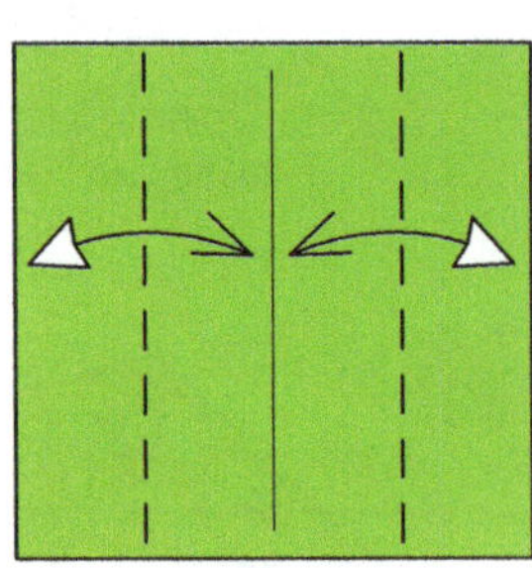

2

Fold and unfold.

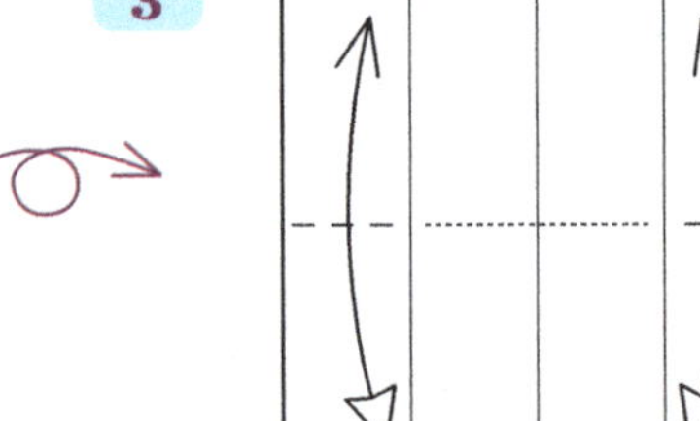

3

Fold and unfold.

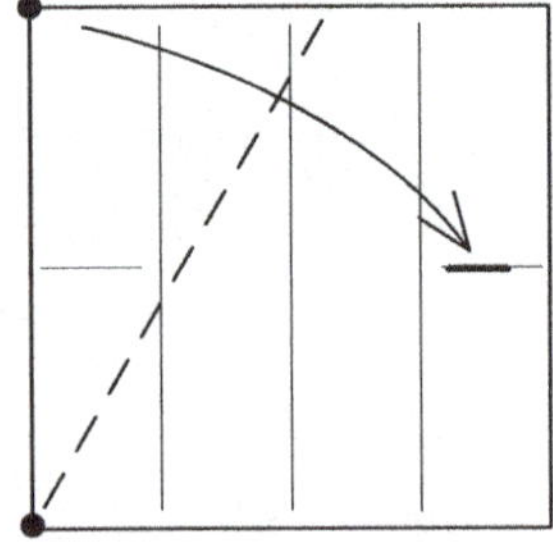

4

Bring the dot to the line.

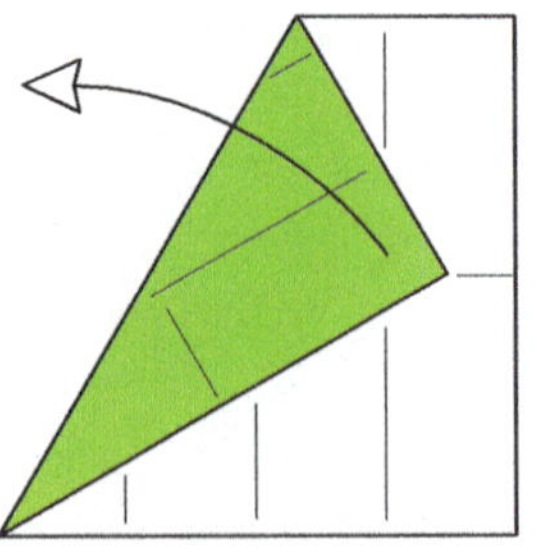

5

Unfold.

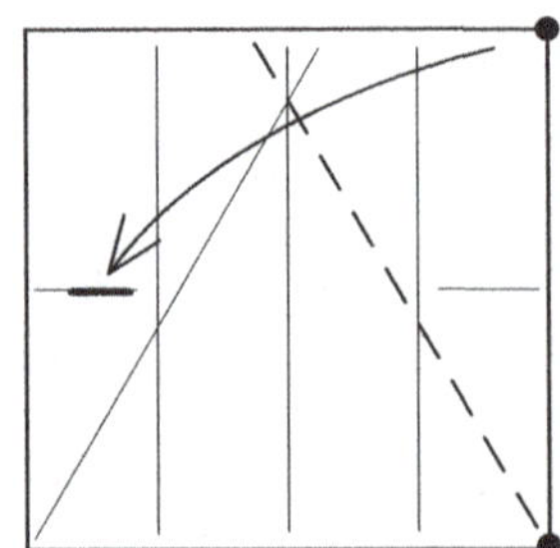

6

Repeat steps 4–5 on the right.

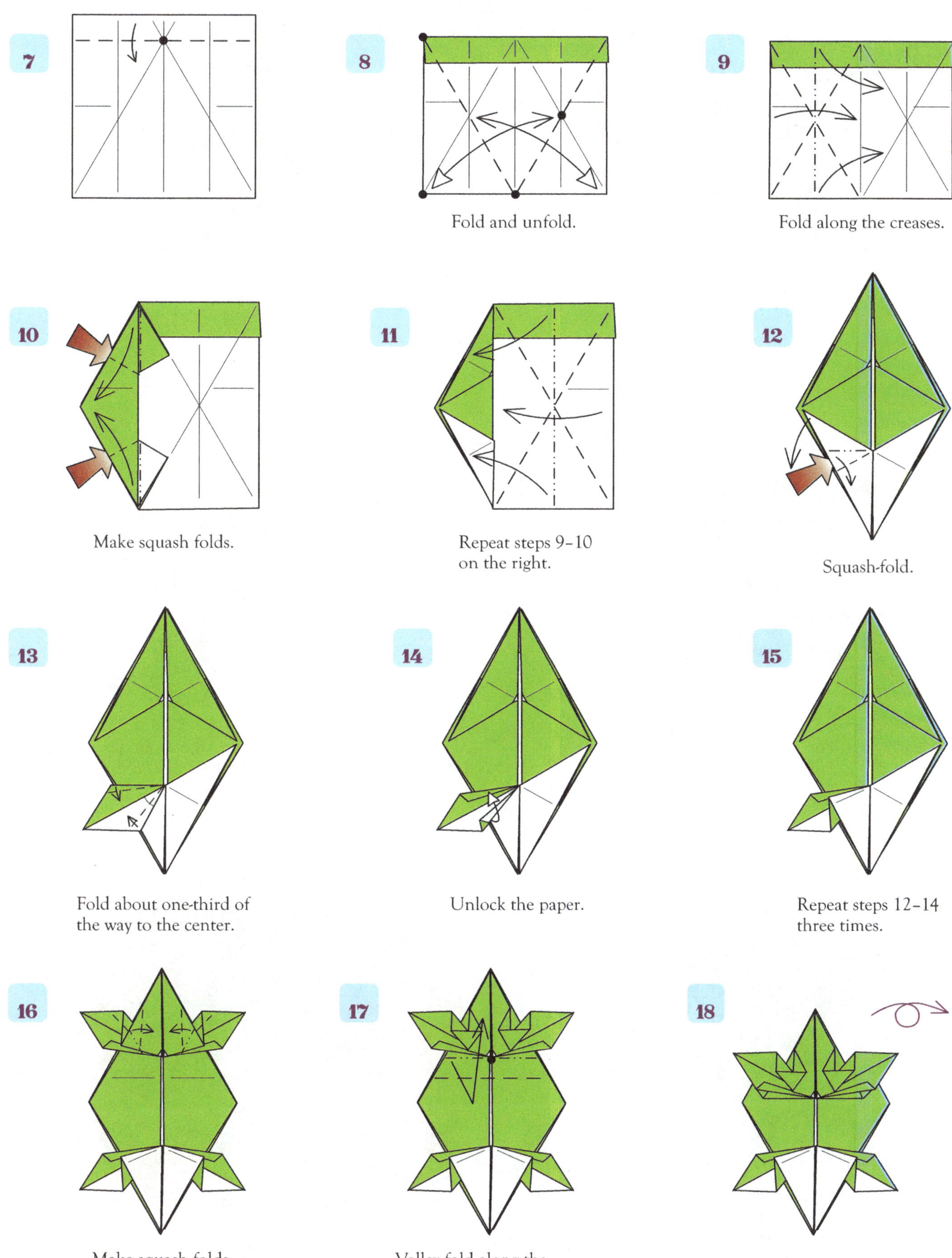

7
8
Fold and unfold.
9
Fold along the creases.
10
Make squash folds.
11
Repeat steps 9–10 on the right.
12
Squash-fold.
13
Fold about one-third of the way to the center.
14
Unlock the paper.
15
Repeat steps 12–14 three times.
16
Make squash folds.
17
Valley-fold along the creases for this pleat fold.
18

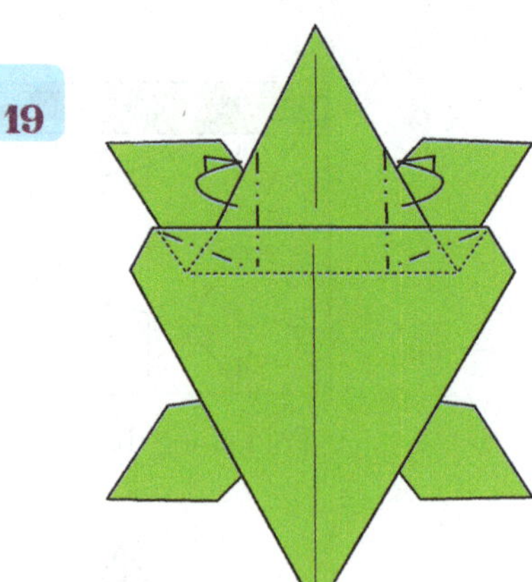

Make squash folds.

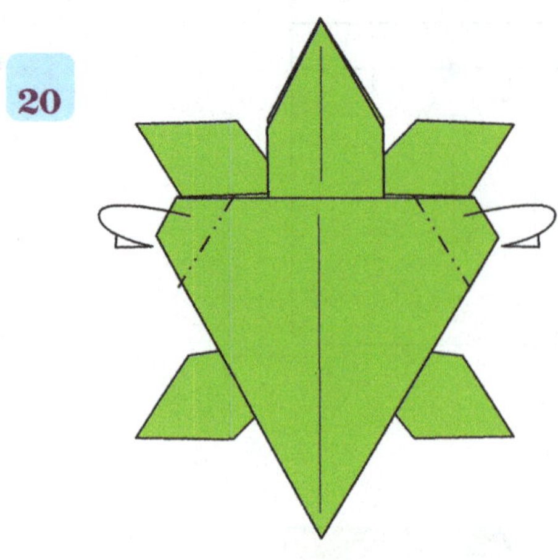

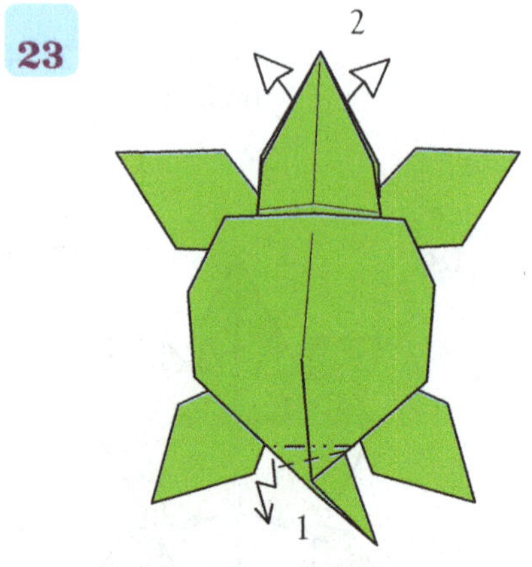

1. Fold behind.
2. Puff out at the dot.

1. Wrap the white layer around.
2. Fold the head up.

1. Pleat-fold.
2. Spread the layers
   of the head.

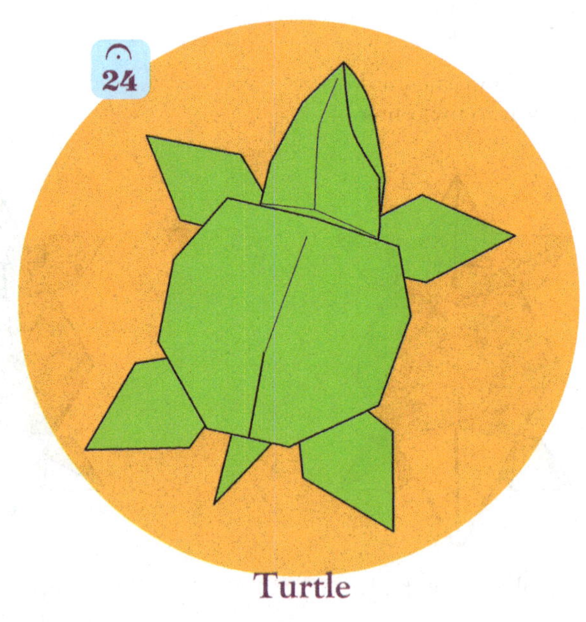

Turtle

Peacock

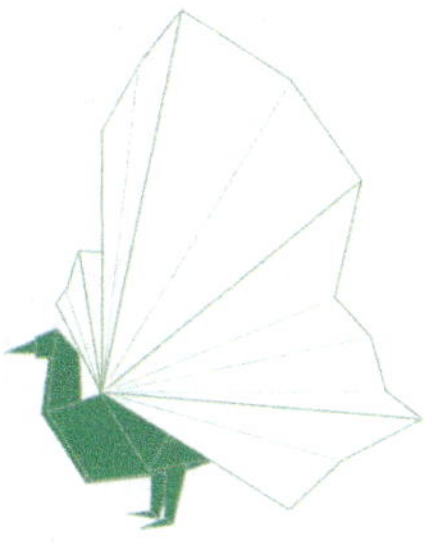

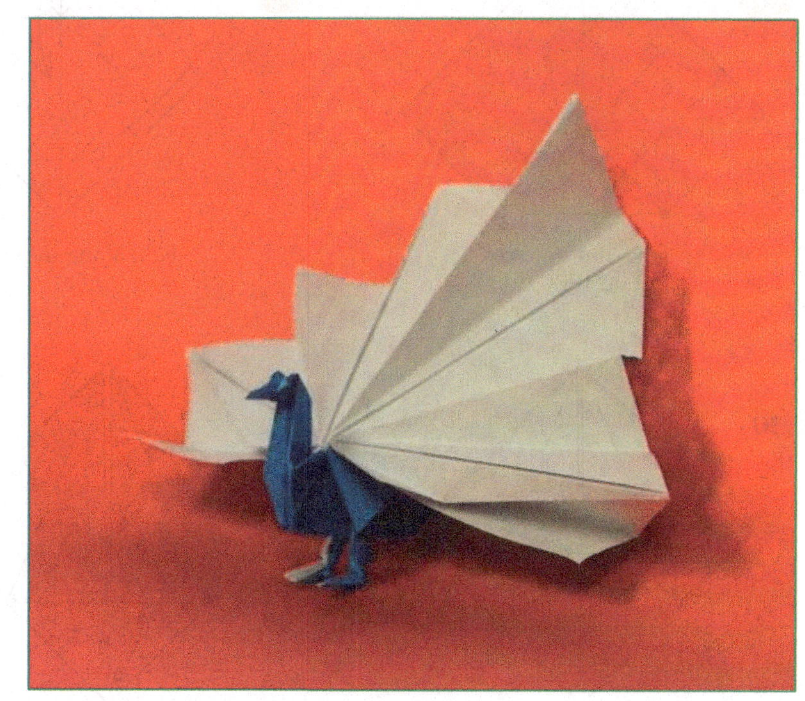

Bold and ostentatious, these large birds have beautiful iridescent tail feathers that have even drawn royalty to keep them as pets because of their extremely luxurious appearance. Strictly speaking, all Peacocks are males, the females being called Peahens.

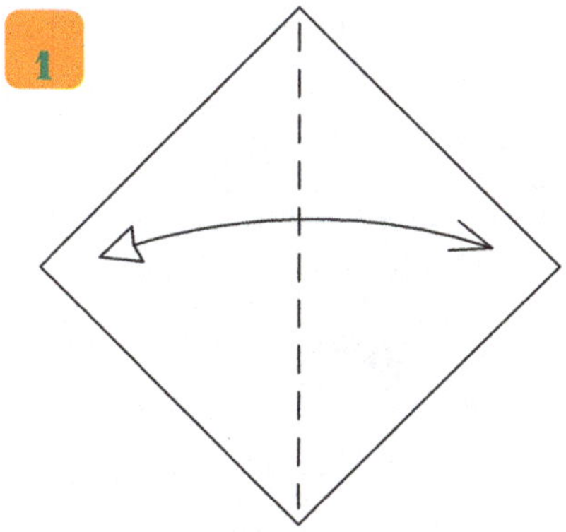

1

Fold and unfold.

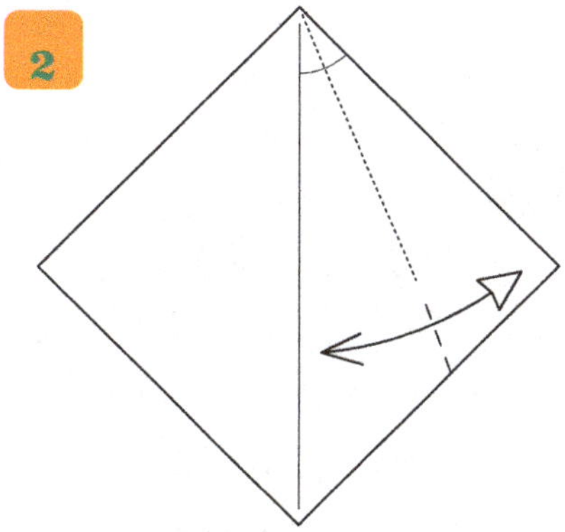

2

Fold and unfold on the edge.

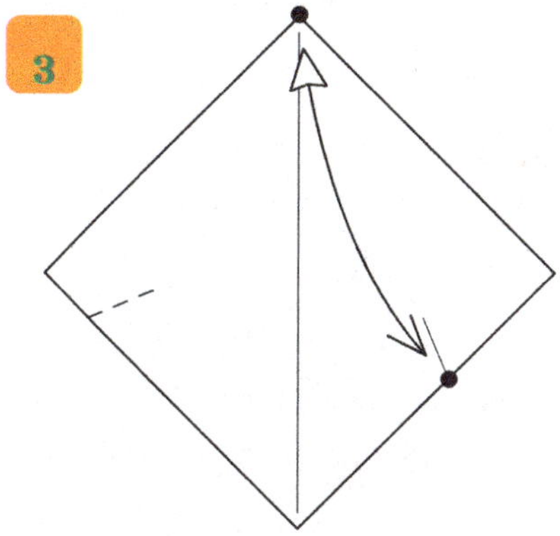

3

Fold and unfold on the edge.

4

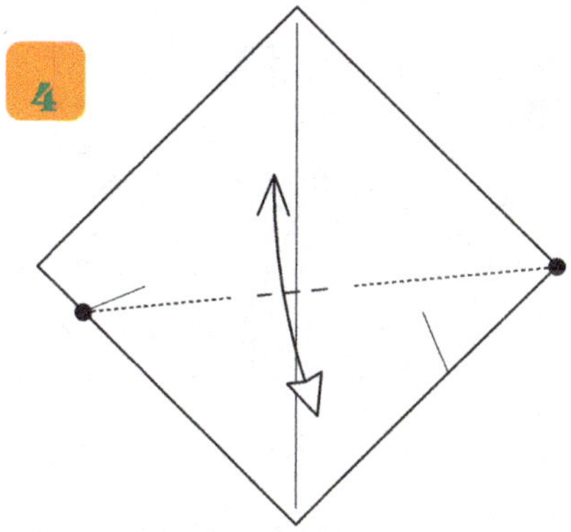

Fold and unfold on the diagonal.

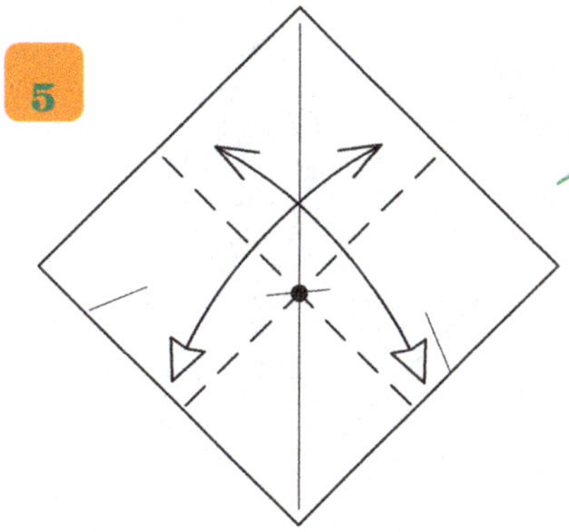

5

The dots will meet.

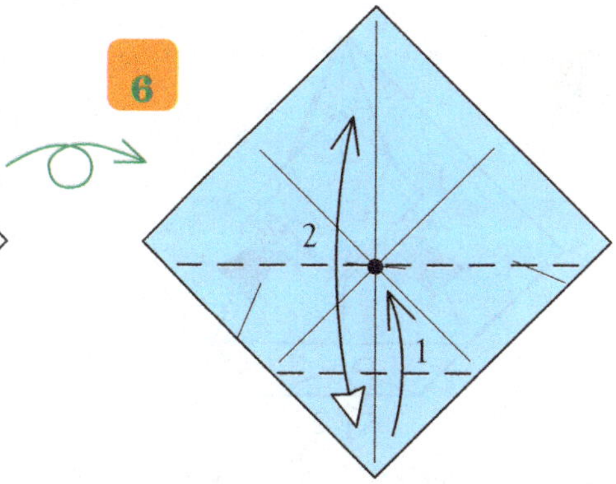

6

1. Fold up.
2. Fold and unfold.

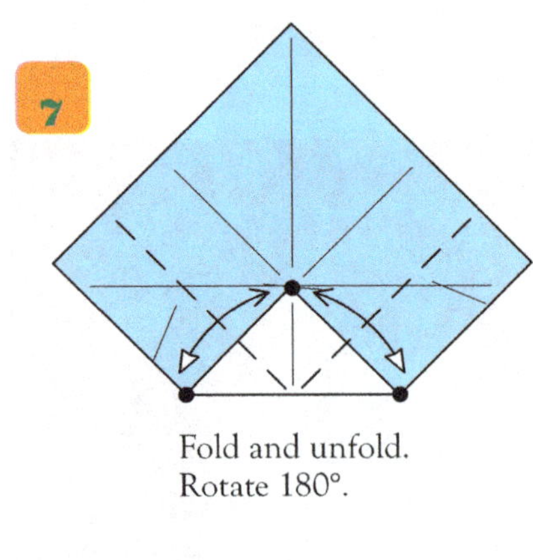

7

Fold and unfold.
Rotate 180°.

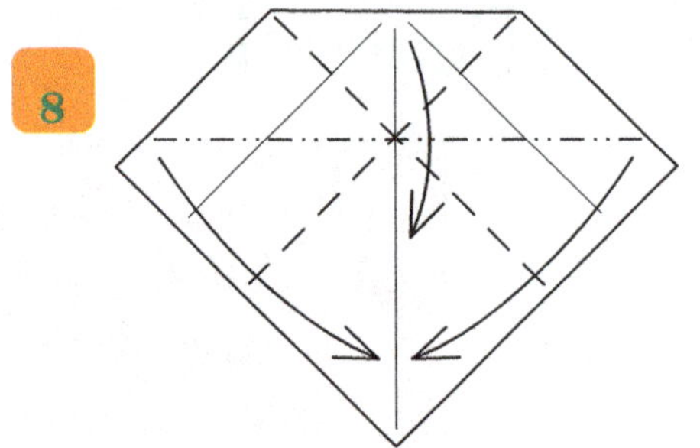

8

Fold along the creases.

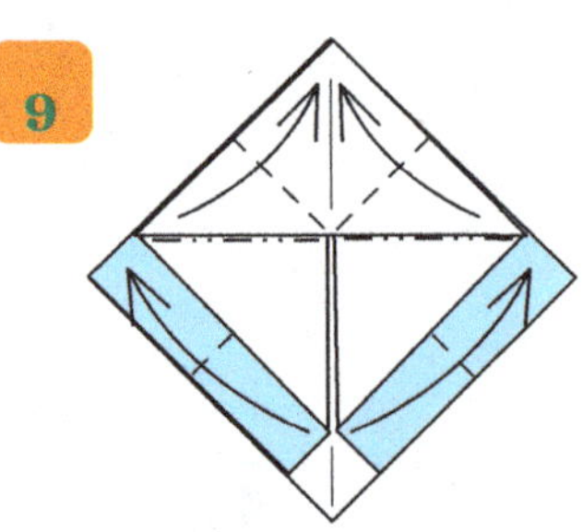

9

Make squash folds.
Fold along the creases.

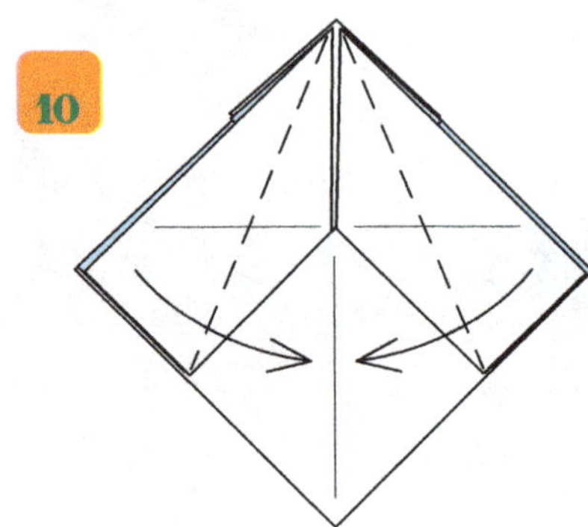

10

Fold the top layers
to the center.

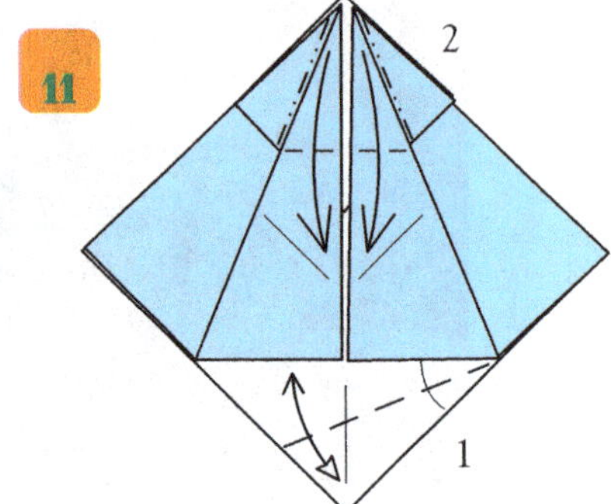

11

1. Fold and unfold.
2. Make squash folds.

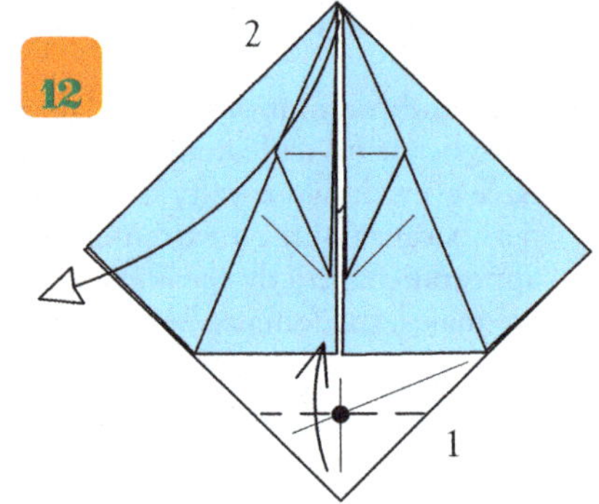

12

1. Fold up.
2. Pull out the
   hidden corner.

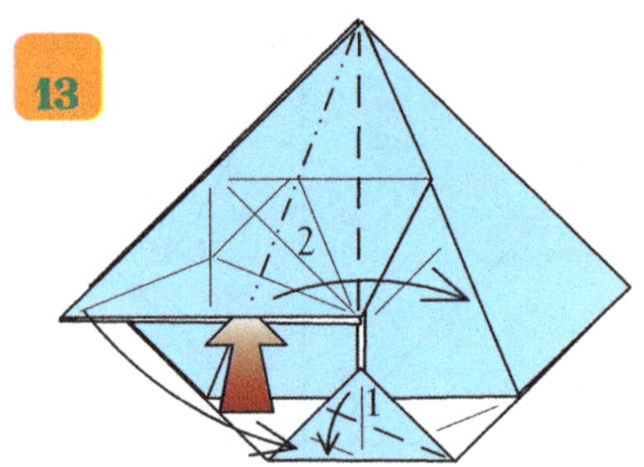

13

1. Fold down.
2. Squash-fold.

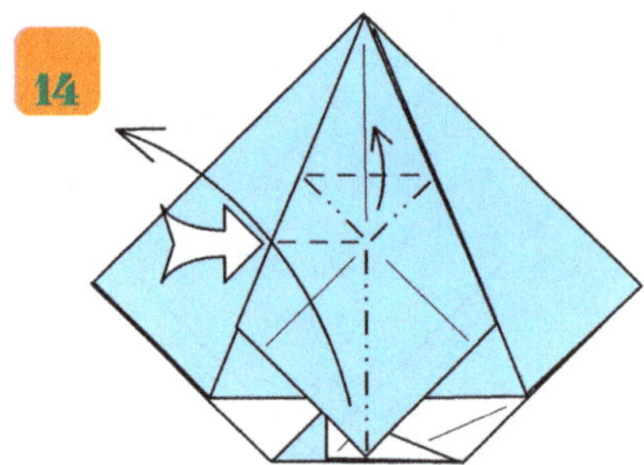

14

Fold along the creases.

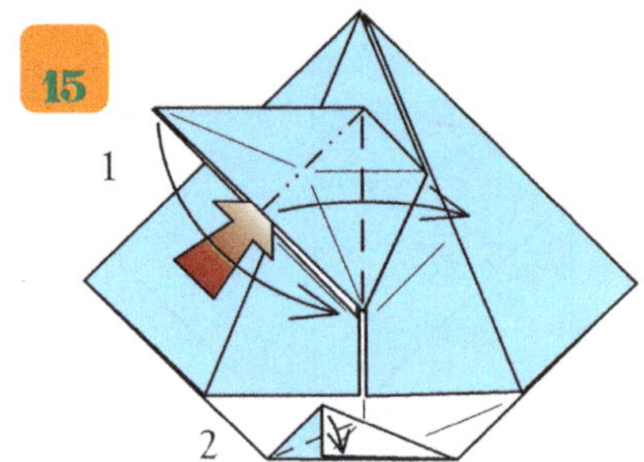

15

1. Squash-fold.
2. Fold down.

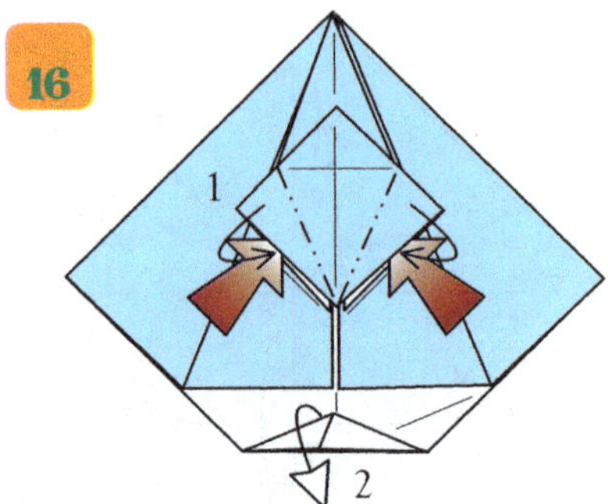

16

1. Make reverse-folds.
2. Unfold.

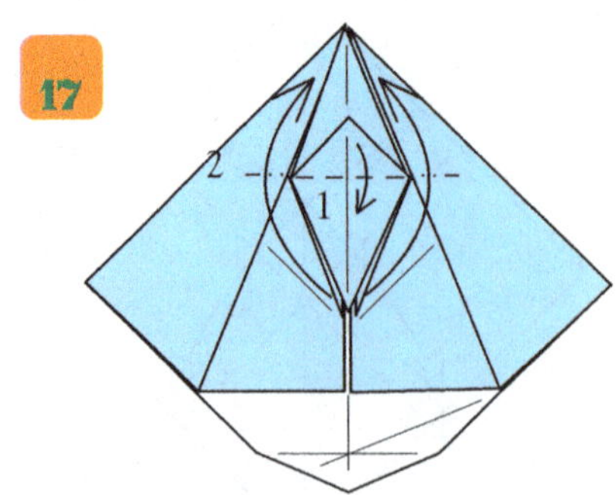

17

1. Fold down.
2. Make reverse-folds.
It is easier to fold these together.

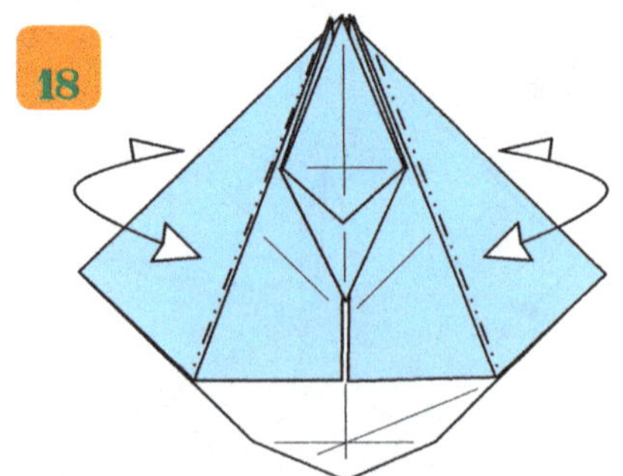

18

Fold and unfold.

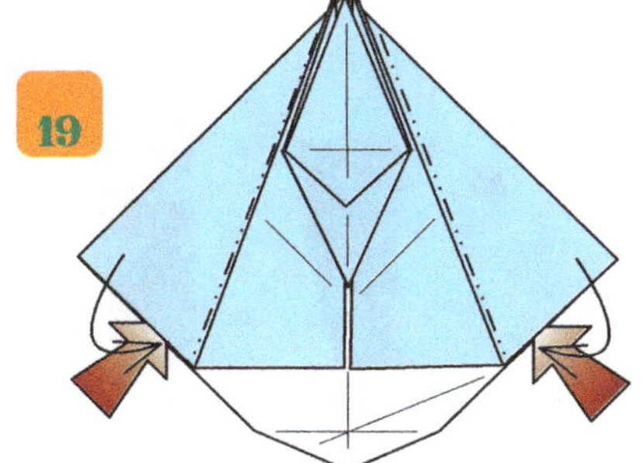

19

Make reverse folds.

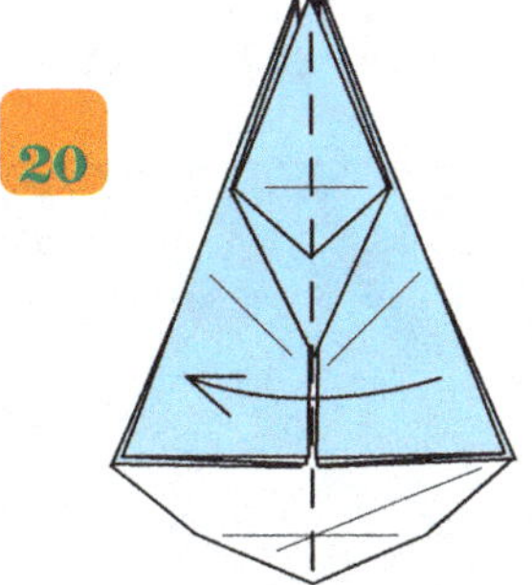

20

Fold in half
and rotate 90°.

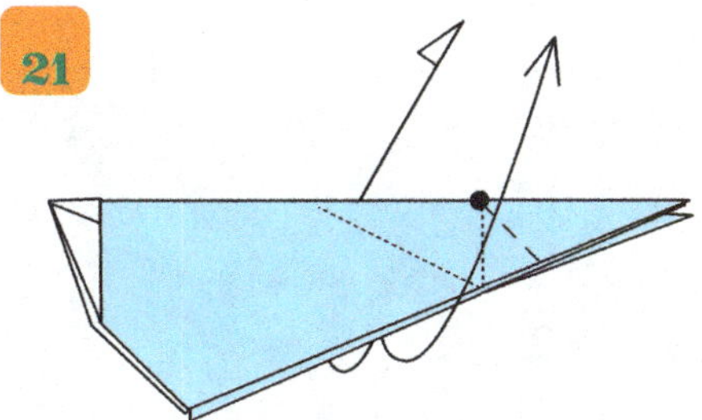

21

Outside-reverse-fold.

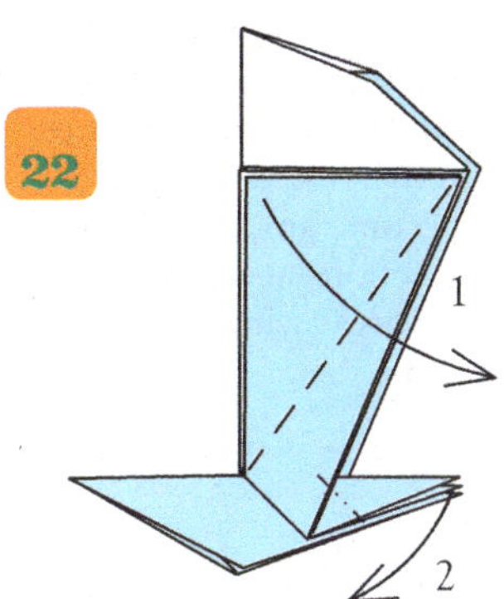

22

1. Fold the top layer.
2. Reverse-fold.
Repeat behind.

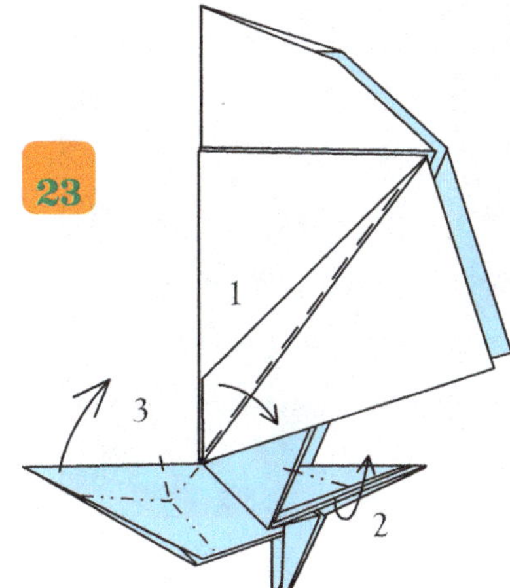

23

1. Valley-fold, repeat behind.
2. Lift up two layers, repeat behind.
3. Double-rabbit-ear.

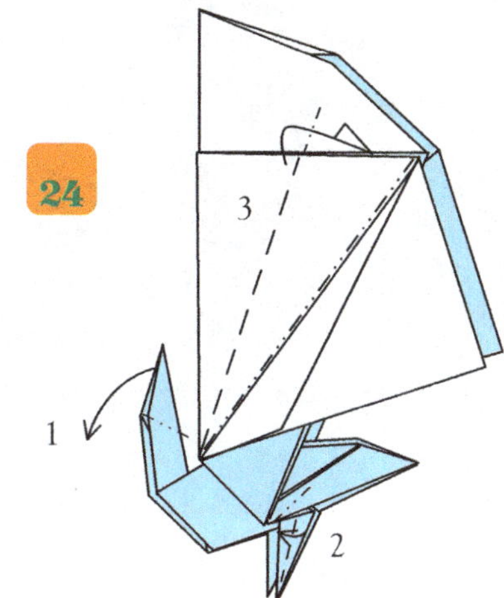

24

1. Reverse-fold.
2. Thin the leg with a small
   reverse fold at the top.
   Repeat behind.
3. Crimp-fold, repeat behind.

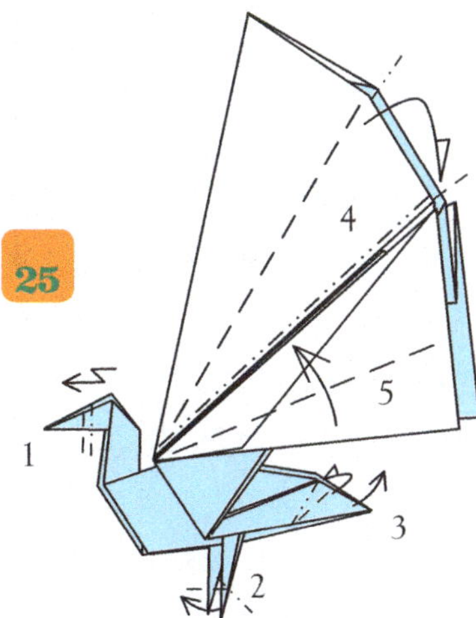

25

1. Reverse-fold.
2. Crimp-fold, repeat behind.
3. Crimp-sink the tail.
4. Crimp-fold.
5. Valley-fold, repeat behind.

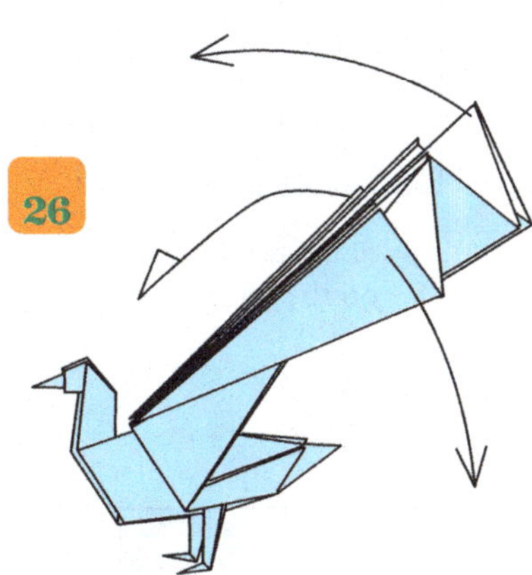

26

Spread the plumes.

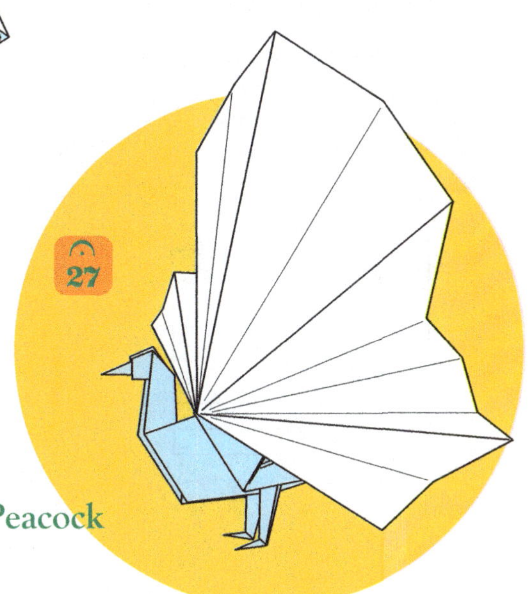

27

Peacock

Panda

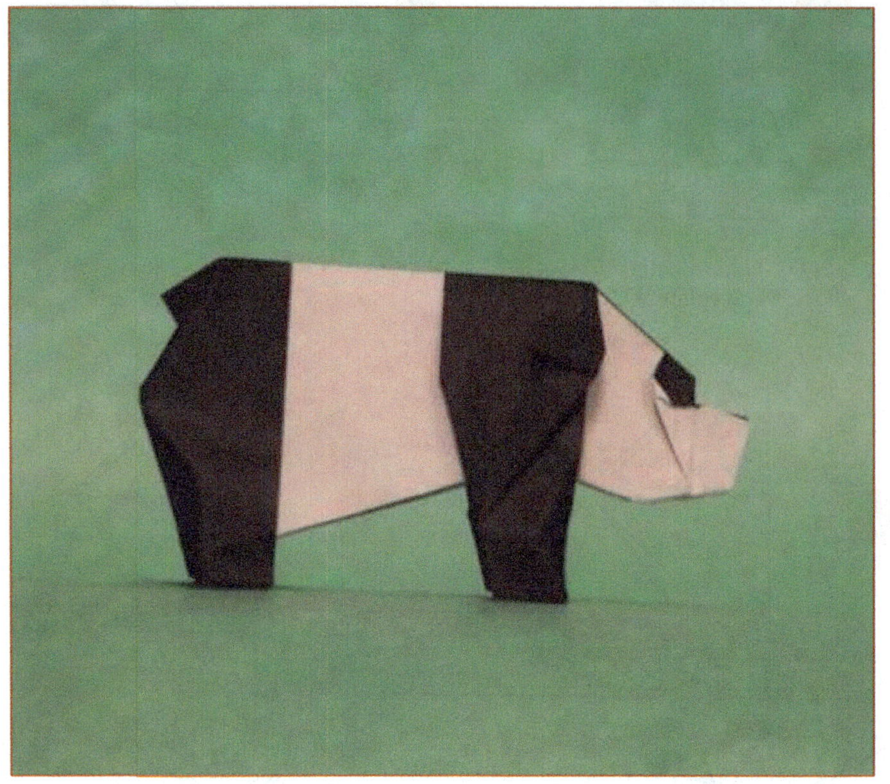

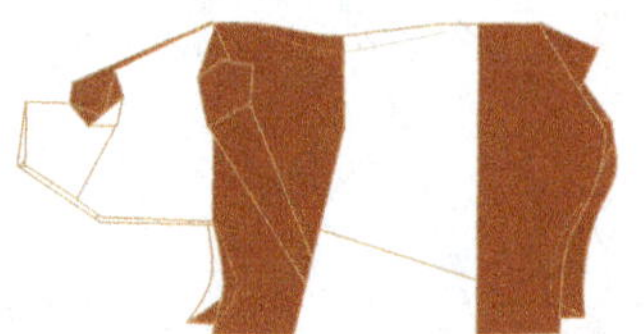

The playful and intelligent Giant Panda Bear's only natural habitat is in the remote mountains of central China, where they live on an abundant supply of bamboo. As concerned humans have sought to protect and increase their species, they have become amongst the most popular attractions at the zoos and conservation areas where they are being studied.

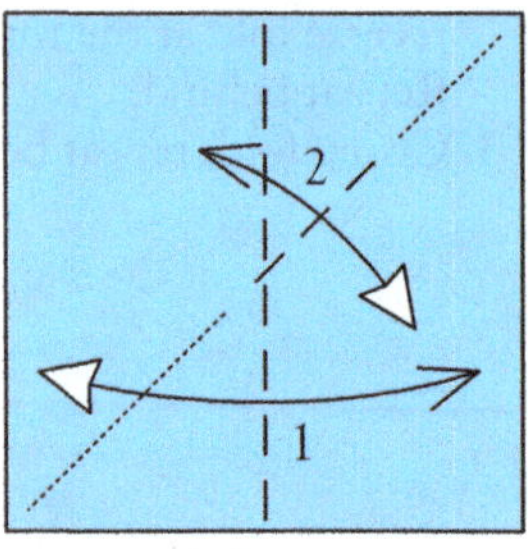

1. Fold and unfold.
2. Fold and unfold
   on the diagonal.

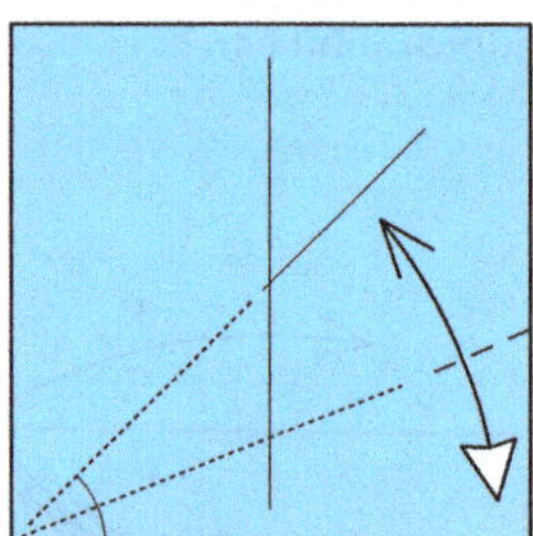

Fold and unfold
on the edge.

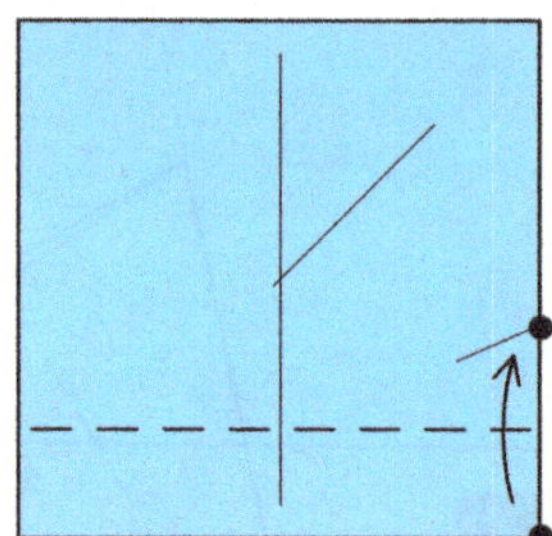

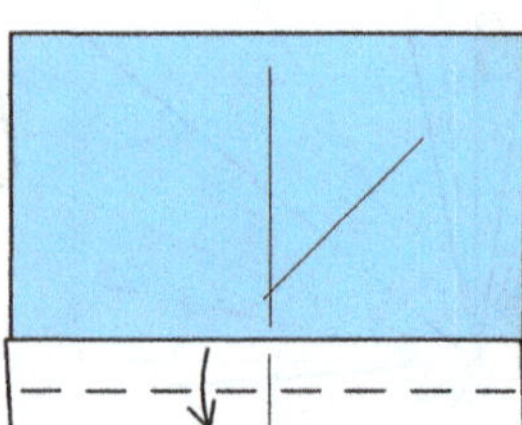

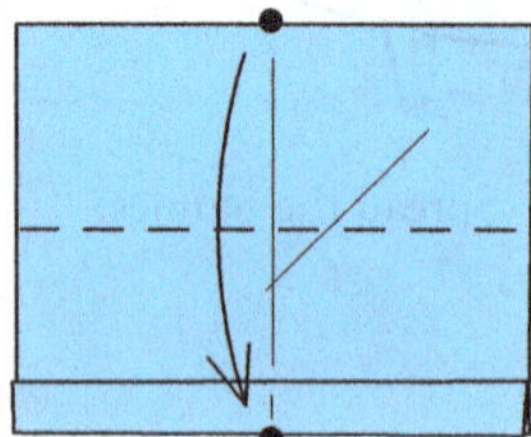

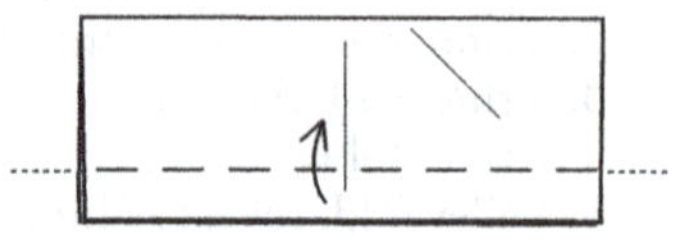

Fold along the
hidden edge.

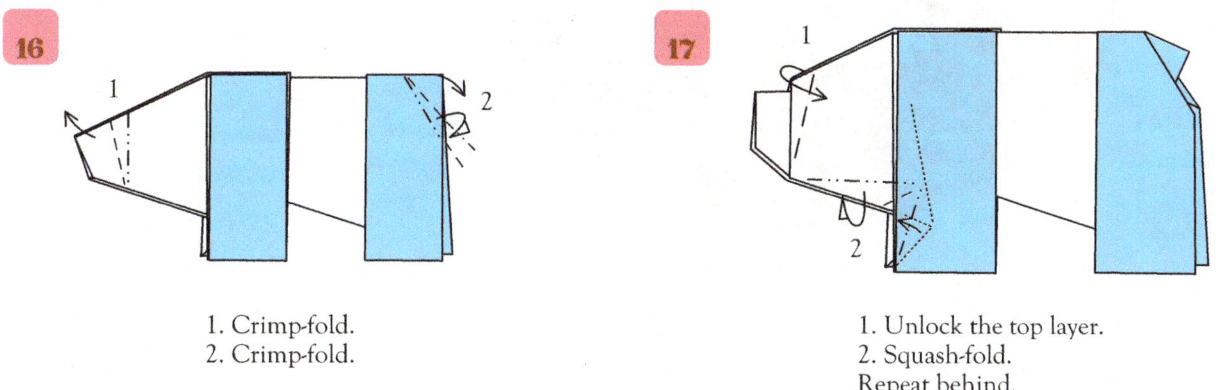

7 Unfold.

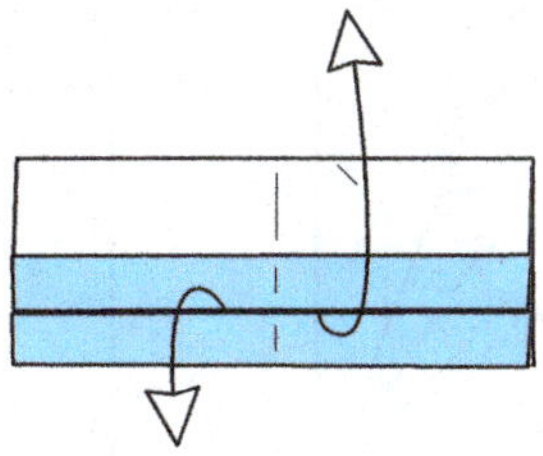

8 Fold to the center.

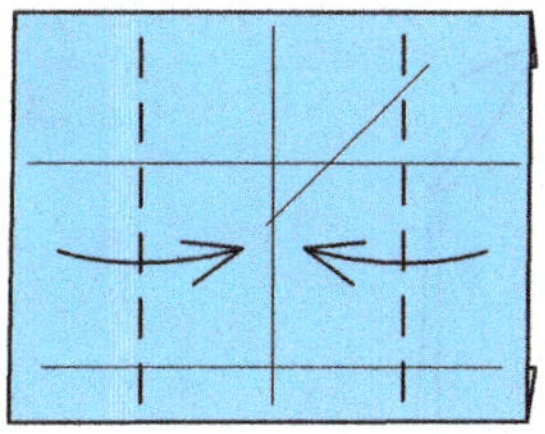

9

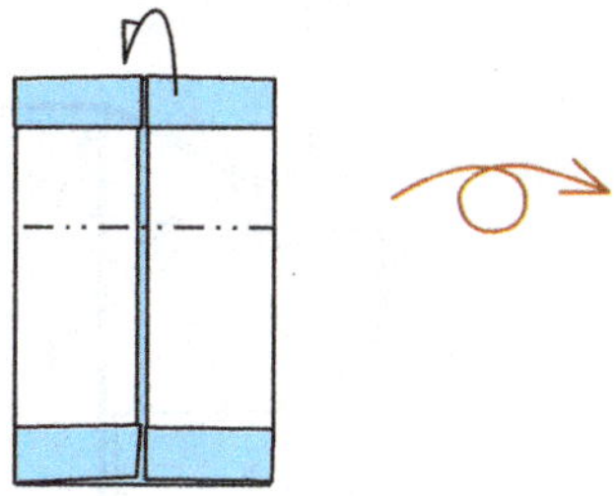

10 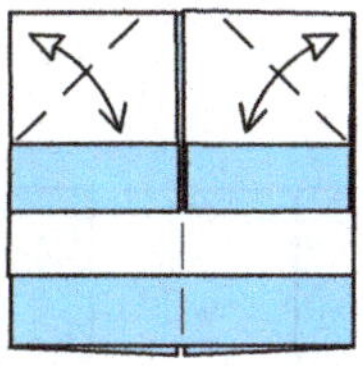 Fold and unfold.

11 Make reverse folds. Rotate 90°.

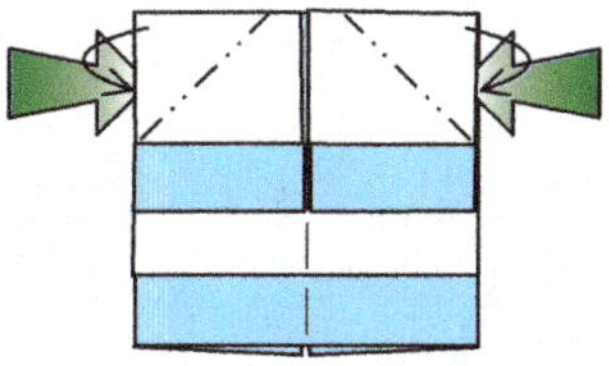

12

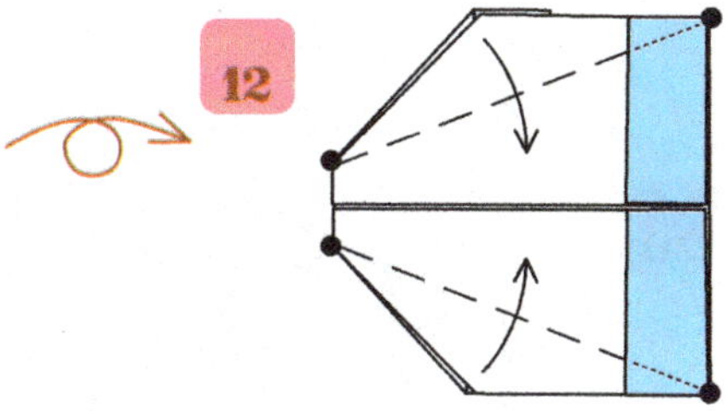

13
1. Fold and unfold. 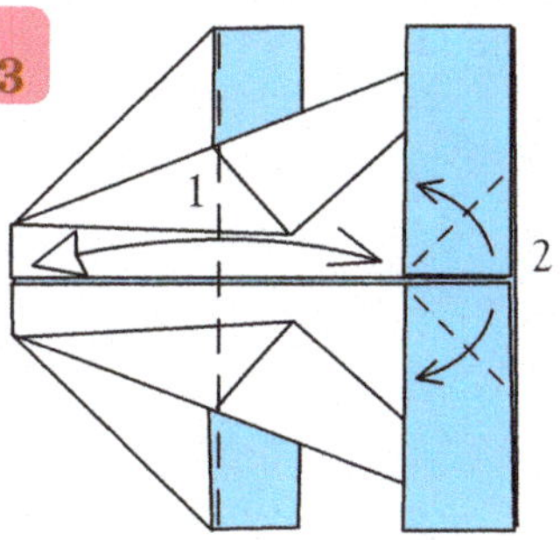
2. Make valley folds.

14

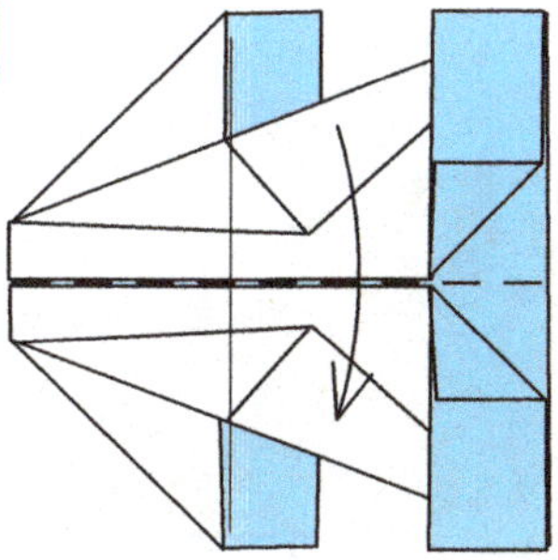

15 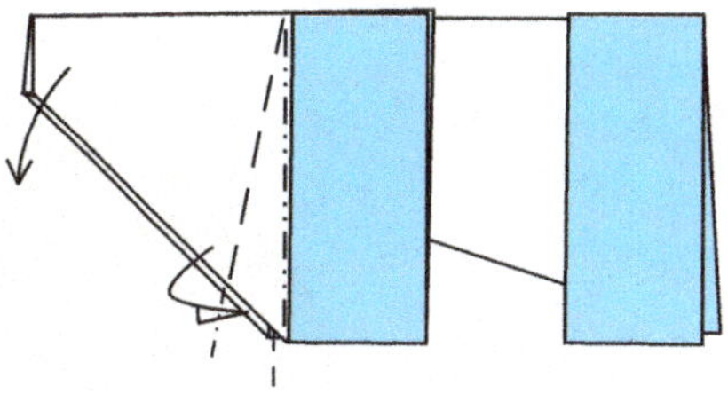 Crimp-fold.

16
1. Crimp-fold.
2. Crimp-fold.

17
1. Unlock the top layer.
2. Squash-fold.
Repeat behind.

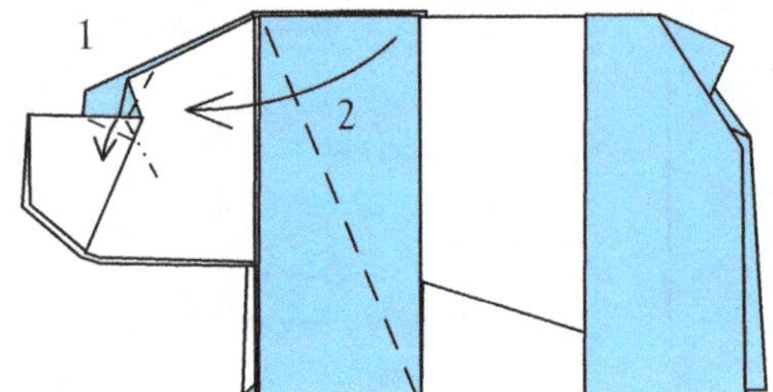

1. Make a small squash fold.
2. Valley-fold.
Repeat behind.

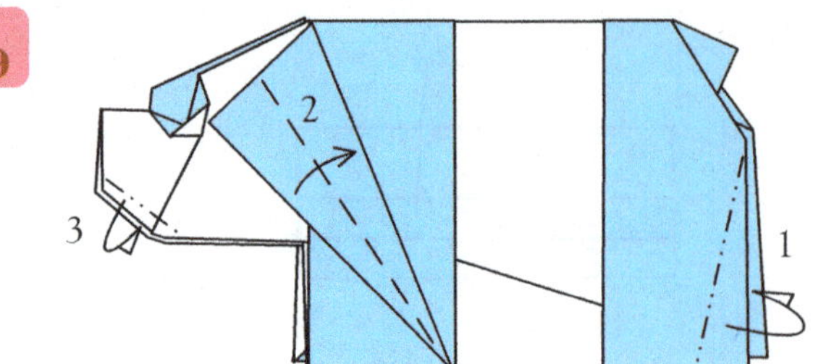

Fold in order. Repeat behind.

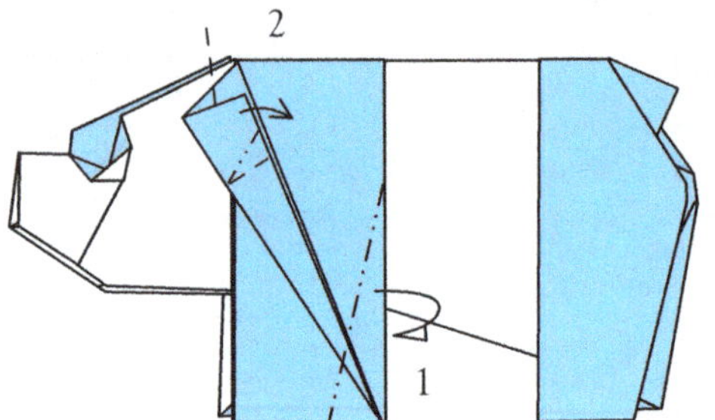

1. Fold behind.
2. Squash-fold.
Repeat behind.

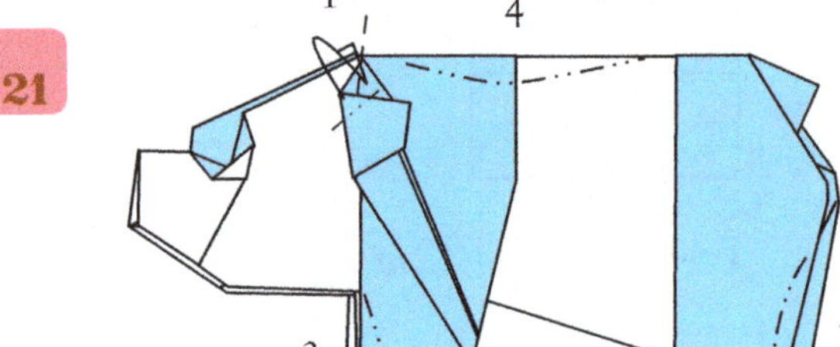

1. Reverse-fold.
2–4. Shape the legs and back.
Repeat behind.

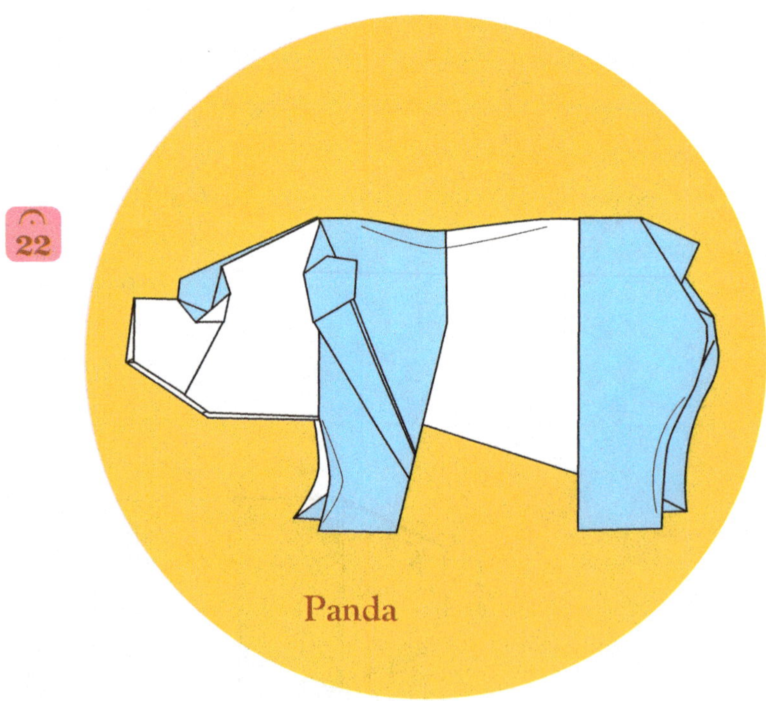

Panda

Koala Bear

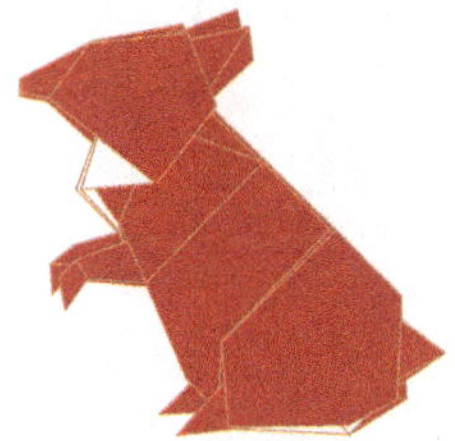

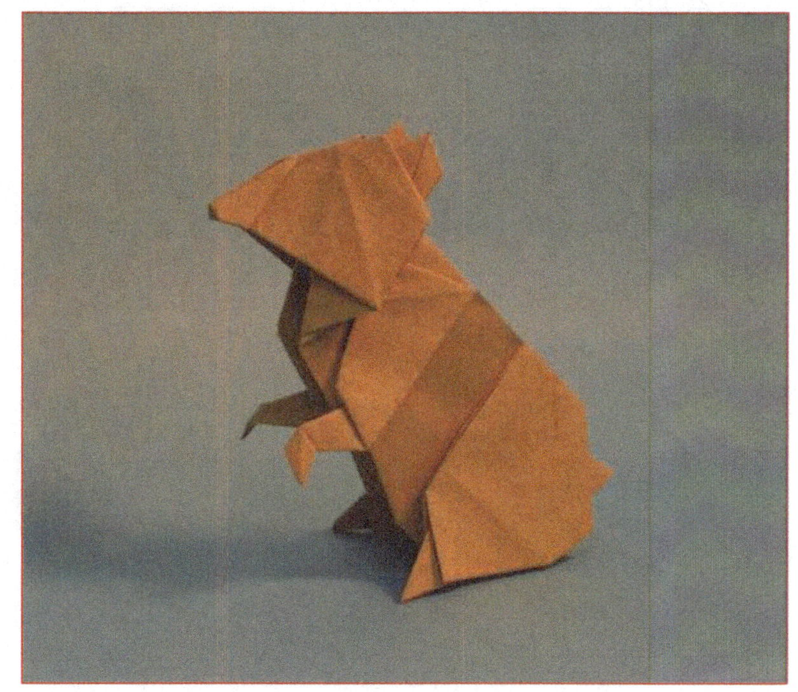

These cuddly favorite Australian creatures are in fact not bears at all, but are marsupials, or pouch-bearing mammals, like their other distant Australian relatives, Kangaroos. They live on Eucalyptus leaves and got their "bear" name from their cute and furry appearance that reminded people of teddy bears.

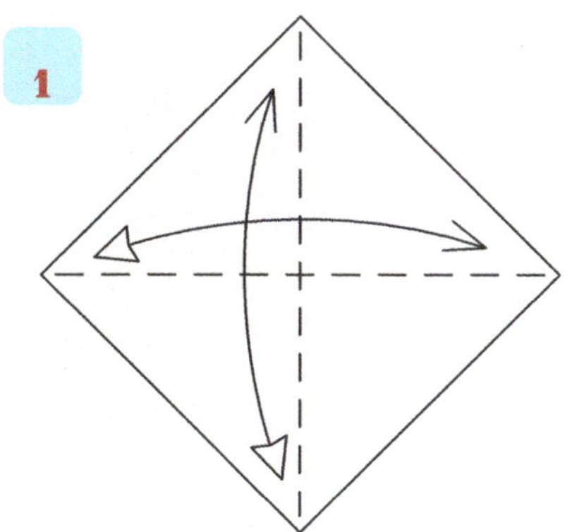

Fold and unfold.

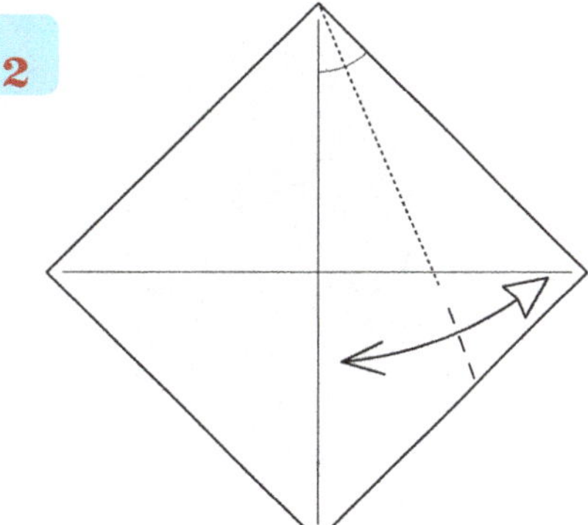

Fold and unfold
on the edge.

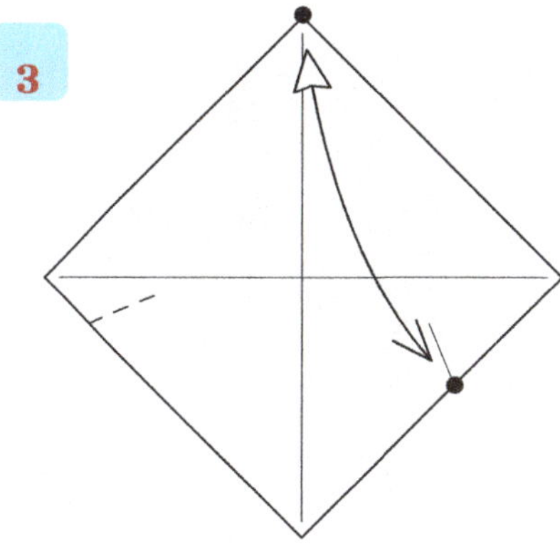

Fold and unfold
on the edge.

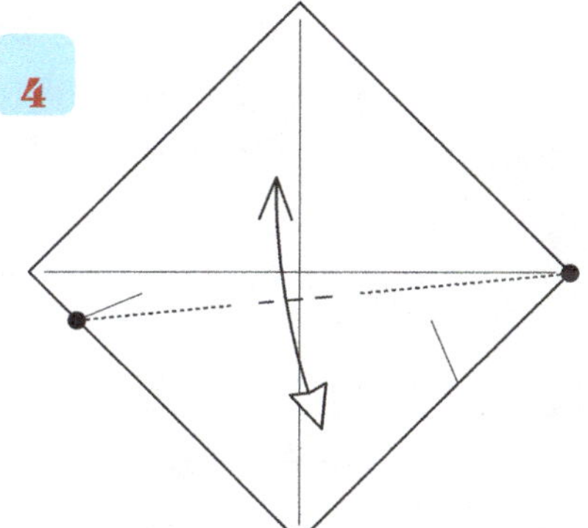

Fold and unfold
on the diagonal.

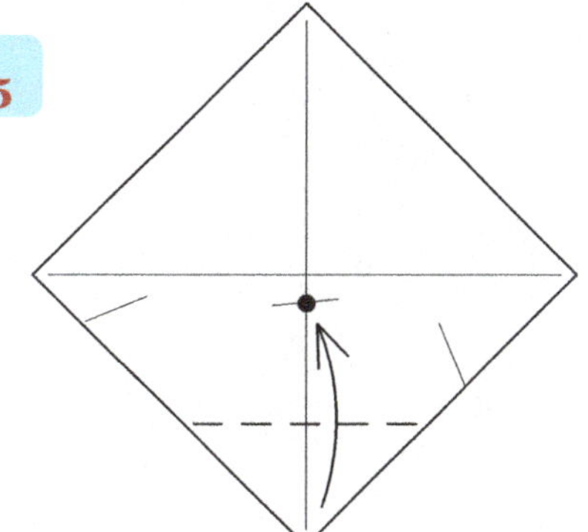

The dots will meet.

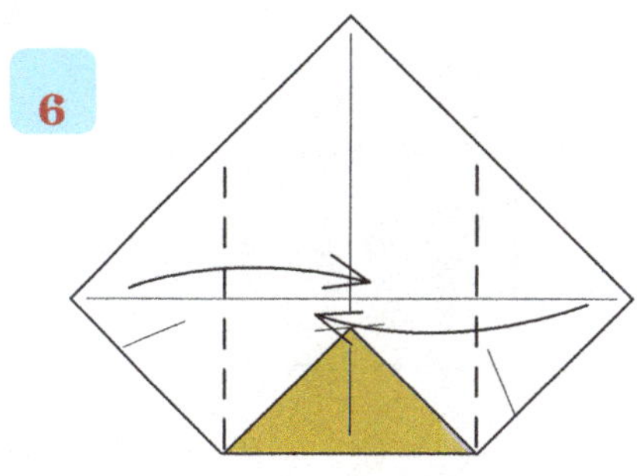

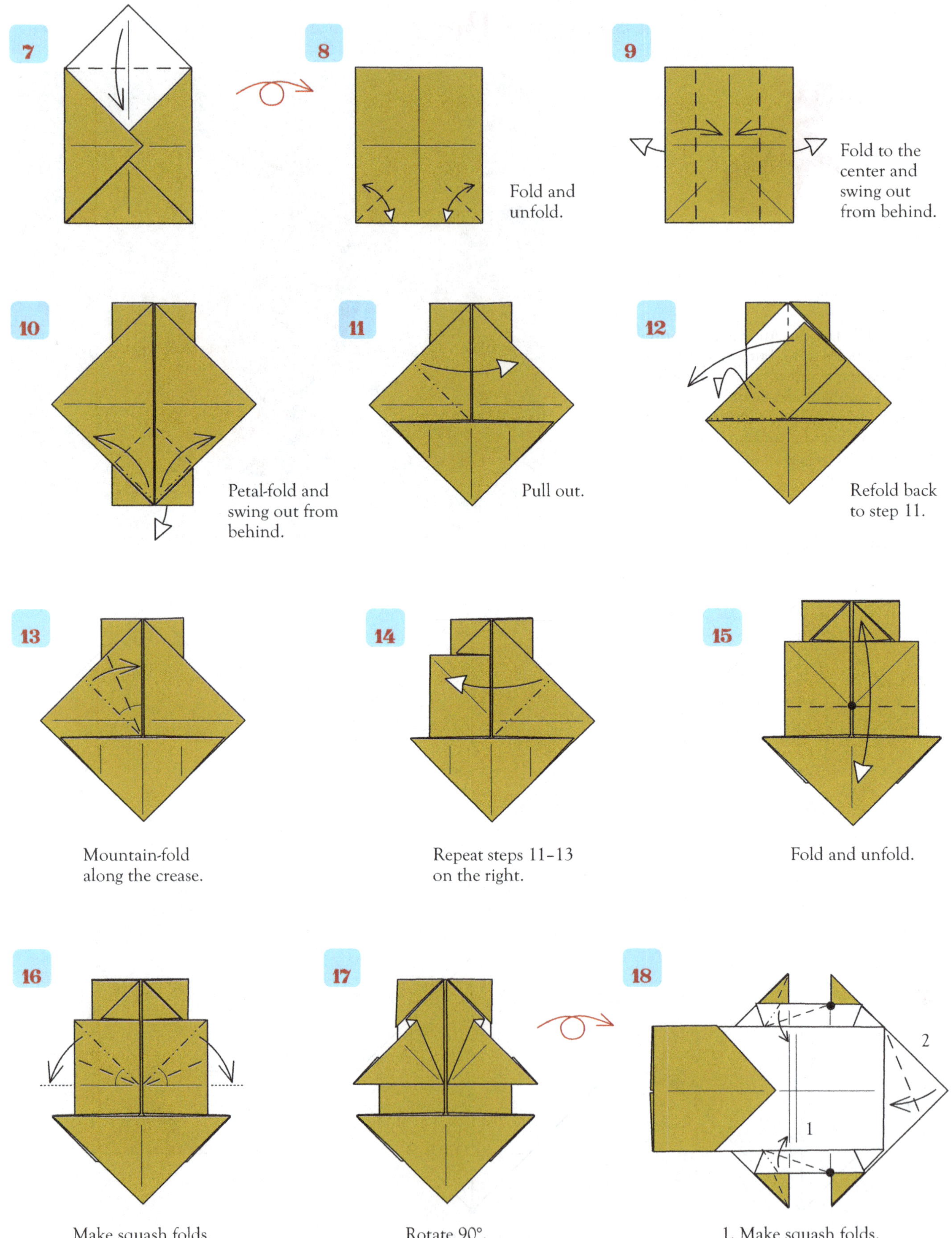

7
8
9
Fold and unfold.
Fold to the center and swing out from behind.
10
11
12
Petal-fold and swing out from behind.
Pull out.
Refold back to step 11.
13
14
15
Mountain-fold along the crease.
Repeat steps 11–13 on the right.
Fold and unfold.
16
17
18
Make squash folds.
Rotate 90°.
1. Make squash folds.
2. Valley-fold.
1
2

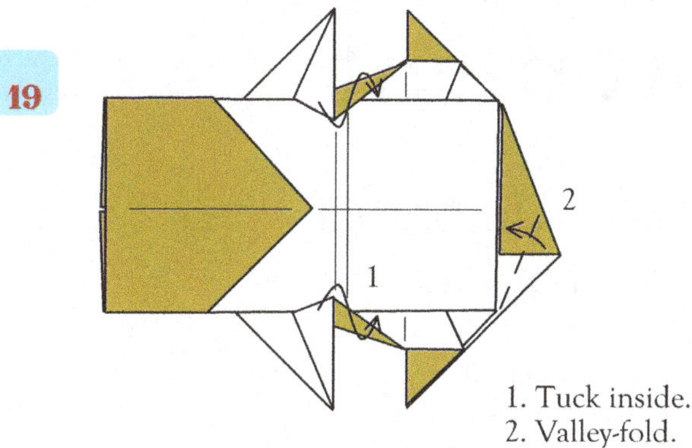

19

1. Tuck inside.
2. Valley-fold.

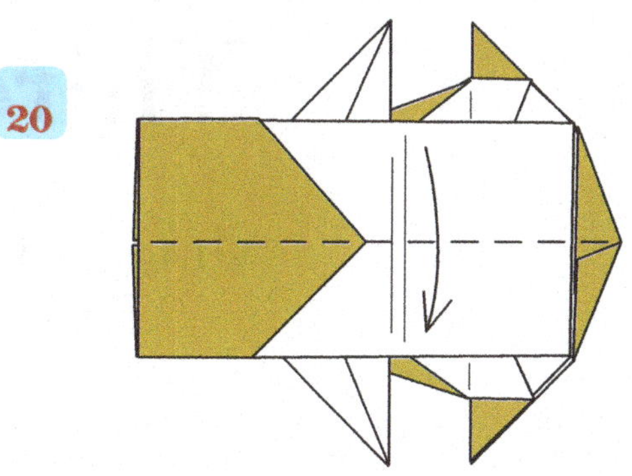

20

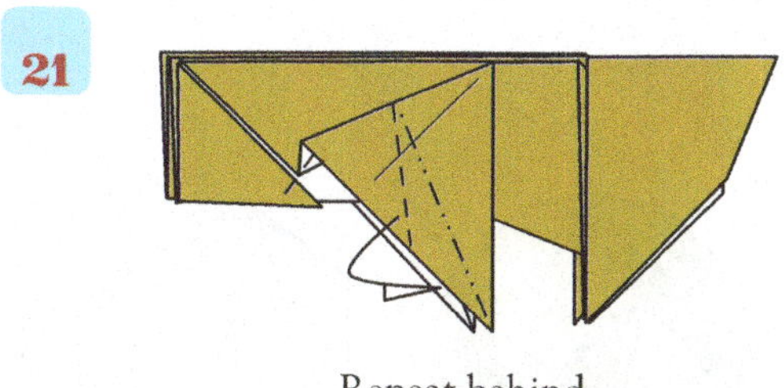

21

Repeat behind.

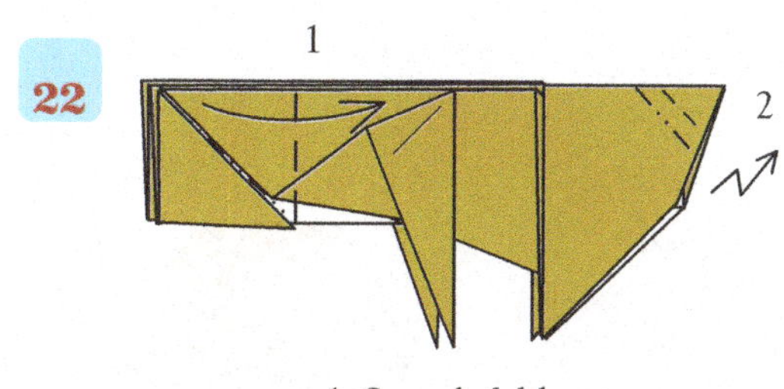
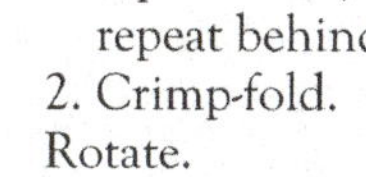

22

1. Squash-fold,
   repeat behind.
2. Crimp-fold.
Rotate.

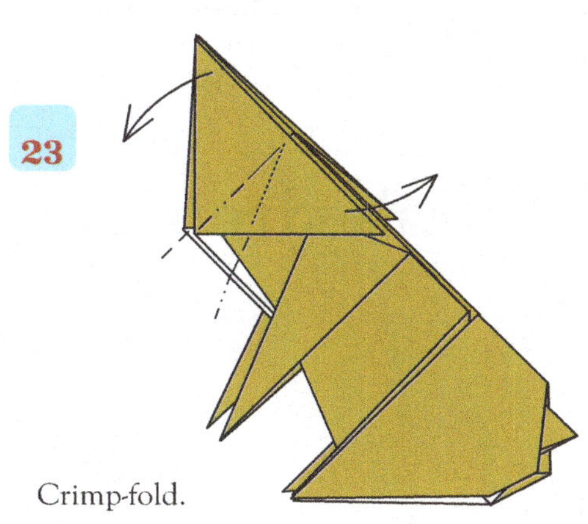

23

Crimp-fold.

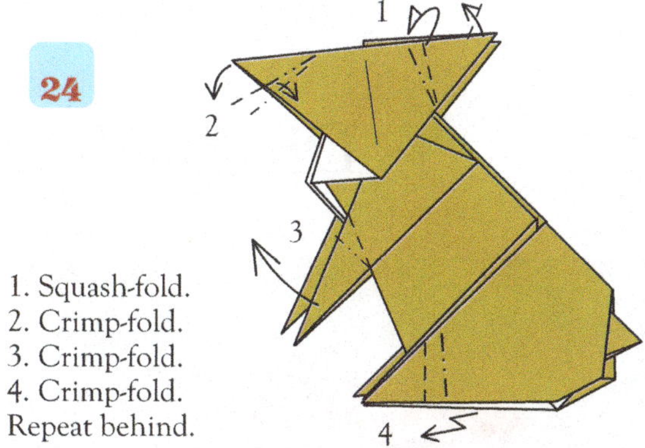

24

1. Squash-fold.
2. Crimp-fold.
3. Crimp-fold.
4. Crimp-fold.
Repeat behind.

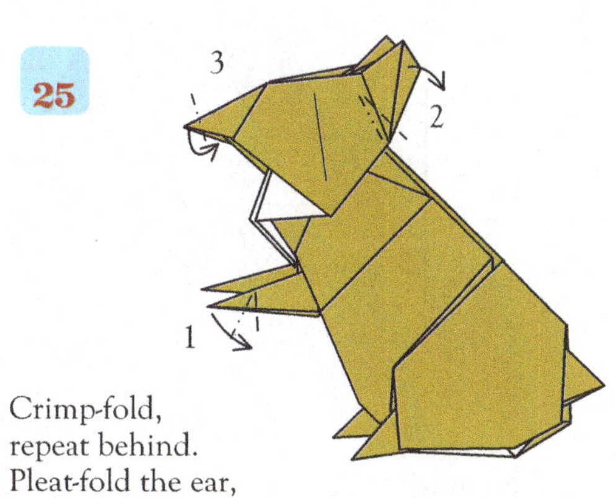

25

1. Crimp-fold,
   repeat behind.
2. Pleat-fold the ear,
   repeat behind.
3. Reverse-fold.

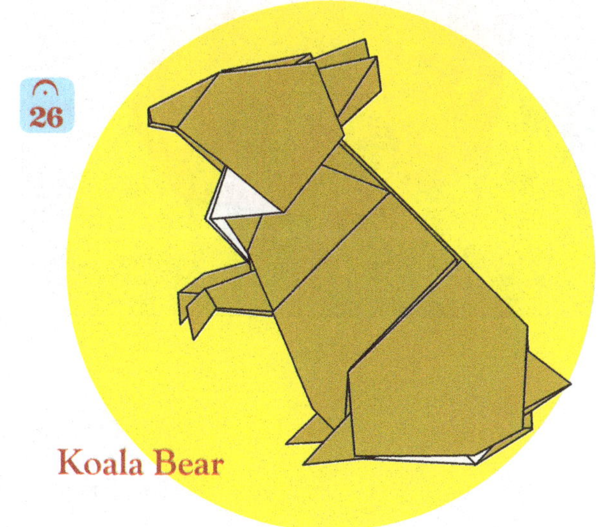

26

Koala Bear

Third Movement

Minuet of Dimpled Polyhedra with a Trio of Archimedean Solids

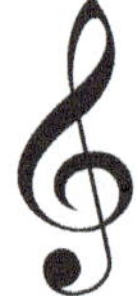 The third movement takes Archimedean Solids and variations of them. Dimpled polyhedra can be formed by folding a Tetrahedron, Cube, Octahedron, or other shape, and sinking the corners. Models range from intermediate to complex. These interesting shapes show the wide range of possibilities with origami.

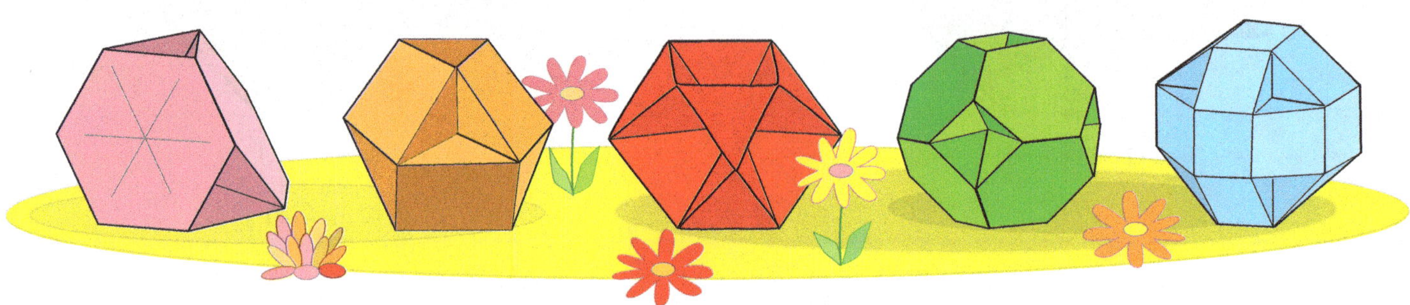

Dimpled Truncated Tetrahedron

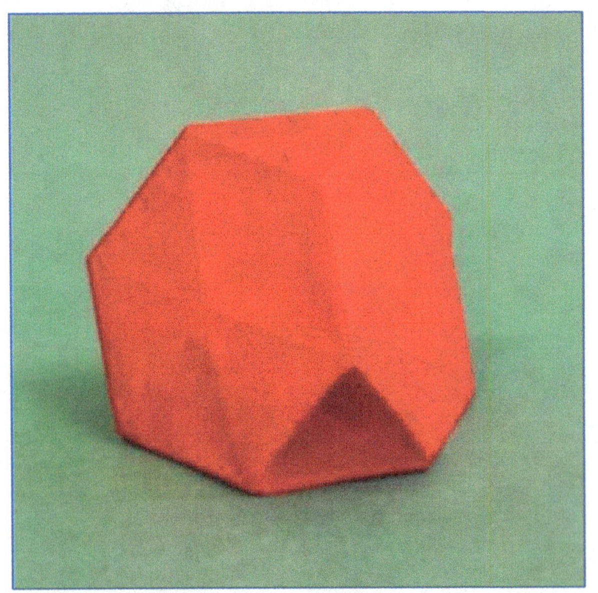

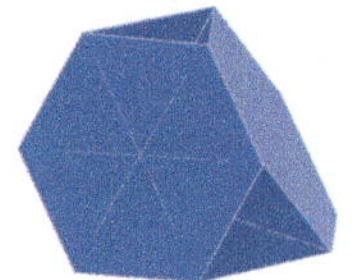

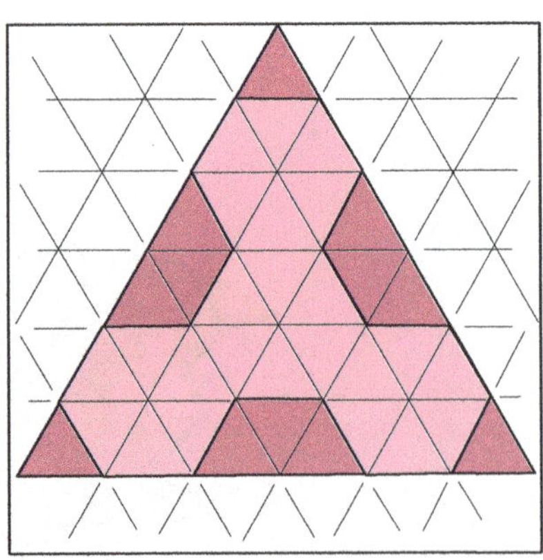

The Dimpled Truncated Tetrahedron is formed from a Tetrahedron. In the crease pattern, the darker regions show the sunken parts.

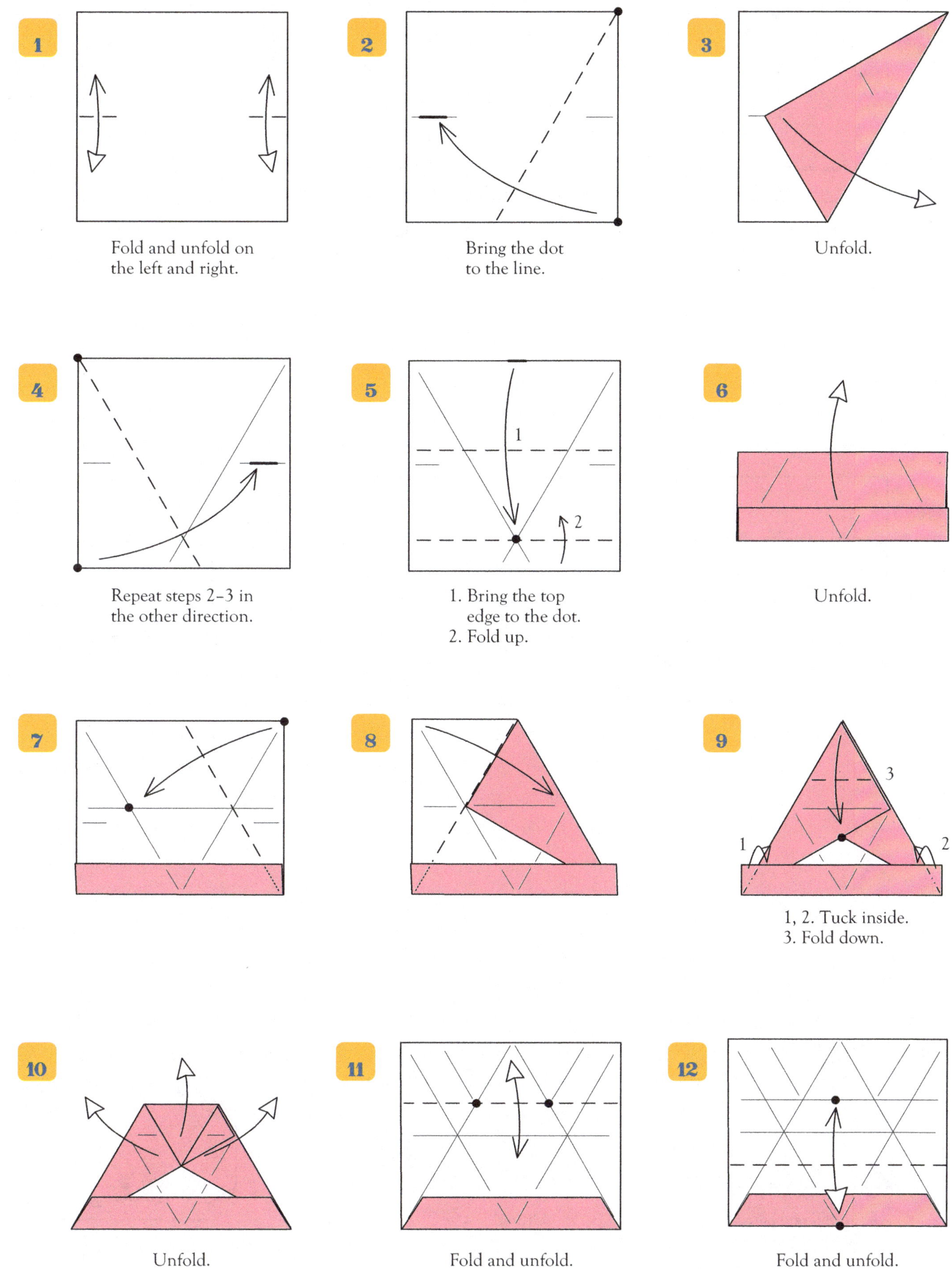

1
Fold and unfold on
the left and right.

2
Bring the dot
to the line.

3
Unfold.

4
Repeat steps 2–3 in
the other direction.

5
1. Bring the top
   edge to the dot.
2. Fold up.

6
Unfold.

7

8

9
1, 2. Tuck inside.
3. Fold down.

10
Unfold.

11
Fold and unfold.

12
Fold and unfold.

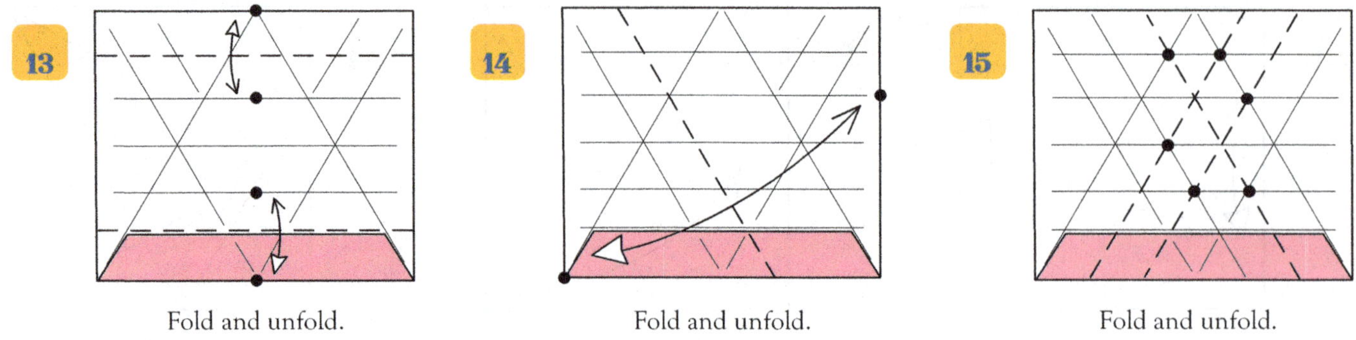

Fold and unfold.

Fold and unfold.

Fold and unfold.

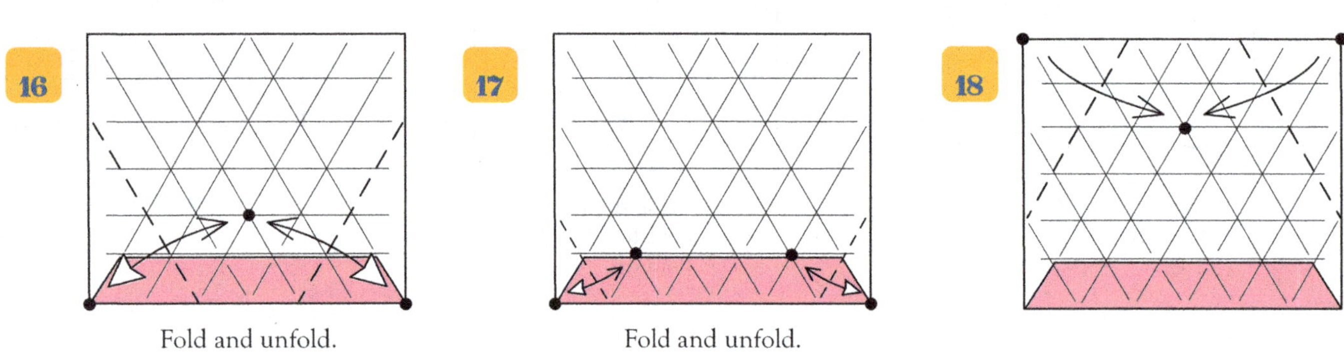

Fold and unfold.

Fold and unfold.

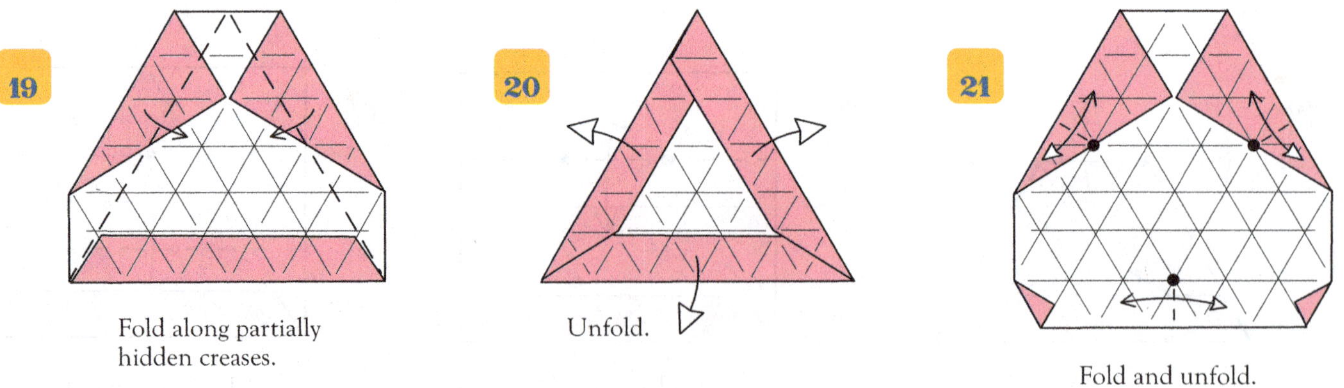

Fold along partially
hidden creases.

Unfold.

Fold and unfold.

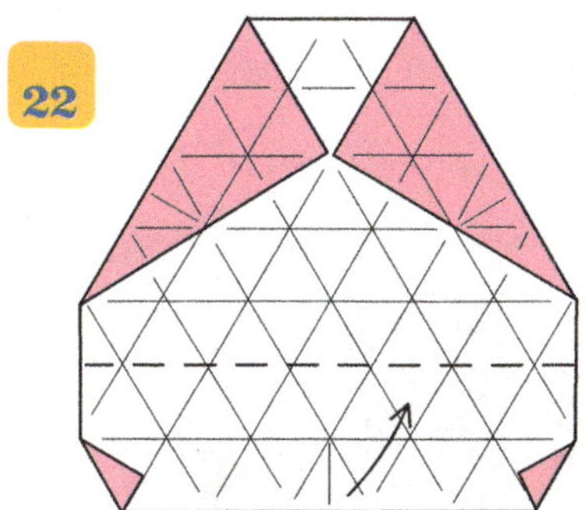

22

Lift up but do not flatten.

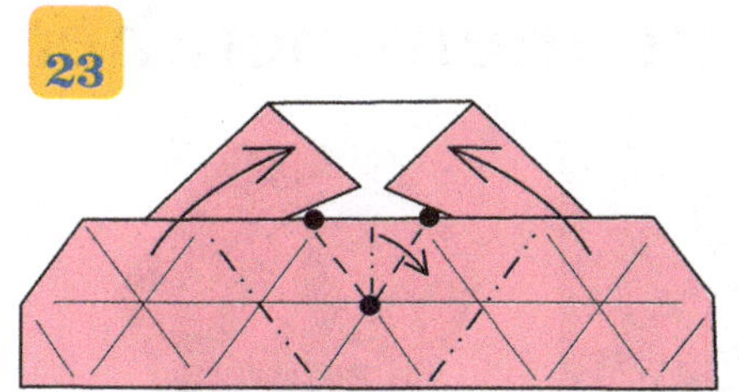

23

Push in at the lower dot. The other dots will meet.

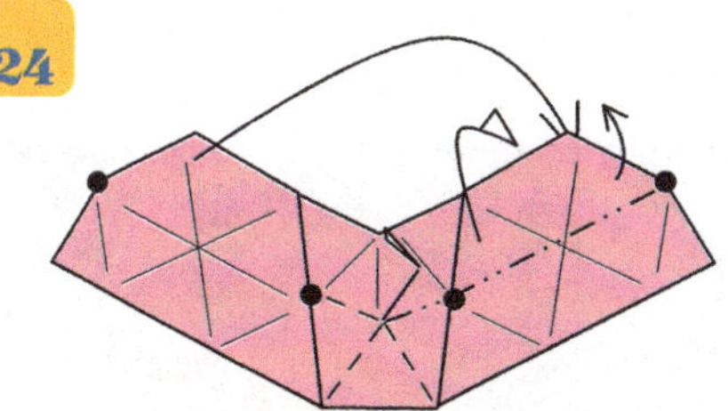

24

Lift up on the left and right. Fold the layers behind on the right to form a sunken triangle in the center (so that the inner pair of dots meet). Flatten the inside layers against the outside ones (so that the outer pair of dots meet).

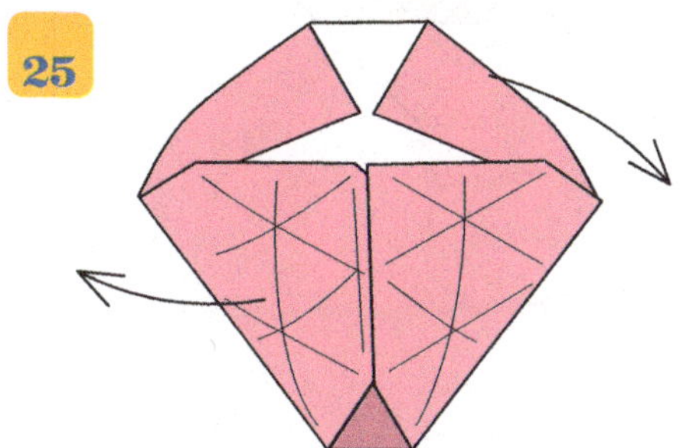

25

Rotate to view the right side.

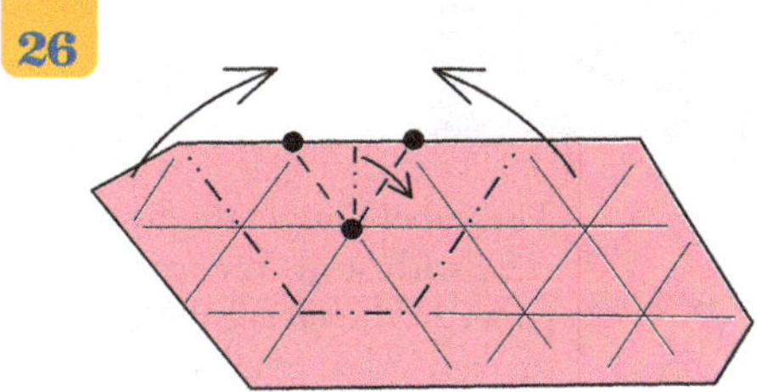

26

Locate the crease from step 21 and repeat steps 23–25 two more times.

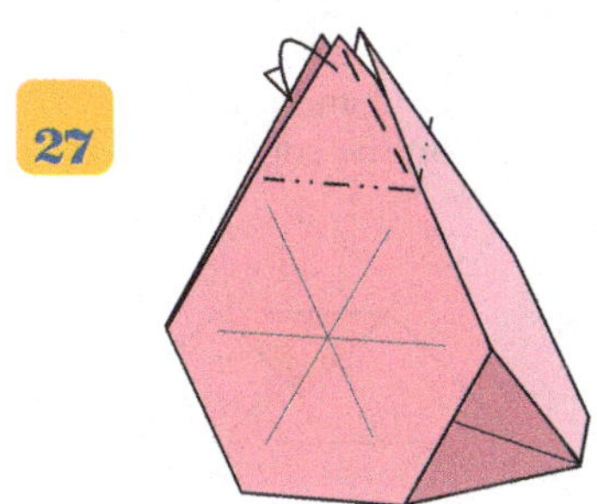

27

Form a sunken triangle with three interlocking reverse folds.

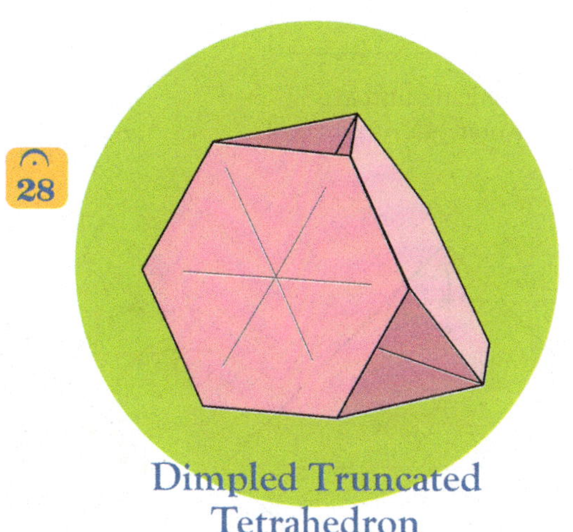

28

Dimpled Truncated Tetrahedron

Cubehemioctahedron

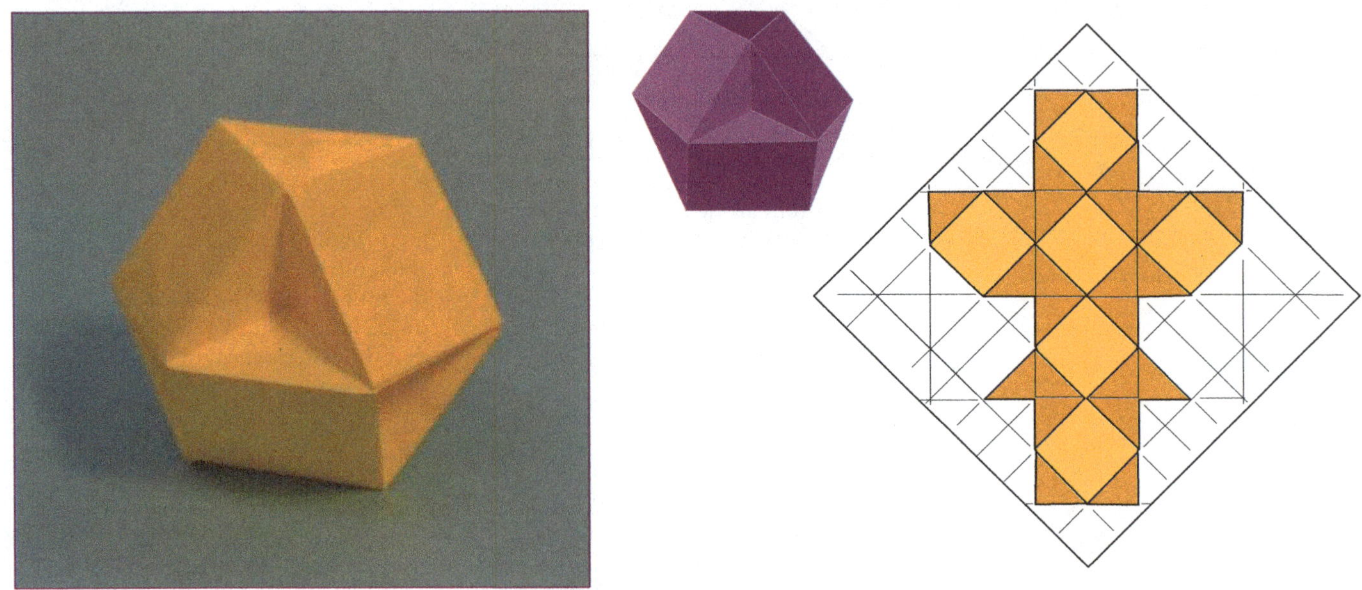

The cubehemioctahedron is basically a cube with sunken corners. The darker paper in the crease pattern shows the sunken sides. Even symmetry is used.

1

Fold and unfold.
Rotate 45°.

2

Fold and unfold.

3

Fold and unfold
on the edges.

4

5

Fold to the center and unfold.

6

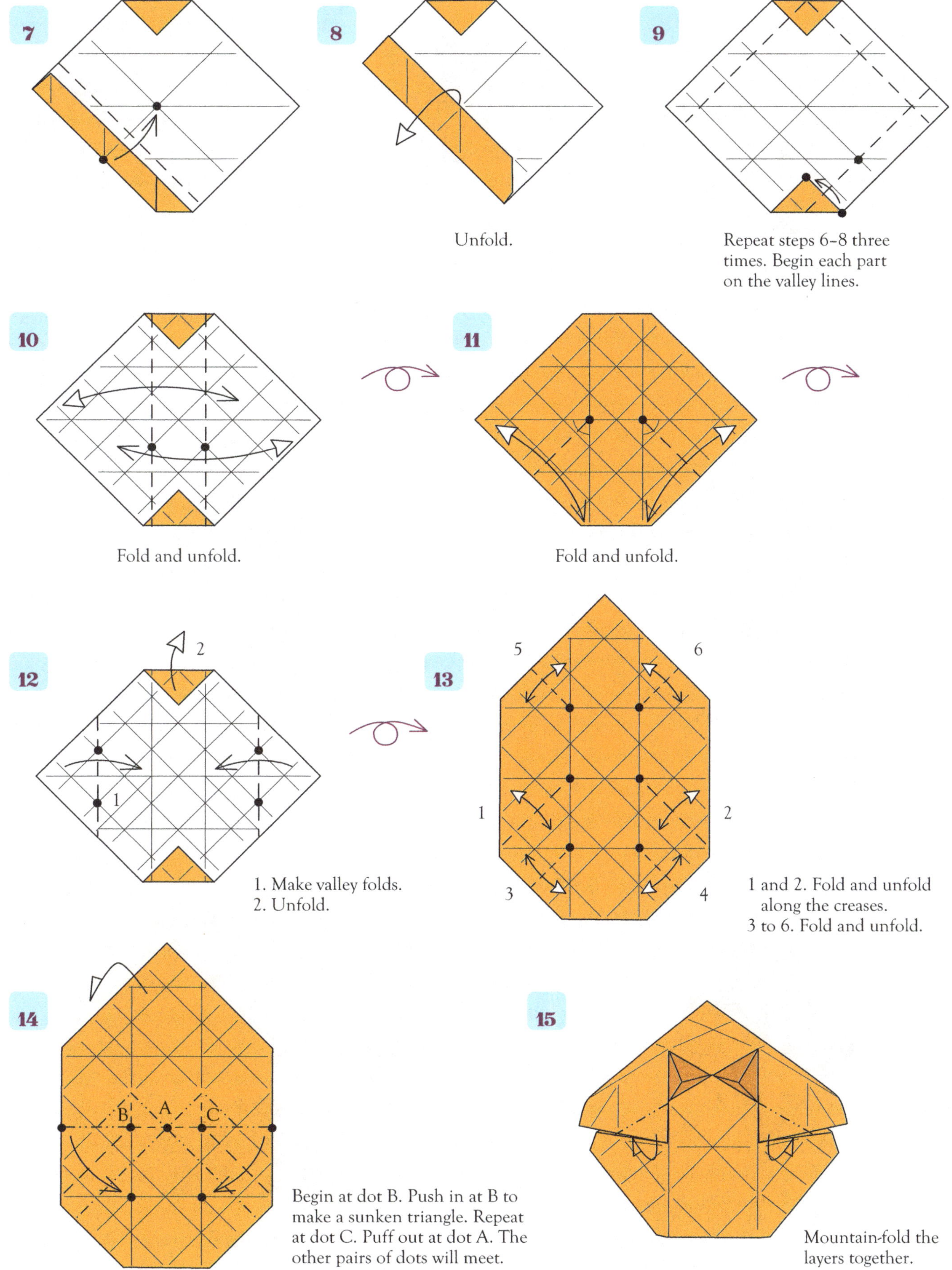

Cubehemioctahedron **73**

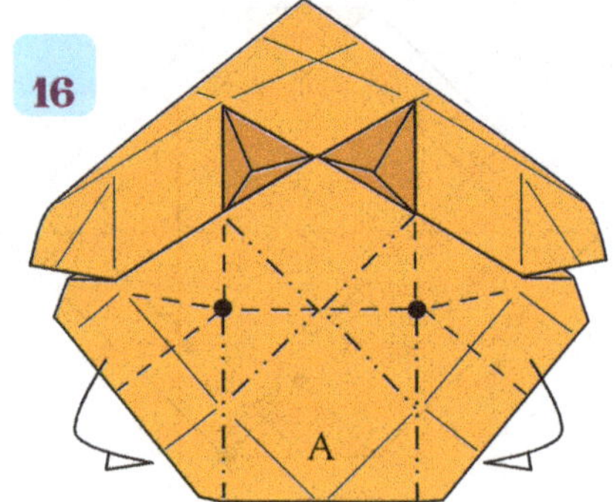

Push in at the dots to form
two sunken triangles. Flatten
the layers behind region A.

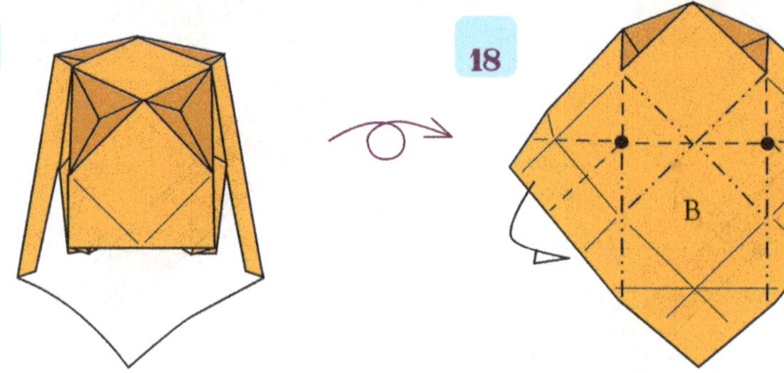

Push in at the dots. Flatten the
layers behind region B. Rotate the
top to the bottom and view region
C, so it becomes front and center.

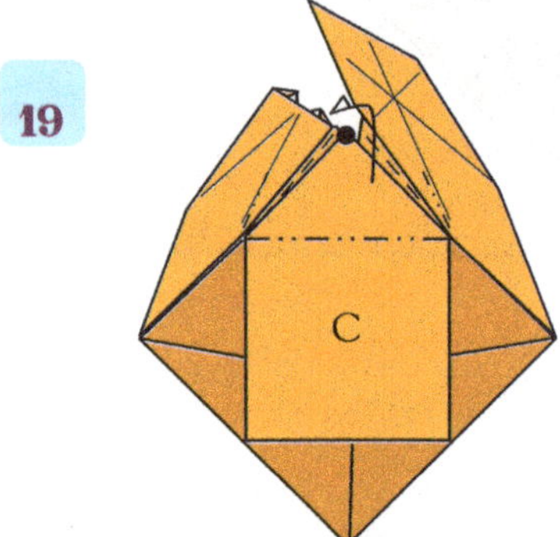

Fold inside towards the center
and repeat behind, so the two
dots (only one drawn) meet.
This begins the formation of
two sunken triangles.

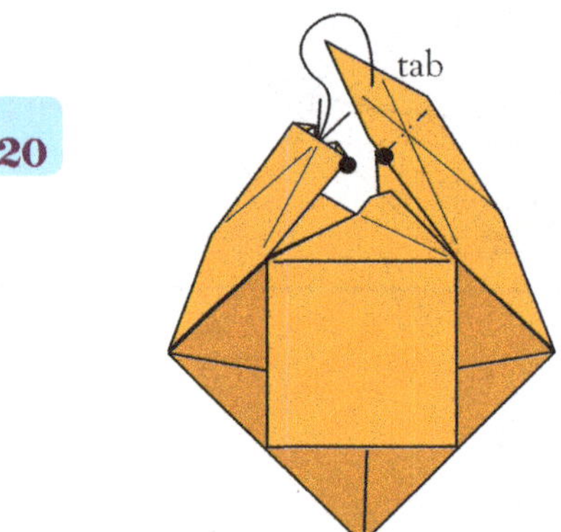

Tuck the tab inside the
pocket so the dots meet.

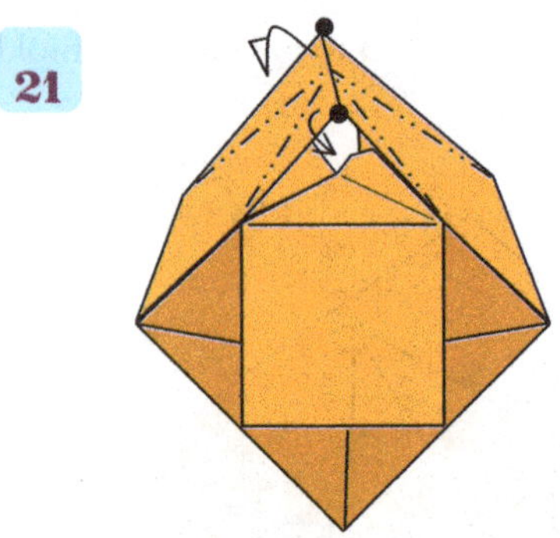

Push in at the dots to complete
the sunken triangles. (Repeat
behind.) This is my favorite step!

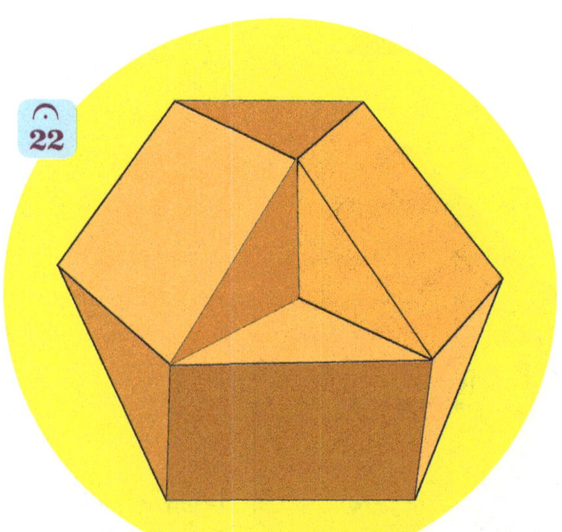

Cubehemioctahedron

Octahemioctahedron

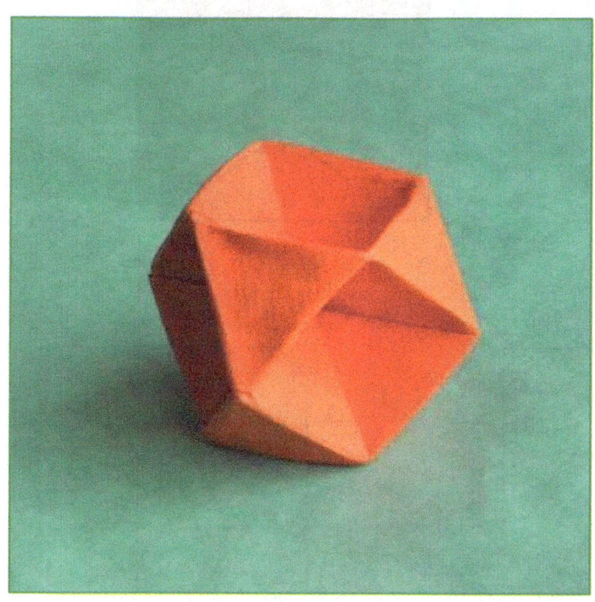

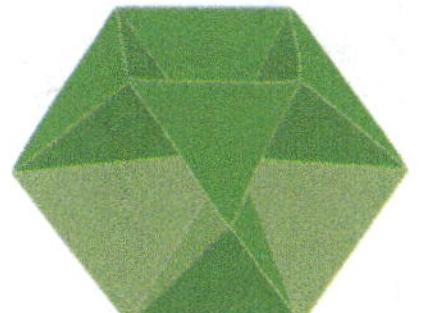

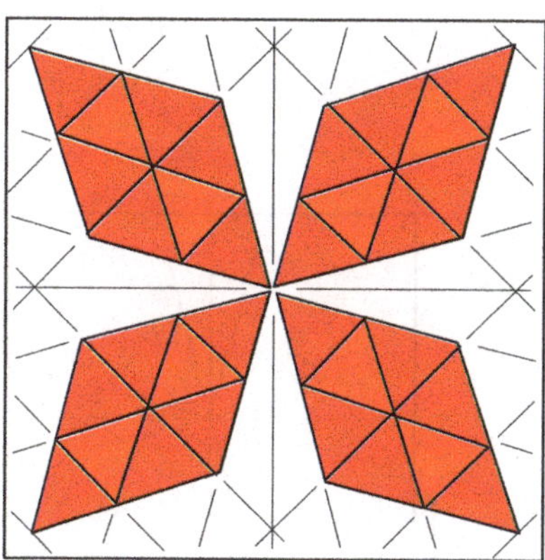

This comes from an octahedron with sunken corners. A similar shape is the cubehemioctahedron which comes from a cube with sunken corners. The darker regions represent the sunken sides.

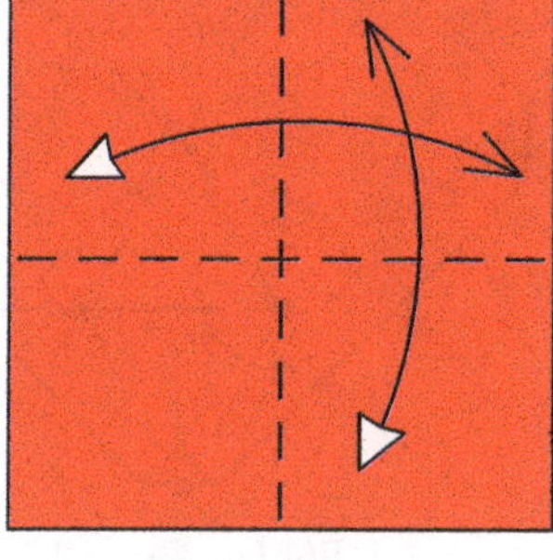

Fold and unfold.

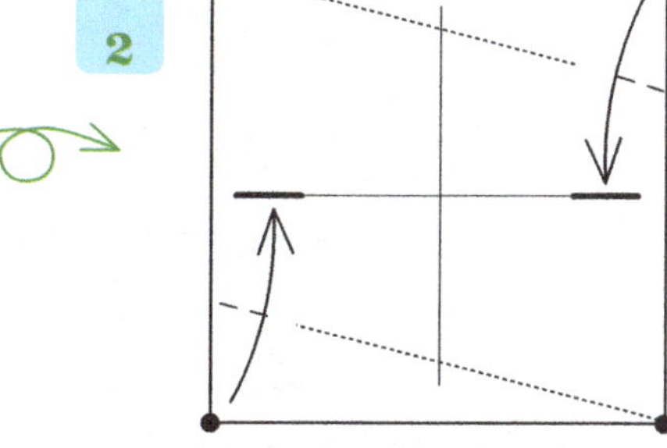

Bring the dots to the lines. Crease on the edges.

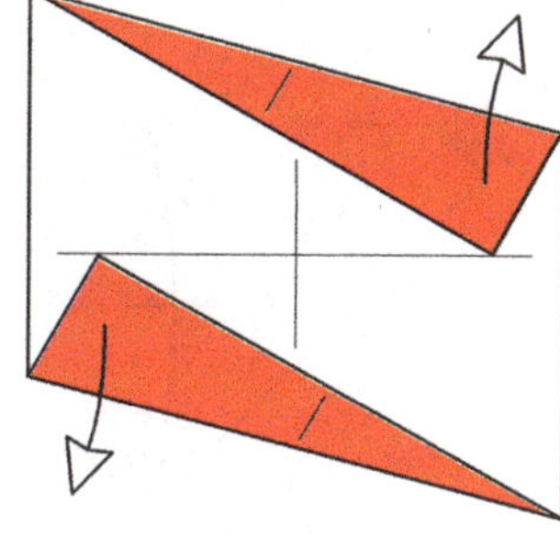

Unfold.

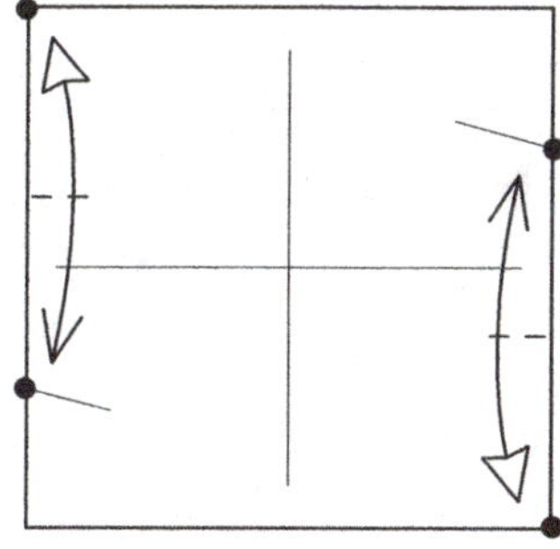

Fold and unfold on the edges.

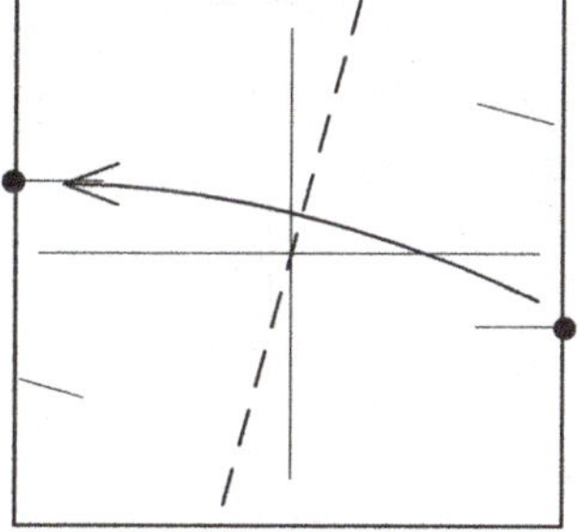

The dots will meet. Rotate 90°.

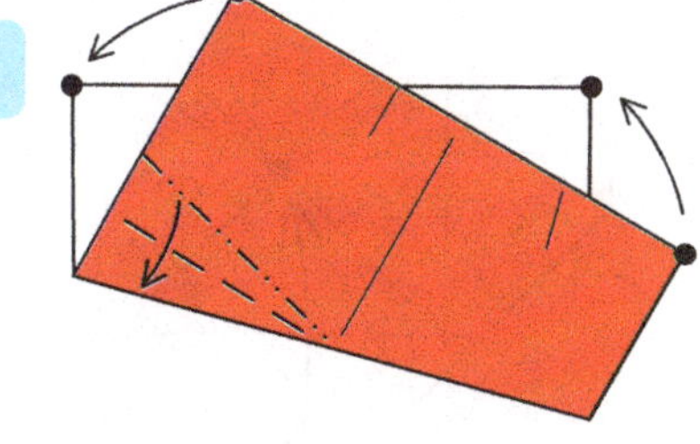

Valley-fold along the crease. Turn over and repeat.

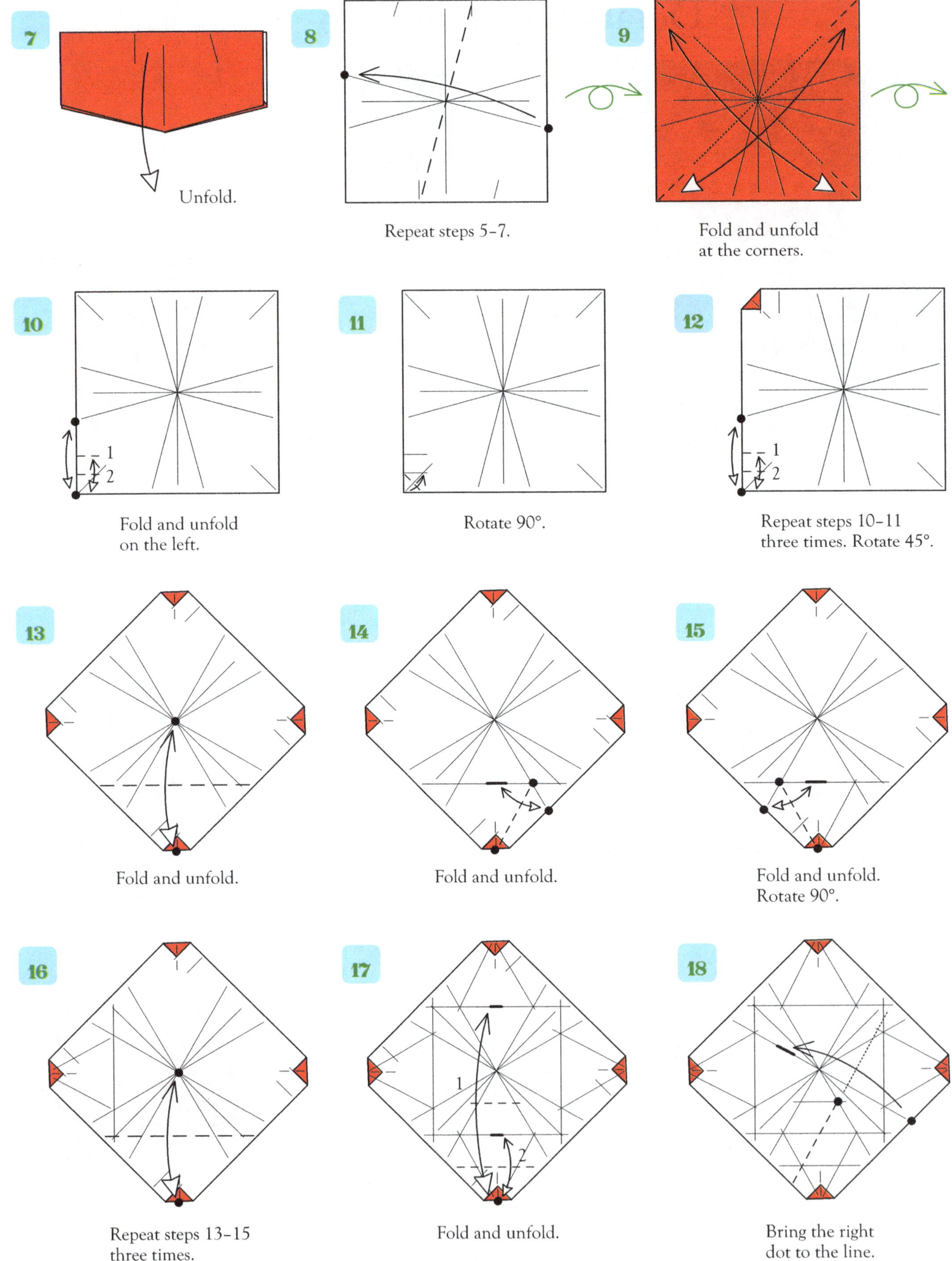

7
Unfold.
8
Repeat steps 5–7.
9
Fold and unfold
at the corners.
10
Fold and unfold
on the left.
1
2
11
Rotate 90°.
12
Repeat steps 10–11
three times. Rotate 45°.
1
2
13
Fold and unfold.
14
Fold and unfold.
15
Fold and unfold.
Rotate 90°.
16
Repeat steps 13–15
three times.
17
Fold and unfold.
1
2
18
Bring the right
dot to the line.

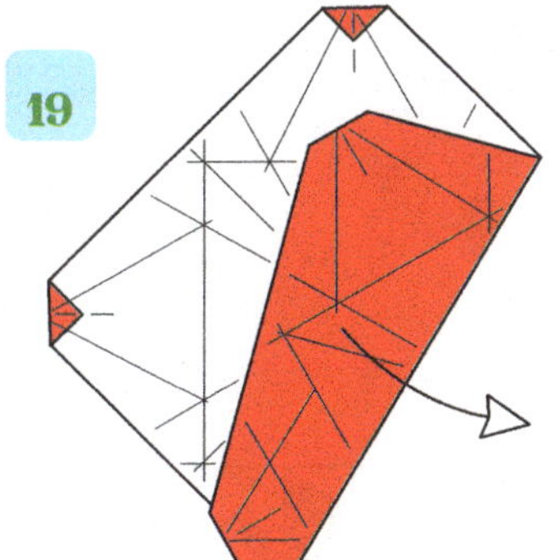

Unfold.

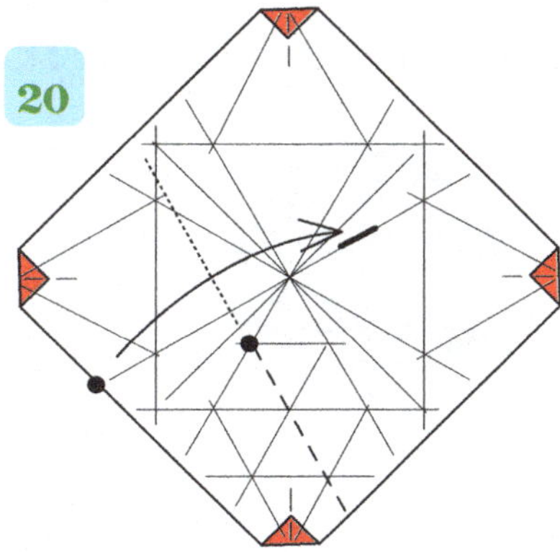

Repeat steps 18–19 in the opposite direction. Rotate 90°.

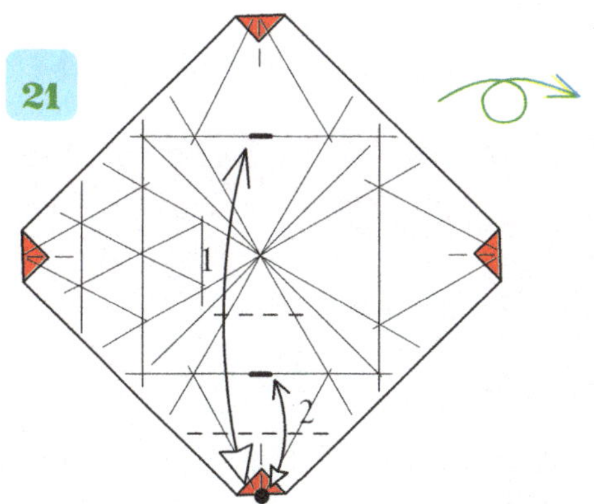

Repeat steps 17–20 three times. Rotate 45°.

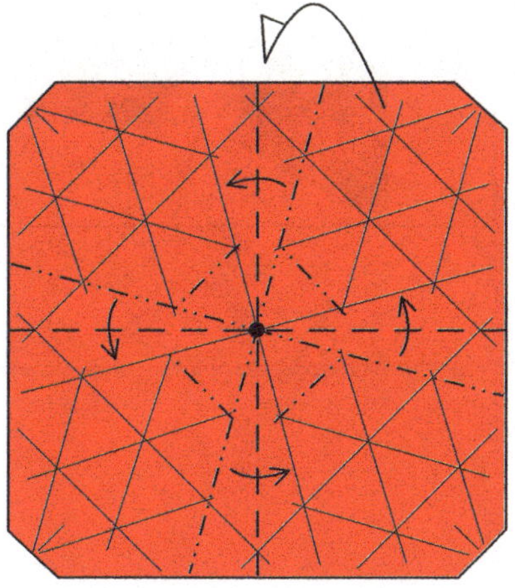

Push in at the dot to form a sunken square.

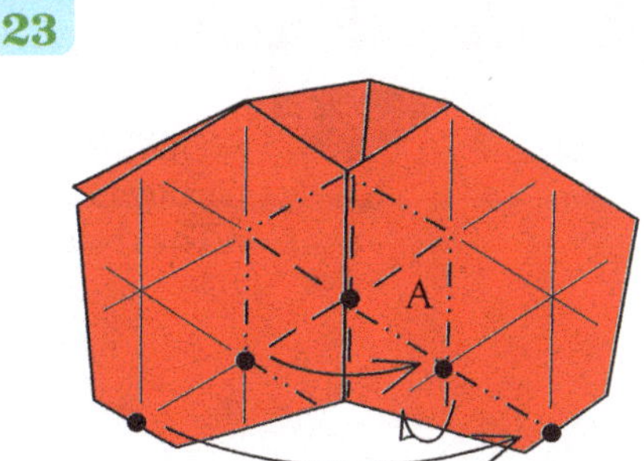

Push in at the upper dot to form another sunken square. The other pairs of dots will meet. Flatten inside, especially under triangle A.

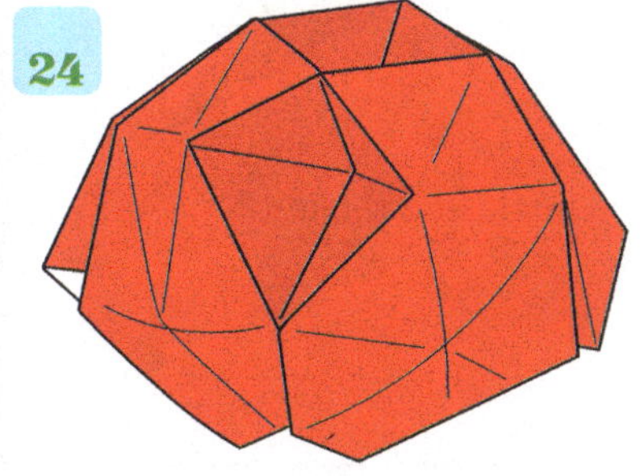

Repeat step 22 on the three other sides.

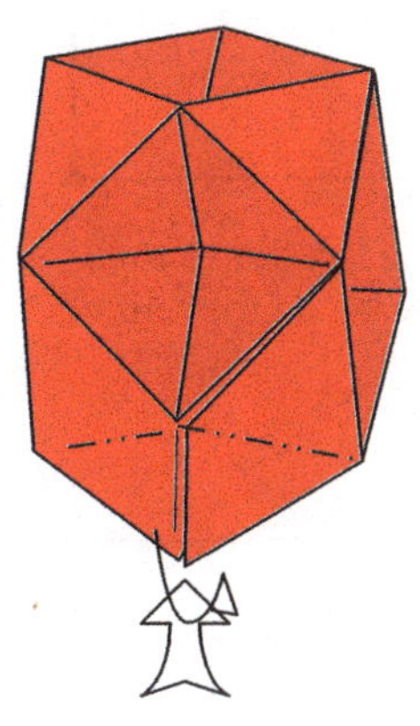

The last sunken square is formed by four connected reverse folds.

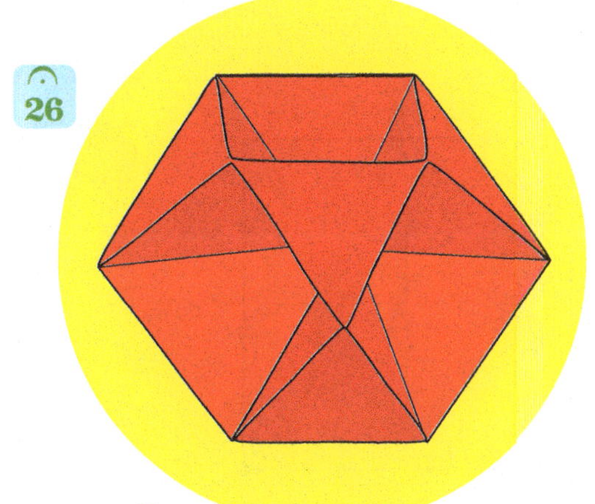

Octahemioctahedron

Dimpled Truncated Octahedron

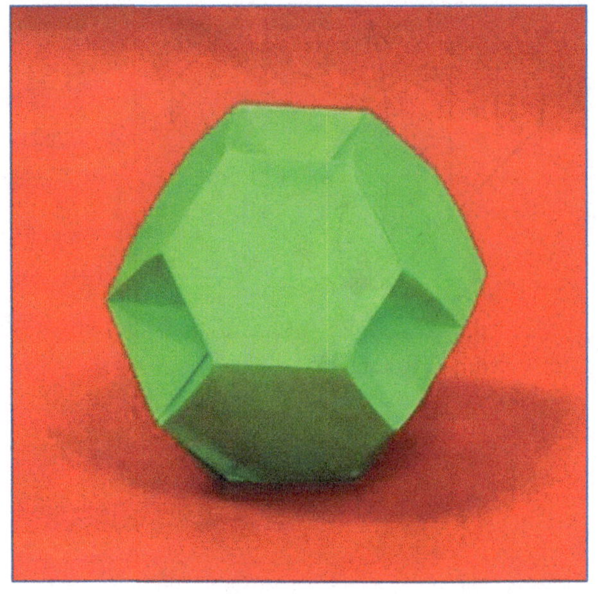

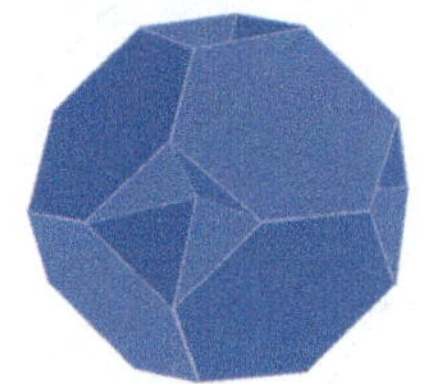

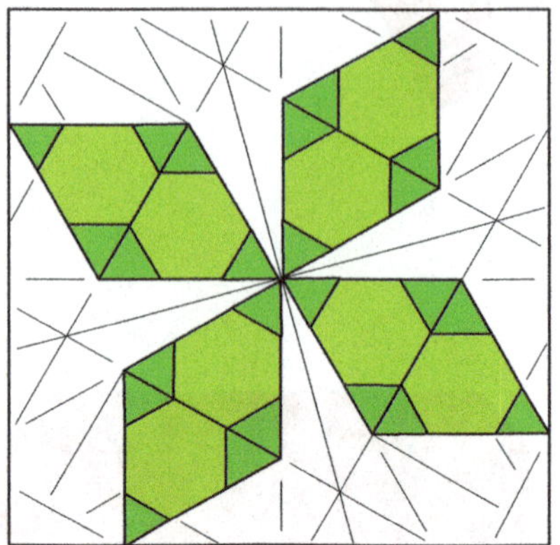

This dimpled truncated octahedron comes from an octahedron design with sunken sides. The crease pattern shows square symmetry.

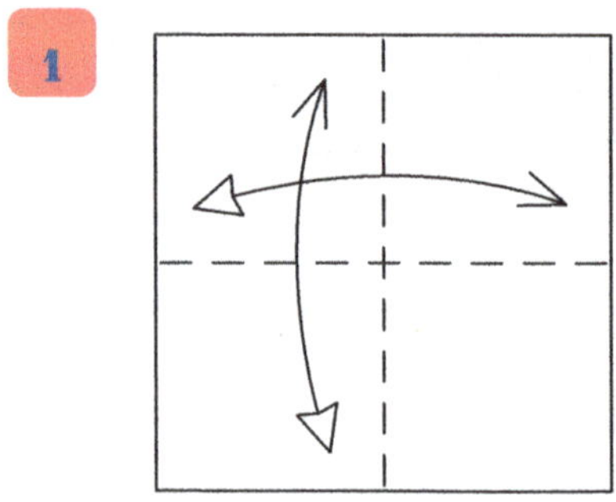

Fold and unfold.

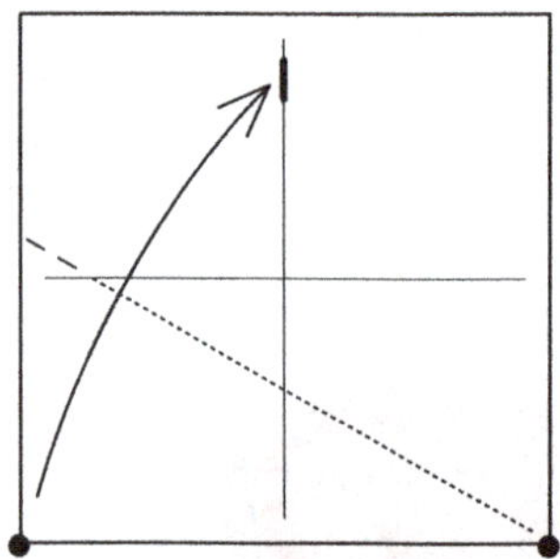

Bring the left dot to the line. Crease on the left.

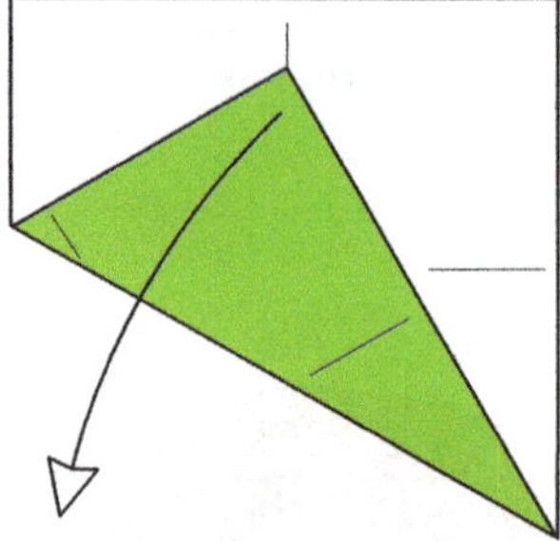

Unfold and rotate 180°.

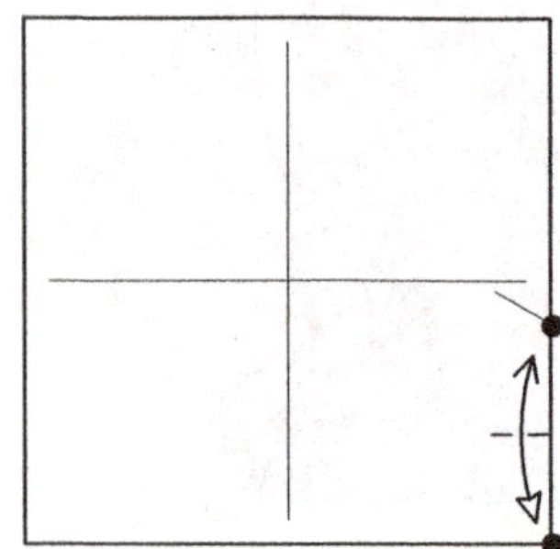

Fold and unfold.

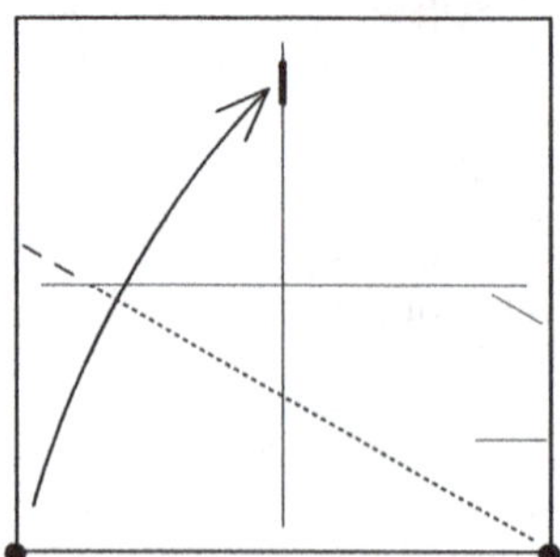

Repeat steps 2–4.

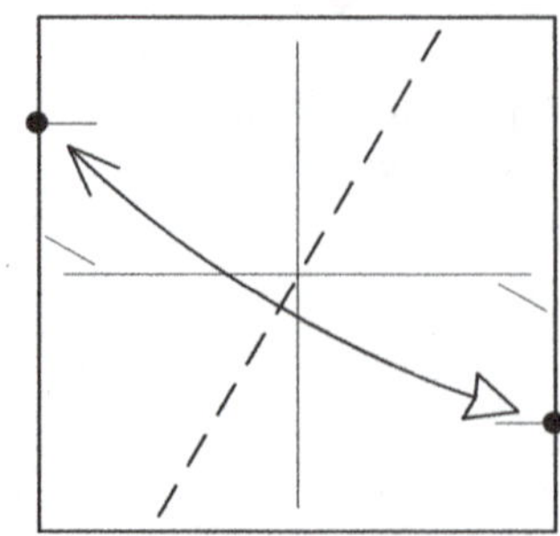

Fold and unfold.

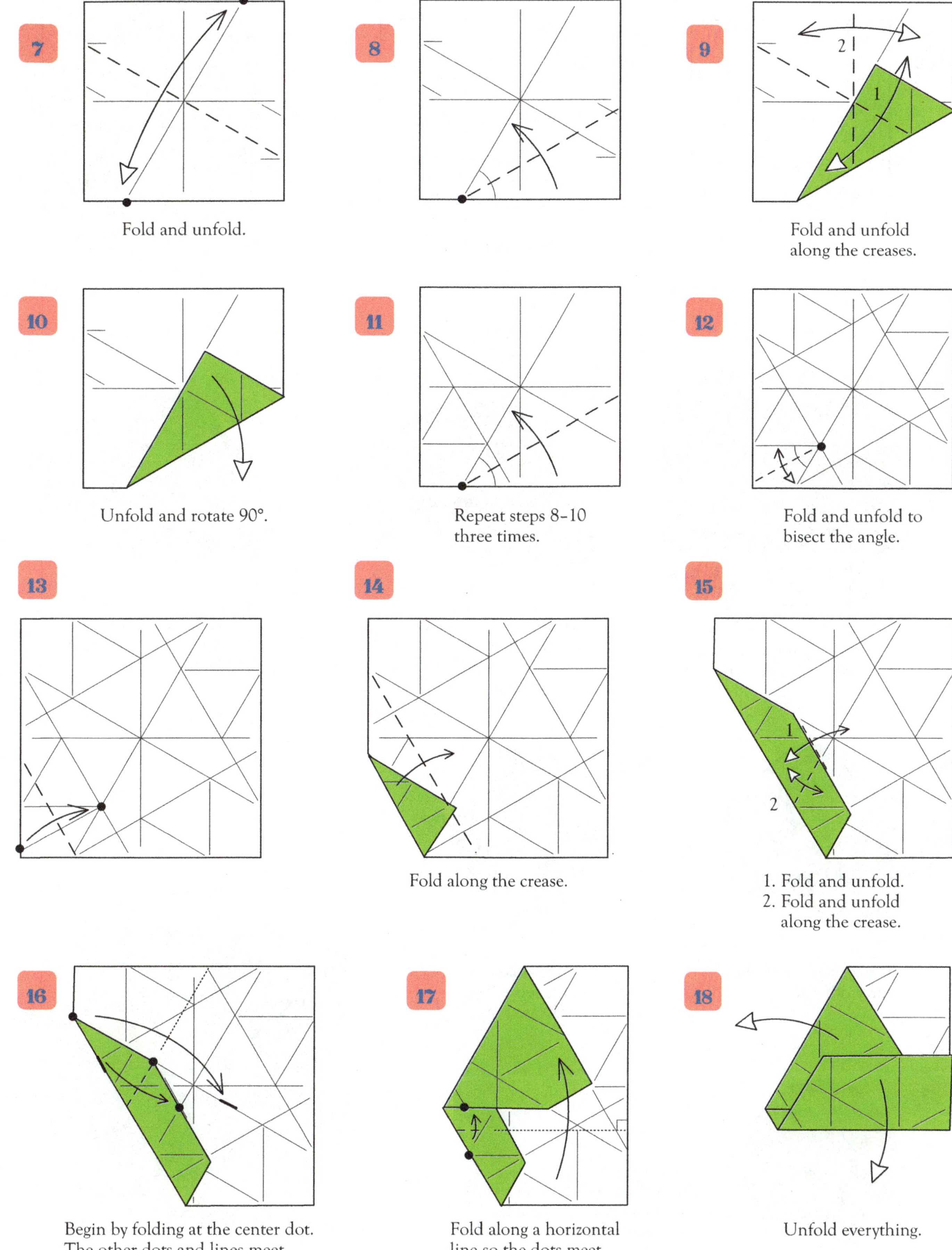

7
8
9
Fold and unfold.
Fold and unfold
along the creases.
10
11
12
Unfold and rotate 90°.
Repeat steps 8–10
three times.
Fold and unfold to
bisect the angle.
13
14
15
Fold along the crease.
1. Fold and unfold.
2. Fold and unfold
along the crease.
16
17
18
Begin by folding at the center dot.
The other dots and lines meet.
Fold along a horizontal
line so the dots meet.
Unfold everything.

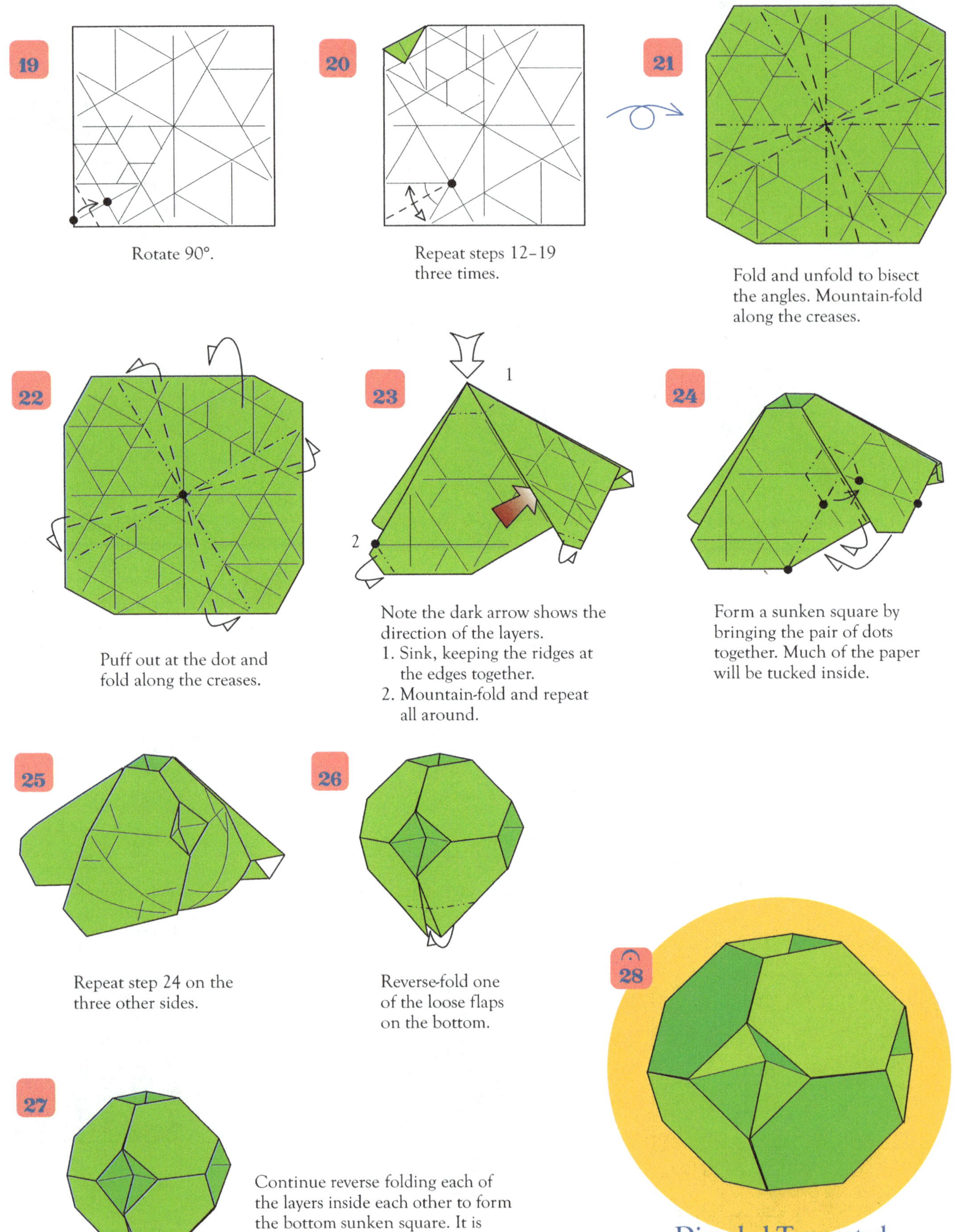

19 Rotate 90°.

20 Repeat steps 12–19 three times.

21 Fold and unfold to bisect the angles. Mountain-fold along the creases.

22 Puff out at the dot and fold along the creases.

23 Note the dark arrow shows the direction of the layers.
1. Sink, keeping the ridges at the edges together.
2. Mountain-fold and repeat all around.

24 Form a sunken square by bringing the pair of dots together. Much of the paper will be tucked inside.

25 Repeat step 24 on the three other sides.

26 Reverse-fold one of the loose flaps on the bottom.

27 Continue reverse folding each of the layers inside each other to form the bottom sunken square. It is possible to inflate at the bottom to round out this polyhedron.

28

Dimpled Truncated Octahedron

Dimpled Rhombicuboctahedron

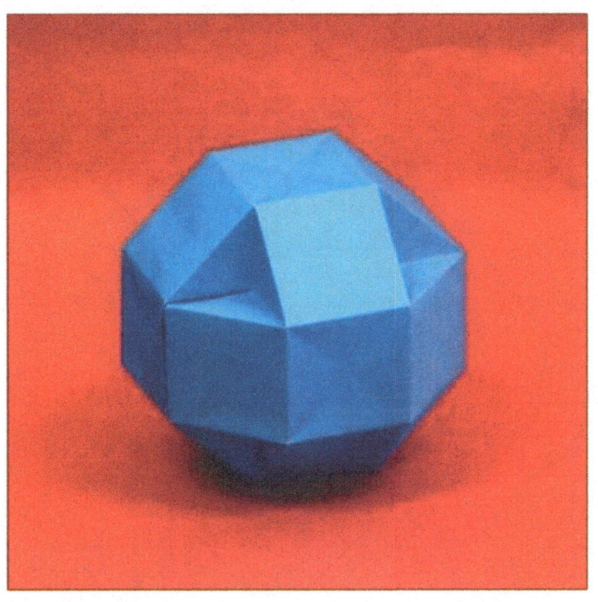

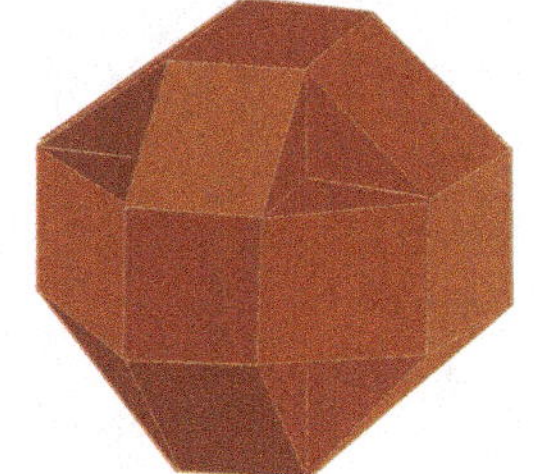

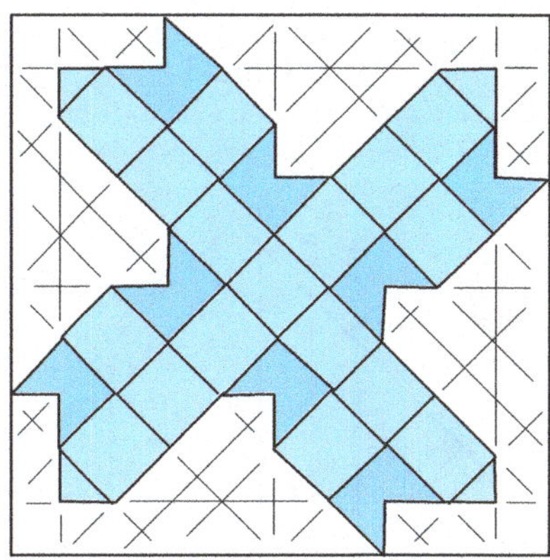

The dimpled rhombicuboctahedron has the same surface as the cube. It has 18 square faces and 8 sunken triangles. The dark regions of the crease pattern show the sunken sides. This model uses square symmetry. The paper is divided into tenths.

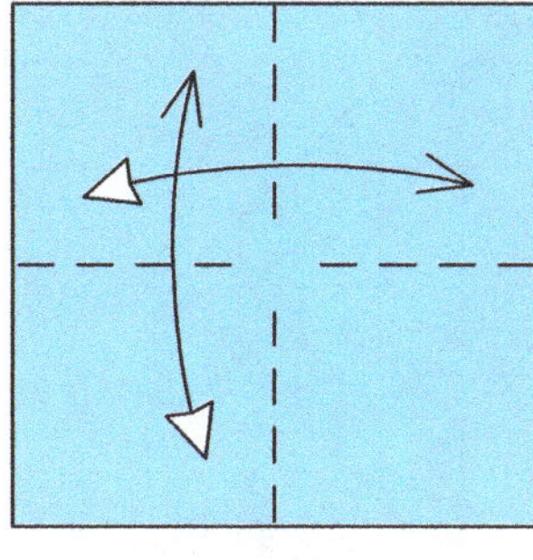

1 Fold and unfold but not in the center.

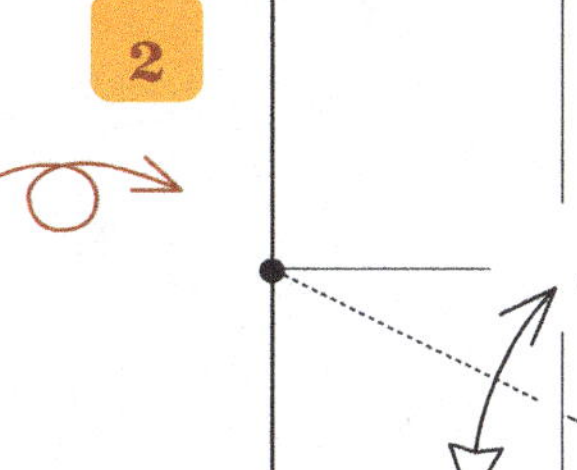

2 Fold and unfold on the intersection.

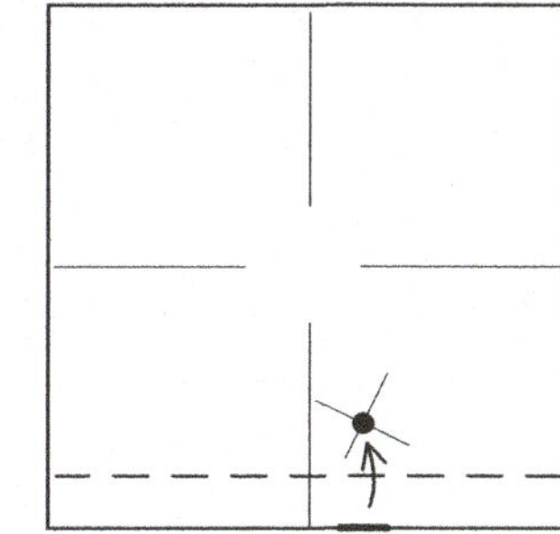

3 Bring the edge to the dot.

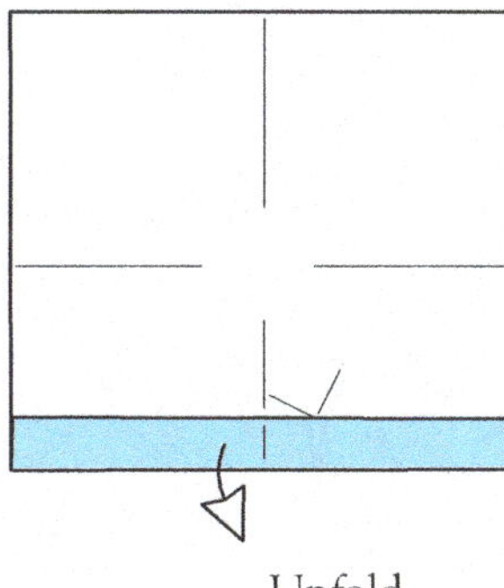

4 Unfold.

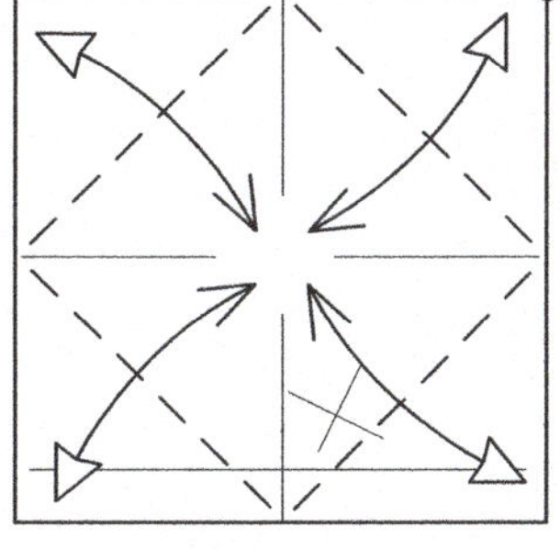

5 Fold the corners to the center and unfold. Rotate the dot to the bottom.

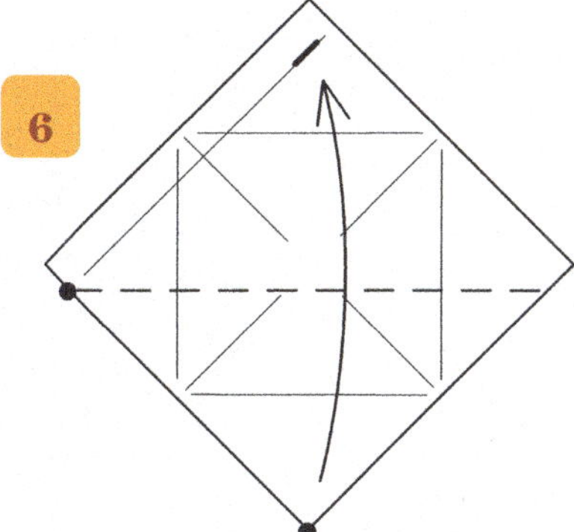

6

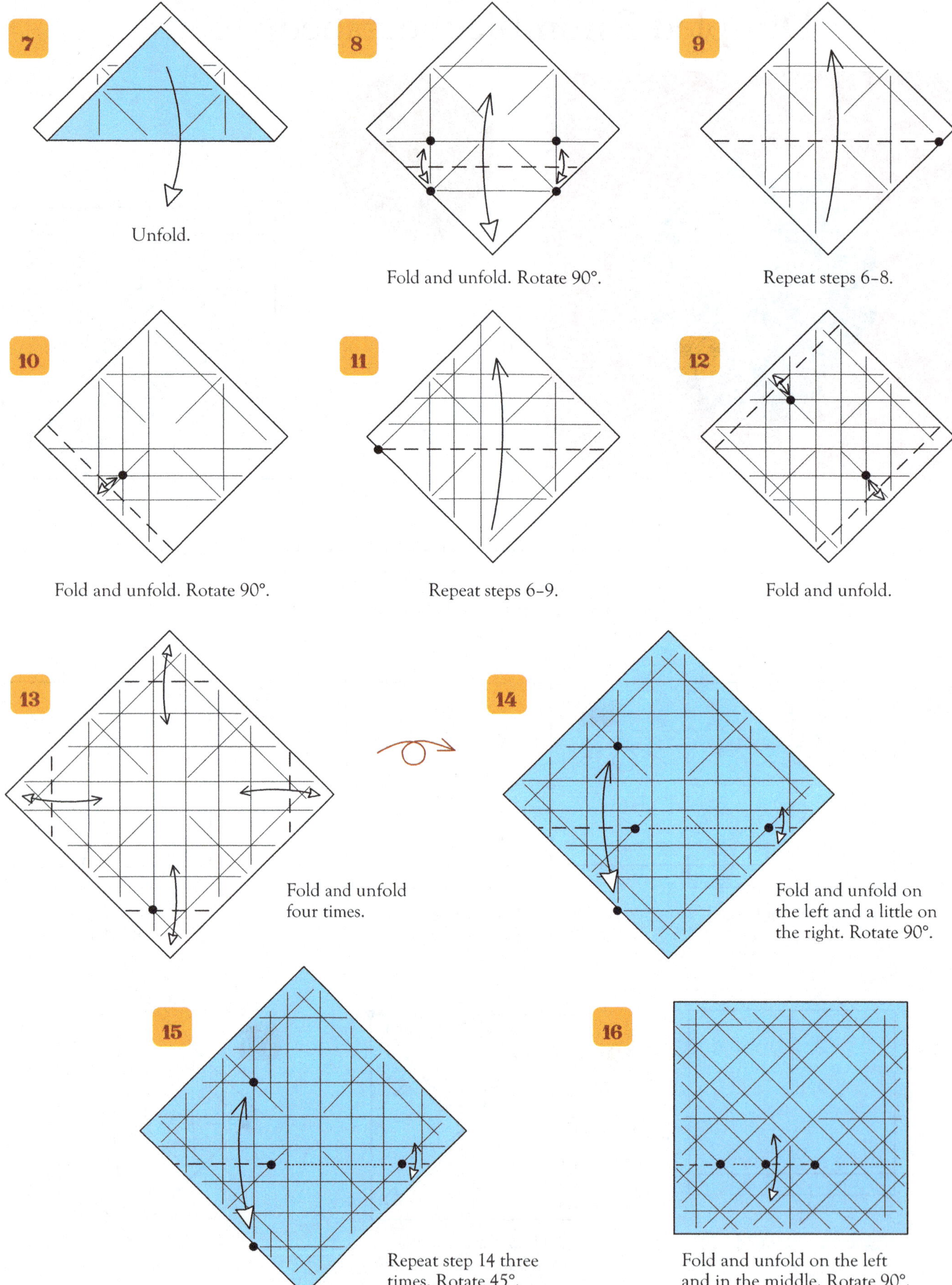

7
Unfold.
8
Fold and unfold. Rotate 90°.
9
Repeat steps 6–8.
10
Fold and unfold. Rotate 90°.
11
Repeat steps 6–9.
12
Fold and unfold.
13
Fold and unfold four times.
14
Fold and unfold on the left and a little on the right. Rotate 90°.
15
Repeat step 14 three times. Rotate 45°.
16
Fold and unfold on the left and in the middle. Rotate 90°.

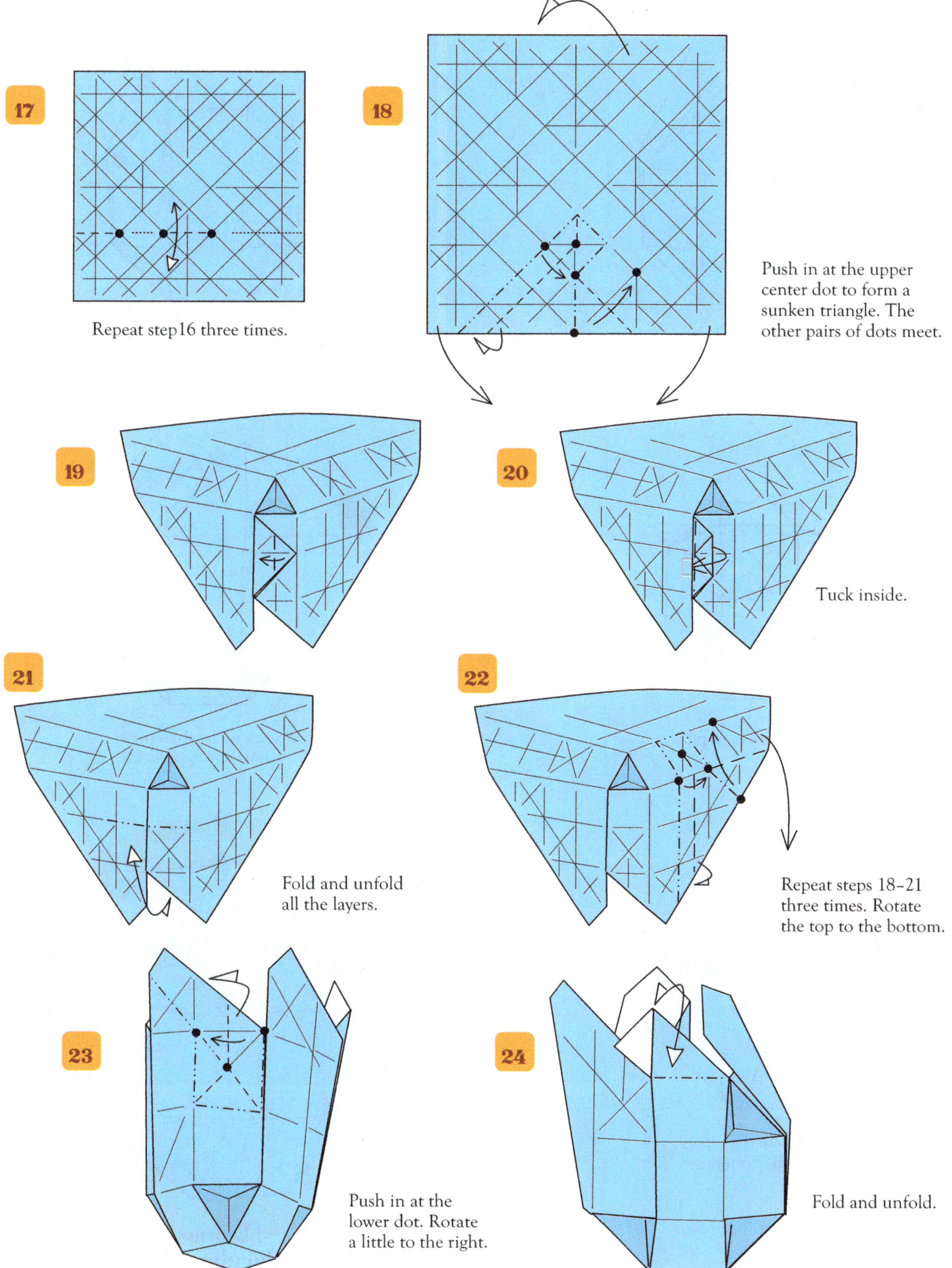

17 Repeat step 16 three times.

18 Push in at the upper center dot to form a sunken triangle. The other pairs of dots meet.

19

20 Tuck inside.

21 Fold and unfold all the layers.

22 Repeat steps 18–21 three times. Rotate the top to the bottom.

23 Push in at the lower dot. Rotate a little to the right.

24 Fold and unfold.

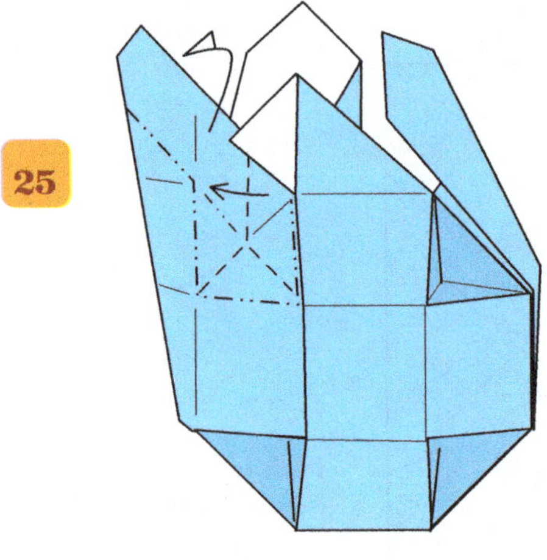

25

Repeat steps 23–24
three times.

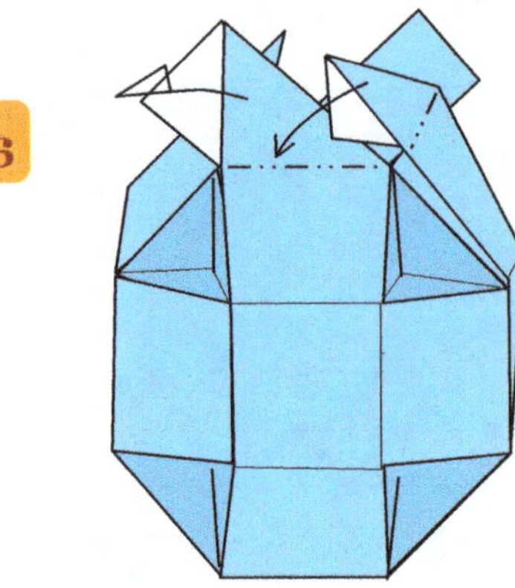

26

Mountain-fold to form
a flat square with four
white triangles.

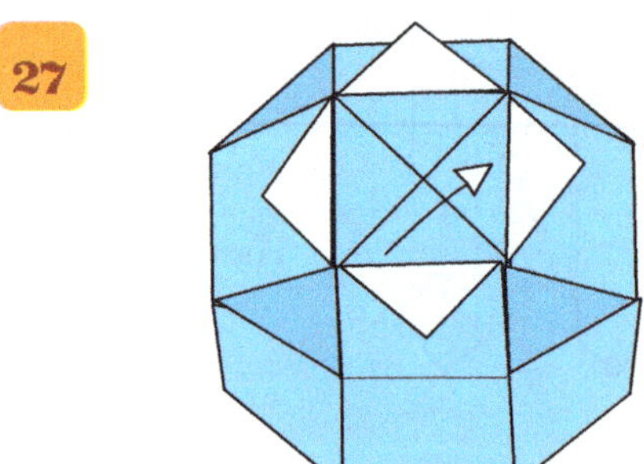

27

Unfold back to step 26.

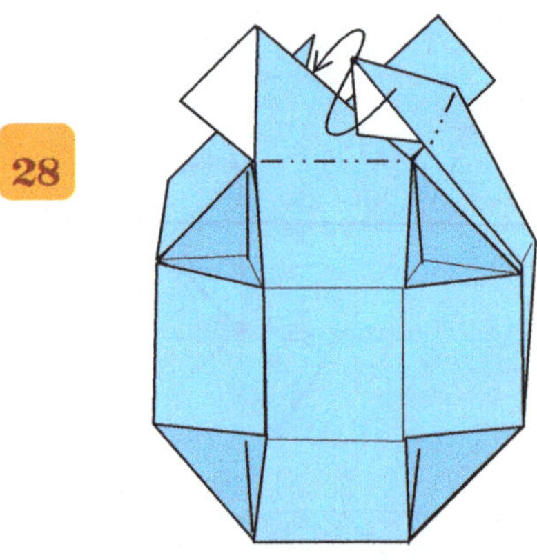

28

Tuck each tab to form
a four-way twist lock.

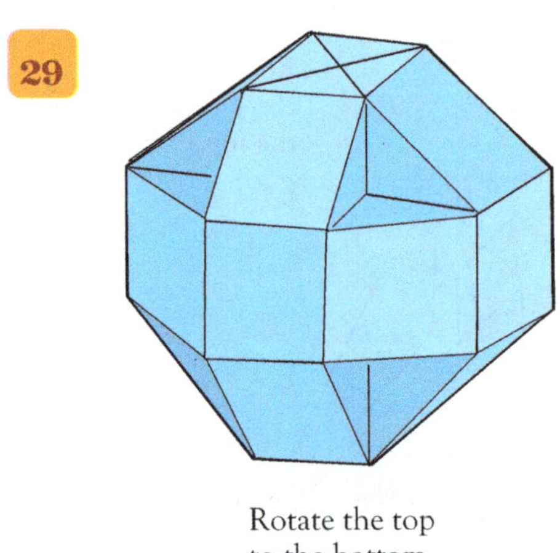

29

Rotate the top
to the bottom.

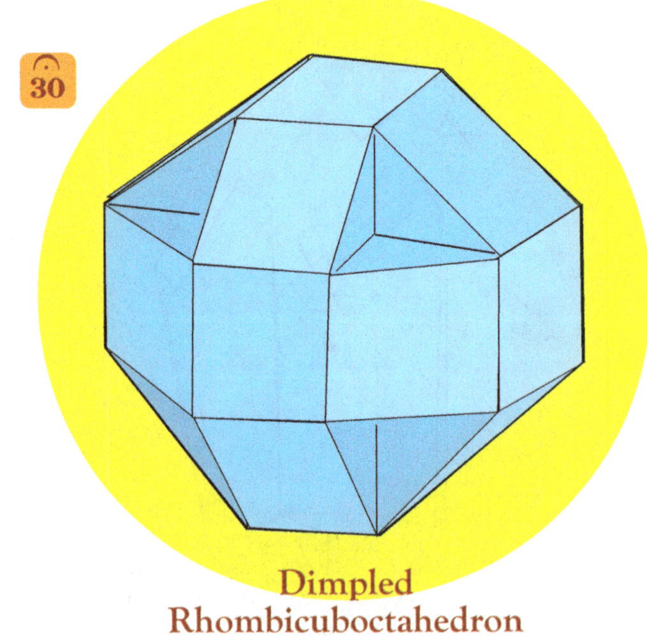

30

**Dimpled
Rhombicuboctahedron**

Trio of Archimedean Solids

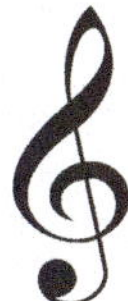

The minuet gives a trio of three of the thirteen Archimedean Solids. Archimedean Solids are convex polyhedra with faces of two or more types of regular polygons, where all the vertices are identical. Dive deep to master these mind-boggling shapes.

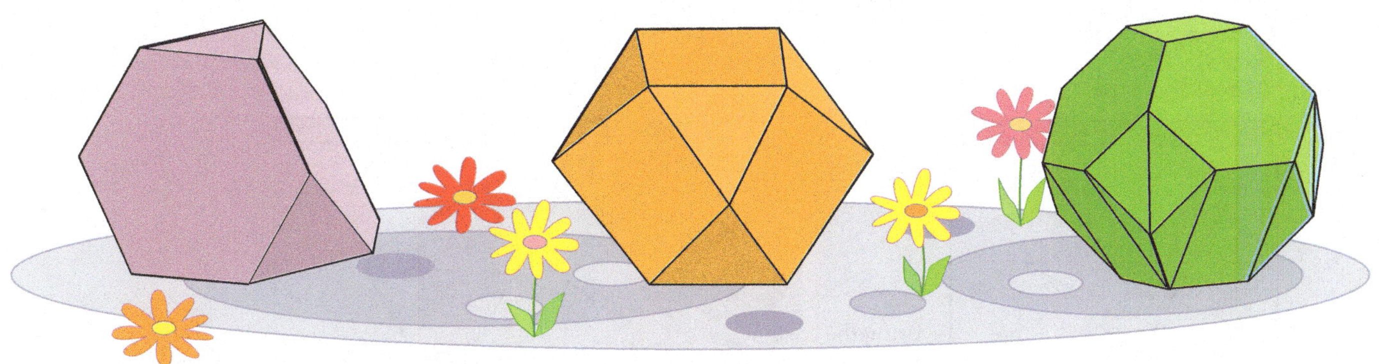

Truncated Tetrahedron

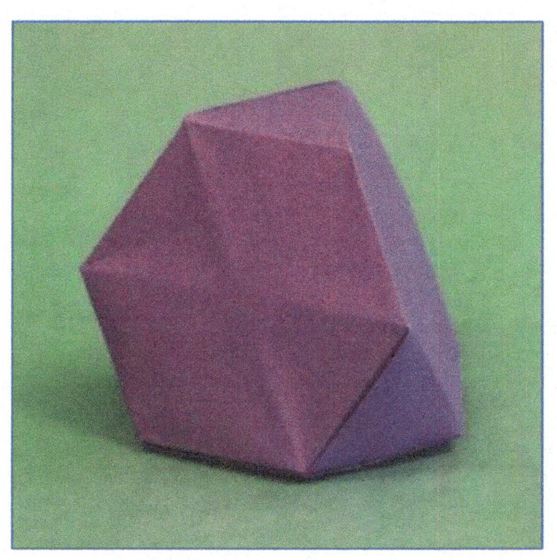

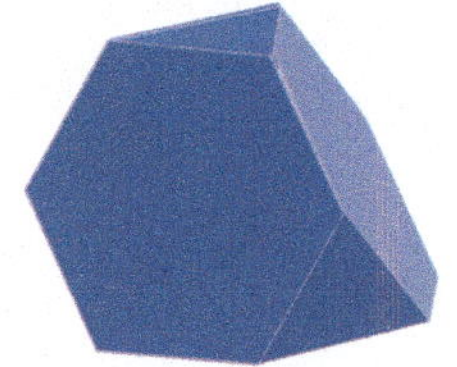

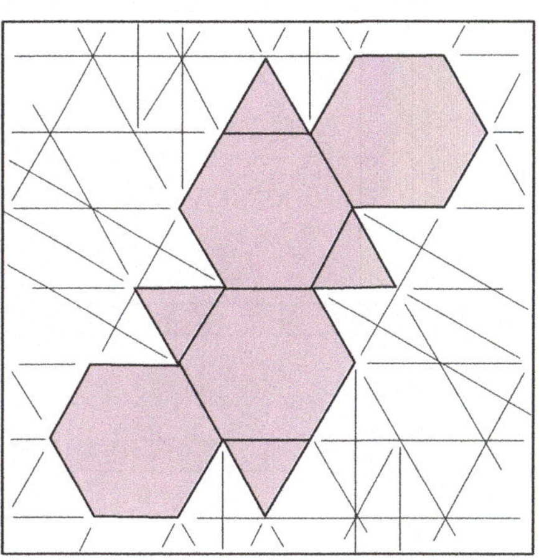

The truncated tetrahedron is an Archimedean solid composed of four triangles and four hexagons. The layout is the same when rotate 180°.

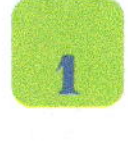

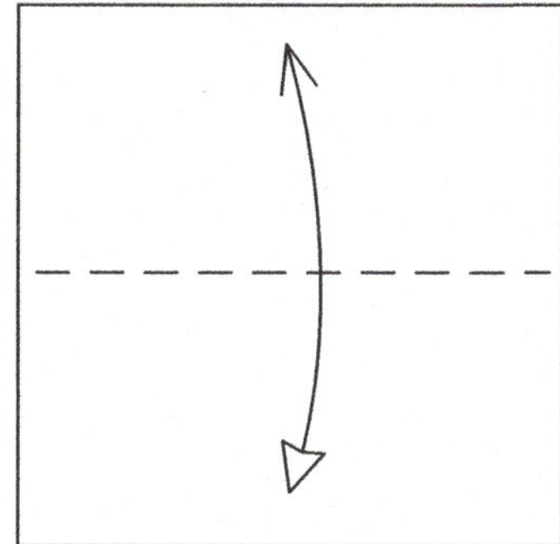

1 Fold and unfold.

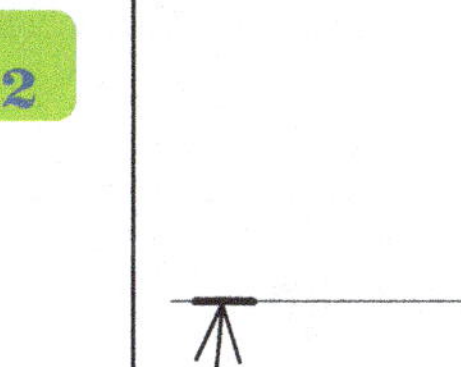

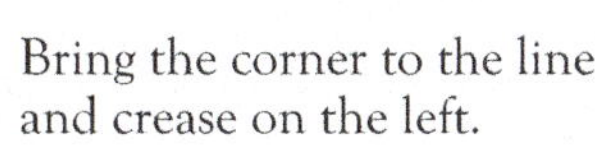

2 Bring the corner to the line and crease on the left.

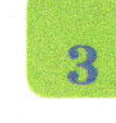

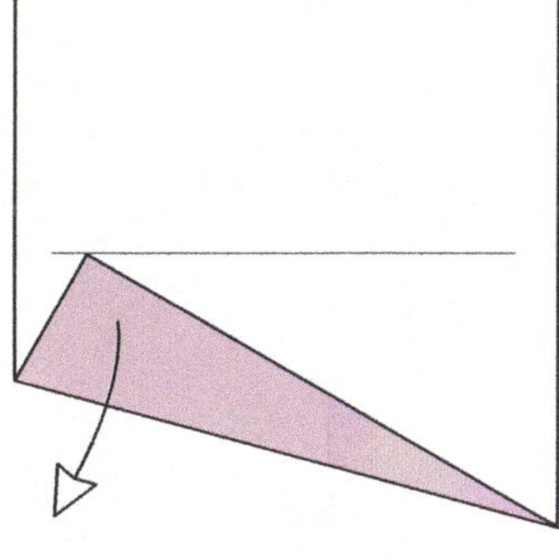

3 Unfold.

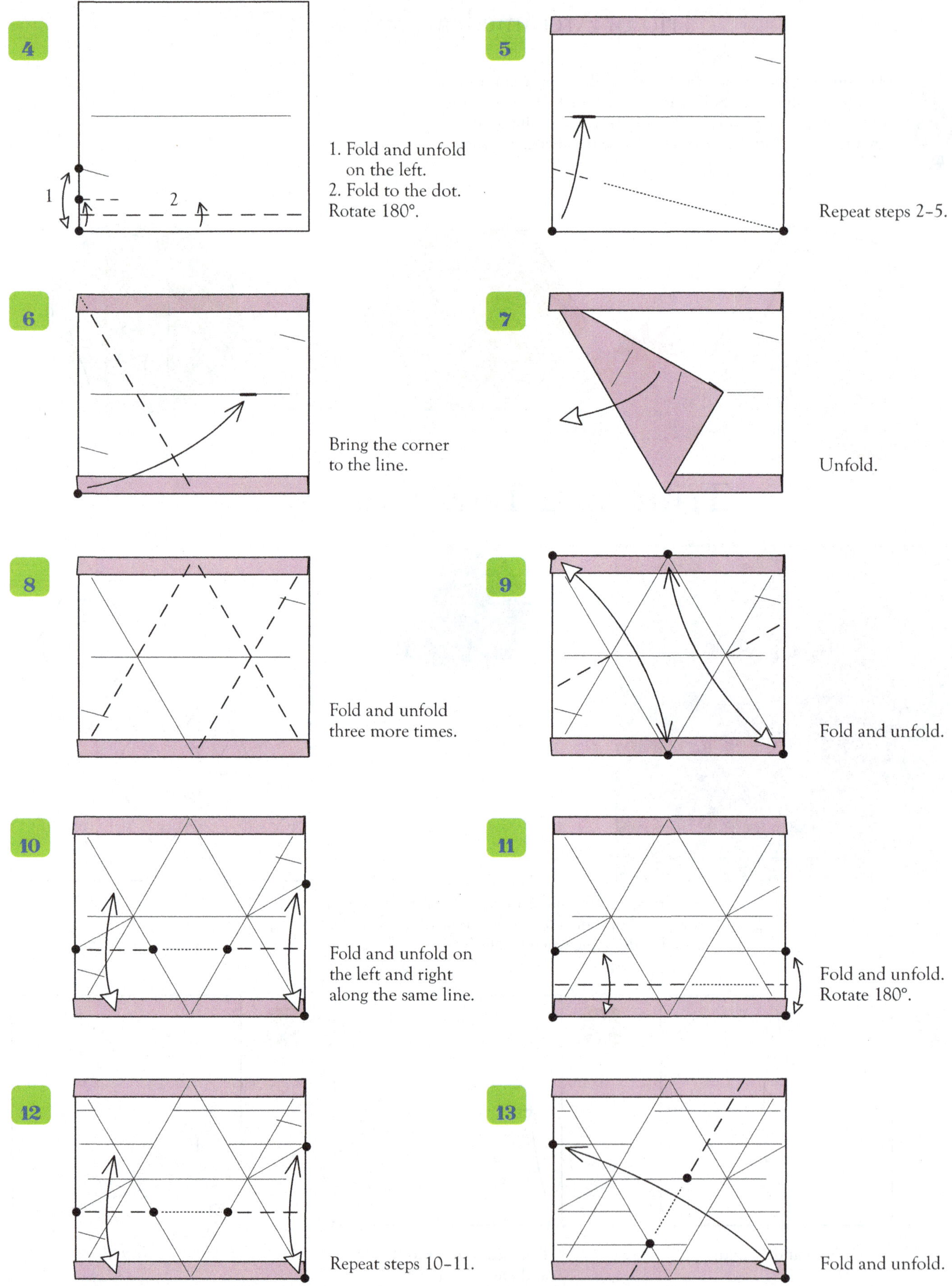

4
1. Fold and unfold on the left.
2. Fold to the dot. Rotate 180°.
5
Repeat steps 2–5.
6
Bring the corner to the line.
7
Unfold.
8
Fold and unfold three more times.
9
Fold and unfold.
10
Fold and unfold on the left and right along the same line.
11
Fold and unfold. Rotate 180°.
12
Repeat steps 10–11.
13
Fold and unfold.

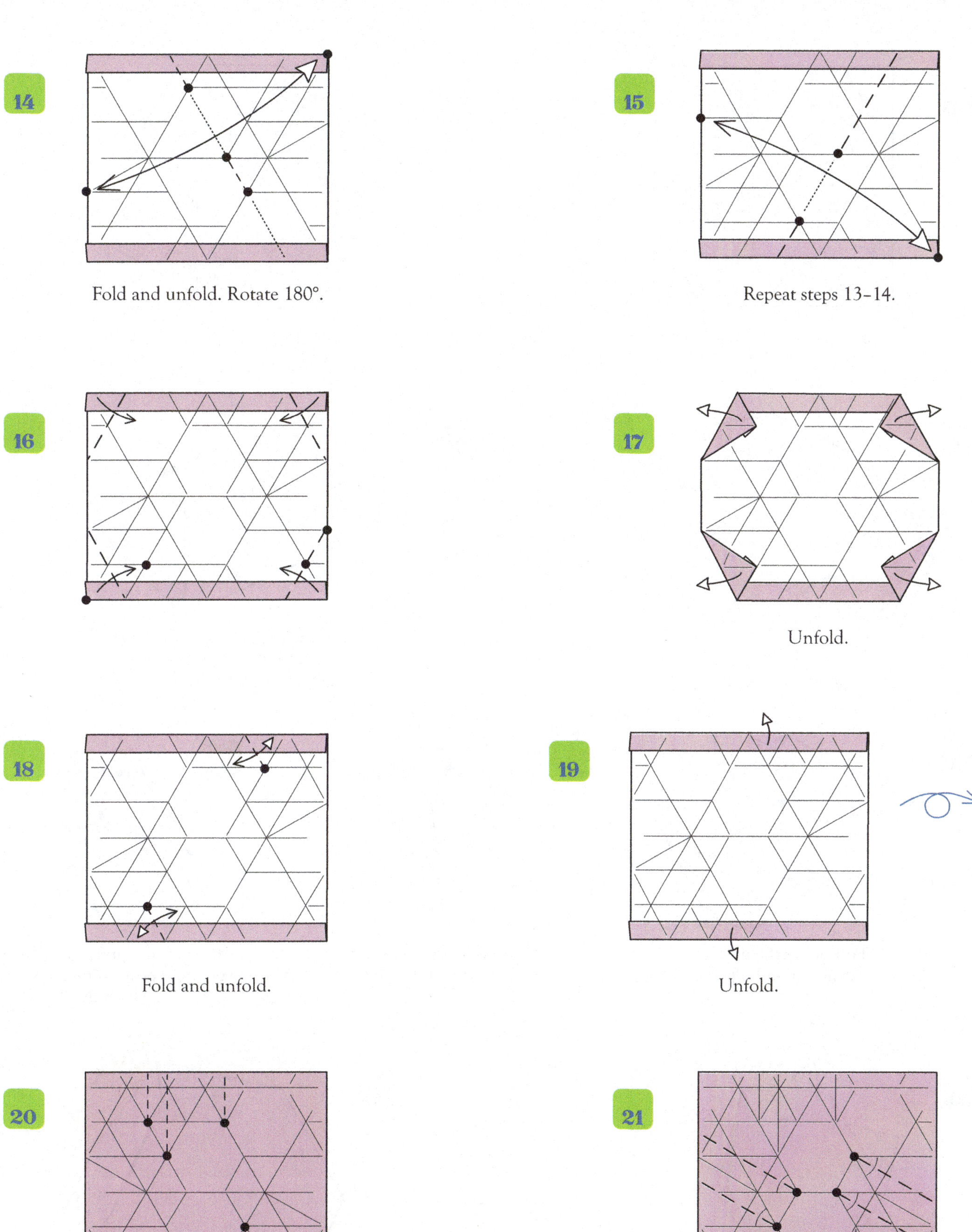

14 Fold and unfold. Rotate 180°.

15 Repeat steps 13–14.

16 Fold and unfold.

17 Unfold.

18 Fold and unfold.

19 Unfold.

20 Fold and unfold.

21 Fold and unfold to bisect the angles.

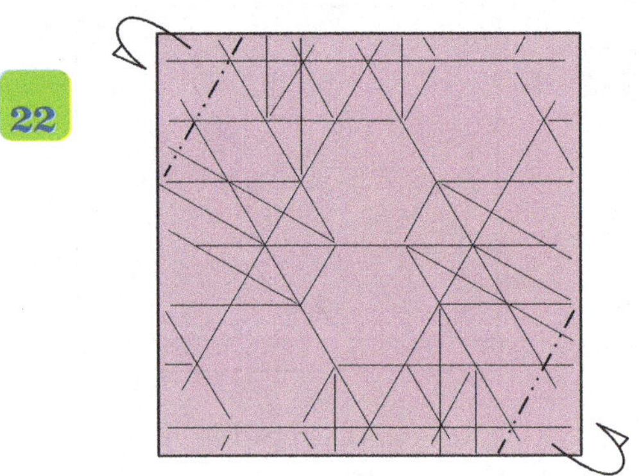

Fold along the creases. Rotate.

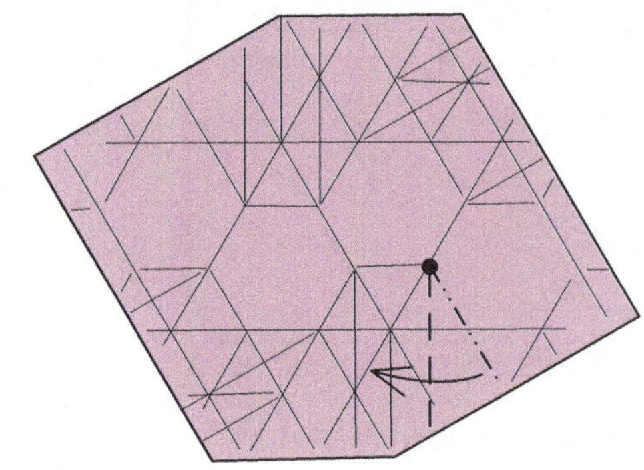

Puff out at the dot.

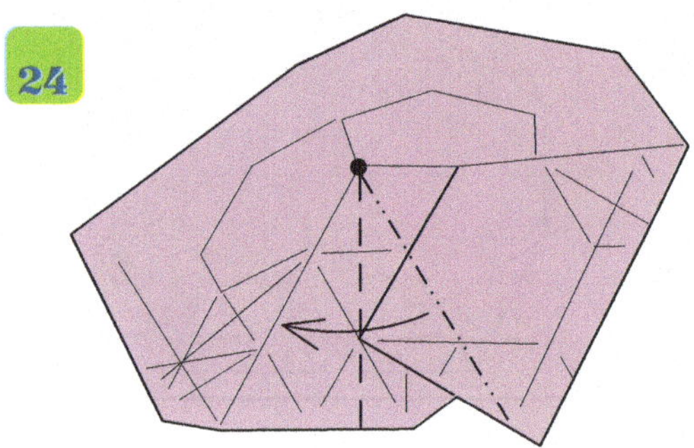

Puff out at the dot.

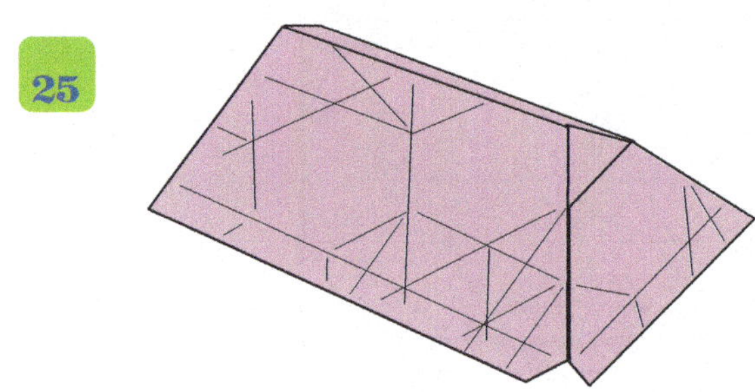

Flatten the layers inside. Turn over and repeat steps 23–24. Then rotate the bottom to the top.

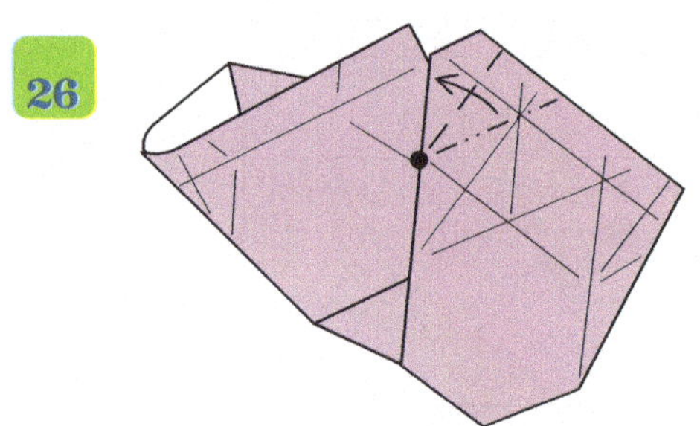

Puff out at the dot.
Turn over and repeat.

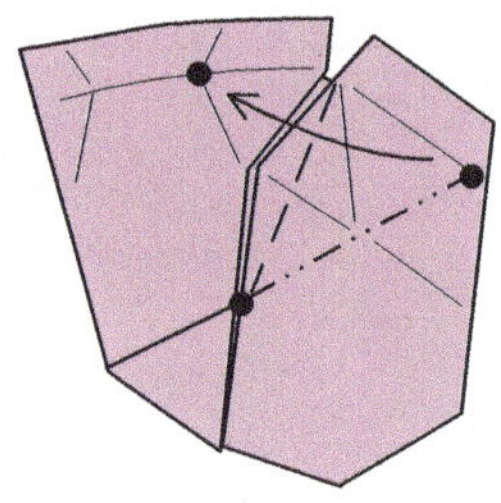

Puff out at the lower dot.
Turn over and repeat.

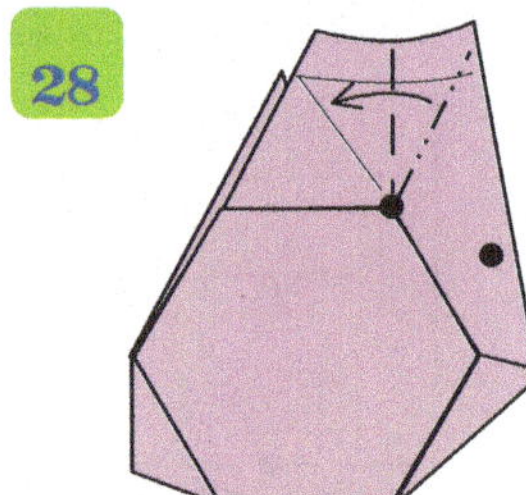

Puff out at the upper dot. Turn over and repeat. Rotate to view the right side with the dot.

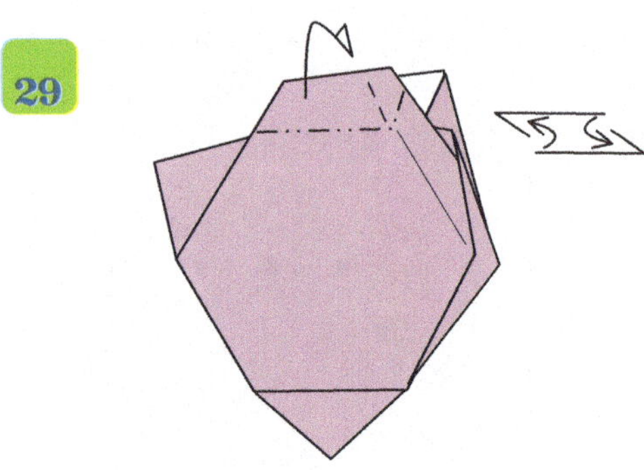

Fold inside, turn over and repeat. Interlock these tabs into each other, as show in the view from above.

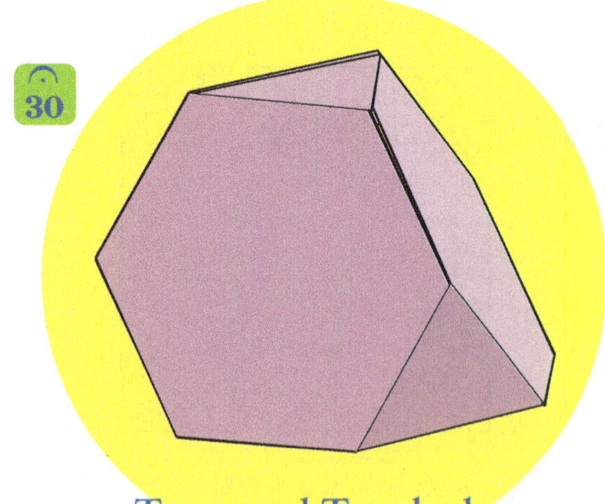

Truncated Tetrahedron

Cuboctahedron

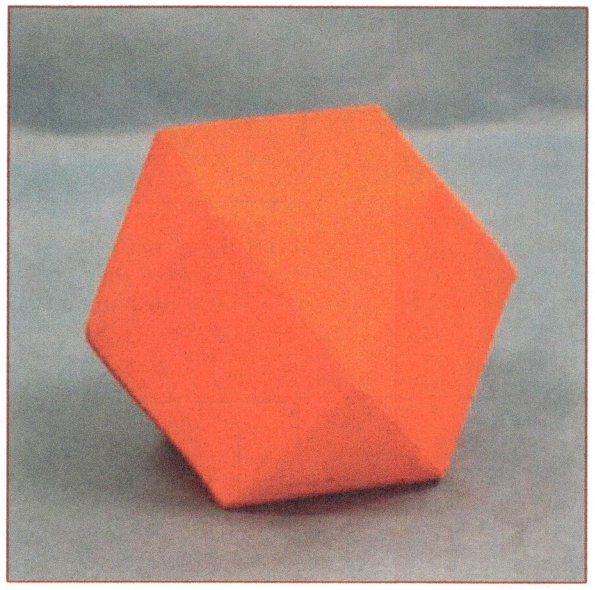

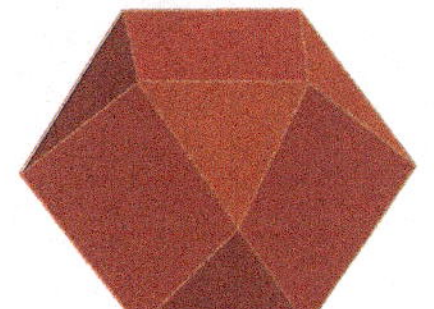

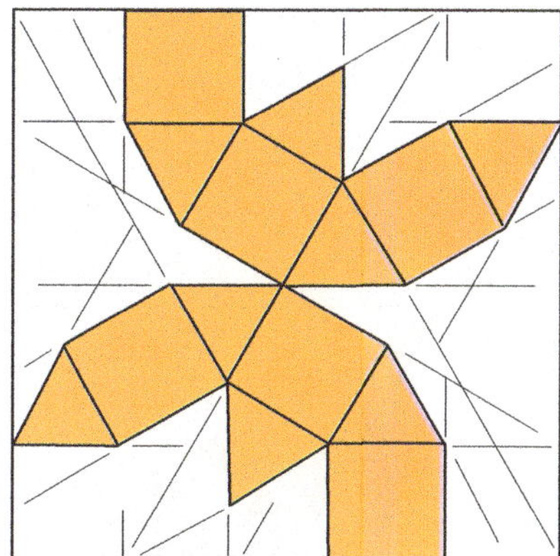

The cuboctahedron has fourteen sides, six squares and eight equilateral triangles. The crease pattern is the same when rotated 180°.

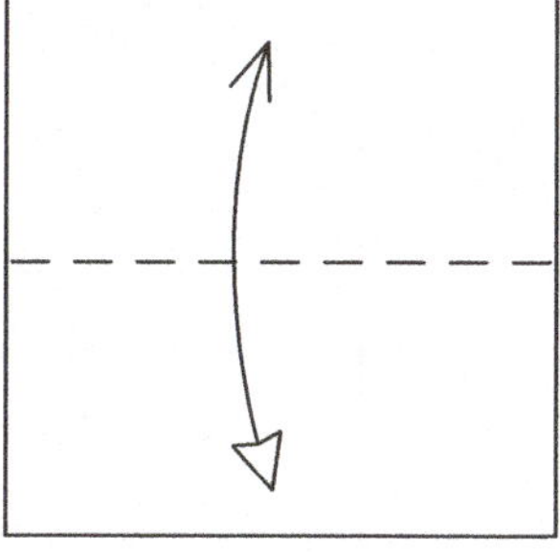

Fold and unfold.

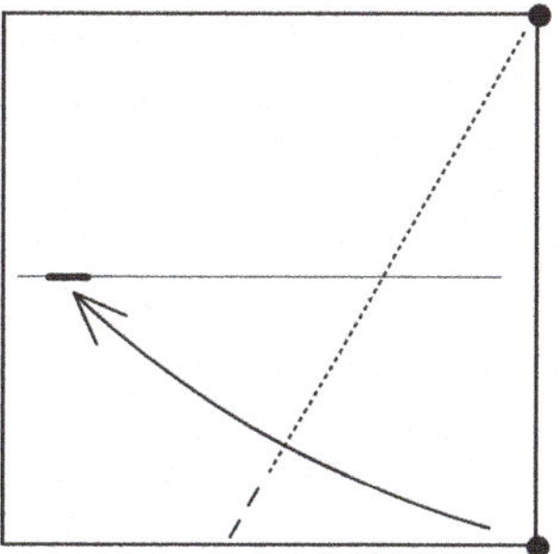

Bring the bottom dot to the line. Crease on the bottom.

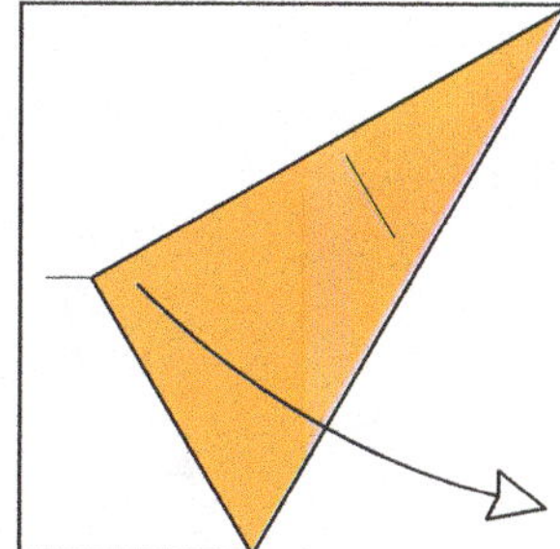

Unfold and rotate 90°.

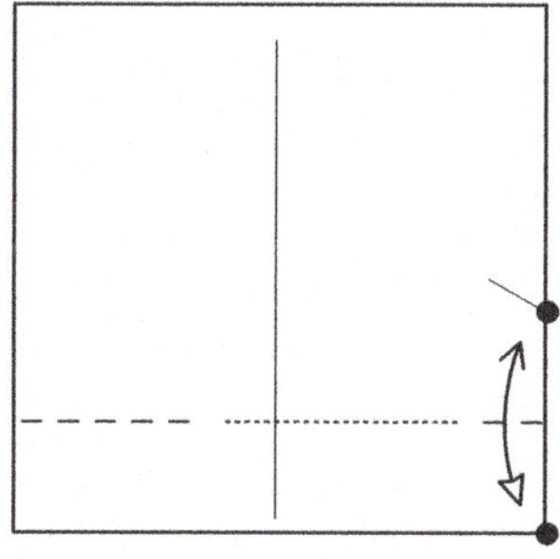

Fold and unfold. Make a small mark on the right and a longer crease on the left. Rotate 90°.

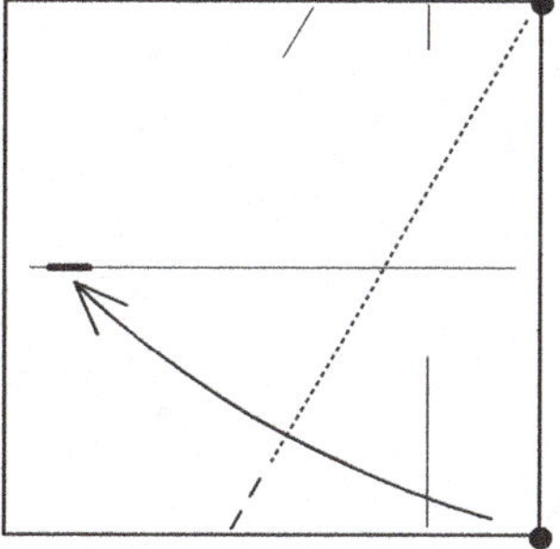

Repeat steps 2–4.

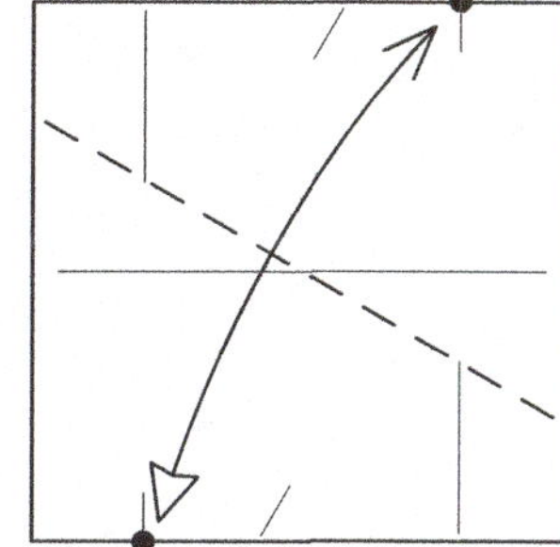

Fold and unfold.

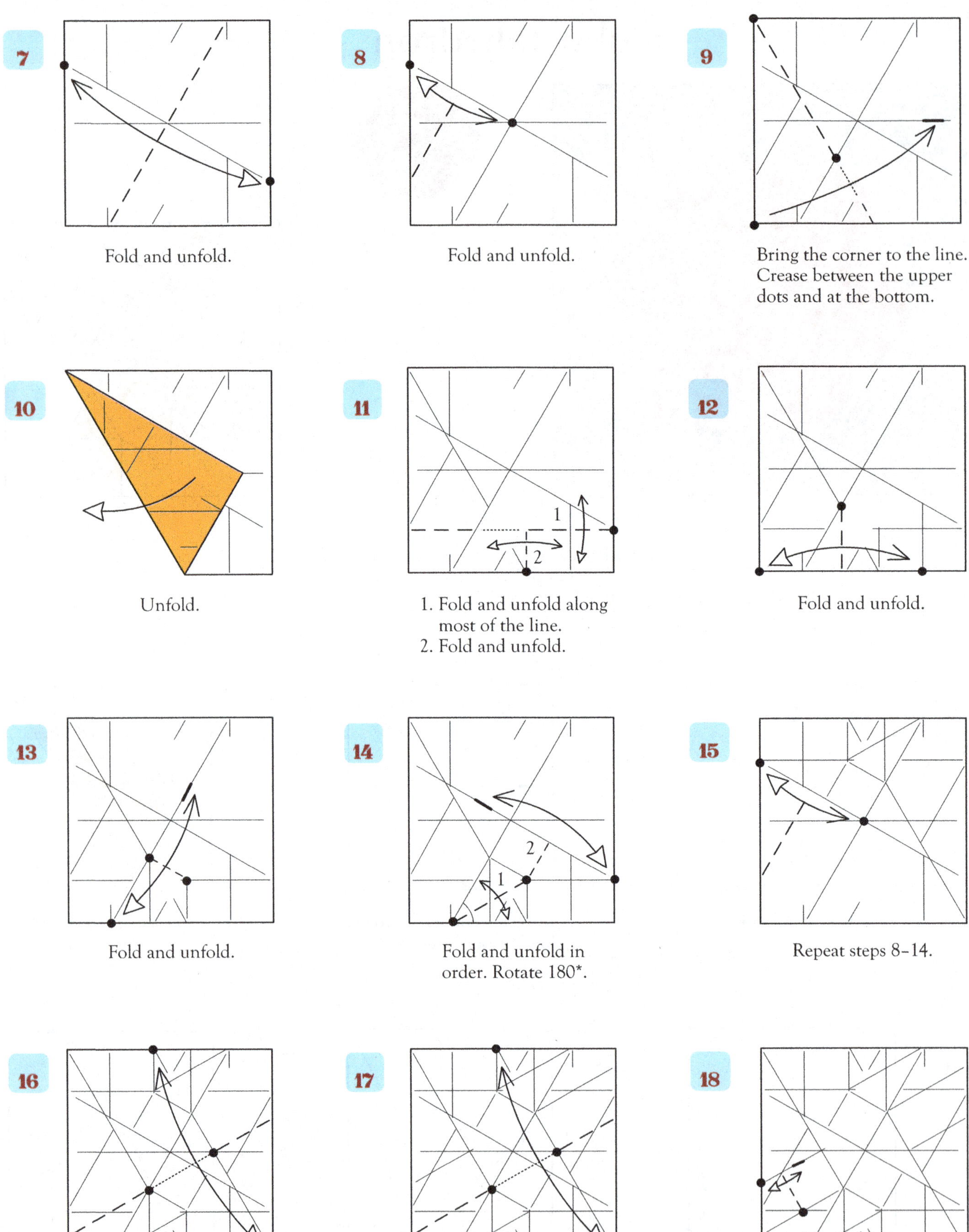

7. Fold and unfold.

8. Fold and unfold.

9. Bring the corner to the line. Crease between the upper dots and at the bottom.

10. Unfold.

11. 1. Fold and unfold along most of the line.
    2. Fold and unfold.

12. Fold and unfold.

13. Fold and unfold.

14. Fold and unfold in order. Rotate 180*.

15. Repeat steps 8–14.

16. Fold and unfold on the left and right. Rotate 180°.

17. Repeat step 16.

18. Fold and unfold.

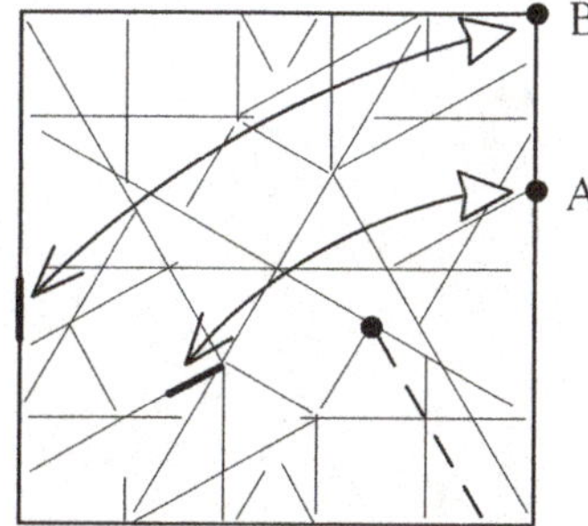

Fold and unfold. Dot A will
meet a line while dot B meets
the left edge. Rotate 180°.

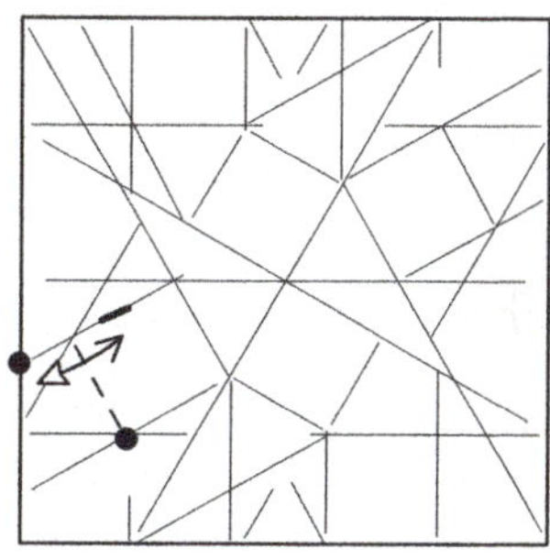

Repeat steps 18–19.

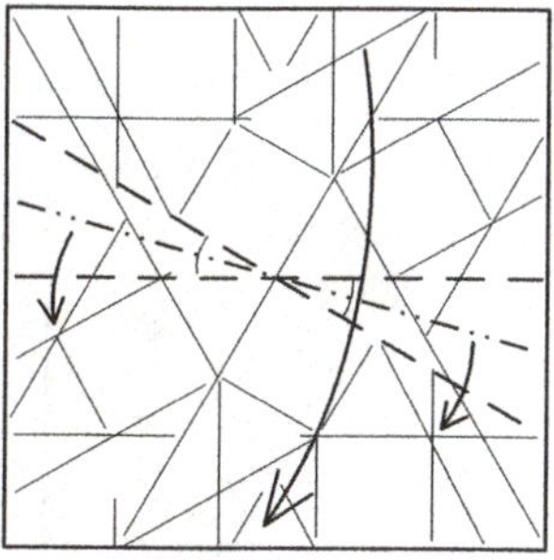

Valley-fold along the creases
and bisect the angles.

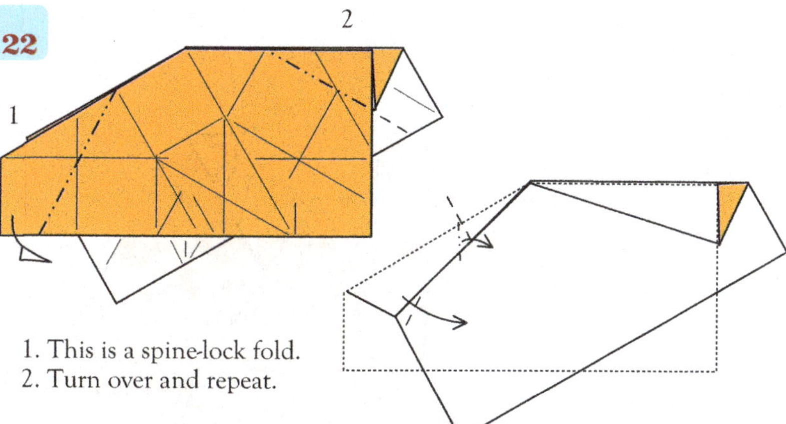

1. This is a spine-lock fold.
2. Turn over and repeat.

The drawing on the right shows an
inside view of the spine-lock fold. The
dotted line is for the upper layer.

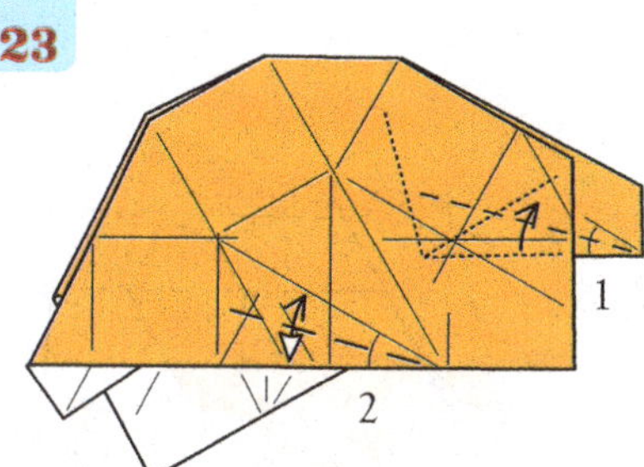

1. Valley-fold a couple layers. Most
   of the folding is hidden, shown
   by the dotted lines.
2. Fold and unfold to bisect the angle.
Turn over and repeat. Rotate the top
to the bottom.

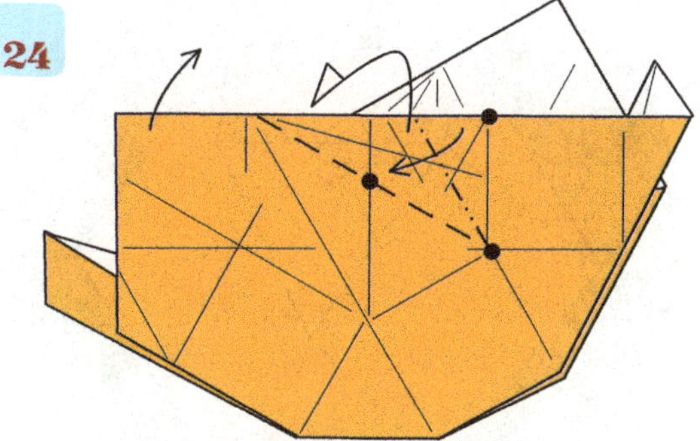

Puff out at the lower dot.
The other dots will meet.

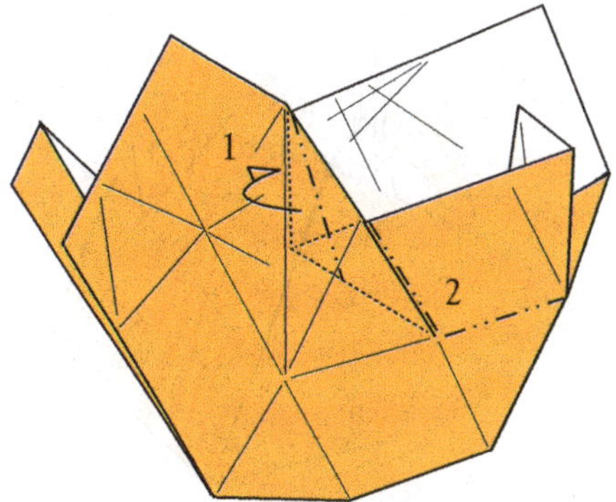

1. Fold the hidden layer
   behind along the crease.
2. Fold and unfold along the
   creases.

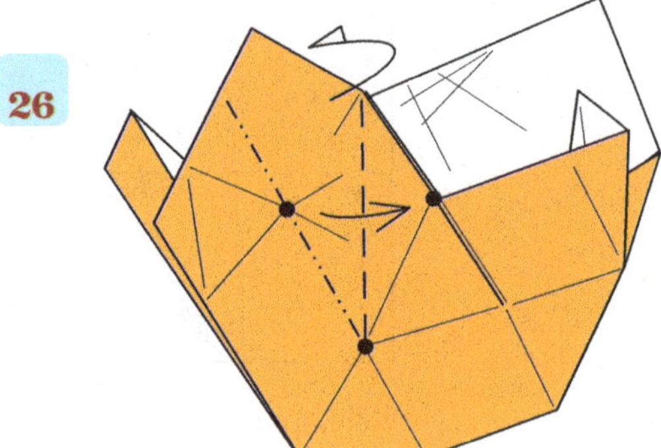

26

Puff out at the lower dot.
The other dots will meet.

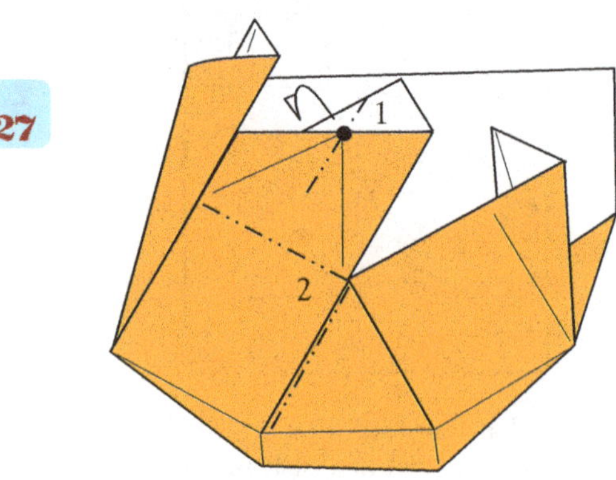

27

1. Fold behind.
2. Fold and unfold
   along the creases.

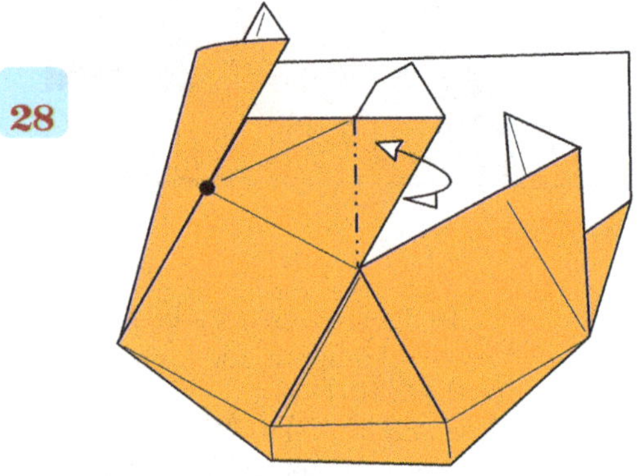

28

1. Fold and unfold along the crease.
2. Turn over and repeat steps 24–28.
3. Rotate so the dot becomes front and center.

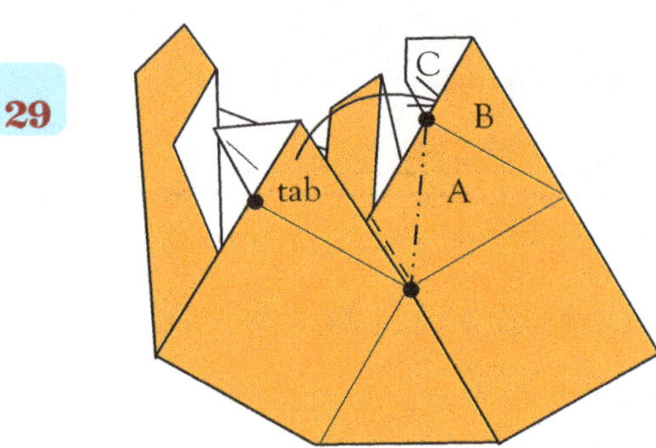

29

Tuck the tab under A and B but above
C. Ths is similar to a reverse fold. Puff
out at the lower dot. The upper dots
will meet. Turn over and repeat.

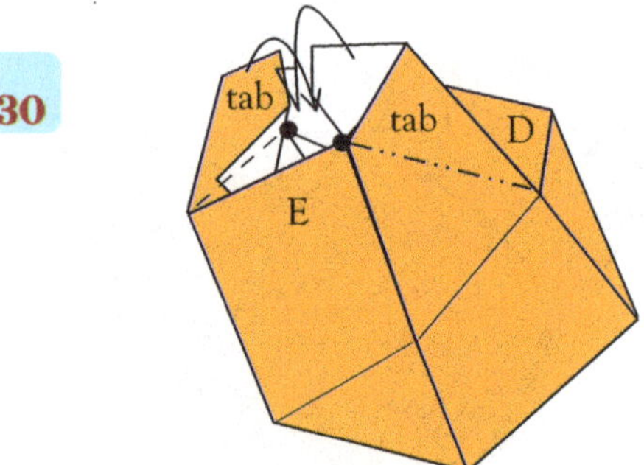

30

The dots will meet as the
tabs interlock and are
tucked under D and E.

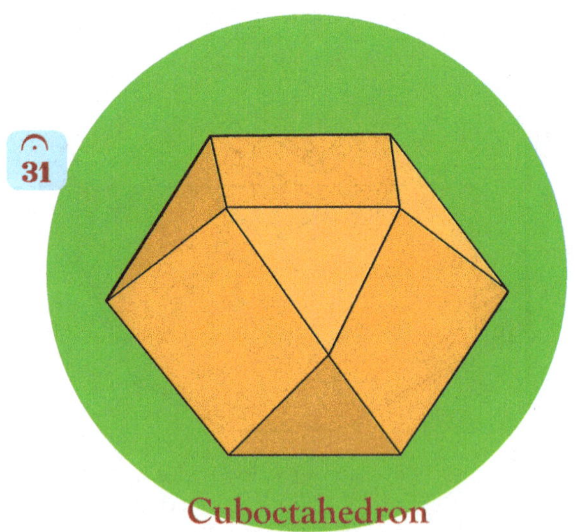

31

Cuboctahedron

Truncated Octahedron

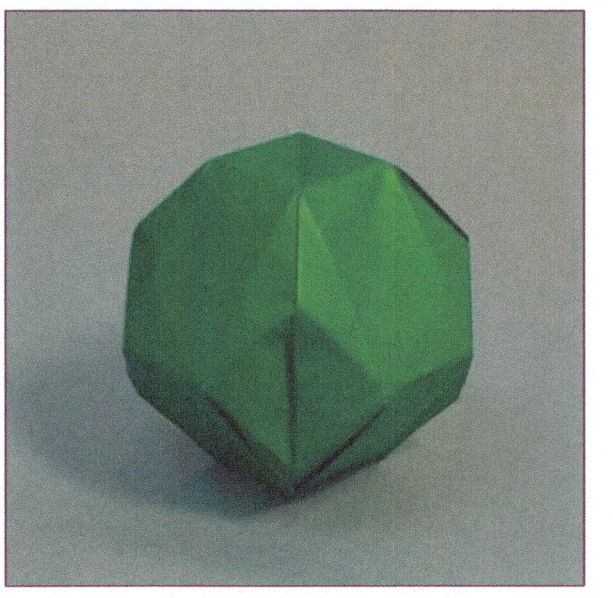

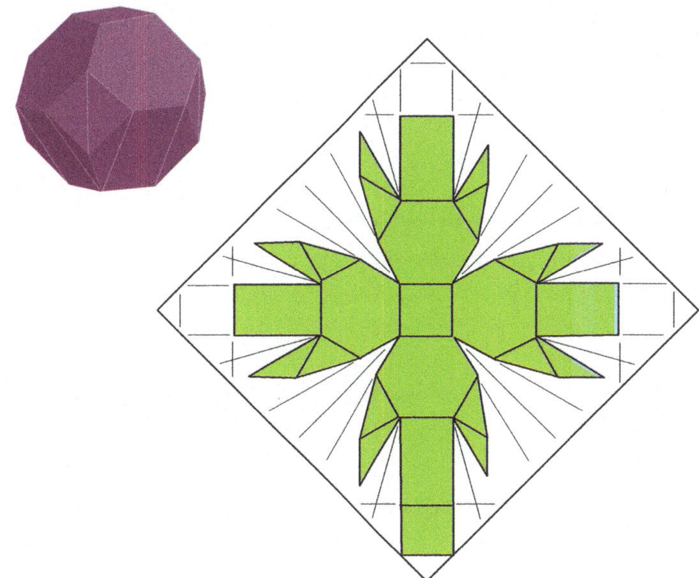

This 14-sided polyhedron is composed of six square and eight hexagonal faces. This beautiful shape is difficult to fold. The layout shows square symmetry, except at the bottom.

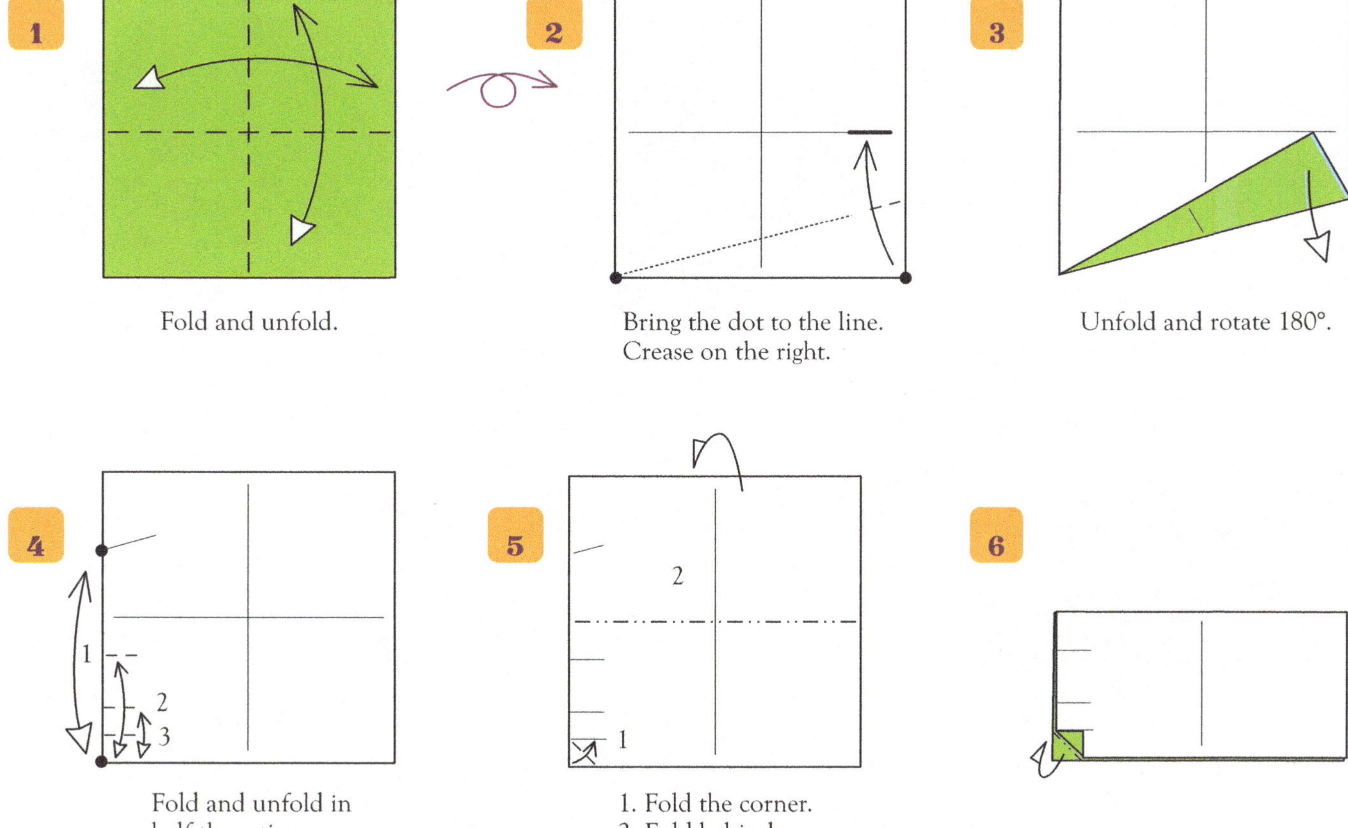

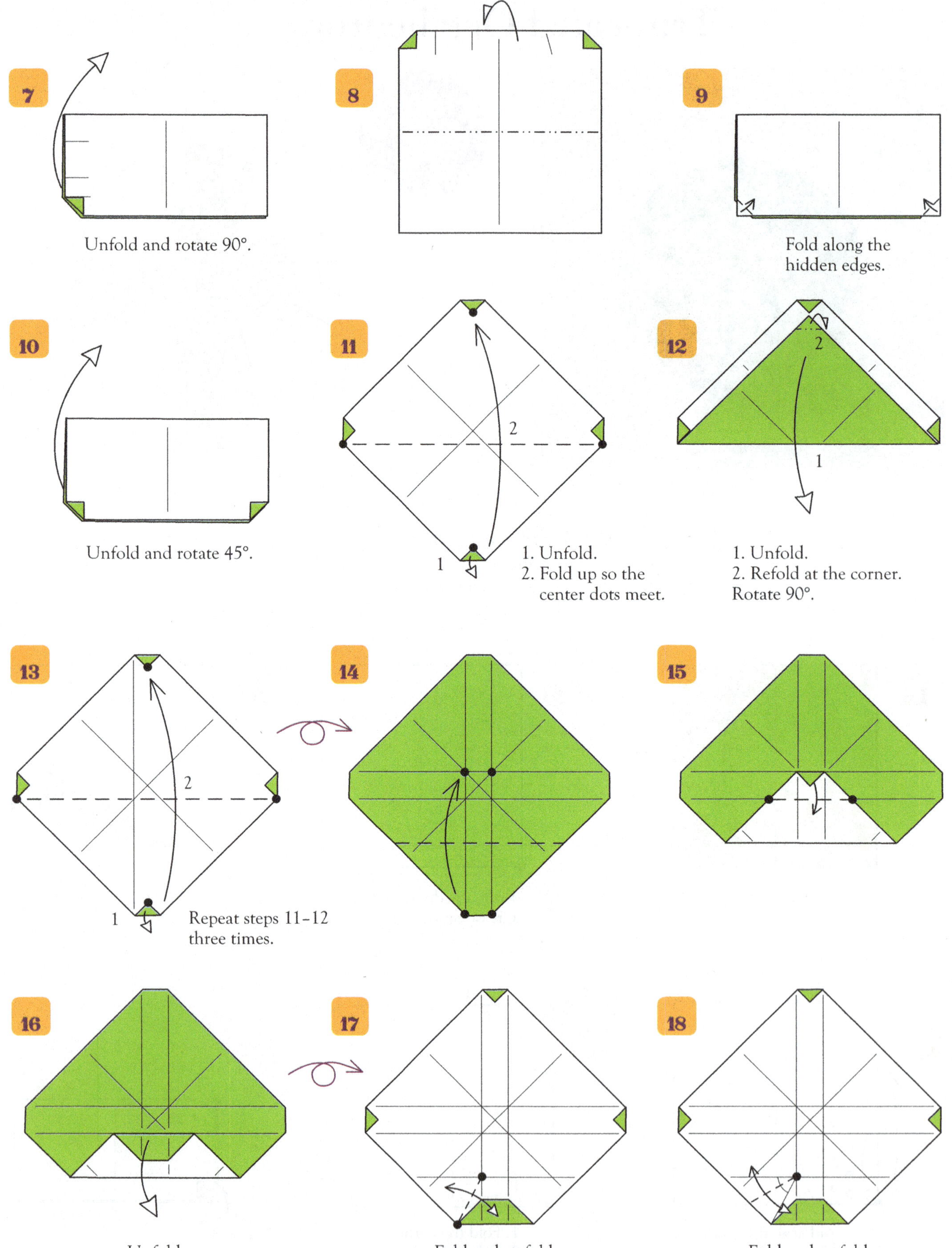

7 Unfold and rotate 90°.

8

9 Fold along the hidden edges.

10 Unfold and rotate 45°.

11
1. Unfold.
2. Fold up so the center dots meet.

12
1. Unfold.
2. Refold at the corner. Rotate 90°.

13 Repeat steps 11–12 three times.

14

15

16 Unfold.

17 Fold and unfold.

18 Fold and unfold.

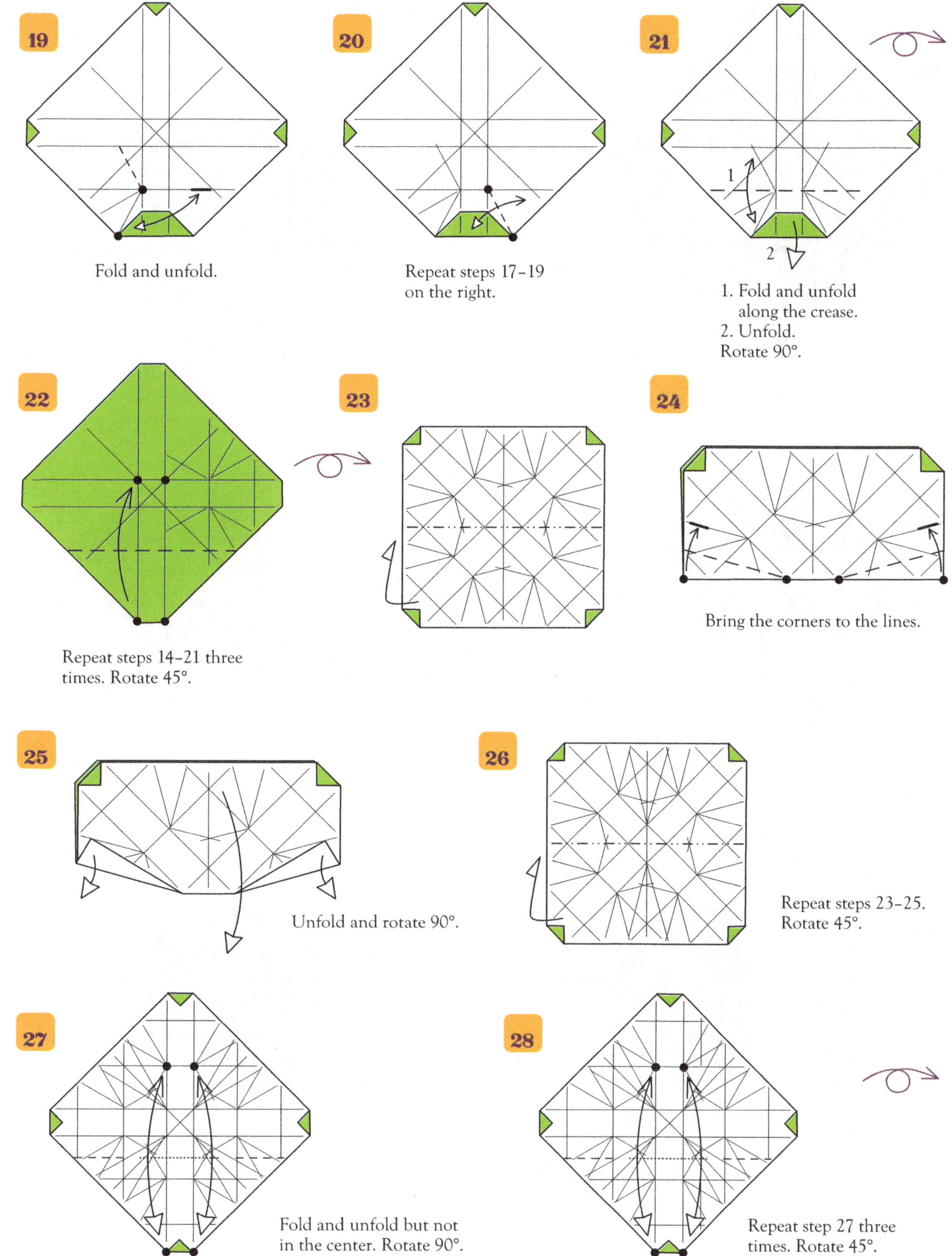

19 Fold and unfold.

20 Repeat steps 17–19 on the right.

21
1. Fold and unfold along the crease.
2. Unfold.
Rotate 90°.

22 Repeat steps 14–21 three times. Rotate 45°.

23

24 Bring the corners to the lines.

25 Unfold and rotate 90°.

26 Repeat steps 23–25. Rotate 45°.

27 Fold and unfold but not in the center. Rotate 90°.

28 Repeat step 27 three times. Rotate 45°.

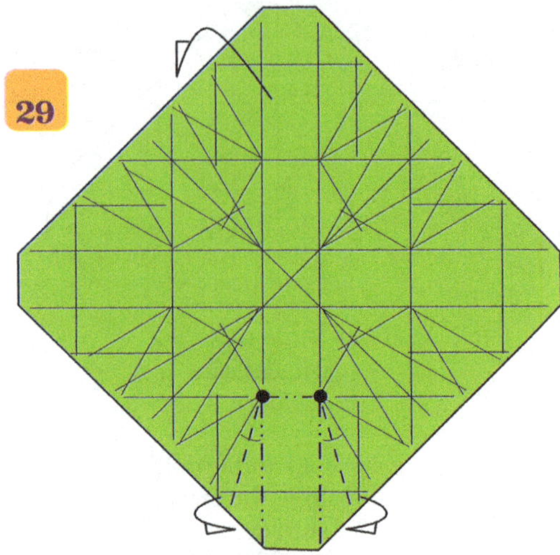

Bisect the angles and
puff out at the dots.

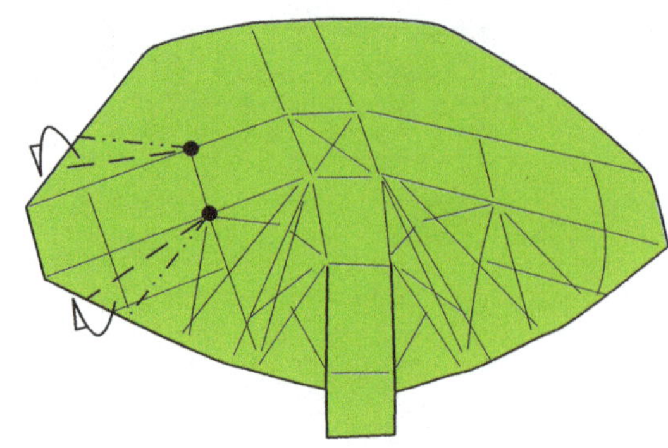

Repeat step 29 three
times. Rotate 45°.

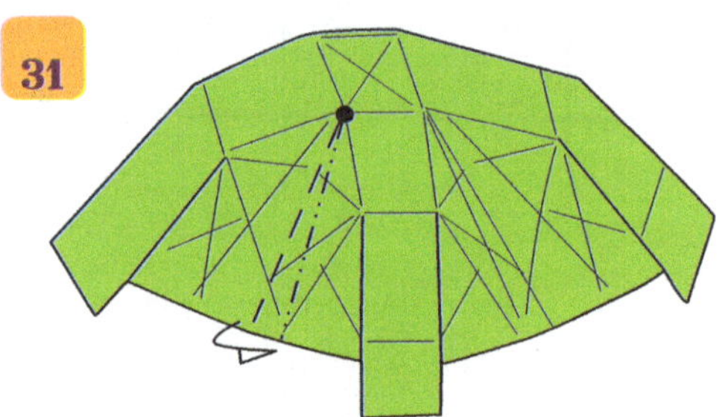

Fold along the creases
and puff out at the dot.

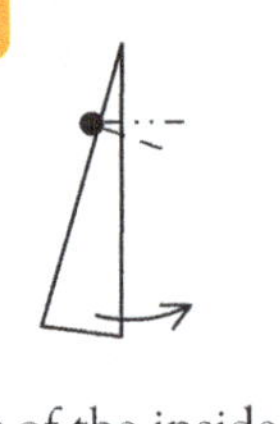

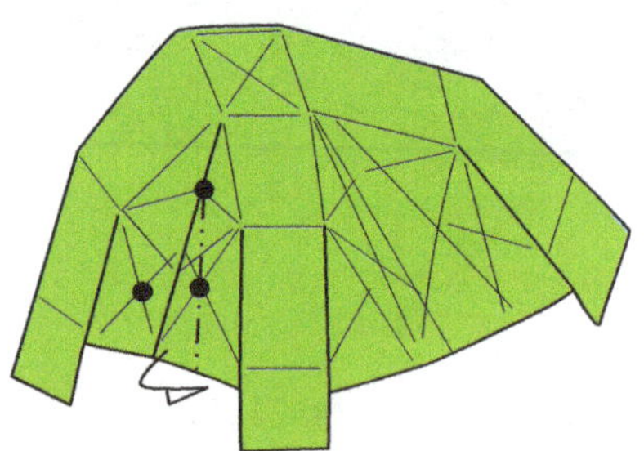

View of the inside,
with the upper dot.

This is a spine-lock fold. Puff out
at the upper dot. The lower dots
will meet. There is a small fold
inside the model at the upper dot.

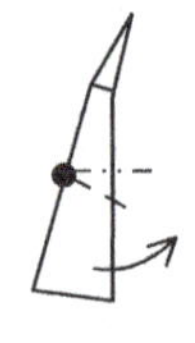

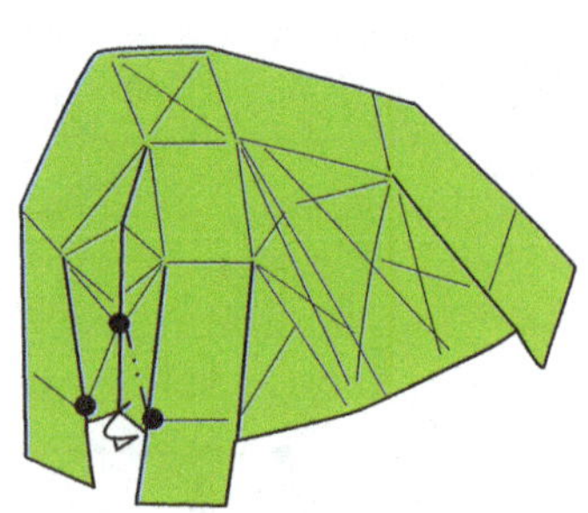

View of the inside,
with the upper dot.

This is a spine-lock fold. Puff out
at the upper dot. The lower dots
will meet. There is a small fold
inside the model at the upper dot.

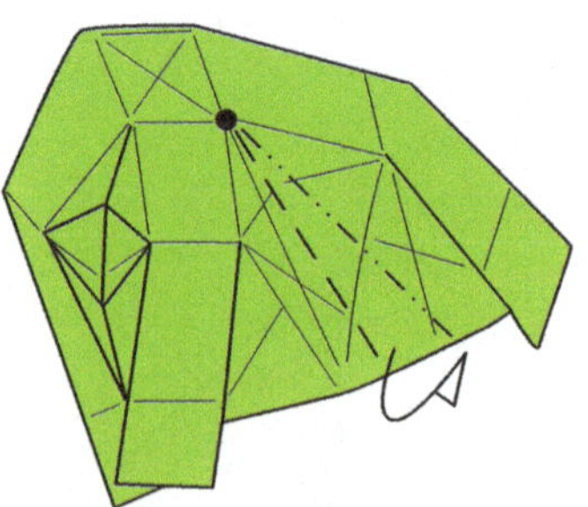

Repeat steps 31–33
three times. Rotate
the top to the bottom.

35

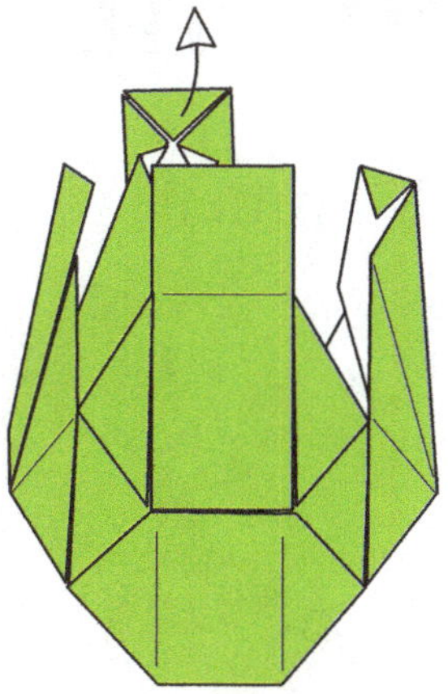

Unfold.

36

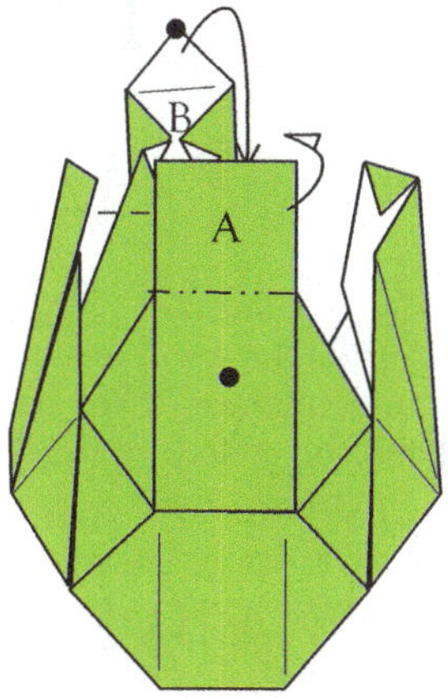

Fold A down so it will be level. Tuck B into A. The dots will meet inside the model. Rotate 90°.

37

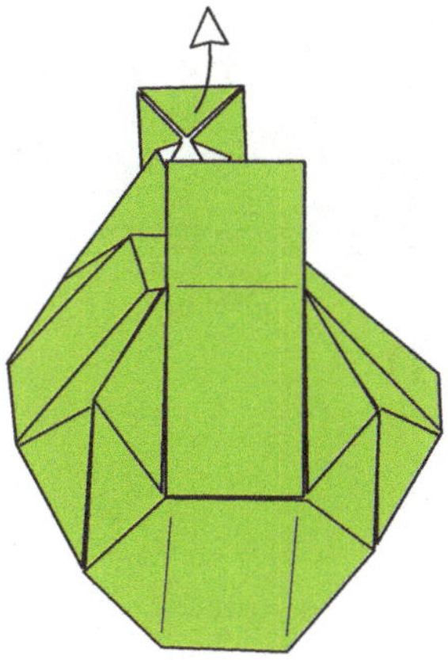

Repeat steps 35–36.

38

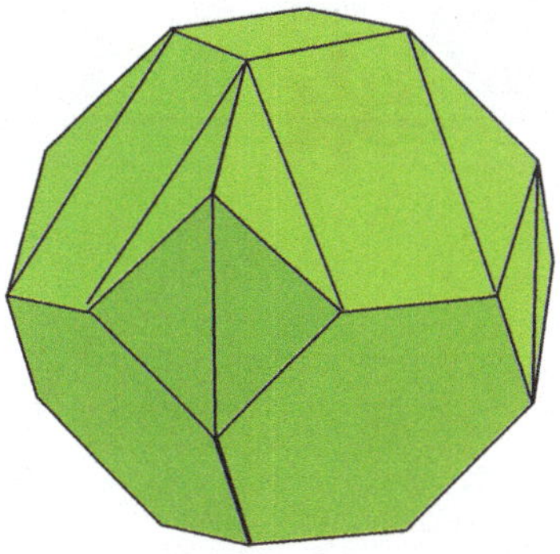

Rotate the top to the bottom.

39

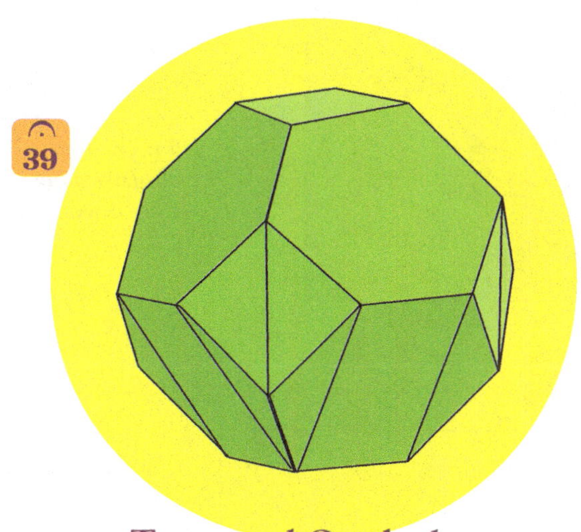

Truncated Octahedron

Fourth Movement

March of the Prehistoric Mammals

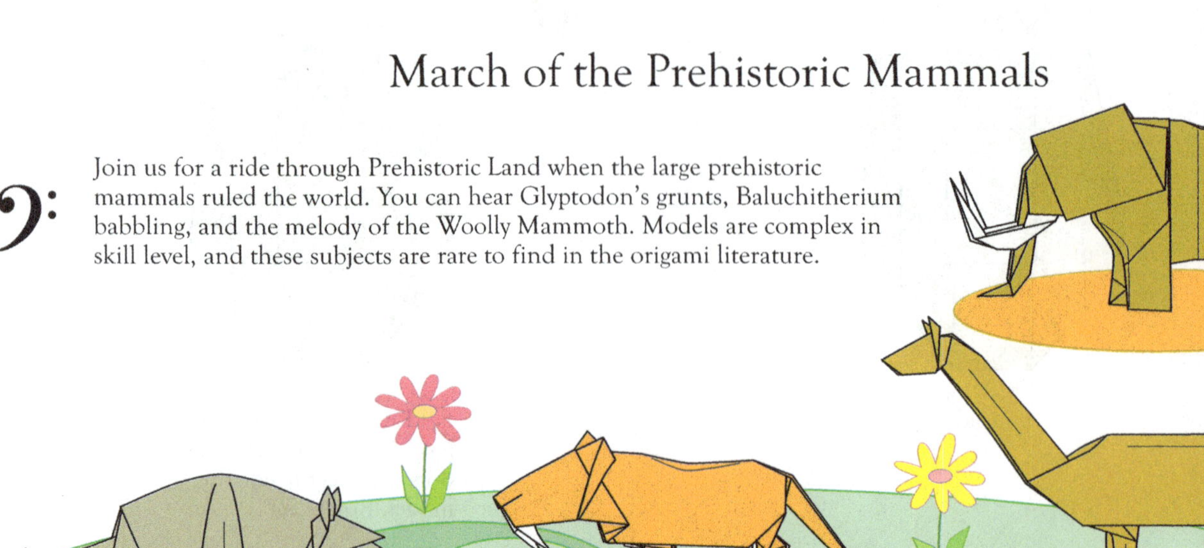

Join us for a ride through Prehistoric Land when the large prehistoric mammals ruled the world. You can hear Glyptodon's grunts, Baluchitherium babbling, and the melody of the Woolly Mammoth. Models are complex in skill level, and these subjects are rare to find in the origami literature.

Megatherium

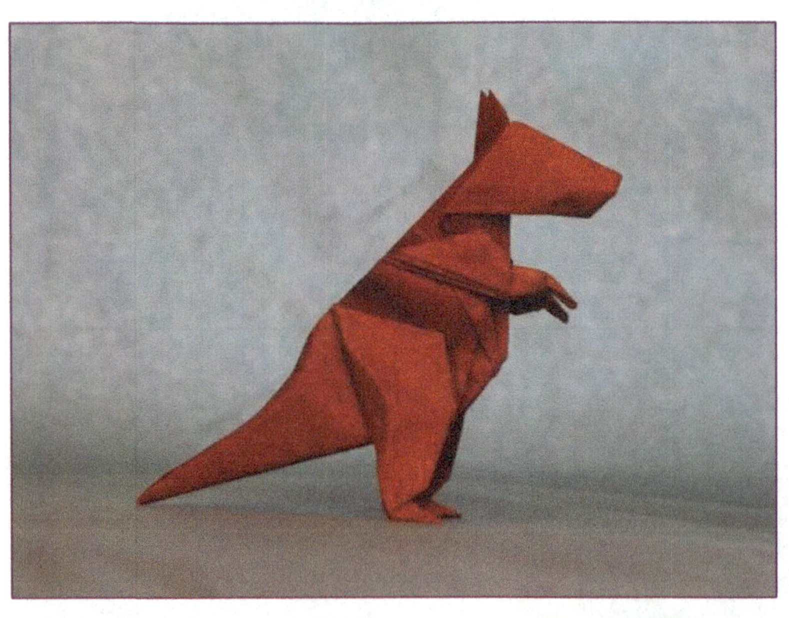

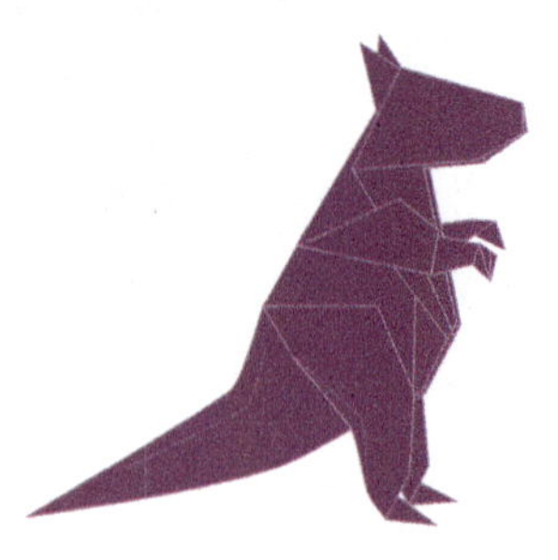

Imagine a sloth the size of an Elephant, and you have the Megatherium. Basically a prehistoric Giant Ground Sloth, the Megatherium roamed the Earth during the Pliocene and Pleistocene Epochs.

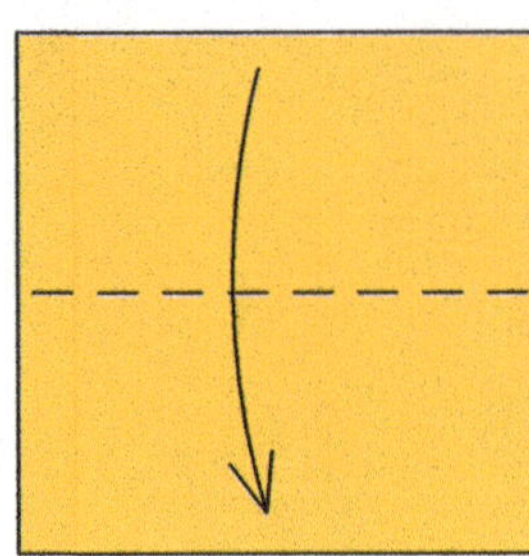

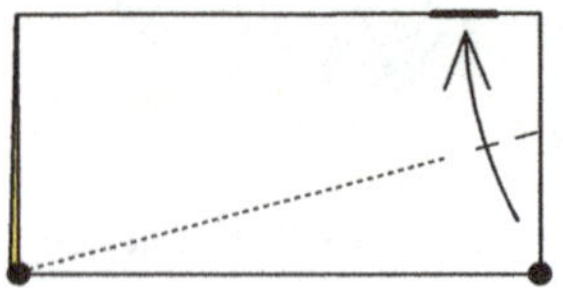

Bring the right dot to the top. Crease on the right.

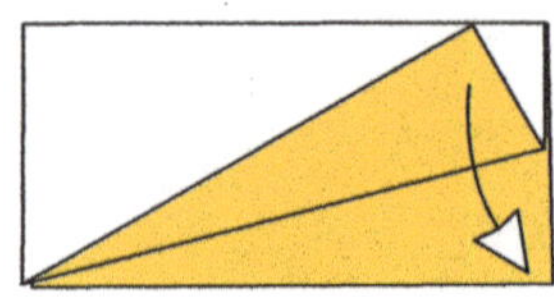

Unfold.

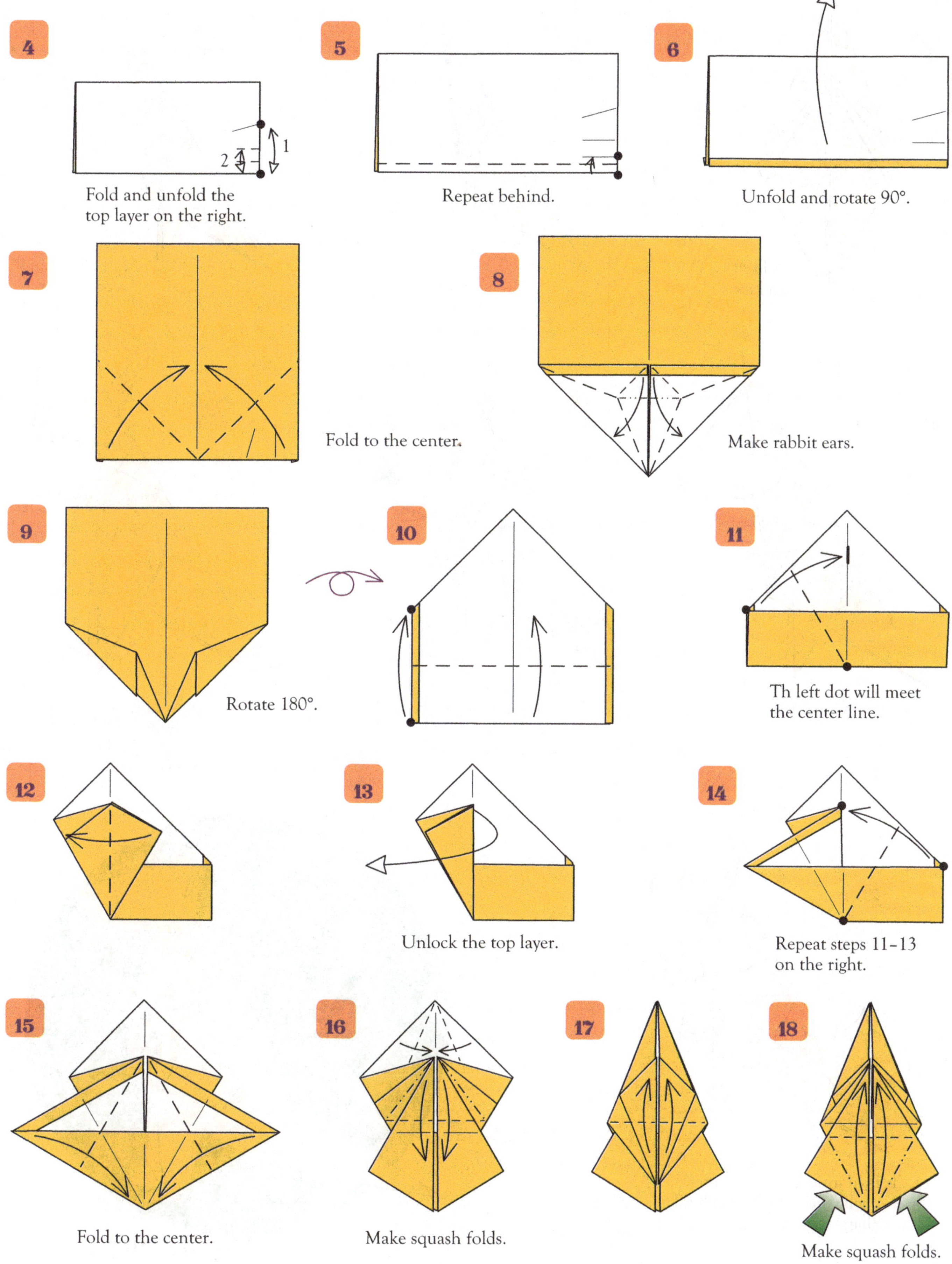

4 Fold and unfold the top layer on the right.

5 Repeat behind.

6 Unfold and rotate 90°.

7 Fold to the center.

8 Make rabbit ears.

9 Rotate 180°.

10

11 Th left dot will meet the center line.

12

13 Unlock the top layer.

14 Repeat steps 11–13 on the right.

15 Fold to the center.

16 Make squash folds.

17

18 Make squash folds.

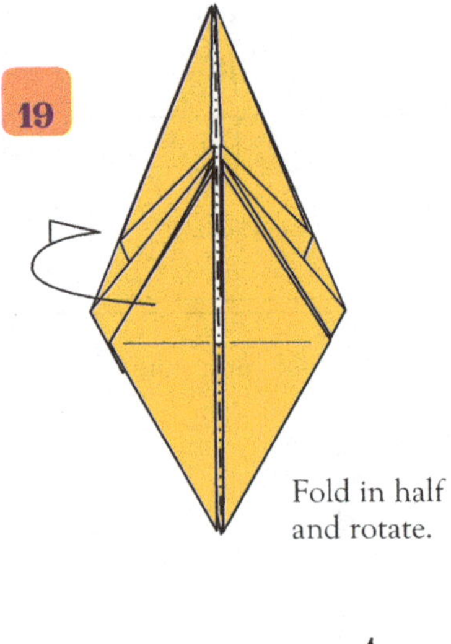

Fold in half
and rotate.

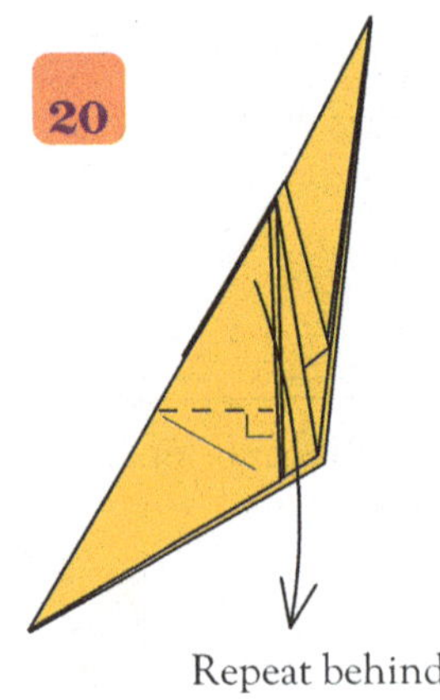

Repeat behind.

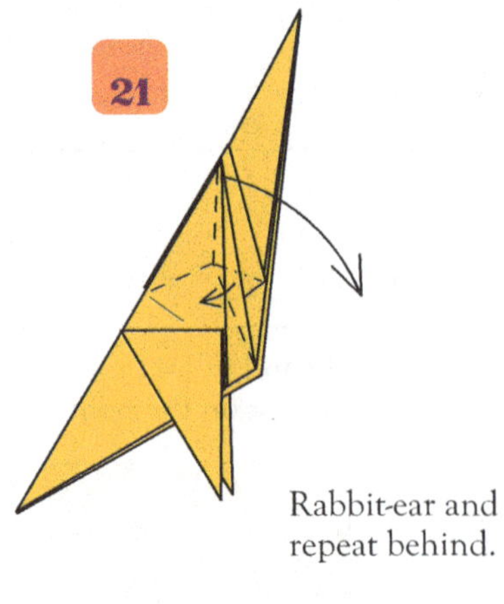

Rabbit-ear and
repeat behind.

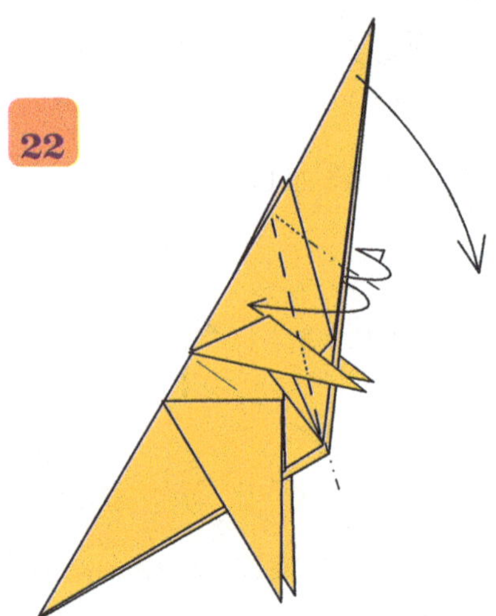

Crimp-fold.

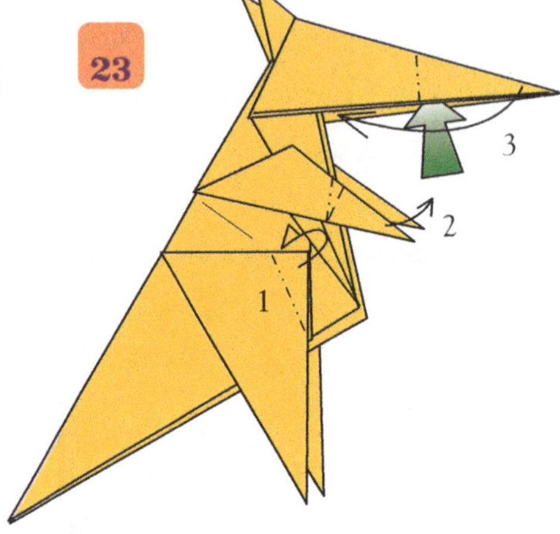

1. Fold inside, repeat behind.
2. Crimp-fold, repeat behind.
3. Reverse-fold.

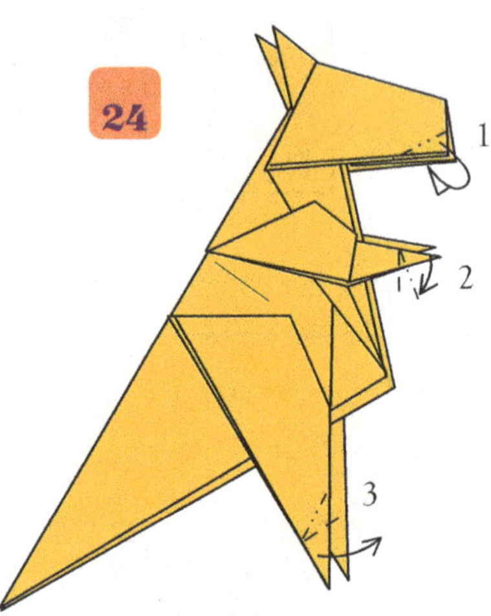

1. Fold inside.
2. Squash-fold.
3. Crimp-fold.
Repeat behind.

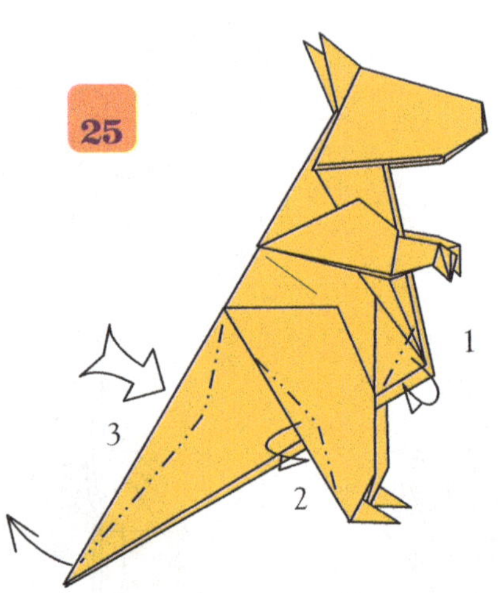
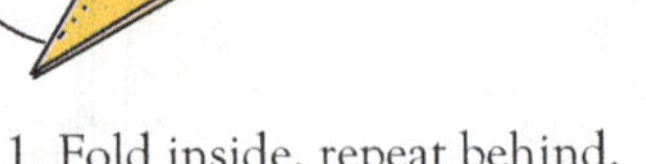

1. Fold inside, repeat behind.
2. Shape the leg, repeat behind.
3. Shape the tail.

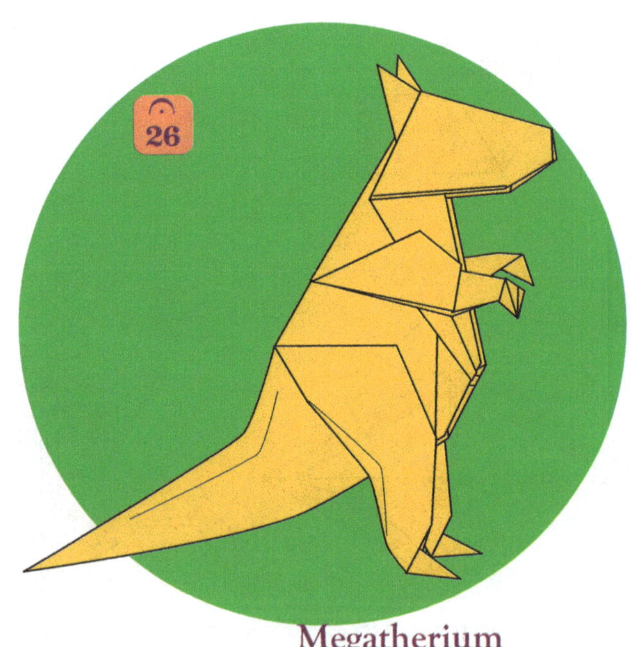

Megatherium

Glyptodon

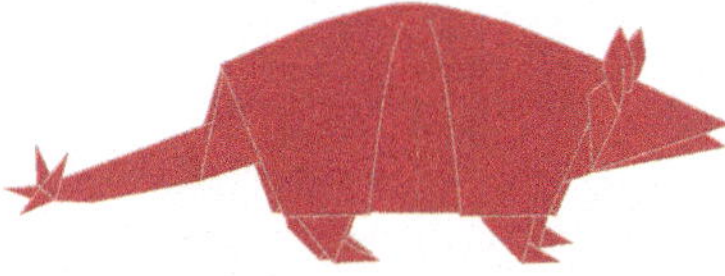

The Glyptodon was a giant prehistoric member of the Armadillo family, with a shell that also bore a resemblance to that of a Turtle. Roughly eleven feet in length and 5 feet in height, these creatures are believed to have had poor eyesight which made it difficult for them to see prey or predators.

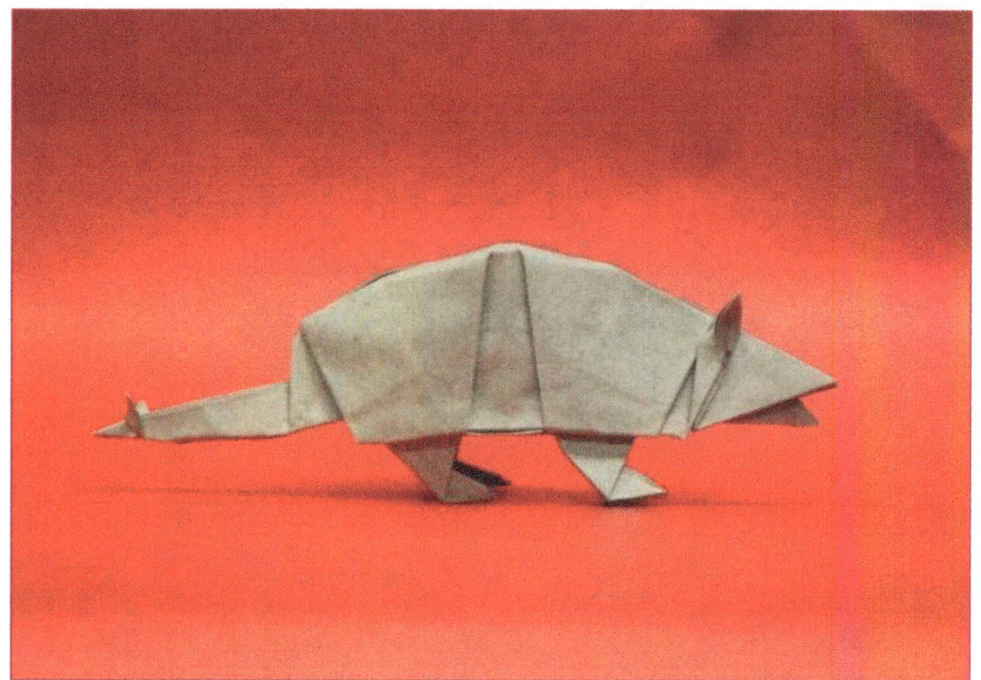

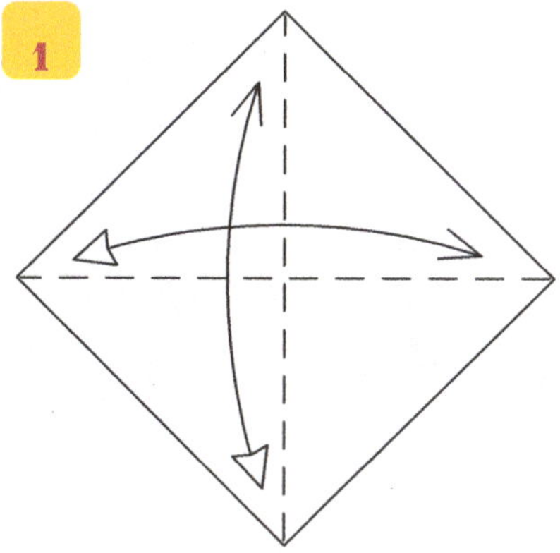

1

Fold and unfold.

2

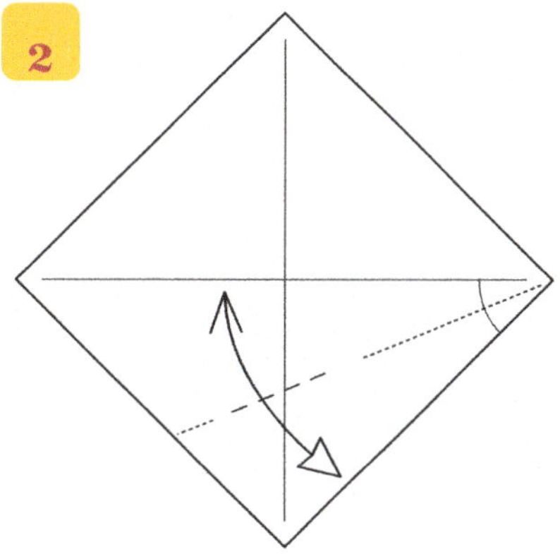

Fold and unfold on the diagonal.

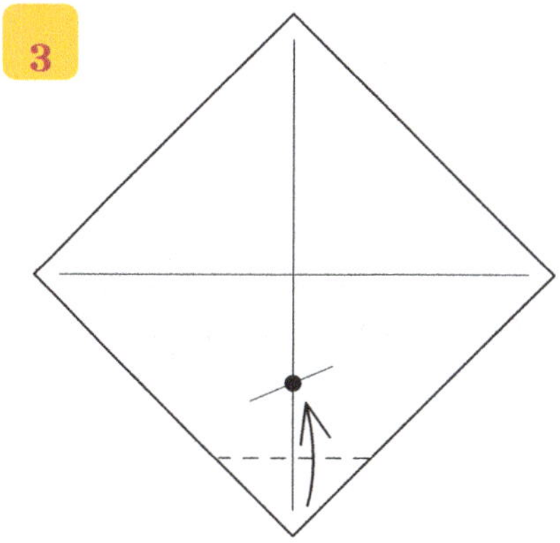

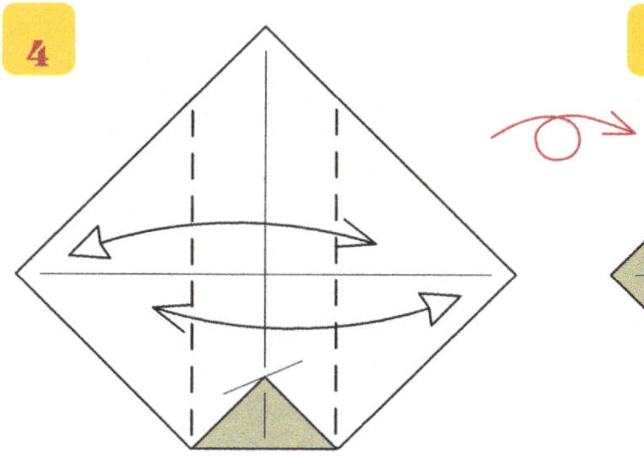

3

4

Fold and unfold.

5

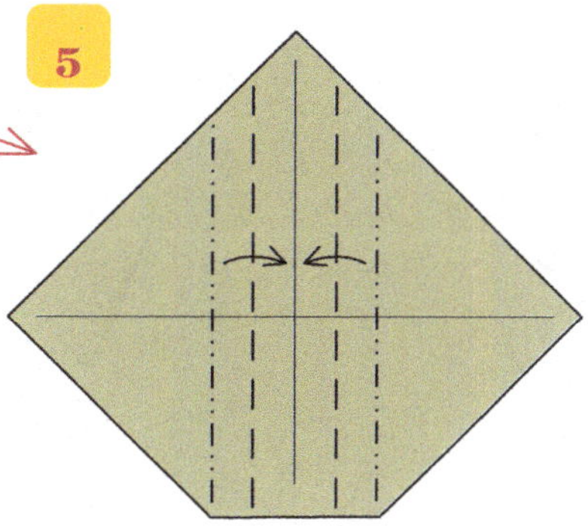

Pleat-fold to the center.

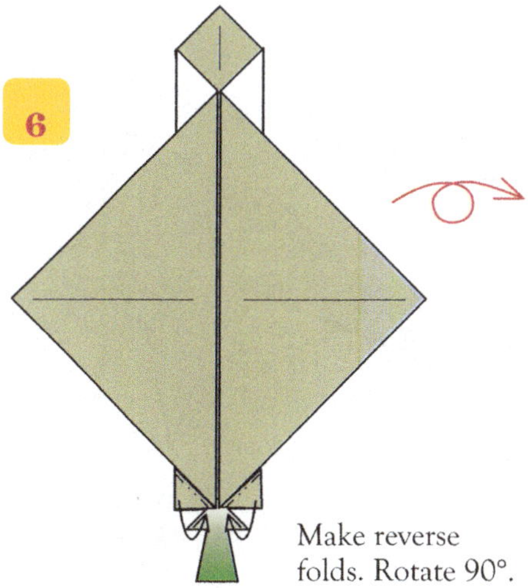

6

Make reverse folds. Rotate 90°.

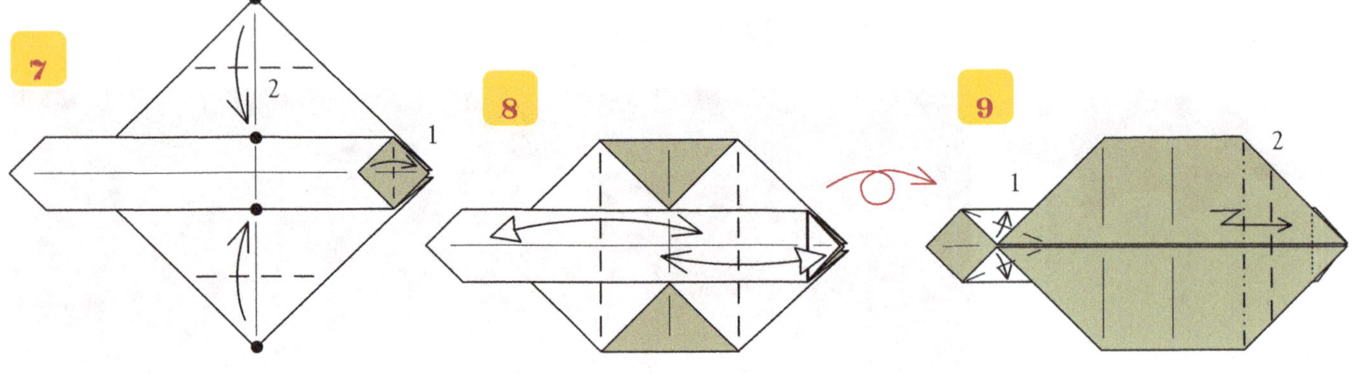

Make three valley folds.

Fold and unfold.

1. Make valley folds.
2. Pleat-fold a little to the
   left of the dotted line.

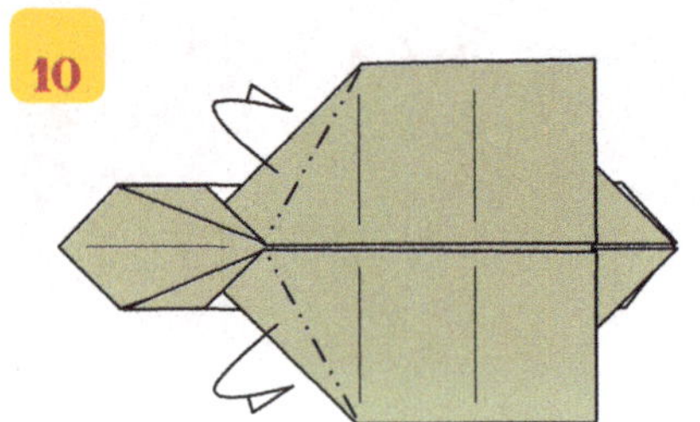

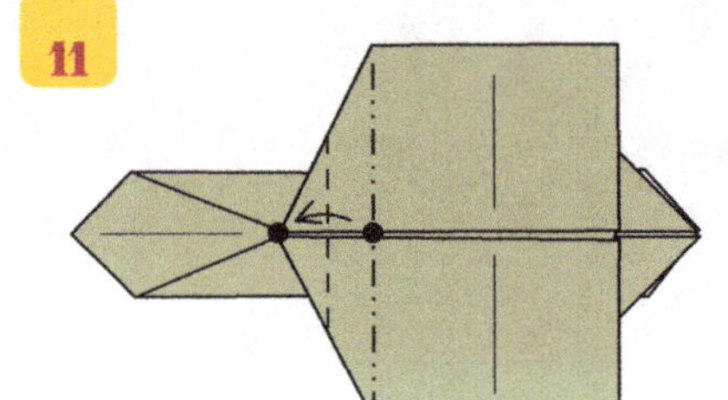

Pleat-fold so the dots meet.

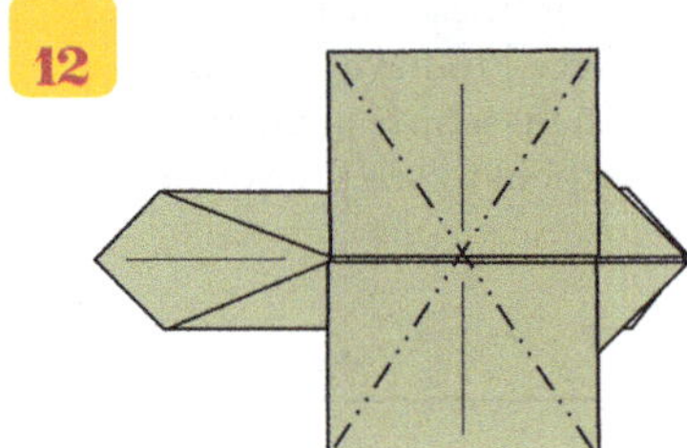

Fold and unfold.

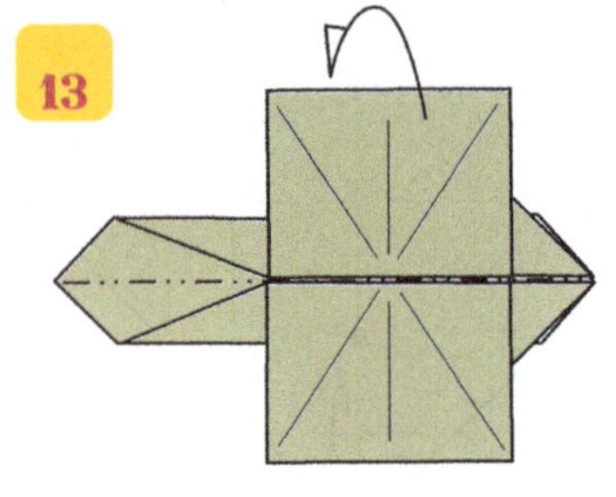

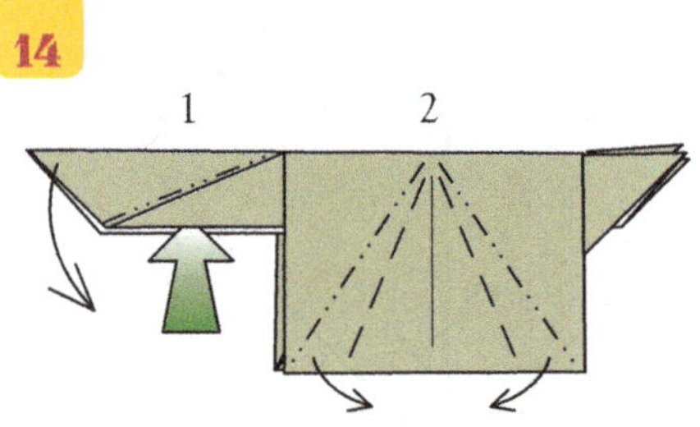

1. Reverse-fold.
2. Make crimp fold.

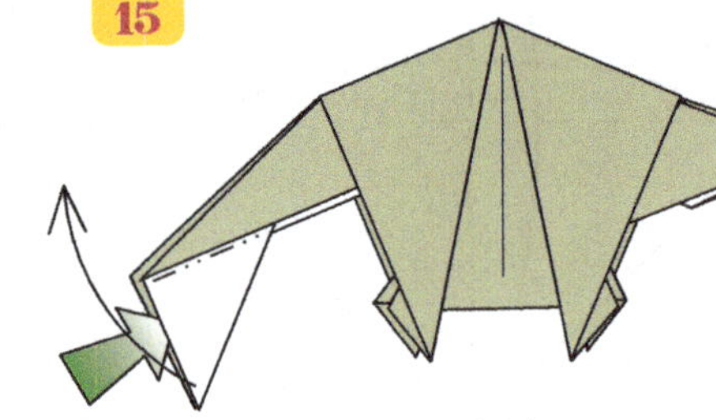

Reverse-fold.

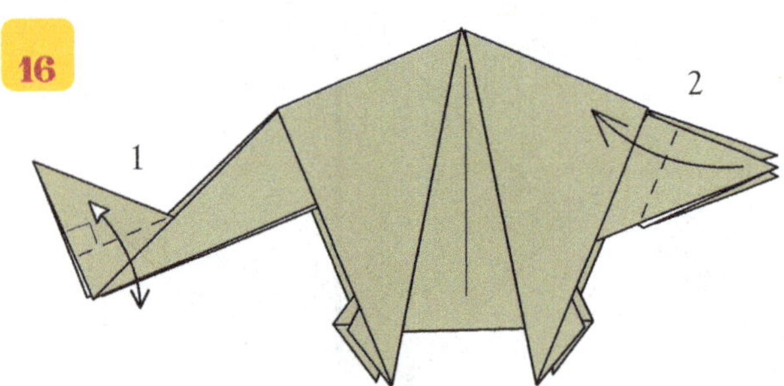

1. Fold and unfold.
2. Repeat behind.

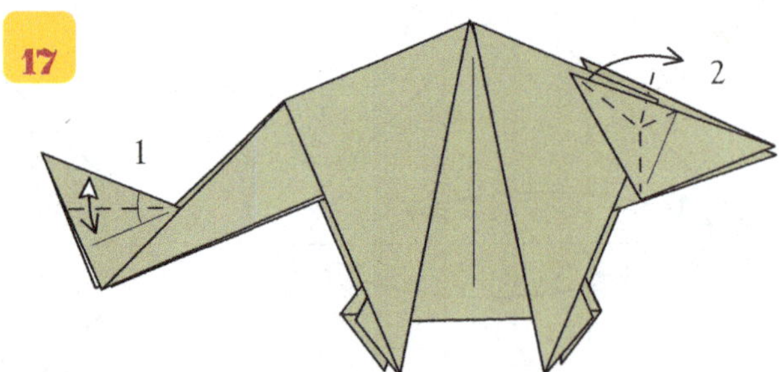

1. Fold and unfold.
2. Rabbit-ear,
   repeat behind.

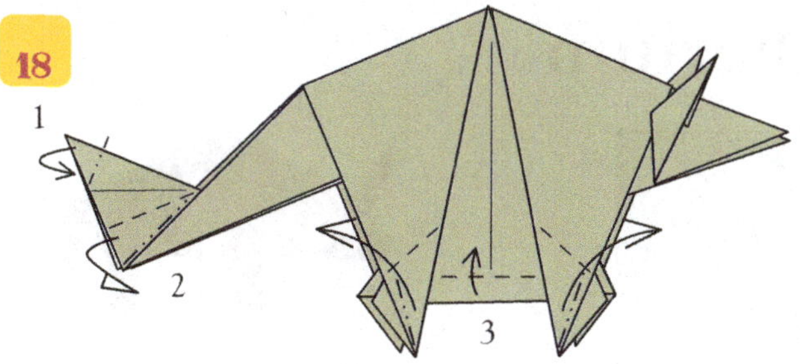

1. Reverse-fold.
2. Crimp-fold.
3. Petal-fold, repeat behind.

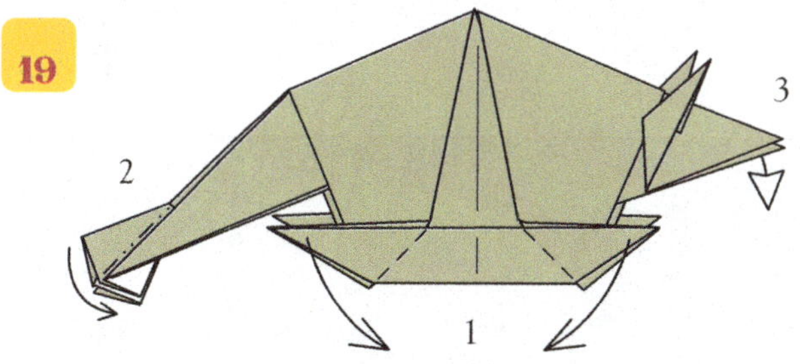

1. Repeat behind.
2. Reverse-fold.
3. Pull the mouth down.

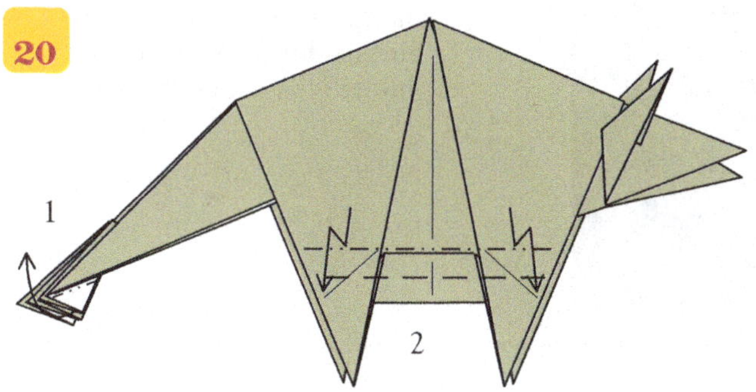

1. Reverse-fold three times.
2. Pleat-fold and spread the
   legs, repeat behind.

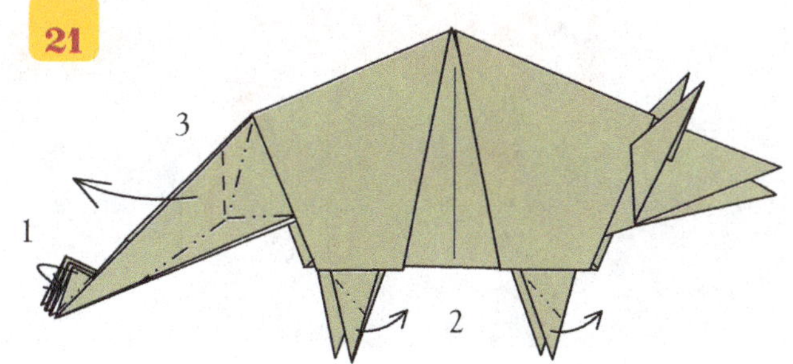

1. Reverse-fold three times.
2. Make reverse-folds, repeat behind.
3. Double-rabbit-ear the tail.

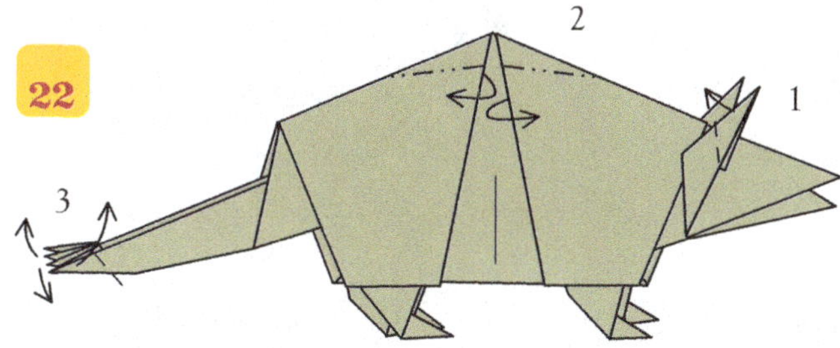

1. Open and shape the ear.
2. Spread at the top to make the body 3D.
3. Fold one spike up, spread the center ones.
Repeat behind.

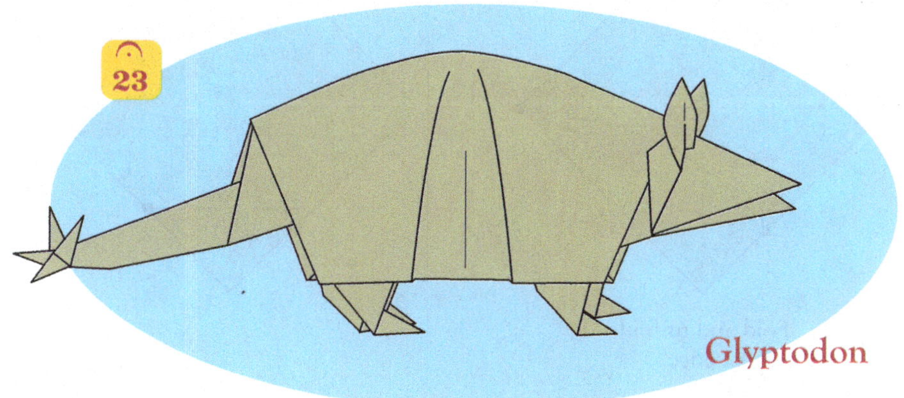

Glyptodon

Elasmotherium

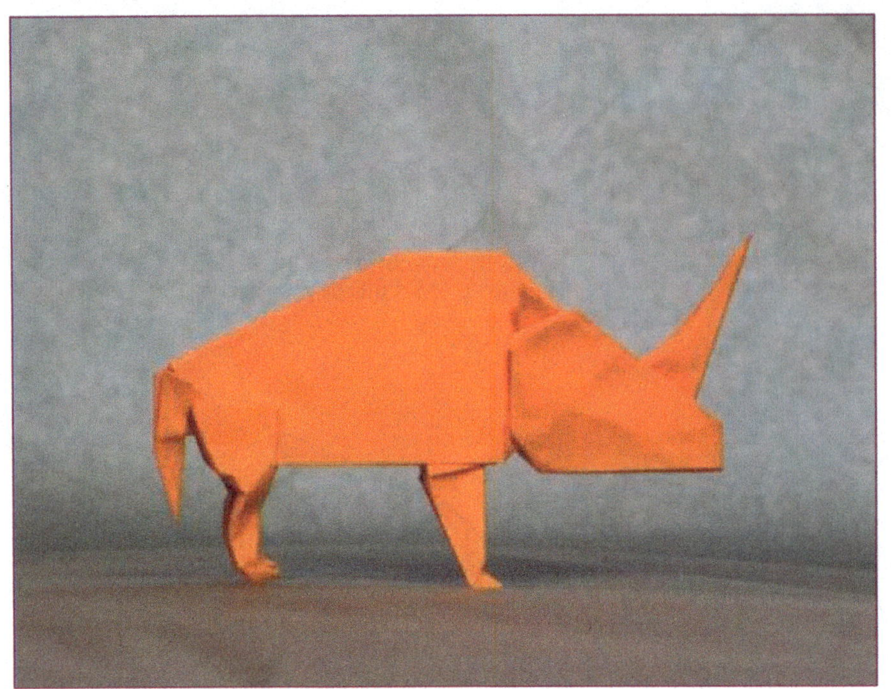

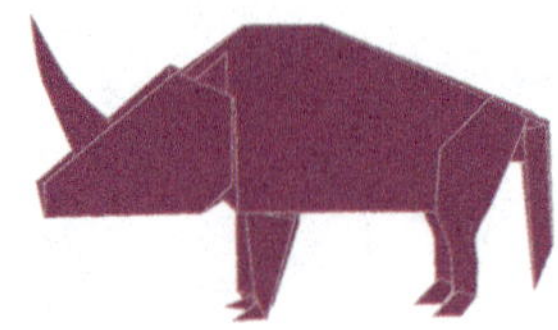

A prehistoric, furry form of Rhinoceros, the Elasmotherium had a distinctive long horn on its snout. The Elasmotherium roamed Eurasia during the Late Pliocene through the Late Pleistocene.

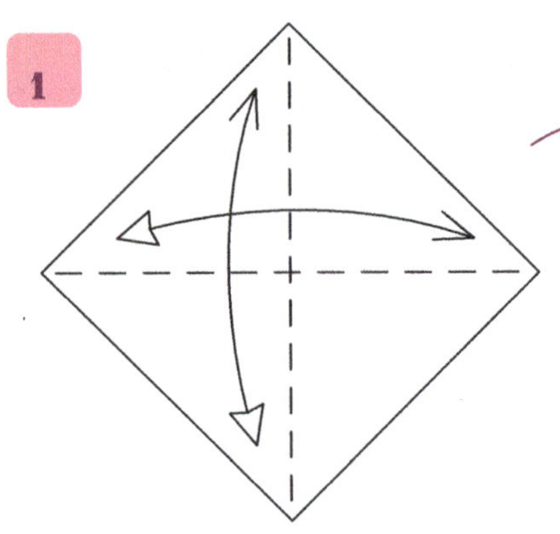

1 Fold and unfold.

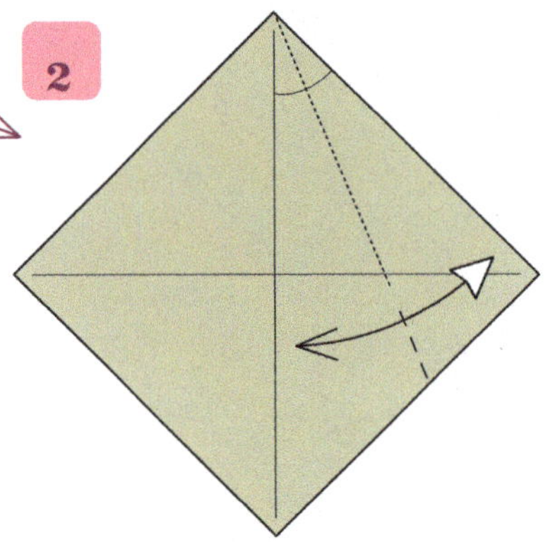

2 Fold and unfold on the edge.

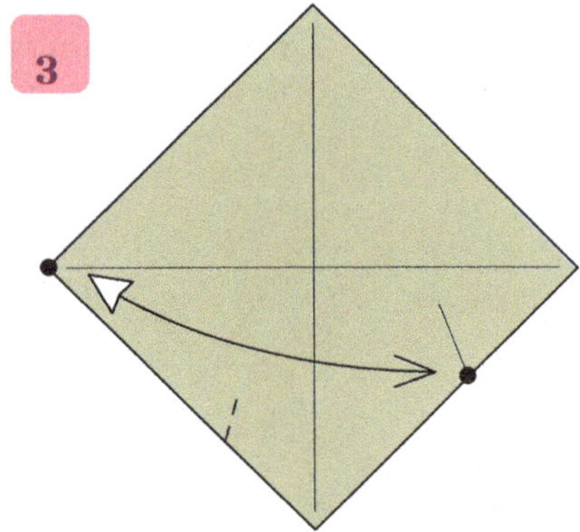

3 Fold and unfold on the edge.

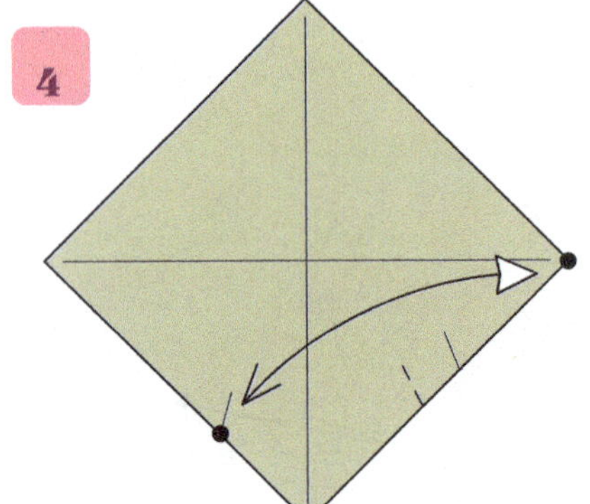

4 Fold and unfold on the edge.

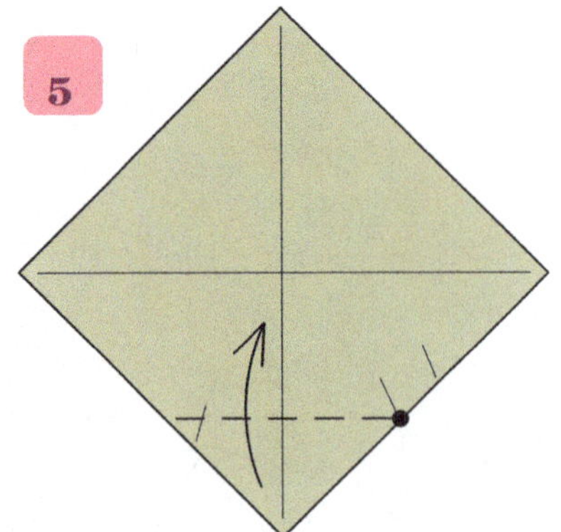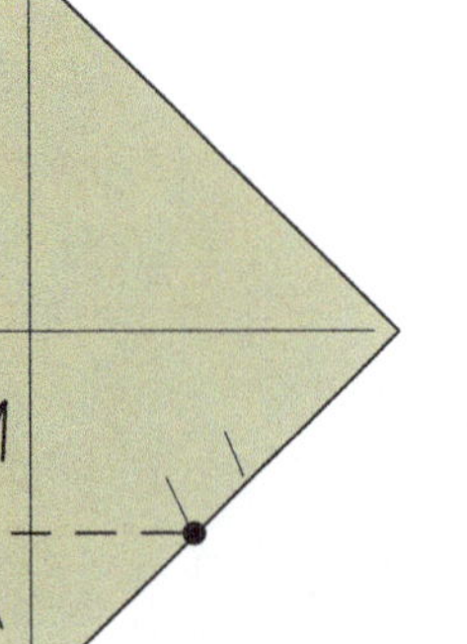

5

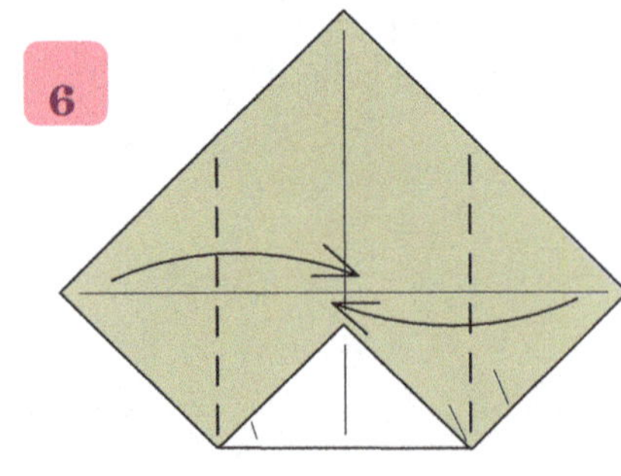

6

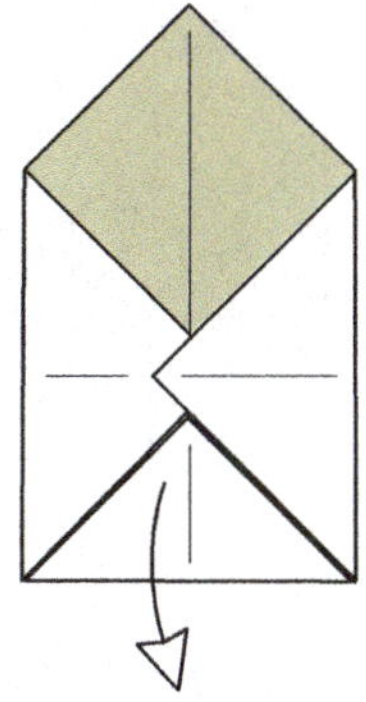

Unfold.

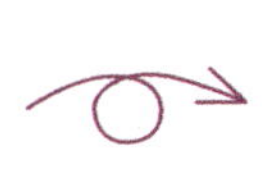 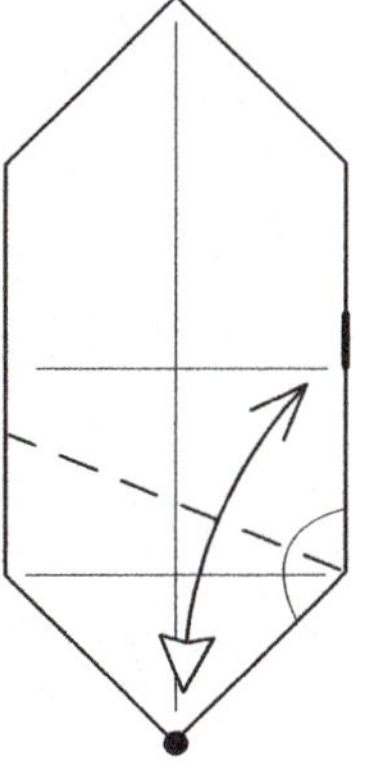

Fold and unfold.

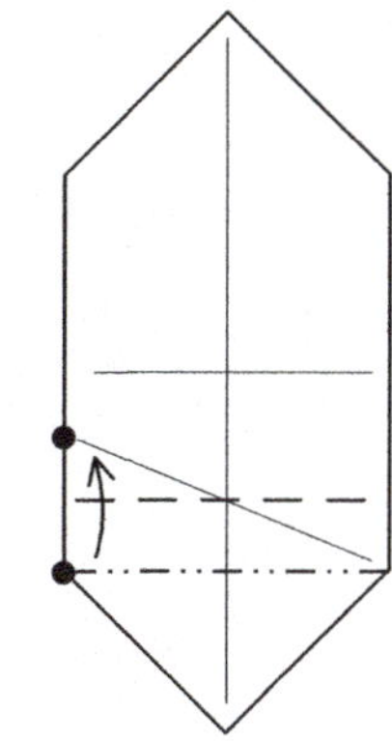

Pleat-fold.

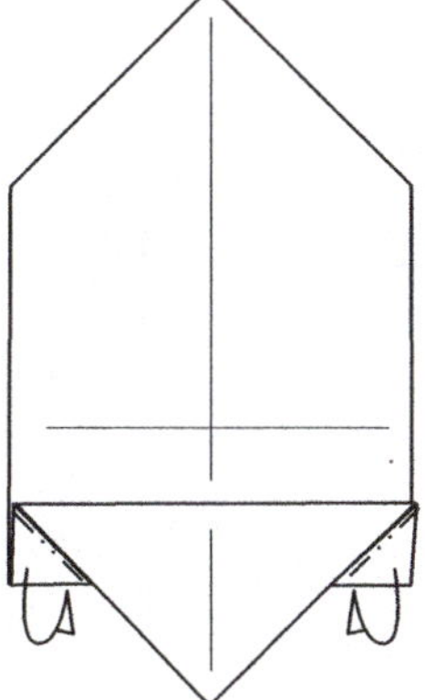

Fold behind.

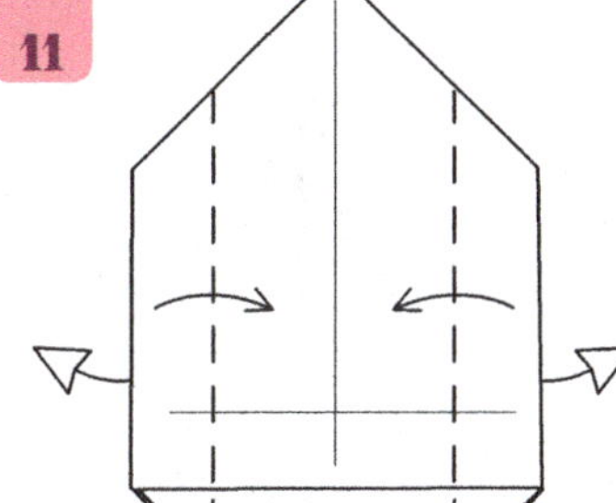

Fold towards the center and
swing out from behind.

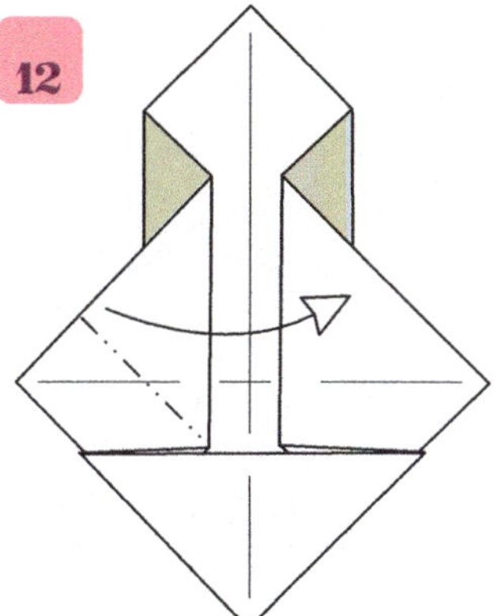

Pull out.

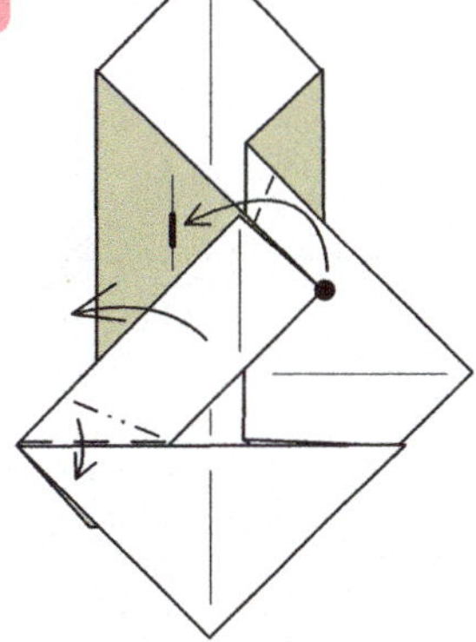

Squash-fold so the dot
meets on the line.

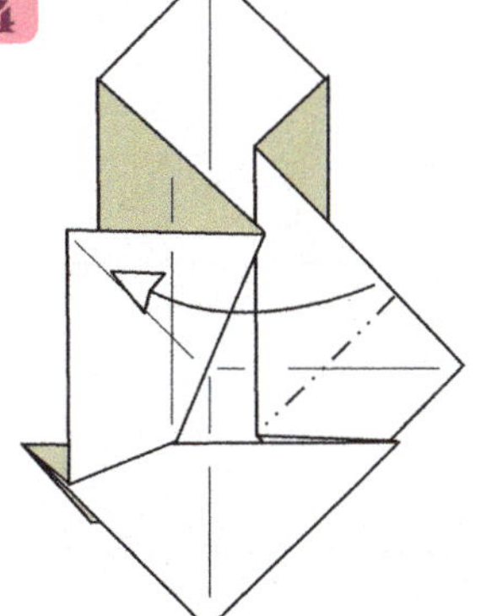

Repeat steps 12–13
on the right.

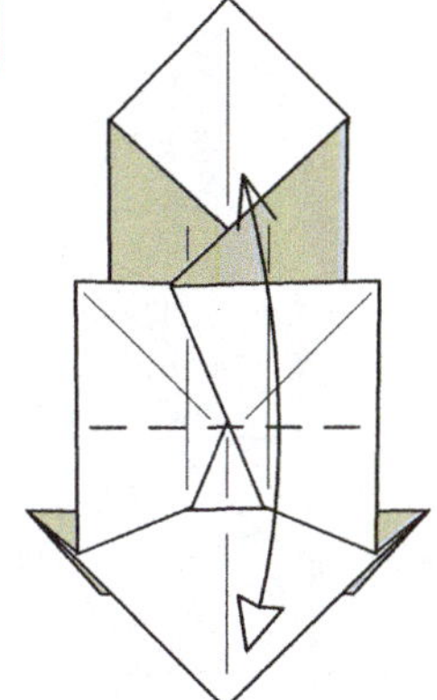

Fold and unfold along
a hidden crease. Turn
over to see the crease.

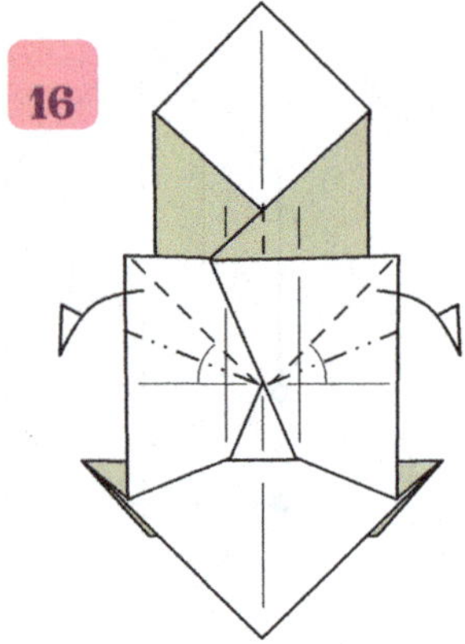

Make squash folds.

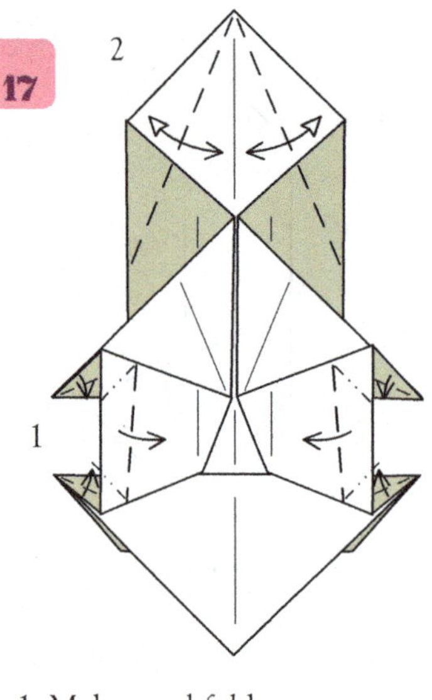

1. Make petal folds.
2. Fold to the center and unfold.

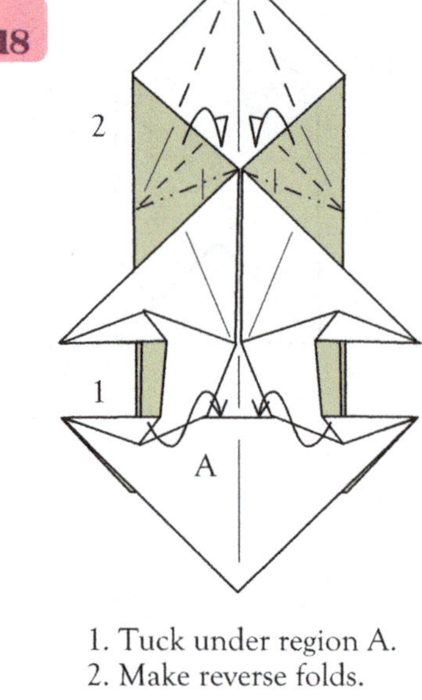

1. Tuck under region A.
2. Make reverse folds.

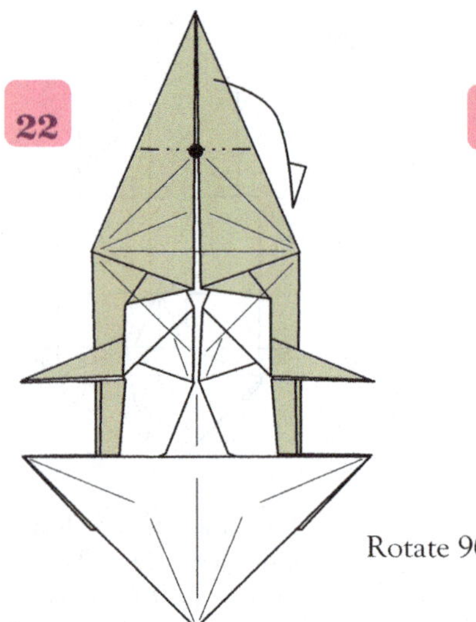

1. Fold and unfold on the
   left and right.
2. This is a combination of
   two squash folds, on the
   left and right.

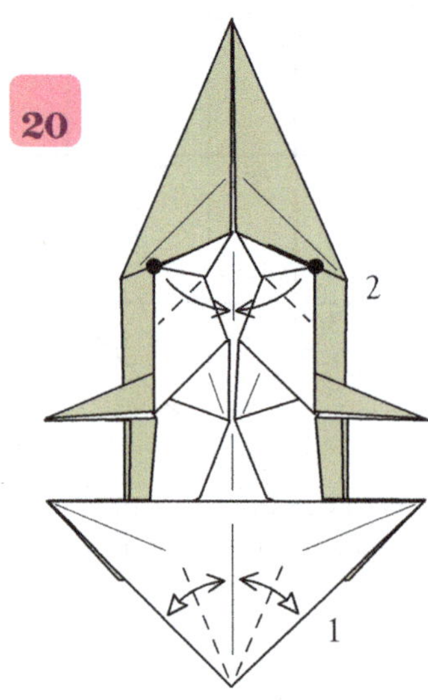

1. Fold and unfold.
2. Bring the dots to the center.

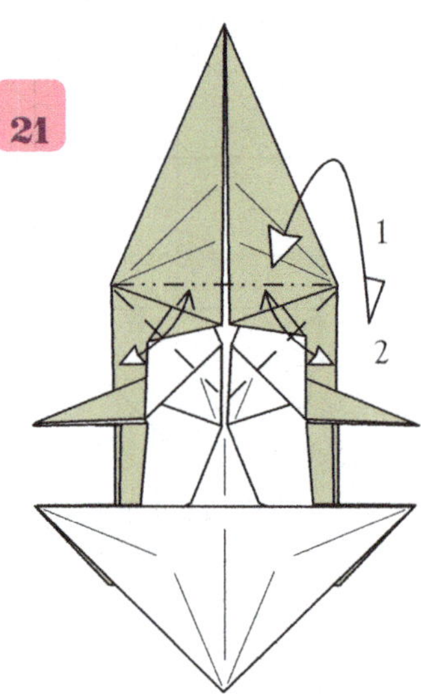

1. Fold and unfold.
2. Fold and unfold on
   the left and right.

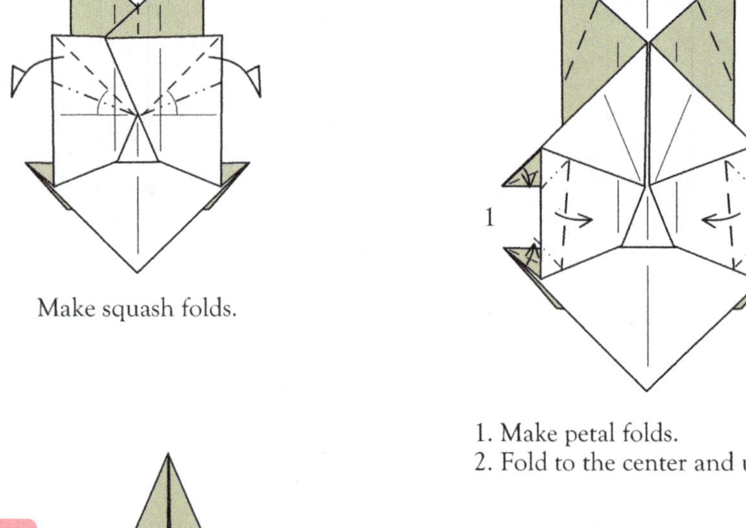

Rotate 90°.

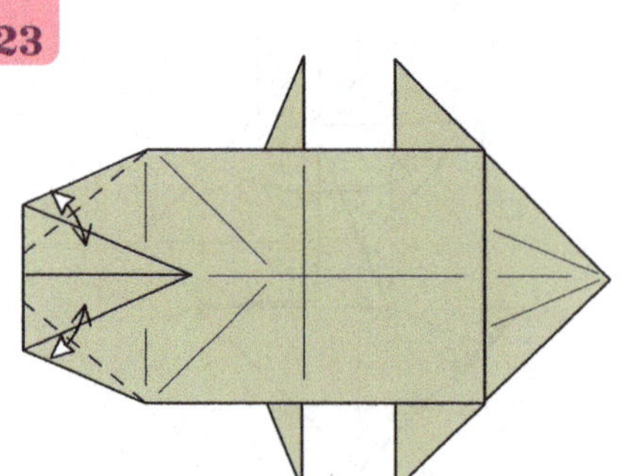

Fold and unfold.

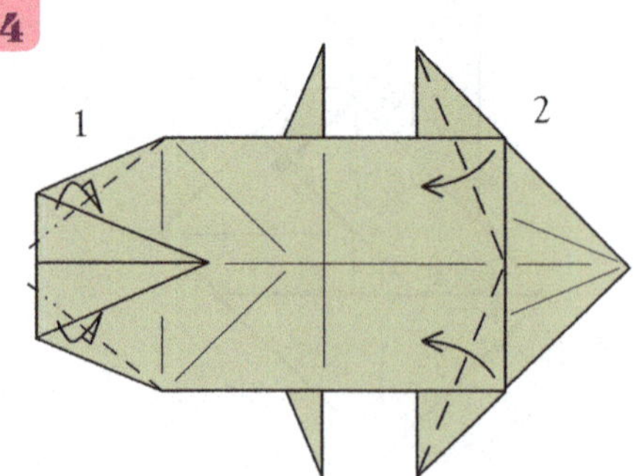

1. Make reverse folds.
2. Fold in front.

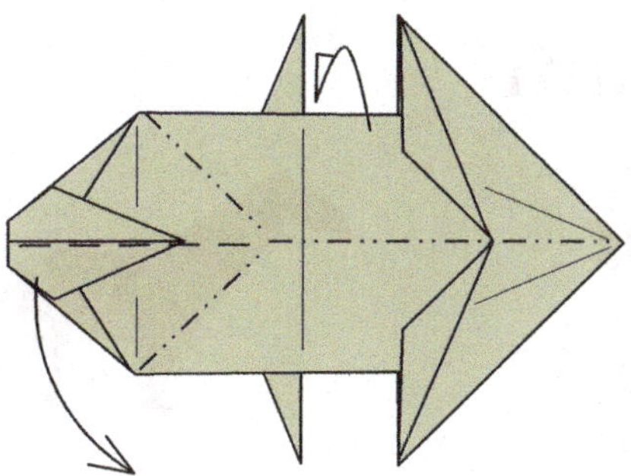

25

Fold along the creases.

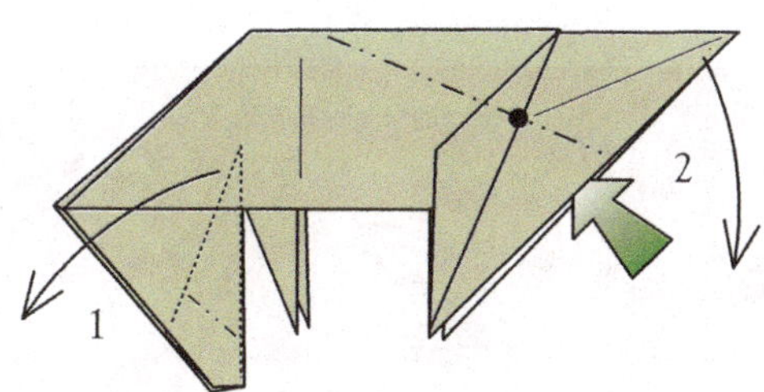

26

1. Reverse-fold.
2. Reverse-fold.

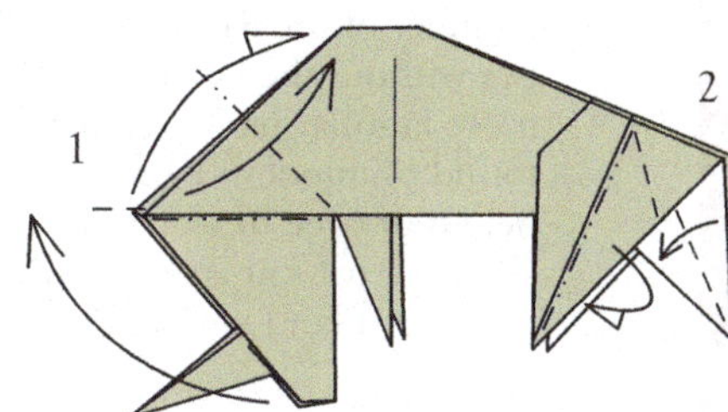

27

1. Crimp-fold.
2. Fold inside to thin
   the tail, repeat behind.

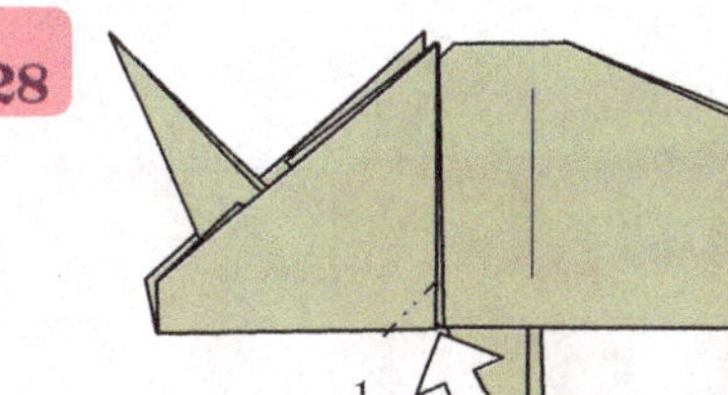

28

1. Spread the paper to sink.
2. Reverse-fold.

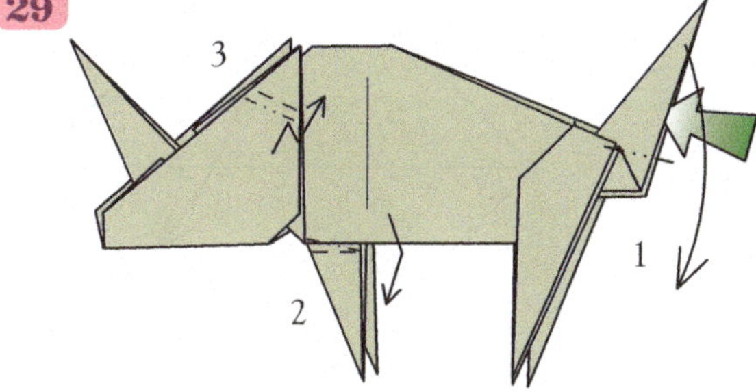

29

1. Reverse-fold.
2. Crimp-fold, repeat behind.
3. Pleat-fold, repeat behind.

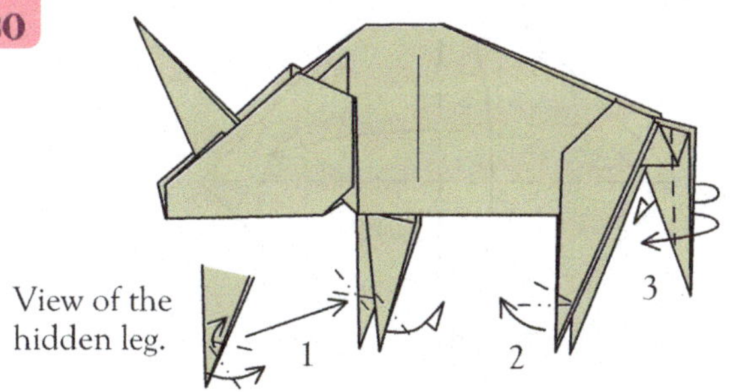

30

View of the hidden leg.

1. Squash-fold, repeat behind.
2. Spread and crimp-fold, repeat behind.
3. Outside-reverse-fold.

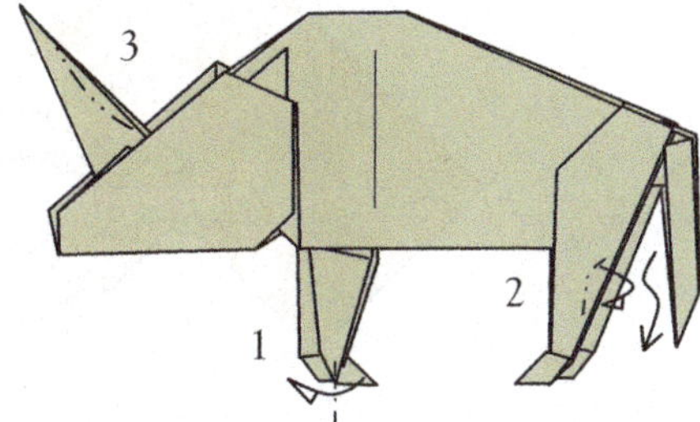

31

1. Fold the foot, repeat behind.
2. Shape the leg, repeat behind.
3. Shape the horn.

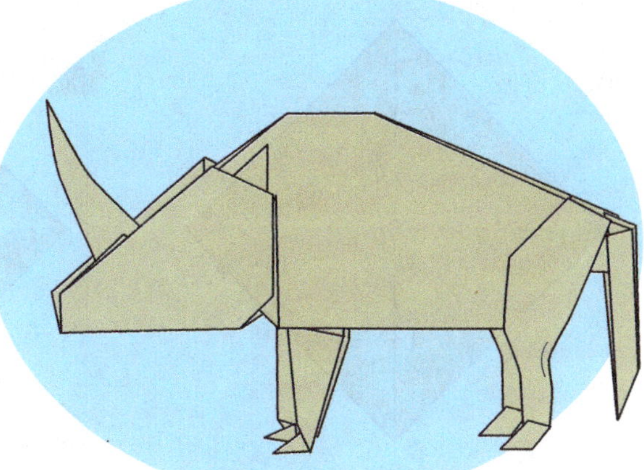

32

Elasmotherium

Baluchitherium

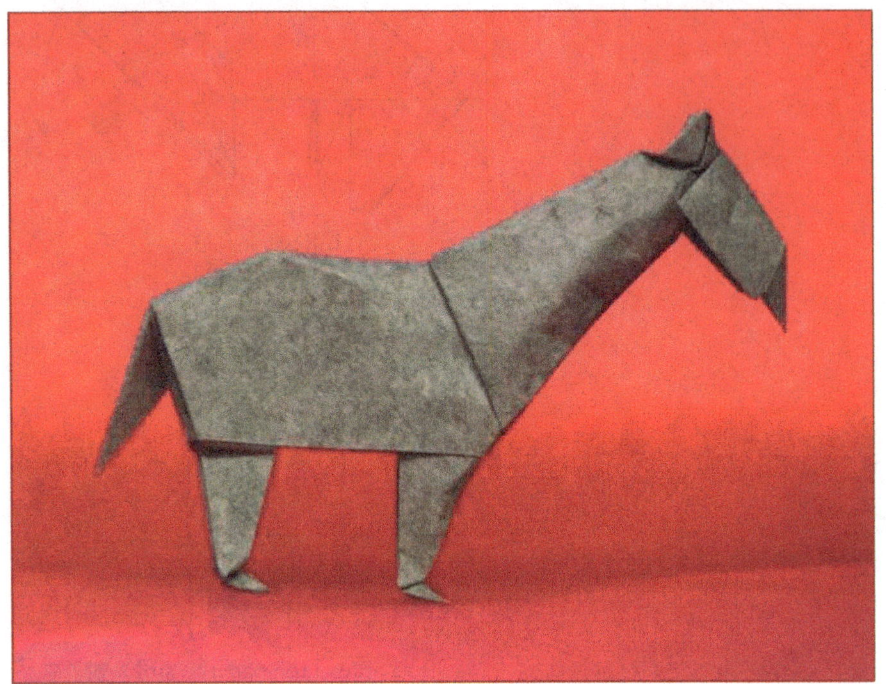

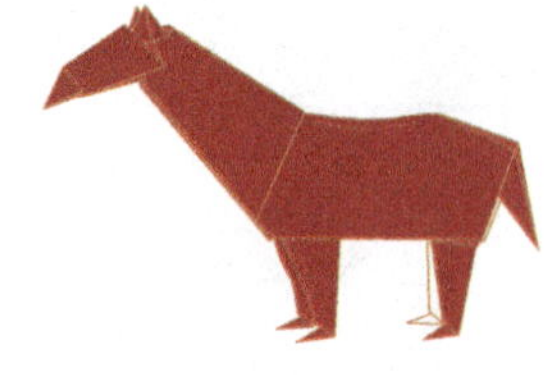

Like the Elasmotherium, the Baluchitherium is also an early member of the Rhinoceros family, but without the horn and with the more familiar hairless, leathery skin found on modern Rhinos. With a height of over 18 feet and weight of about 10 tons, it is probably one of the largest land mammals.

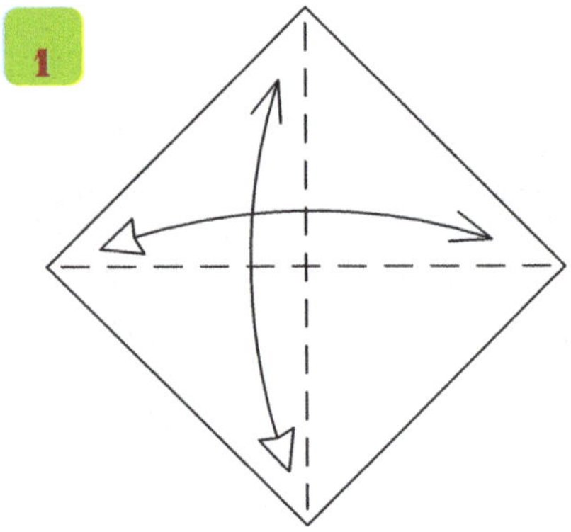

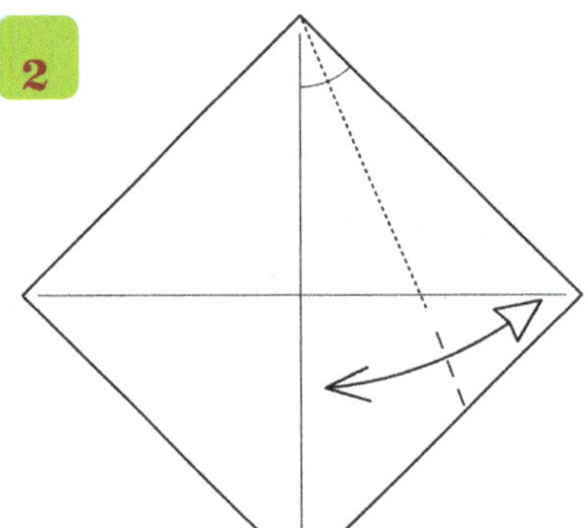

Fold and unfold.

Fold and unfold on the edge.

Fold and unfold on the edge.

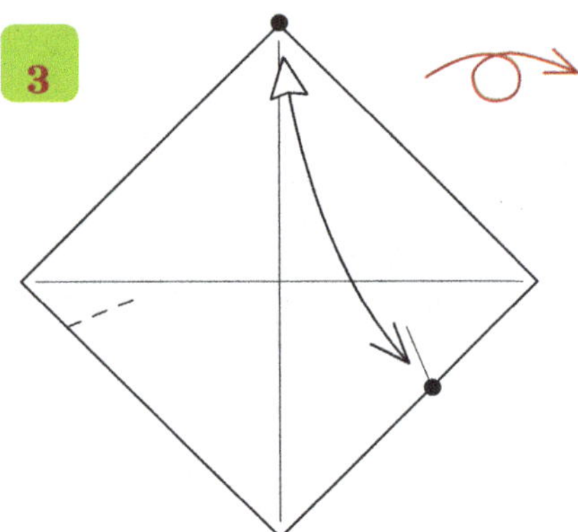

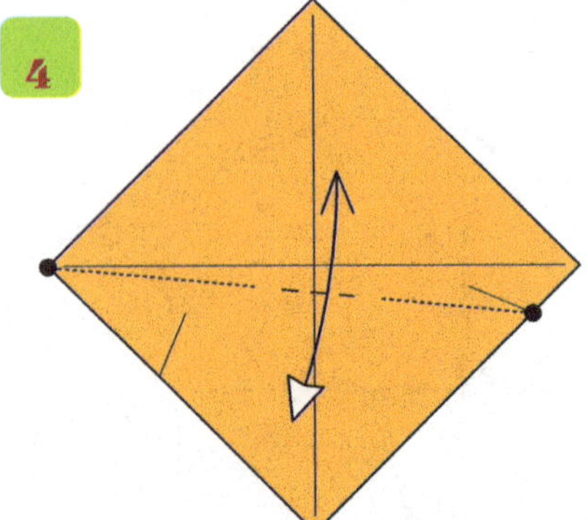

Fold and unfold on the diagonal.

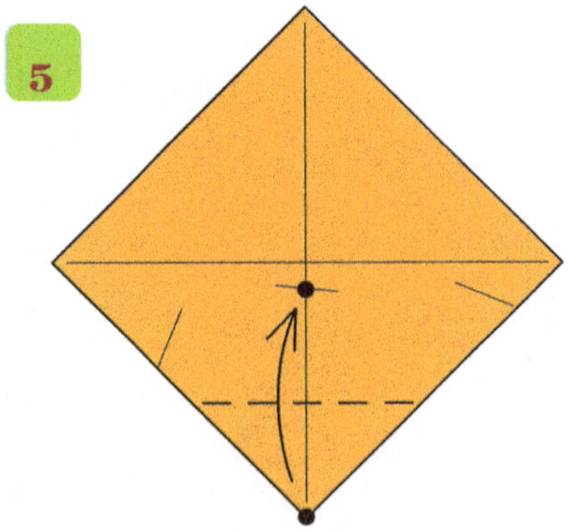

The dots will meet.

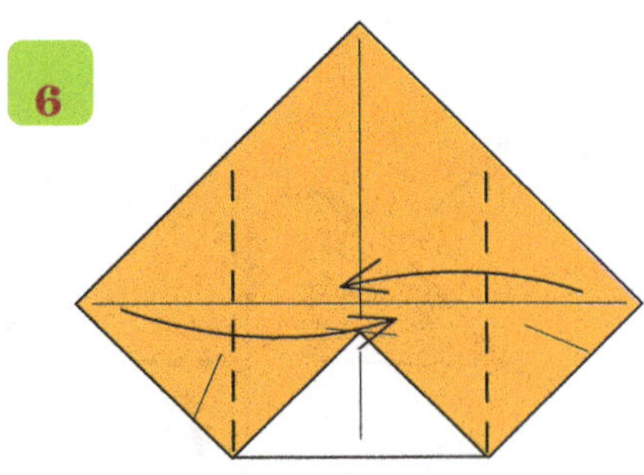

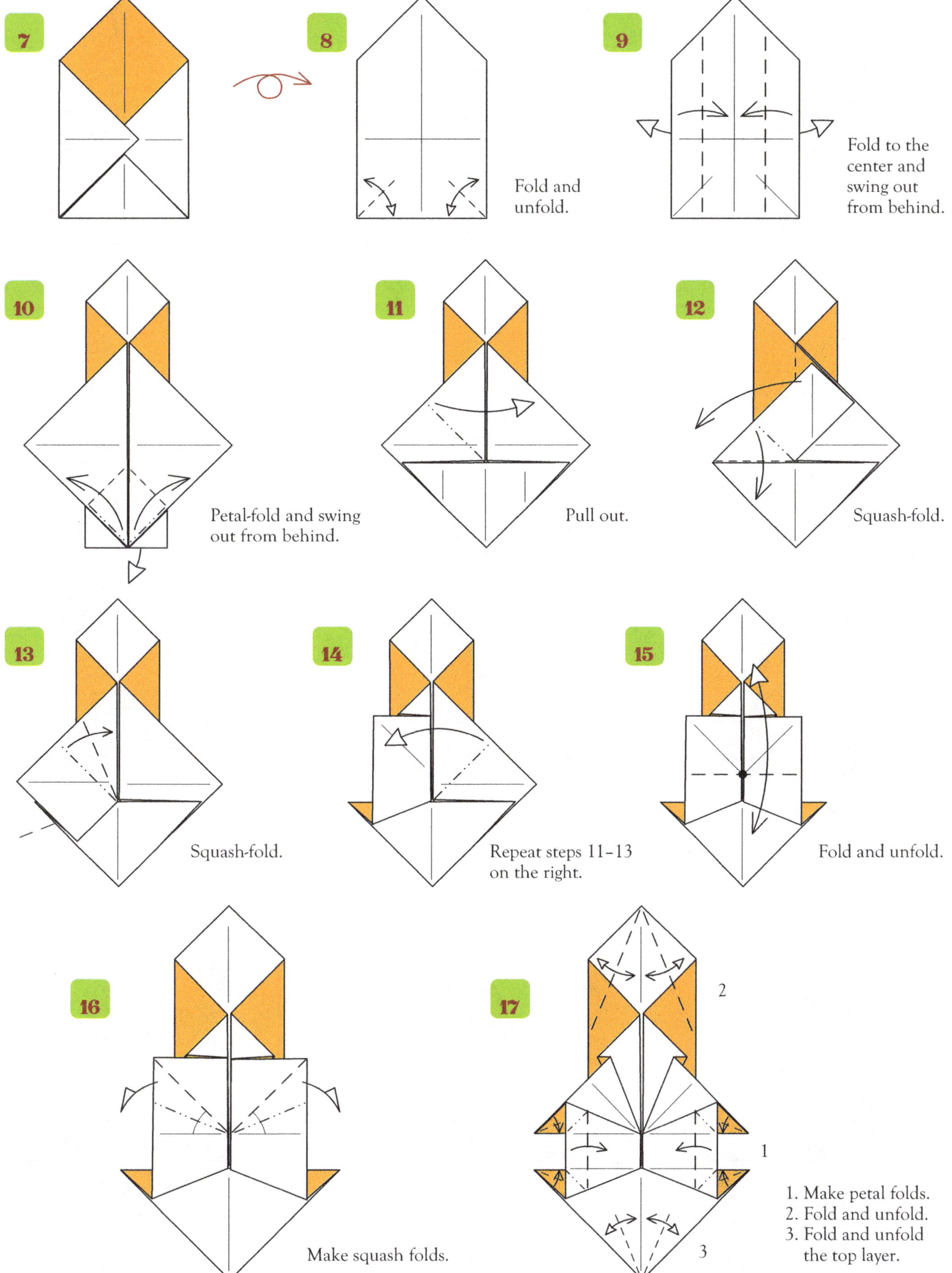

7
8
Fold and unfold.
9
Fold to the center and swing out from behind.
10
Petal-fold and swing out from behind.
11
Pull out.
12
Squash-fold.
13
Squash-fold.
14
Repeat steps 11–13 on the right.
15
Fold and unfold.
16
Make squash folds.
17
1
2
3
1. Make petal folds.
2. Fold and unfold.
3. Fold and unfold the top layer.

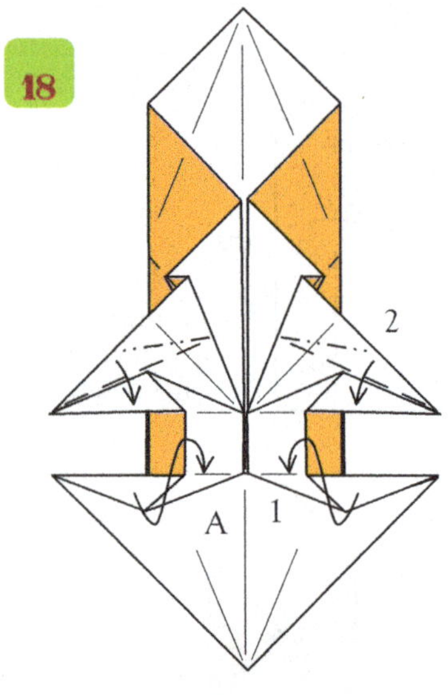

1. Tuck under region A.
2. Make squash folds.

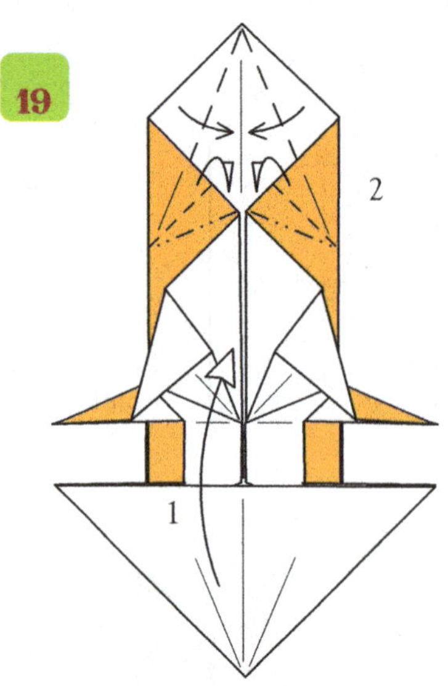

1. Unfold.
2. This is similar to
   a reverse fold.

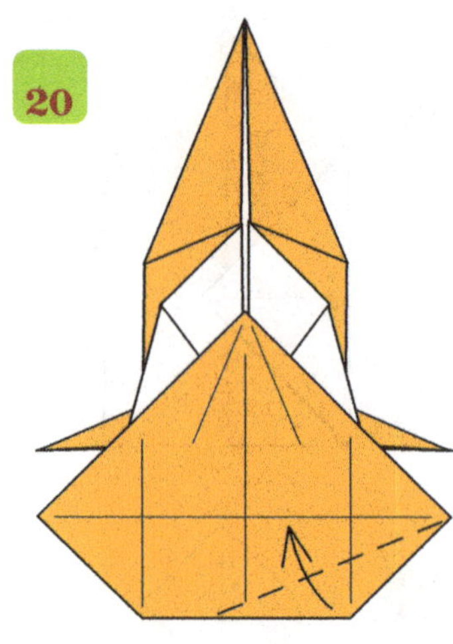

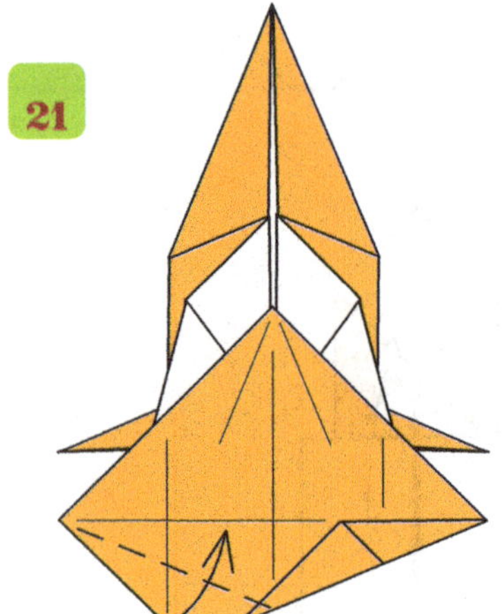

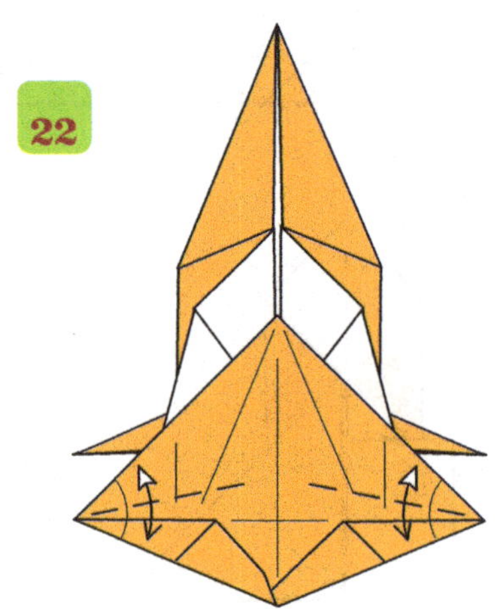

Fold and unfold.

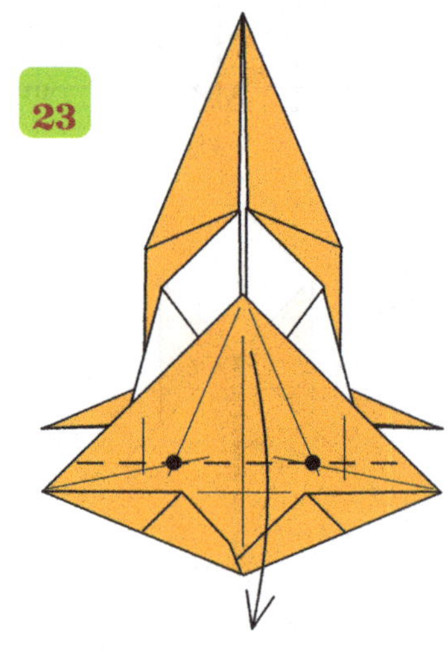

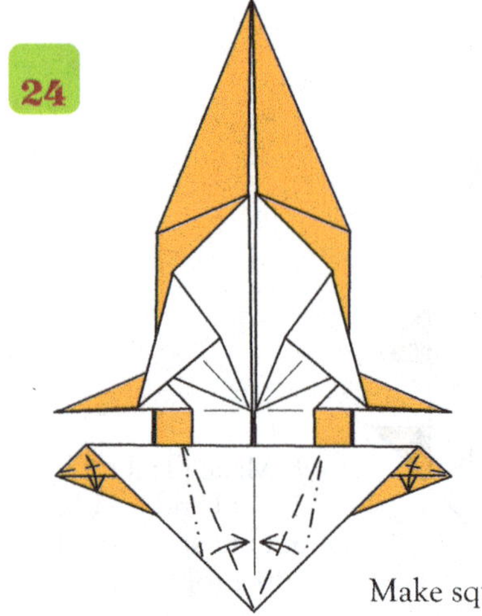

Make squash folds.

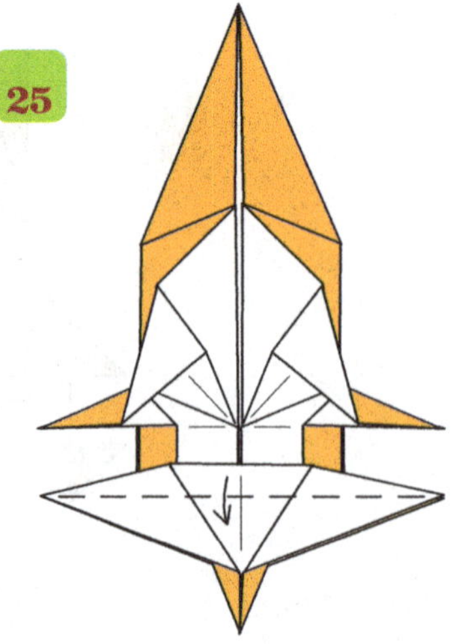

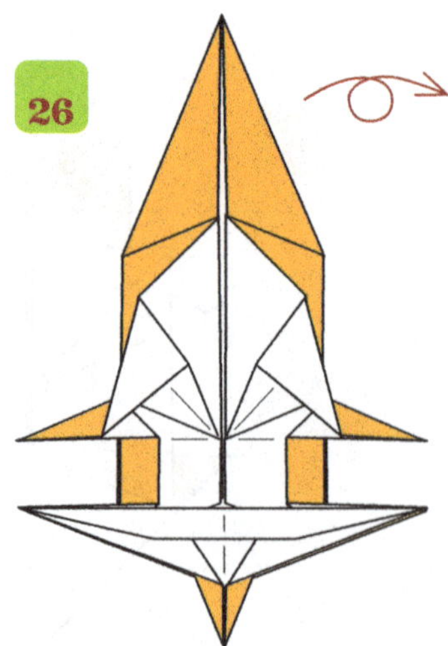

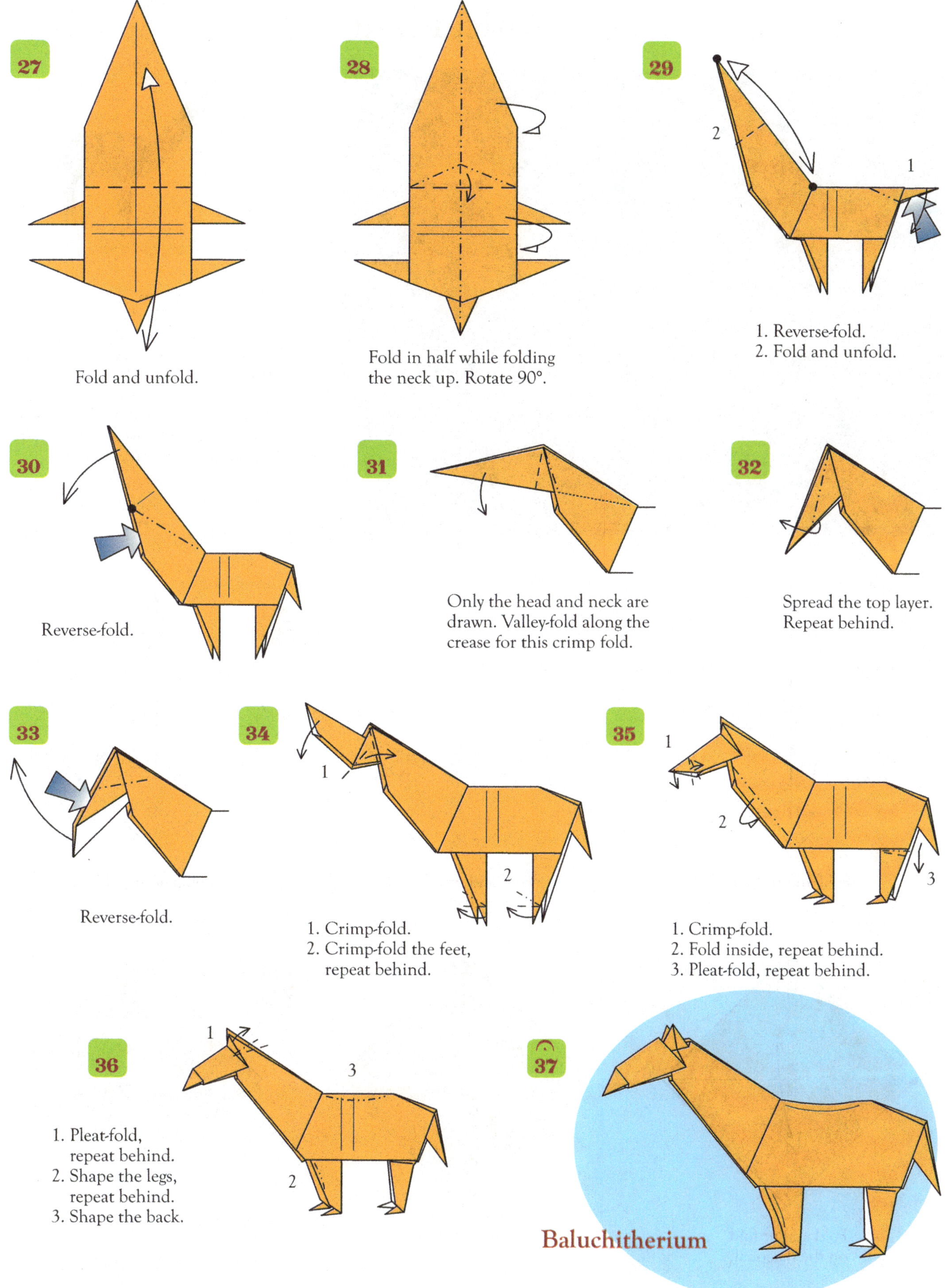

27 Fold and unfold.

28 Fold in half while folding the neck up. Rotate 90°.

29
1. Reverse-fold.
2. Fold and unfold.

30 Reverse-fold.

31 Only the head and neck are drawn. Valley-fold along the crease for this crimp fold.

32 Spread the top layer. Repeat behind.

33 Reverse-fold.

34
1. Crimp-fold.
2. Crimp-fold the feet, repeat behind.

35
1. Crimp-fold.
2. Fold inside, repeat behind.
3. Pleat-fold, repeat behind.

36
1. Pleat-fold, repeat behind.
2. Shape the legs, repeat behind.
3. Shape the back.

37 Baluchitherium

Alticamelus

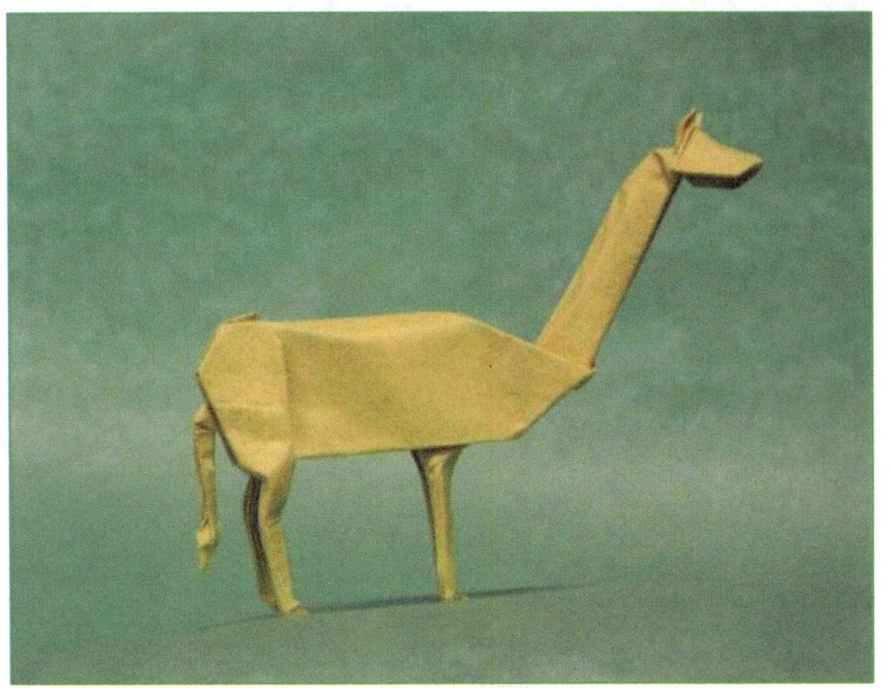

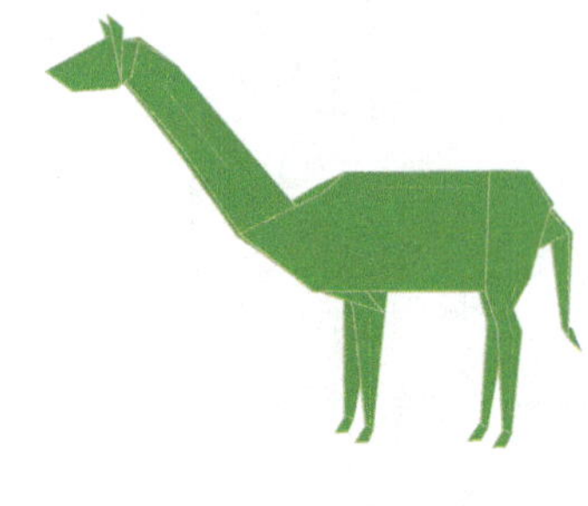

Looking like a cross between a Camel and a Giraffe, these long-necked, furry relatives of the Camel lived during the Miocene. They are now also known as Aepycamelus and lived on the prairies of prehistoric North America.

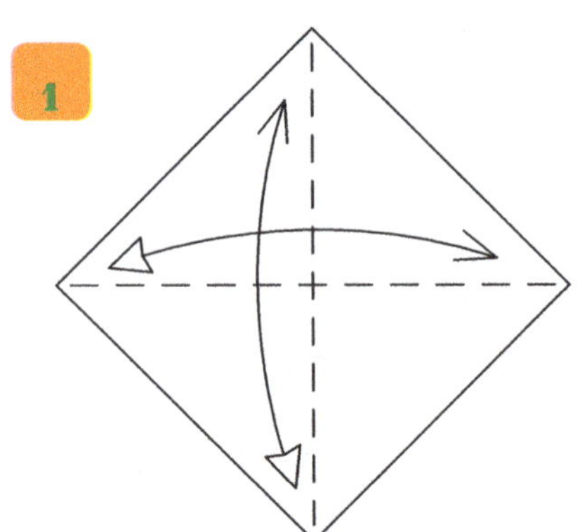

Fold and unfold.

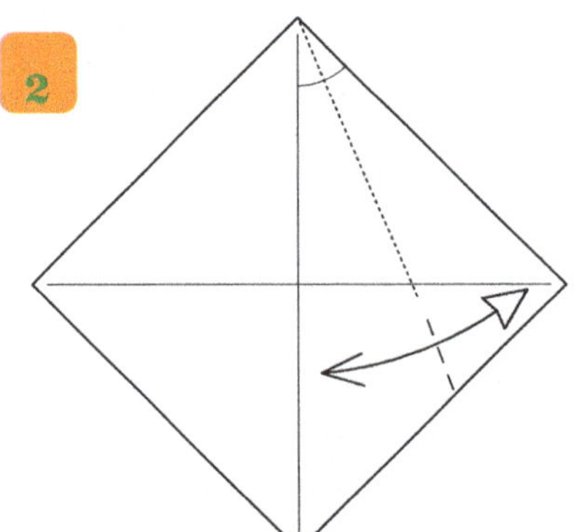

Fold and unfold
on the edge.

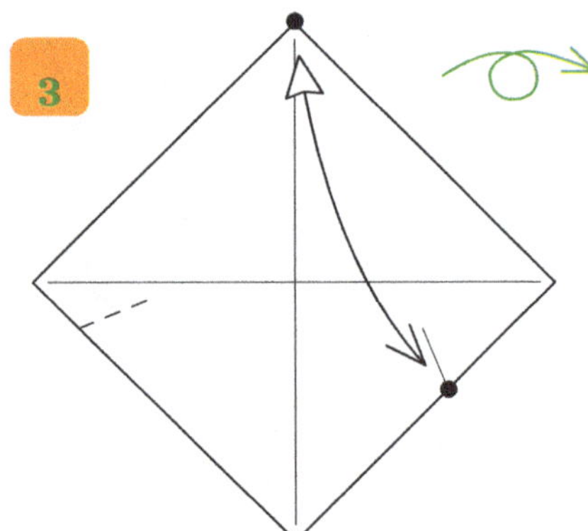

Fold and unfold
on the edge.

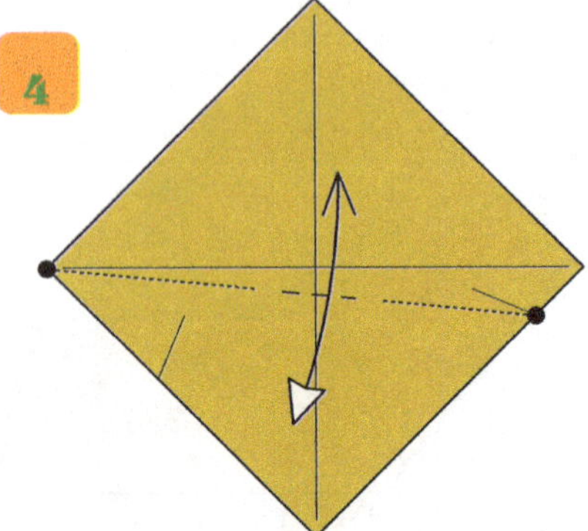

Fold and unfold
on the diagonal.

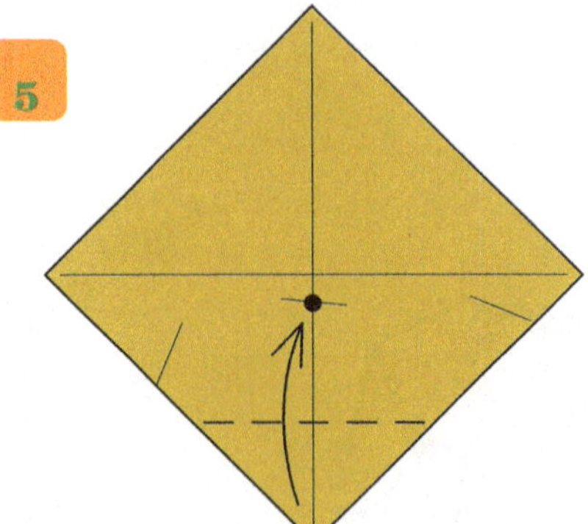

The dots will meet.

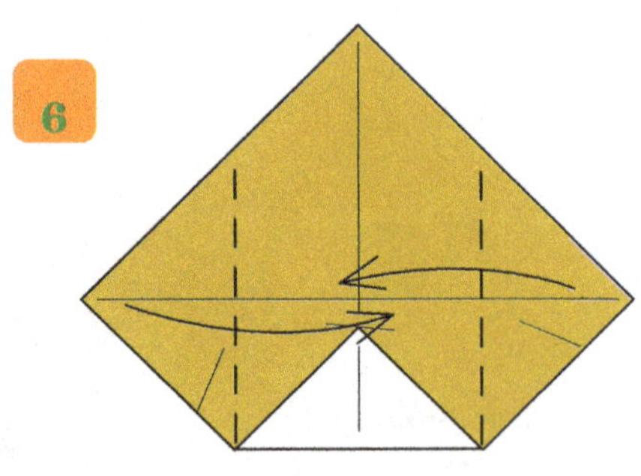

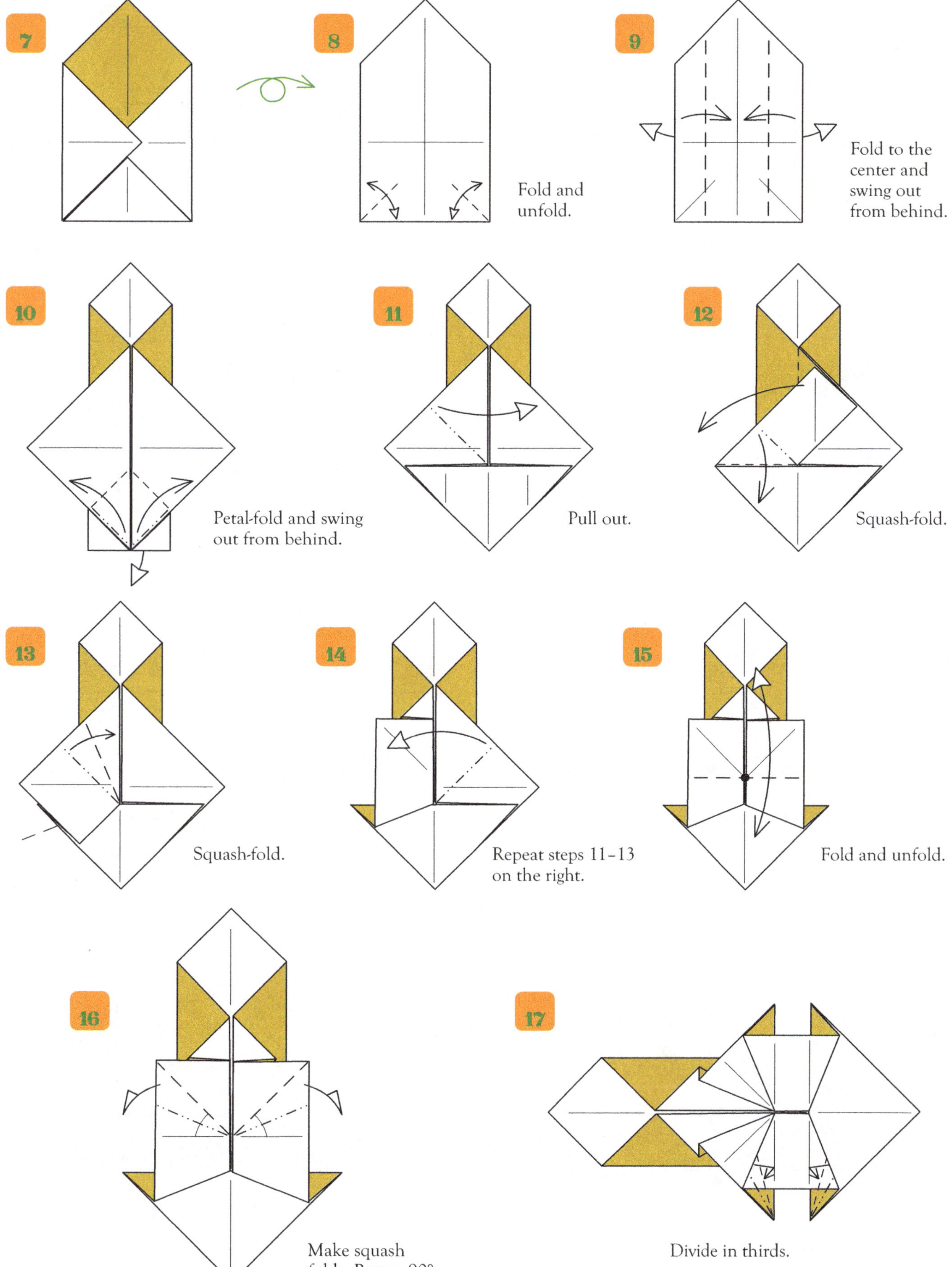

7

8

Fold and unfold.

9

Fold to the center and swing out from behind.

10

Petal-fold and swing out from behind.

11

Pull out.

12

Squash-fold.

13

Squash-fold.

14

Repeat steps 11–13 on the right.

15

Fold and unfold.

16

Make squash folds. Rotate 90°.

17

Divide in thirds.

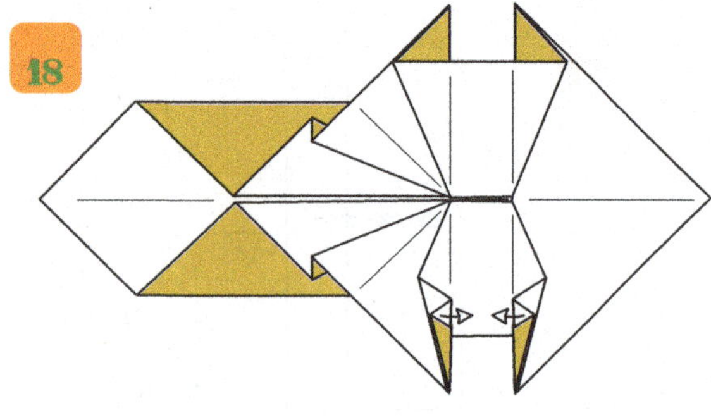

Unfold.

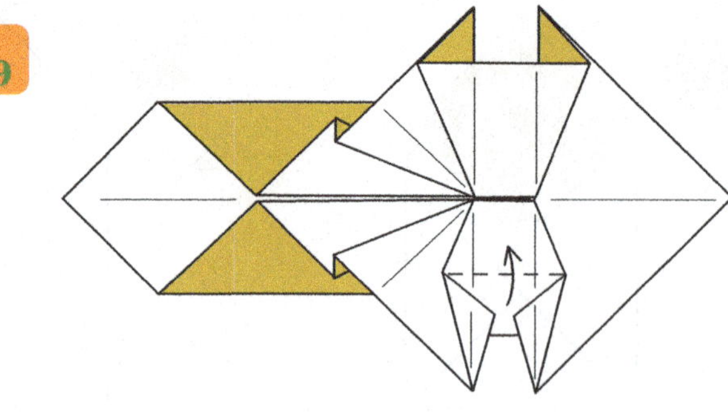

Lift up.

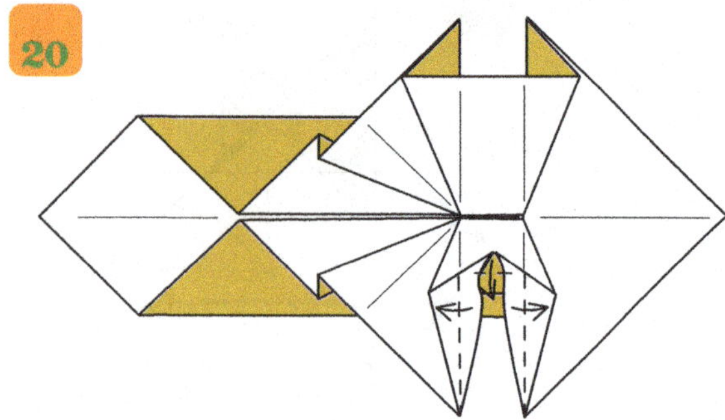

This is 3D. Flatten.

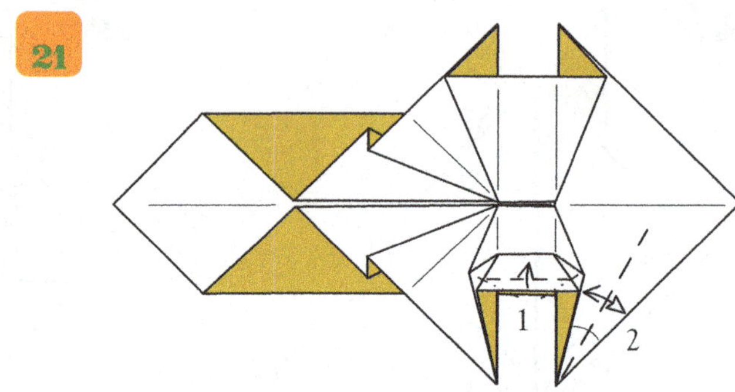

1. Make a thin petal fold.
2. Fold and unfold all the layers.

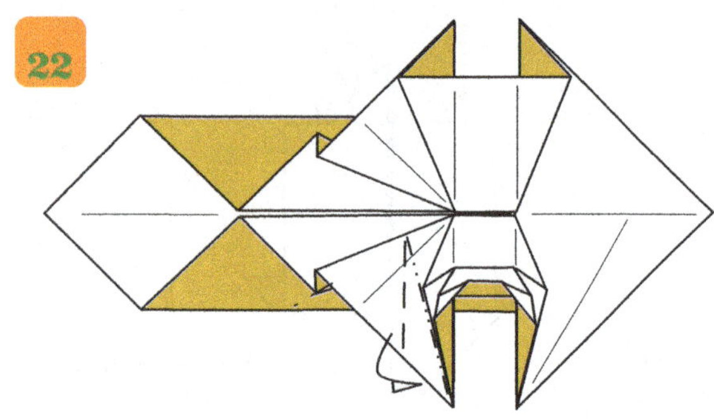

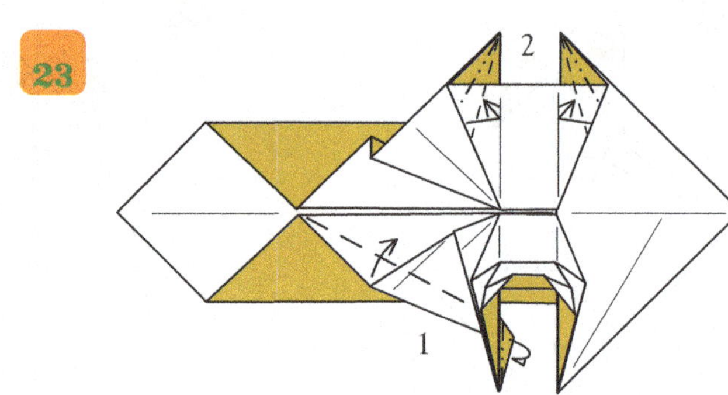

1. Thin the leg.
2. Repeat steps 17–23
   on the top.

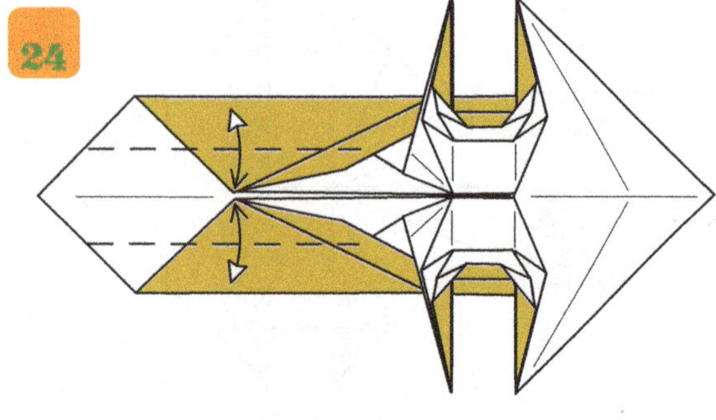

Fold to the center
and unfold.

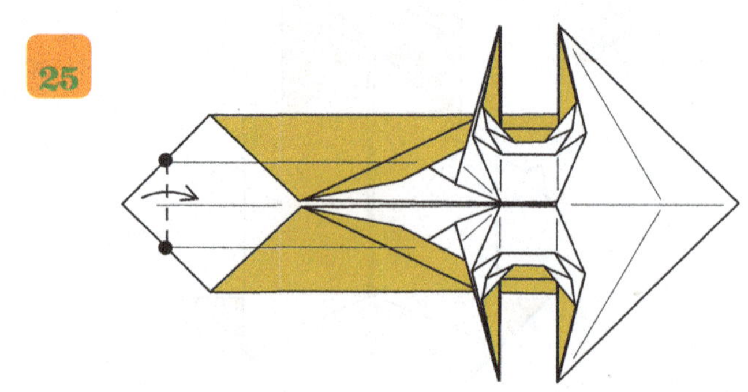

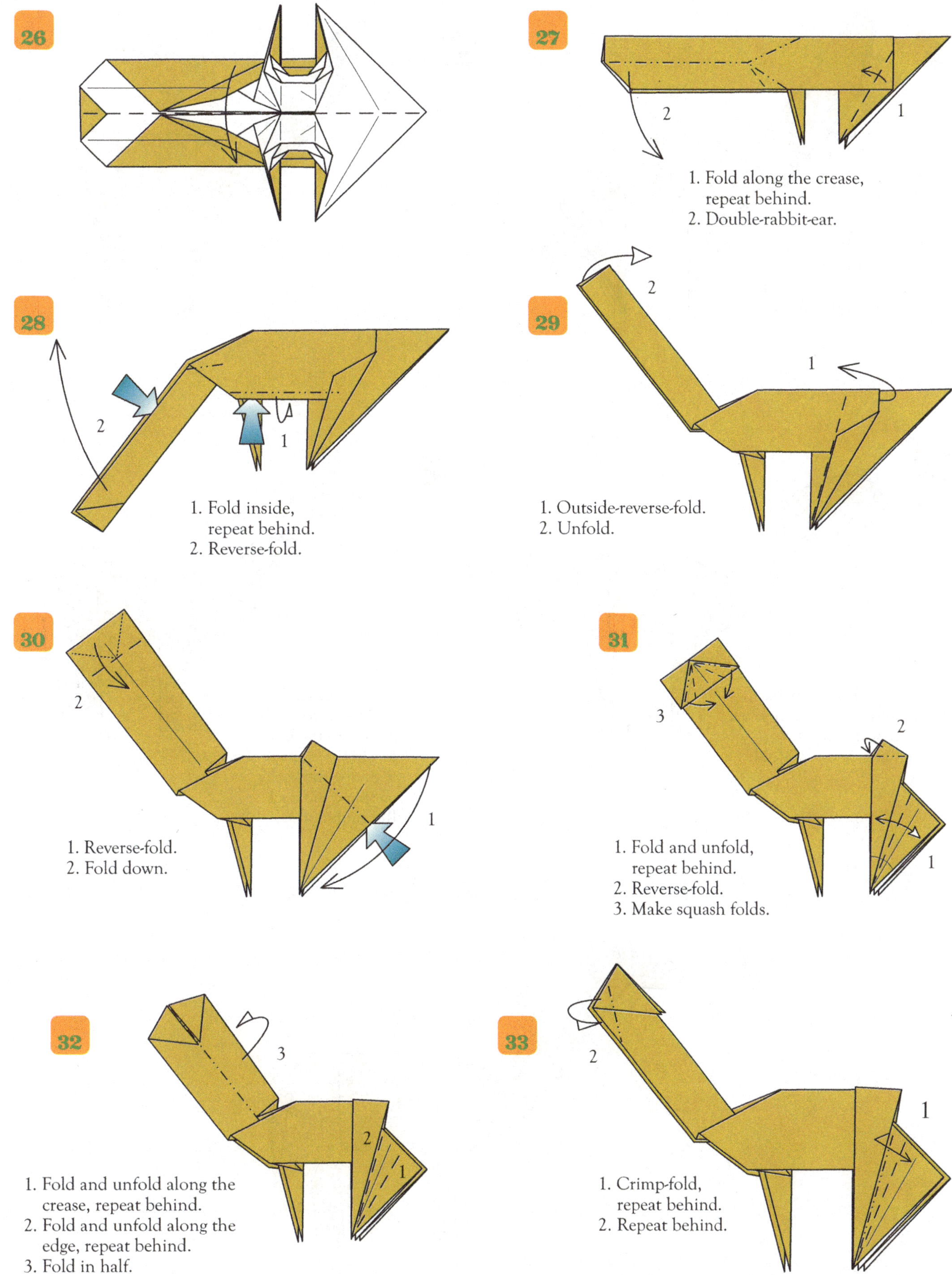
26
27
1. Fold along the crease,
repeat behind.
2. Double-rabbit-ear.
28
1. Fold inside,
repeat behind.
2. Reverse-fold.
29
1. Outside-reverse-fold.
2. Unfold.
30
1. Reverse-fold.
2. Fold down.
31
1. Fold and unfold,
repeat behind.
2. Reverse-fold.
3. Make squash folds.
32
1. Fold and unfold along the
crease, repeat behind.
2. Fold and unfold along the
edge, repeat behind.
3. Fold in half.
33
1. Crimp-fold,
repeat behind.
2. Repeat behind.

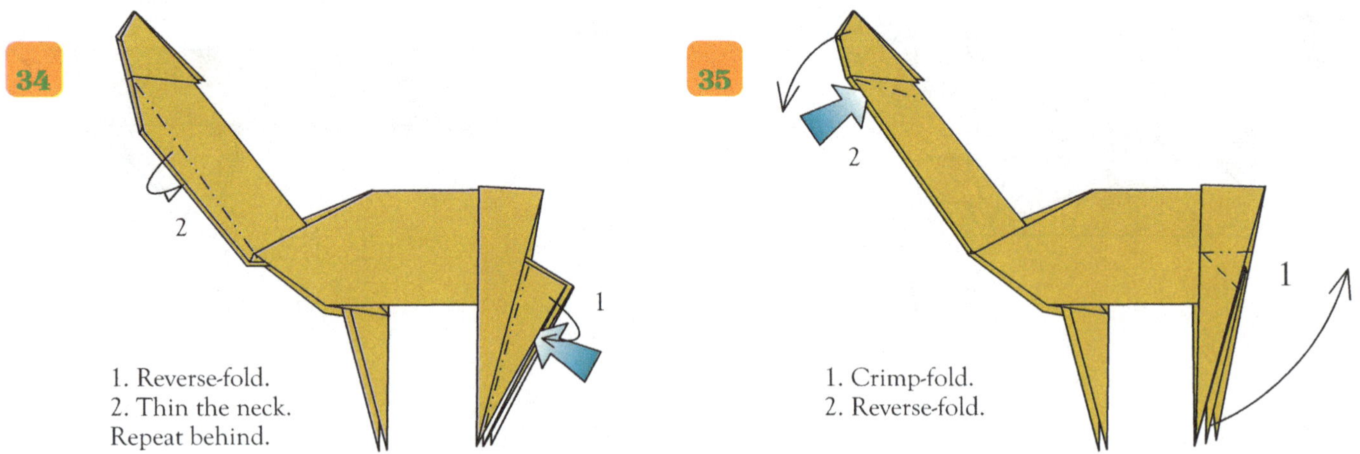

34

1. Reverse-fold.
2. Thin the neck.
Repeat behind.

35

1. Crimp-fold.
2. Reverse-fold.

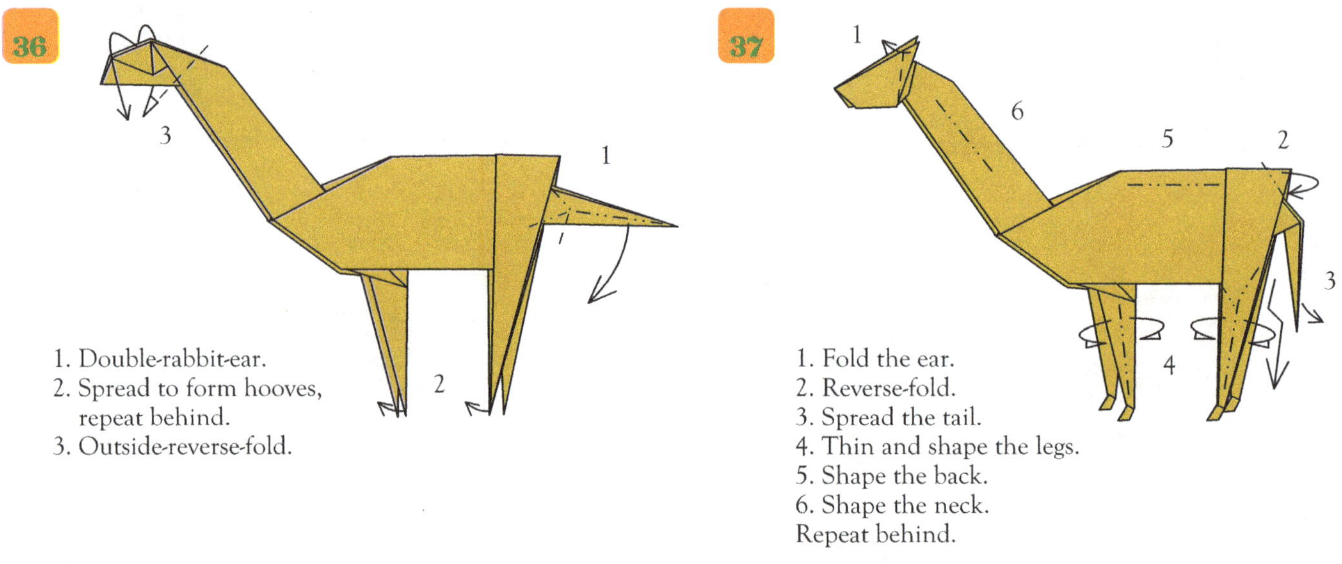

36

1. Double-rabbit-ear.
2. Spread to form hooves,
   repeat behind.
3. Outside-reverse-fold.

37

1. Fold the ear.
2. Reverse-fold.
3. Spread the tail.
4. Thin and shape the legs.
5. Shape the back.
6. Shape the neck.
Repeat behind.

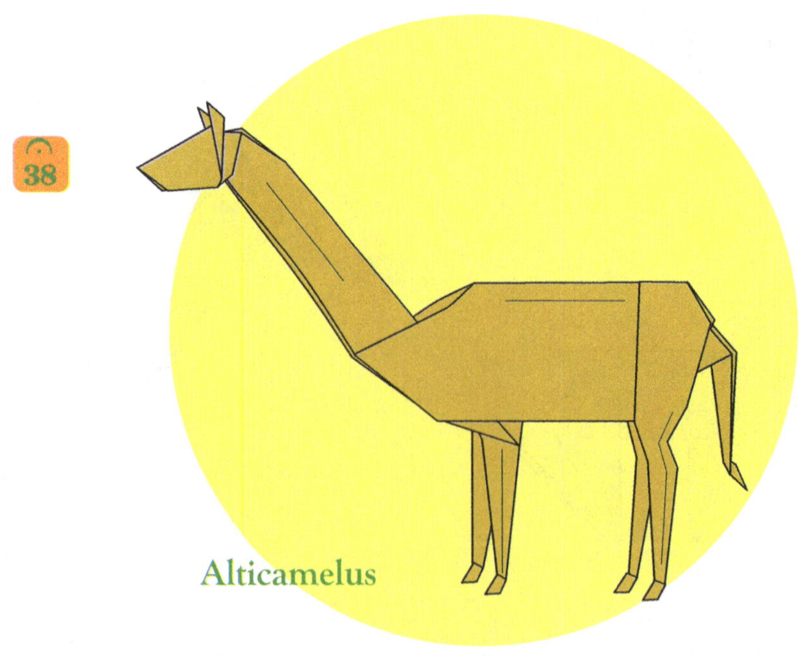

38

Alticamelus

Smilodon

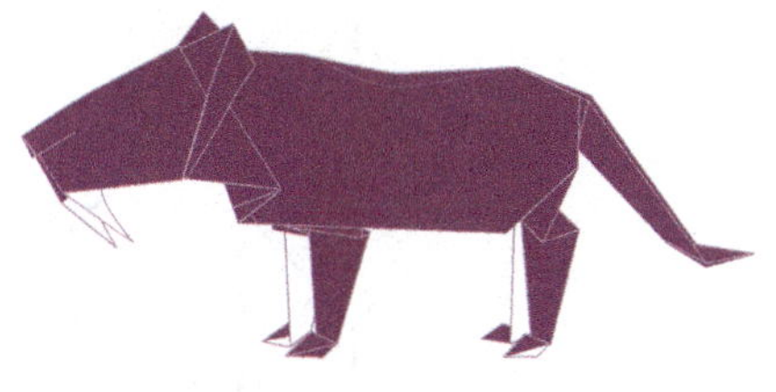

Also known as the famous Saber-Toothed Tiger, the Smilodon is actually not related to modern Cats, nor was it a Tiger. These ferocious creatures hunted Camels and Bison and other large herbivores.

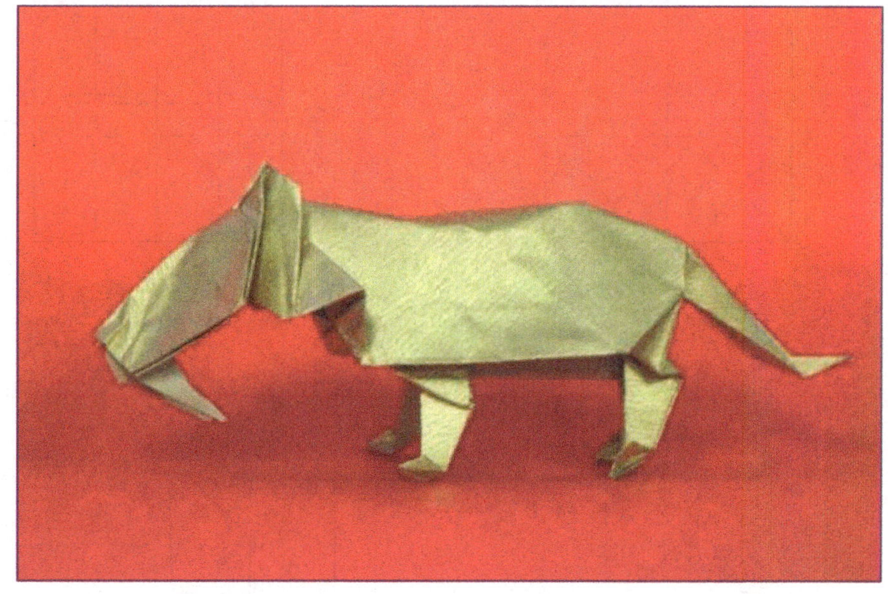

1

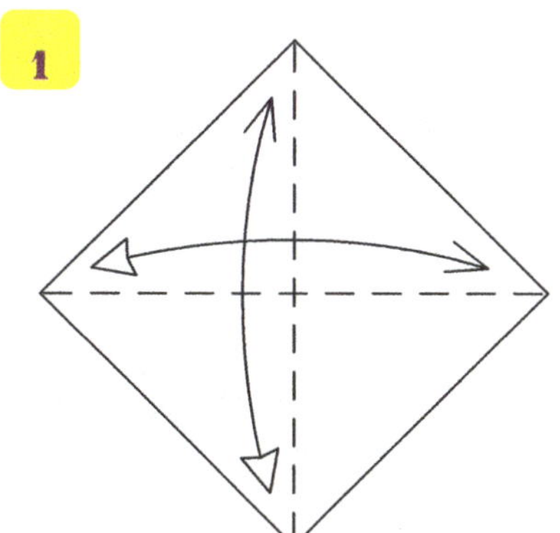

Fold and unfold.

2

Fold to the center and unfold.

3

Fold and unfold to find the quarter mark.

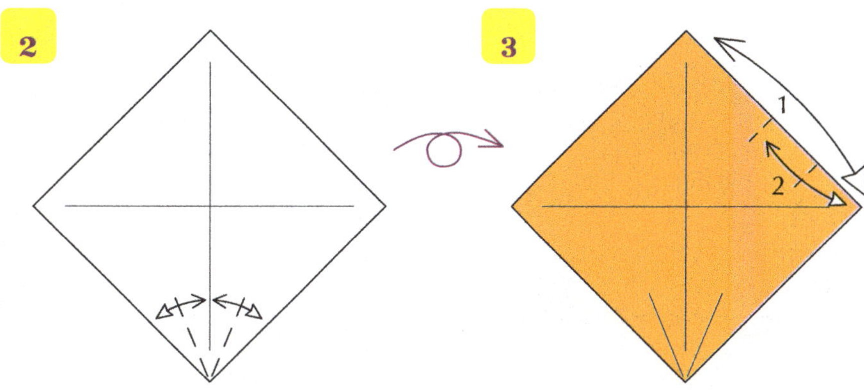

4

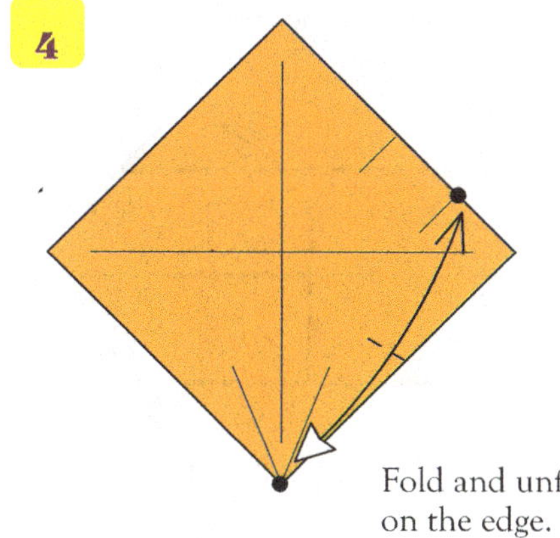

Fold and unfold on the edge.

5

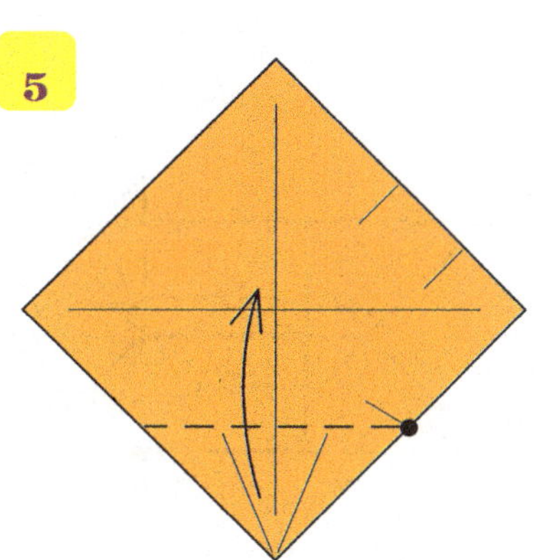

6

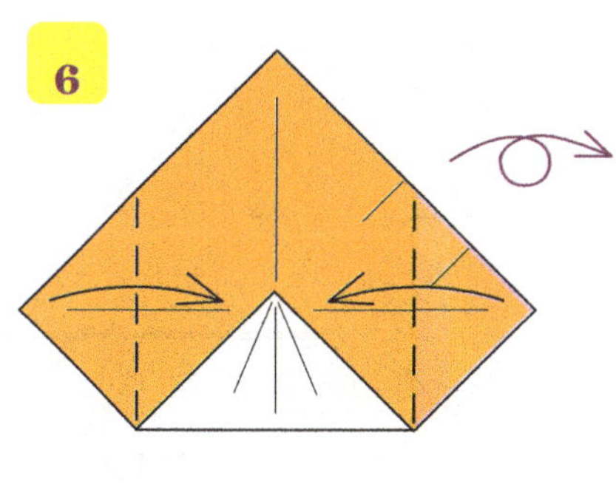

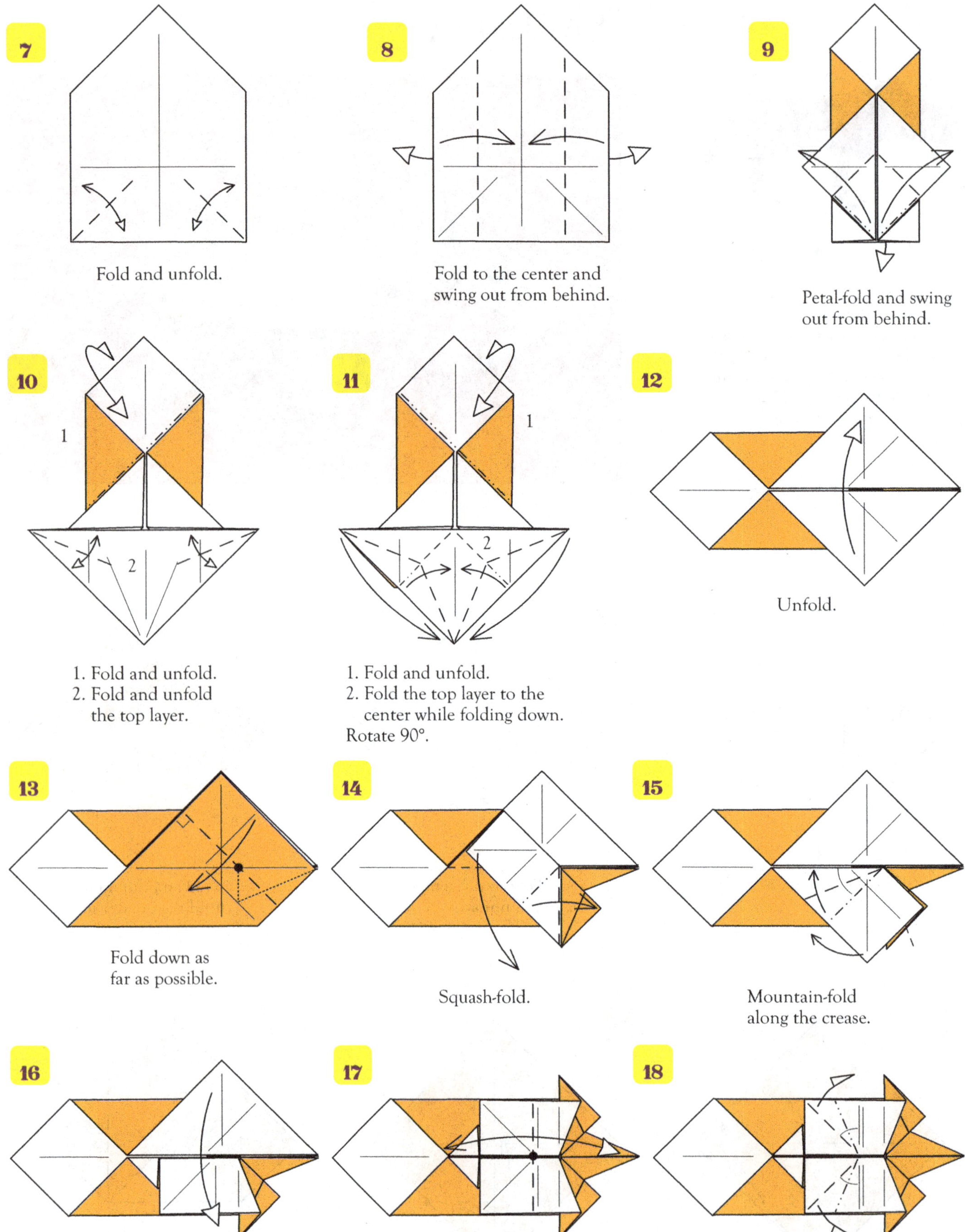

7 Fold and unfold.

8 Fold to the center and swing out from behind.

9 Petal-fold and swing out from behind.

10
1. Fold and unfold.
2. Fold and unfold the top layer.

11
1. Fold and unfold.
2. Fold the top layer to the center while folding down. Rotate 90°.

12 Unfold.

13 Fold down as far as possible.

14 Squash-fold.

15 Mountain-fold along the crease.

16 Repeat steps 12–15 on the top.

17 Fold and unfold.

18 Make squash folds.

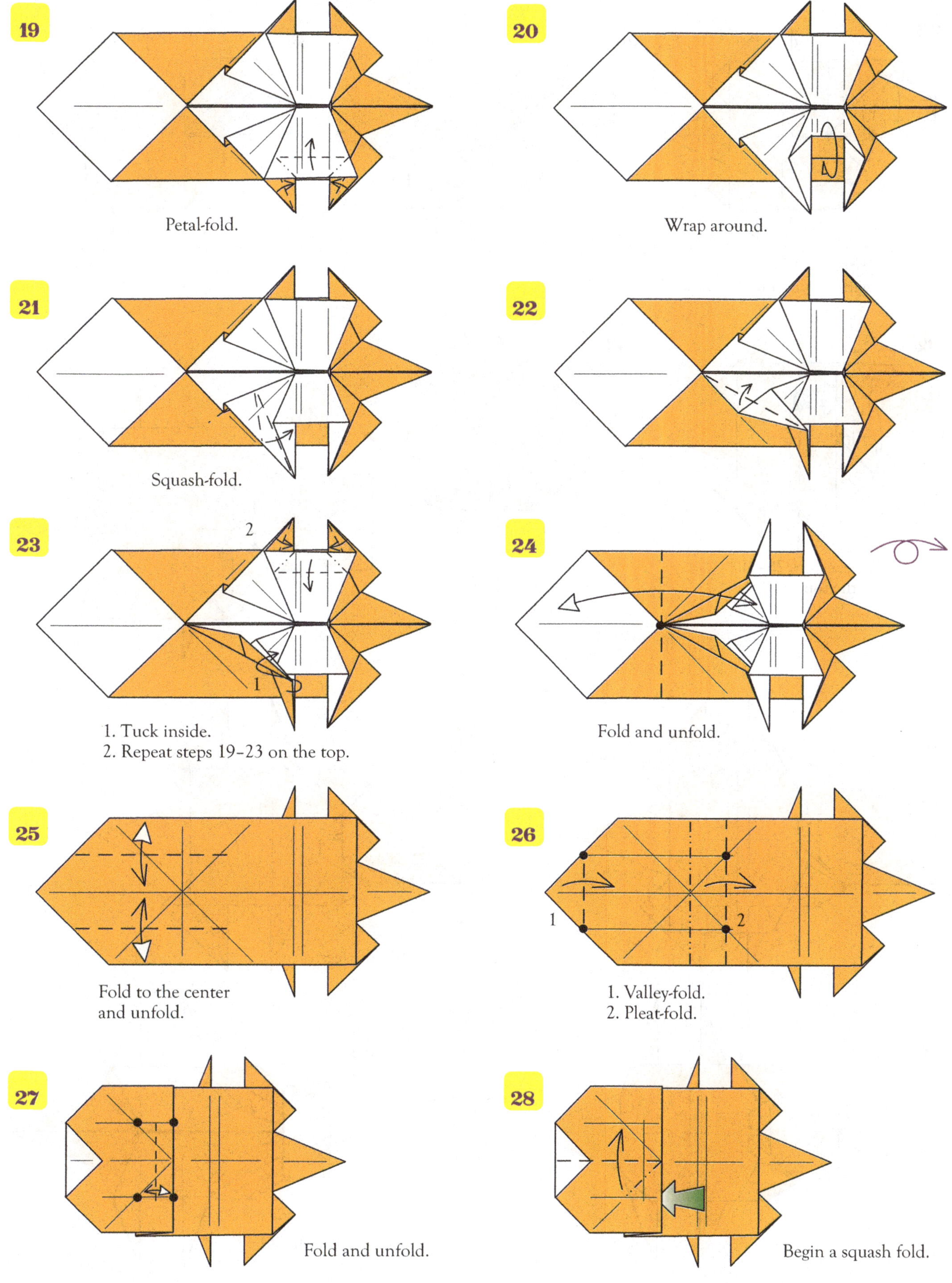

19 Petal-fold.

20 Wrap around.

21 Squash-fold.

22

23
1. Tuck inside.
2. Repeat steps 19–23 on the top.

24 Fold and unfold.

25 Fold to the center and unfold.

26
1. Valley-fold.
2. Pleat-fold.

27 Fold and unfold.

28 Begin a squash fold.

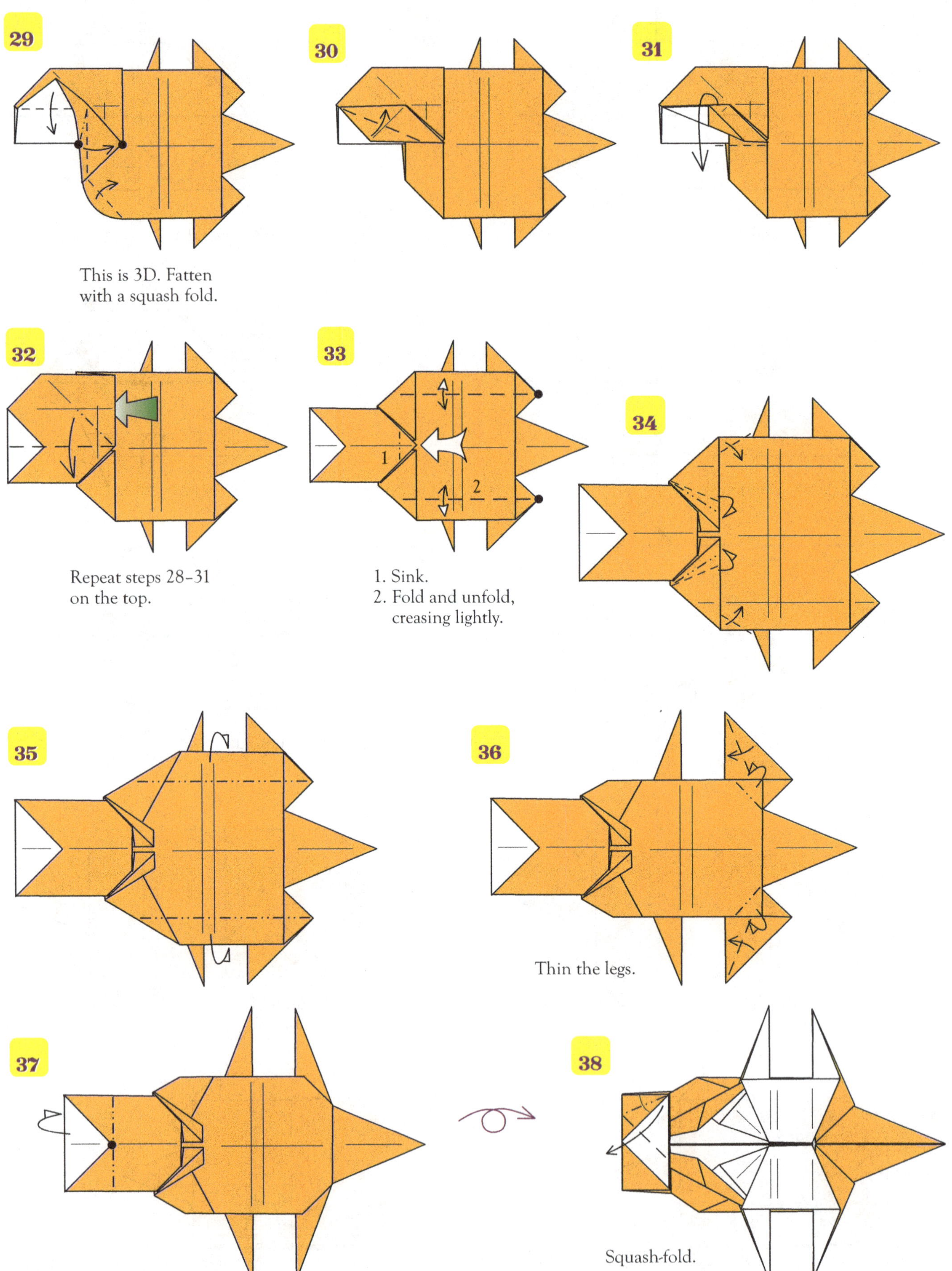

This is 3D. Fatten
with a squash fold.

Repeat steps 28–31
on the top.

1. Sink.
2. Fold and unfold,
   creasing lightly.

Thin the legs.

Squash-fold.

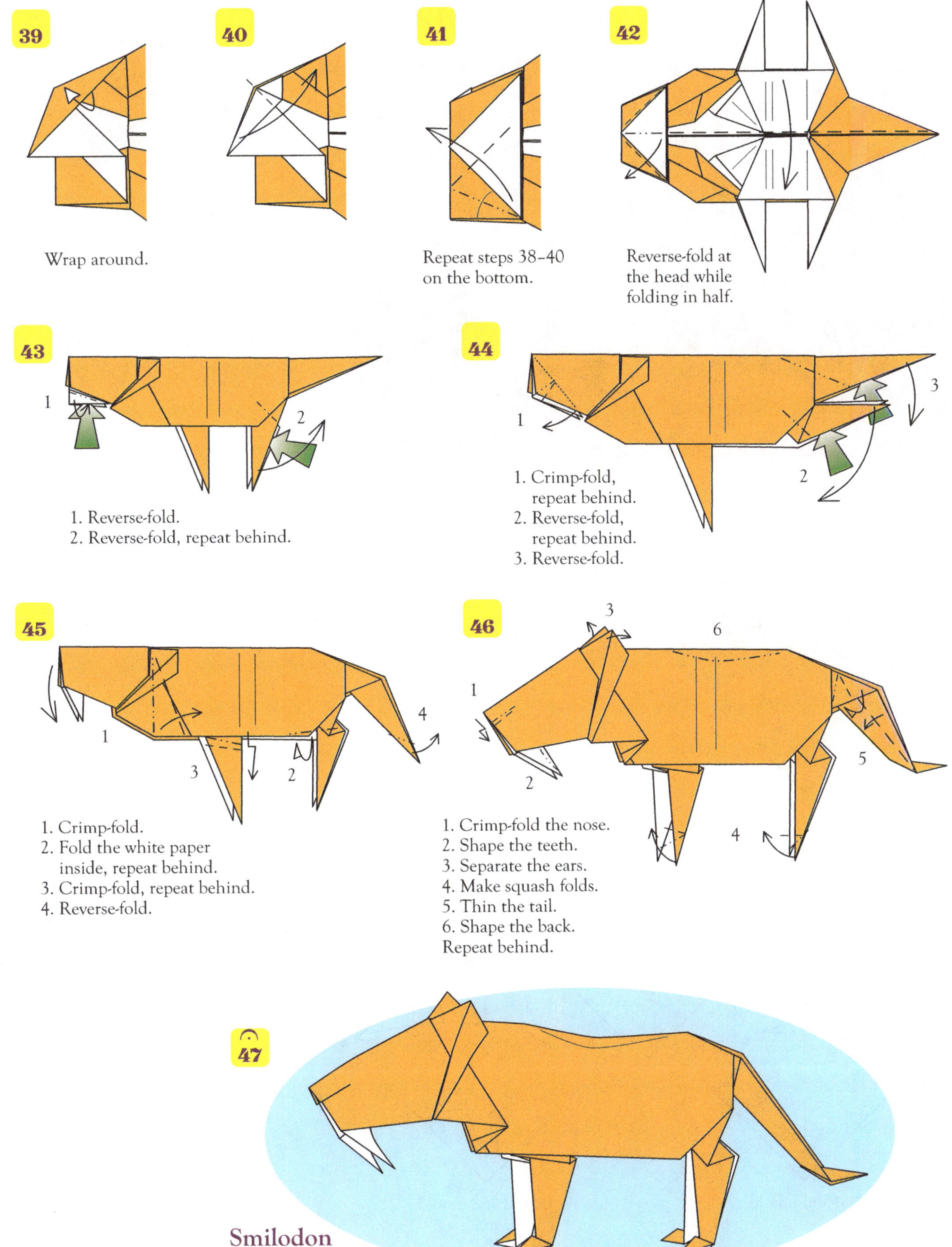

39

Wrap around.

40

41

Repeat steps 38–40
on the bottom.

42

Reverse-fold at
the head while
folding in half.

43

1. Reverse-fold.
2. Reverse-fold, repeat behind.

44

1. Crimp-fold,
   repeat behind.
2. Reverse-fold,
   repeat behind.
3. Reverse-fold.

45

1. Crimp-fold.
2. Fold the white paper
   inside, repeat behind.
3. Crimp-fold, repeat behind.
4. Reverse-fold.

46

1. Crimp-fold the nose.
2. Shape the teeth.
3. Separate the ears.
4. Make squash folds.
5. Thin the tail.
6. Shape the back.
Repeat behind.

47

Smilodon

Woolly Mammoth

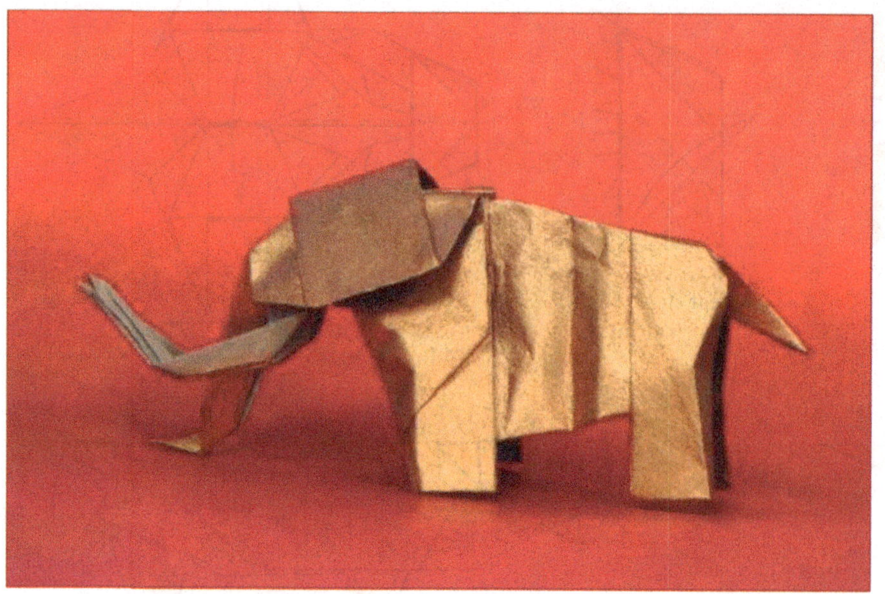

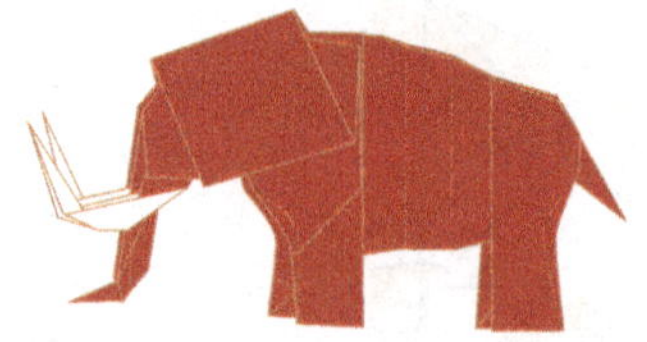

A large, furry relative of the Elephant, the Woolly Mammoth lived alongside early Humans and was used by Humans as food, to make tools from its bones and as the subject of early art.

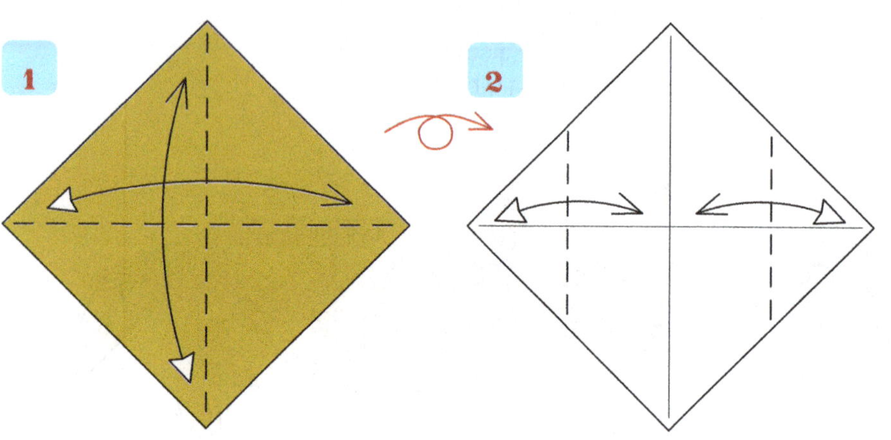

1 Fold and unfold.

2 Fold to the center and unfold.

3 Fold to the center and unfold.

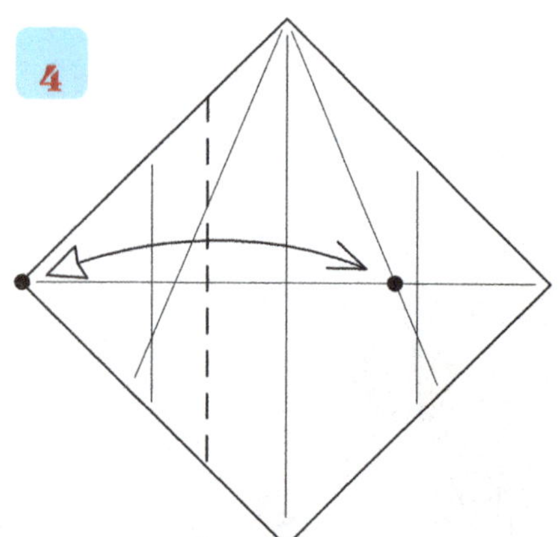

4 Fold and unfold.

5
1. Fold and unfold.
2. Fold up.
Rotate 180°.

6 The dots will meet.

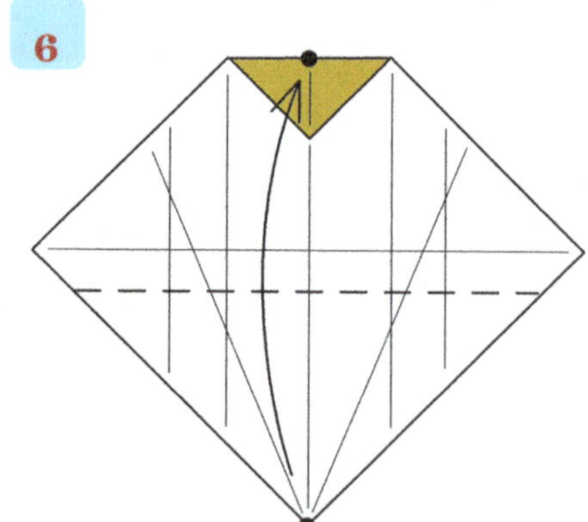

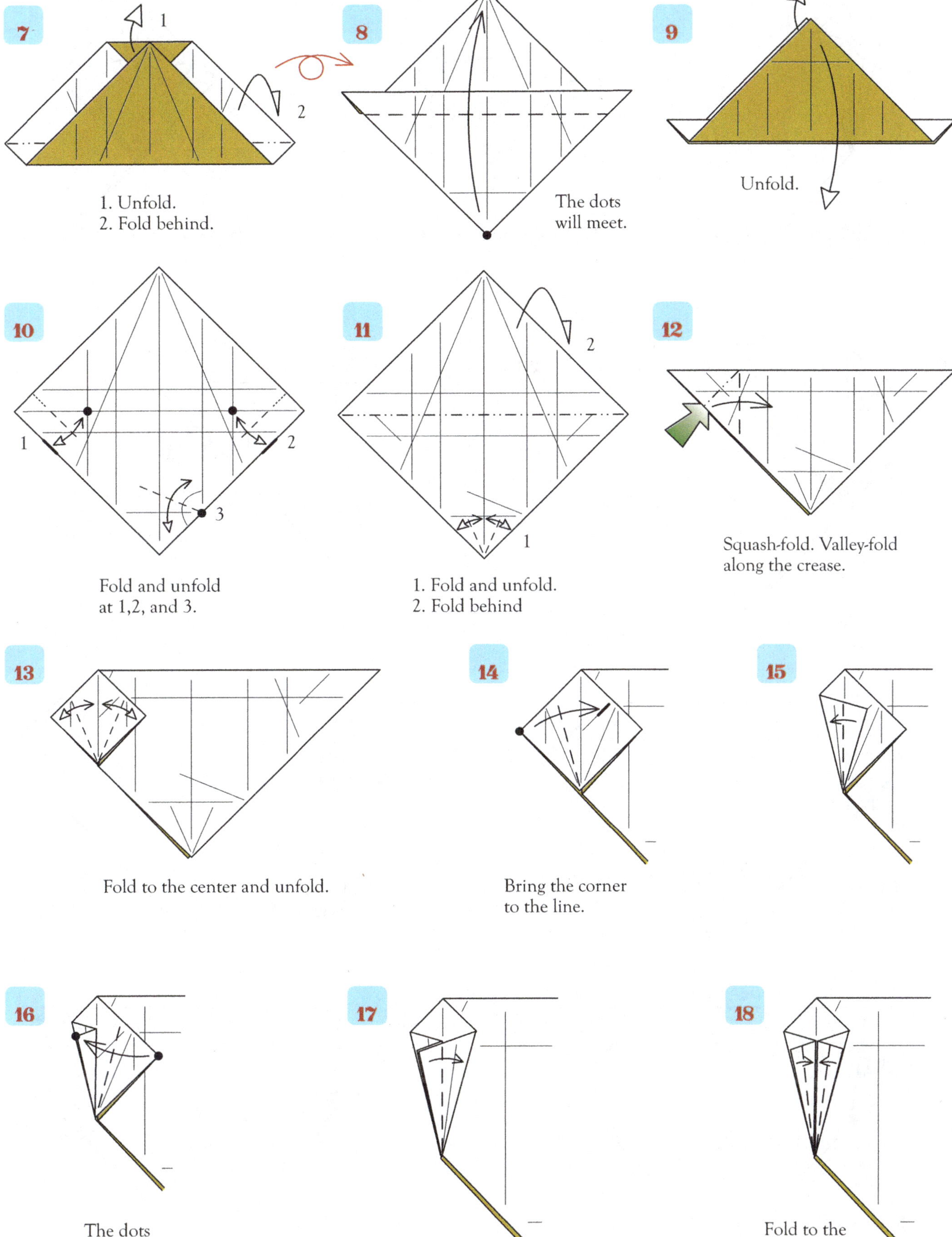

7
1. Unfold.
2. Fold behind.

8
The dots will meet.

9
Unfold.

10
Fold and unfold at 1, 2, and 3.

11
1. Fold and unfold.
2. Fold behind

12
Squash-fold. Valley-fold along the crease.

13
Fold to the center and unfold.

14
Bring the corner to the line.

15

16
The dots will meet.

17

18
Fold to the center.

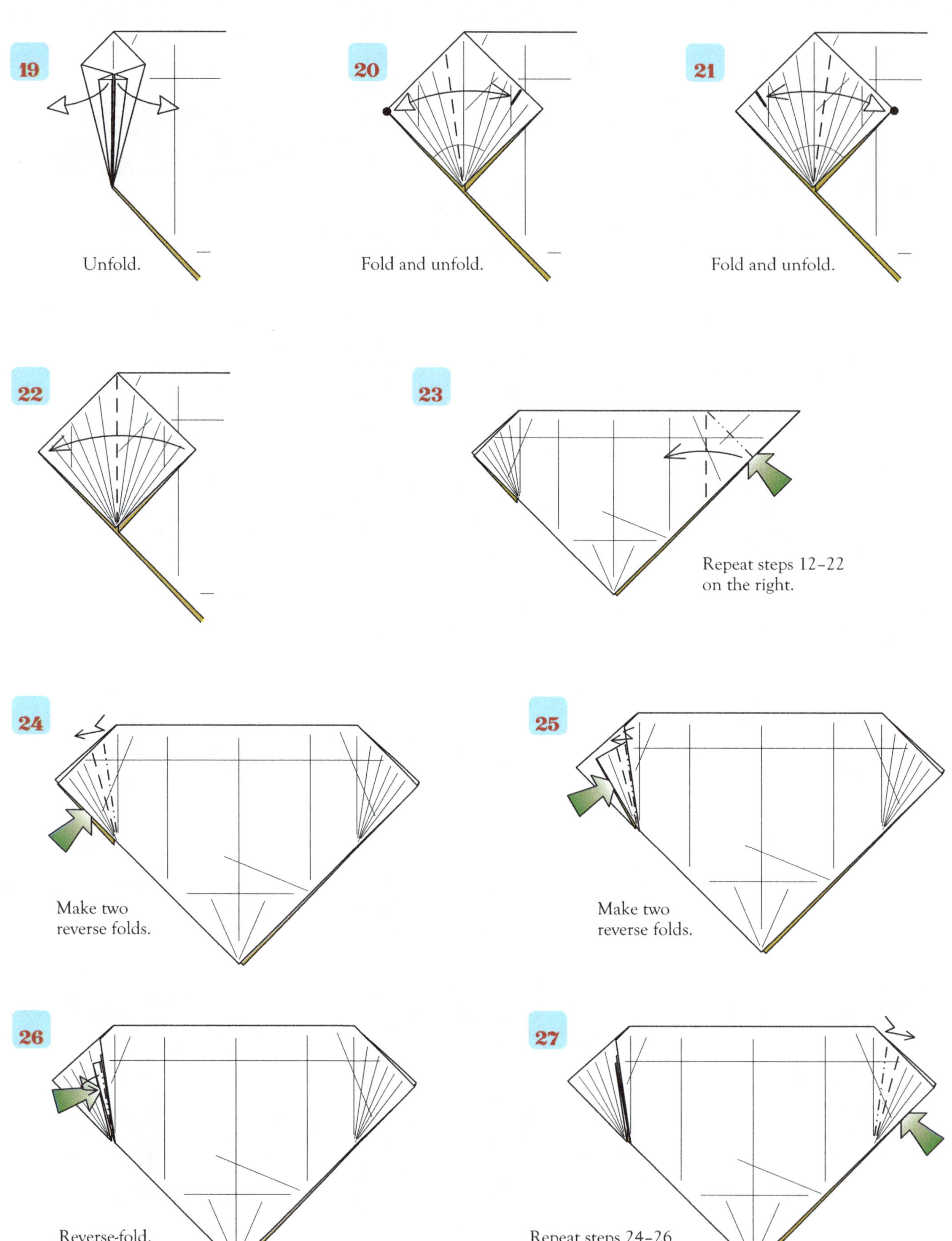

19
Unfold.
20
Fold and unfold.
21
Fold and unfold.
22
23
Repeat steps 12–22
on the right.
24
Make two
reverse folds.
25
Make two
reverse folds.
26
Reverse-fold.
27
Repeat steps 24–26
three times, behind
and on the right.

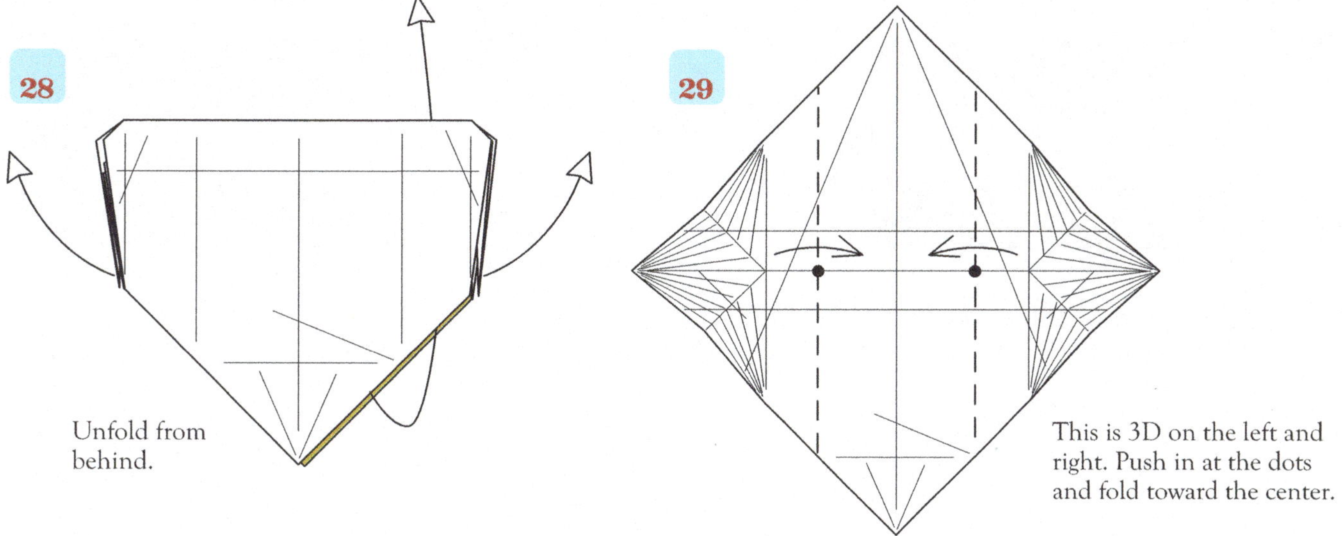

28

Unfold from behind.

29

This is 3D on the left and right. Push in at the dots and fold toward the center.

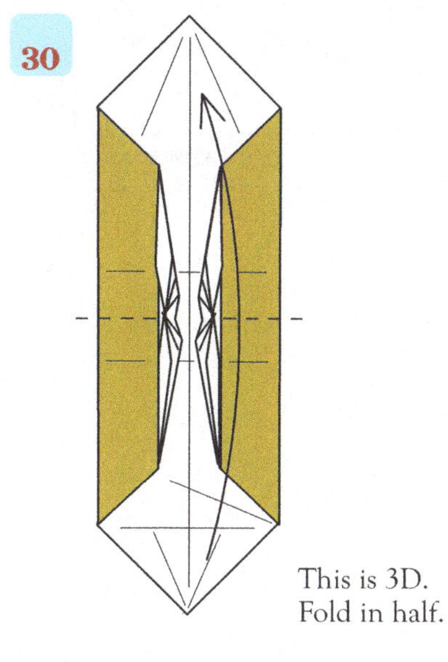

30

This is 3D.
Fold in half.

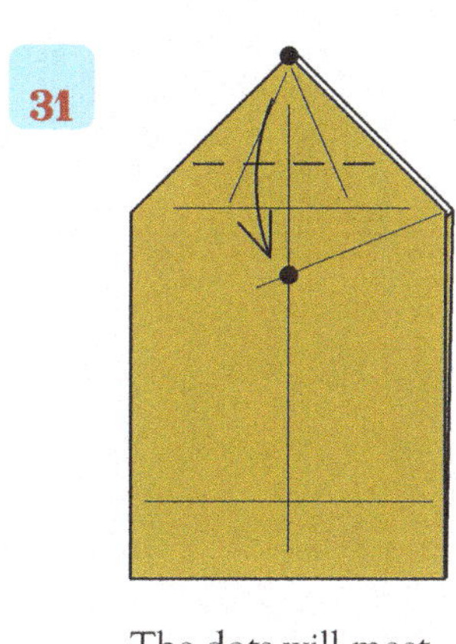

31

The dots will meet.

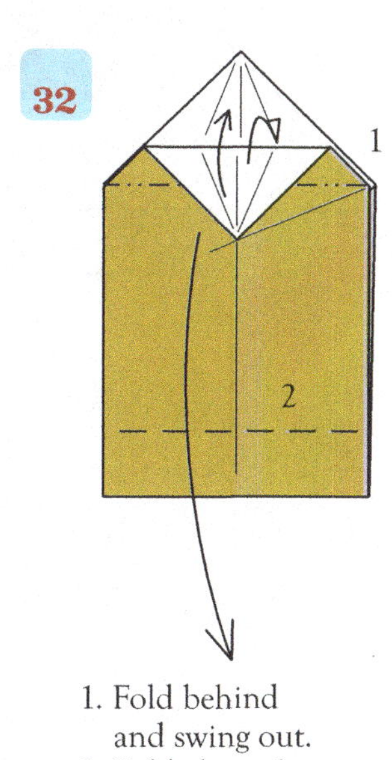

32

1. Fold behind and swing out.
2. Fold along the crease.

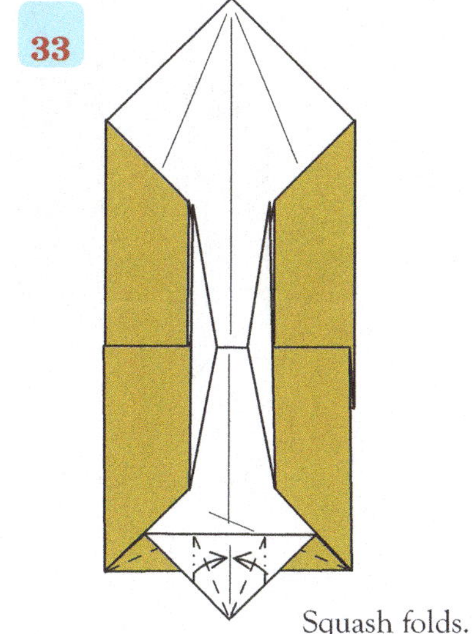

33

Squash folds.

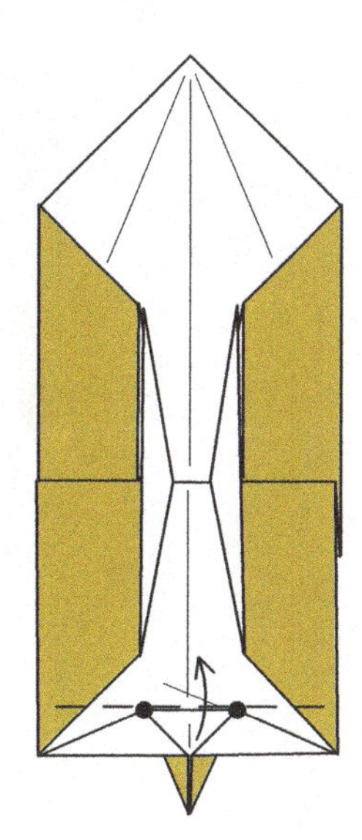

34

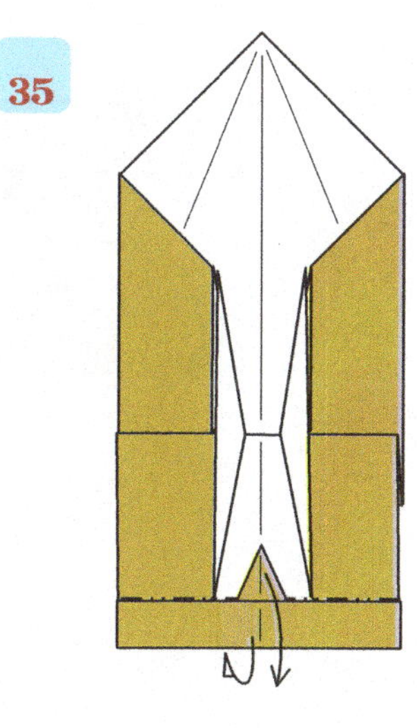

35

Rotate 90°.

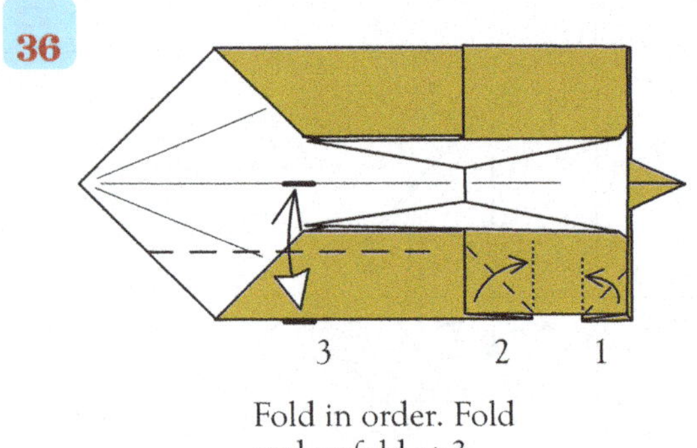

Fold in order. Fold
and unfold at 3.

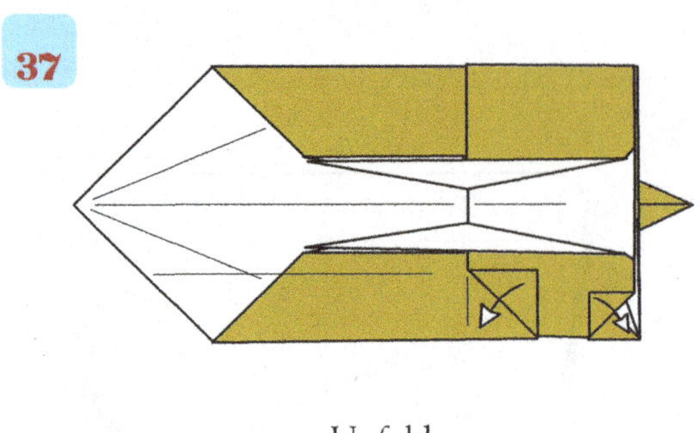

Unfold.

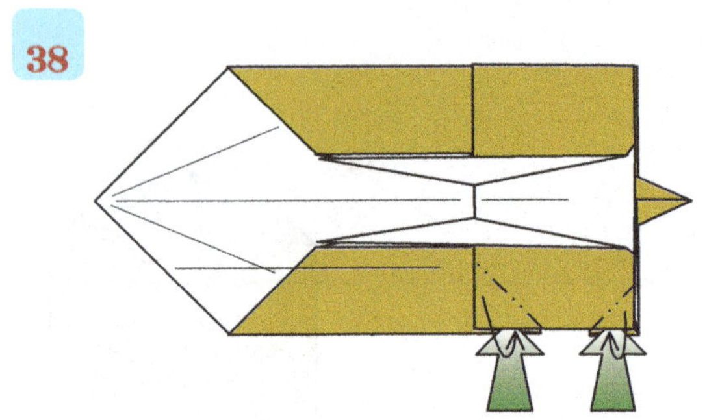

Reverse folds.

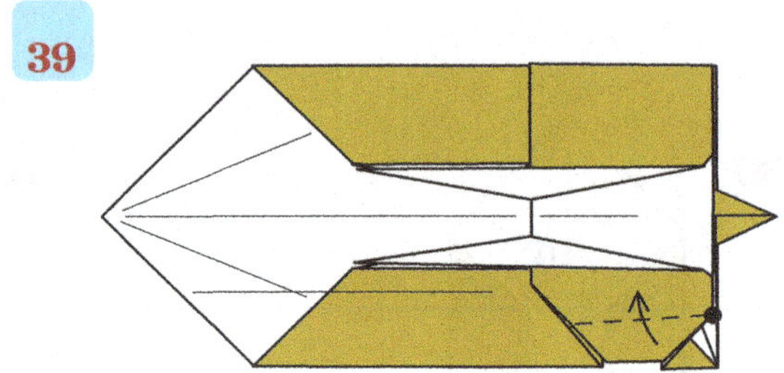

Fold up at an angle and
spread the paper at the dot.

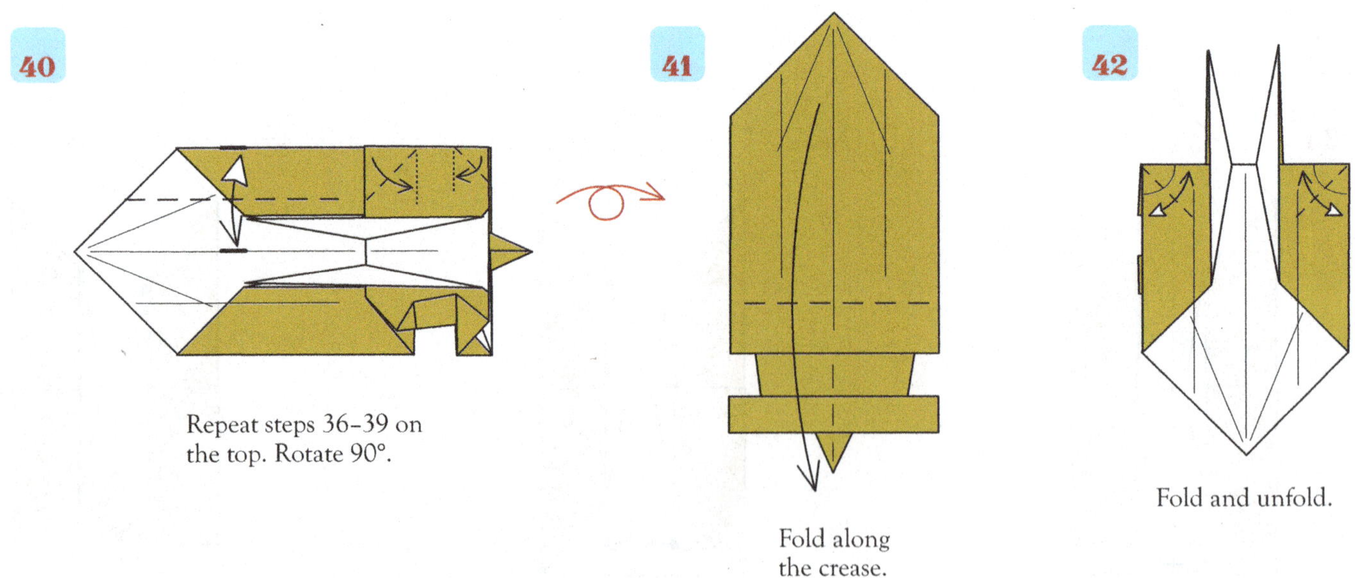

Repeat steps 36–39 on
the top. Rotate 90°.

Fold along
the crease.

Fold and unfold.

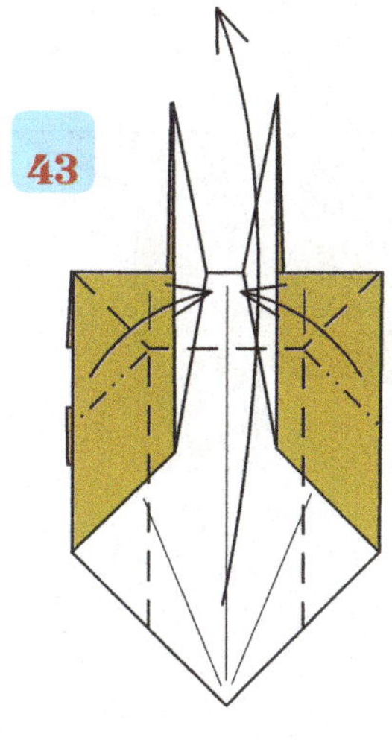

43

Fold along
the creases.

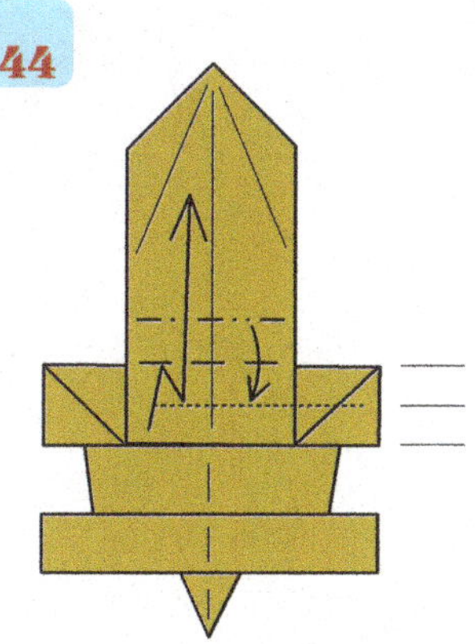

44

Pleat-fold to the
center of the region.

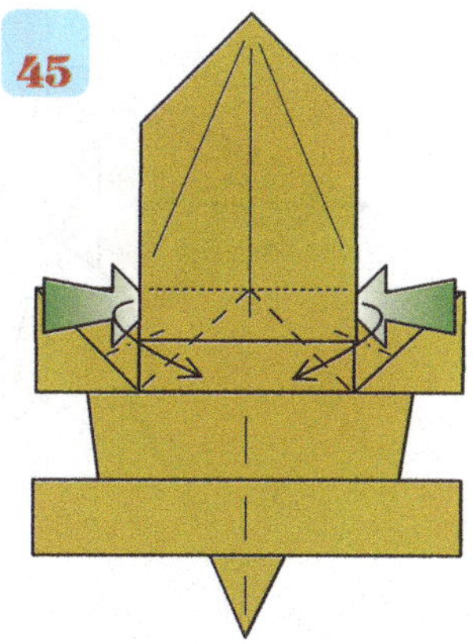

45

This is similar
to reverse folds.

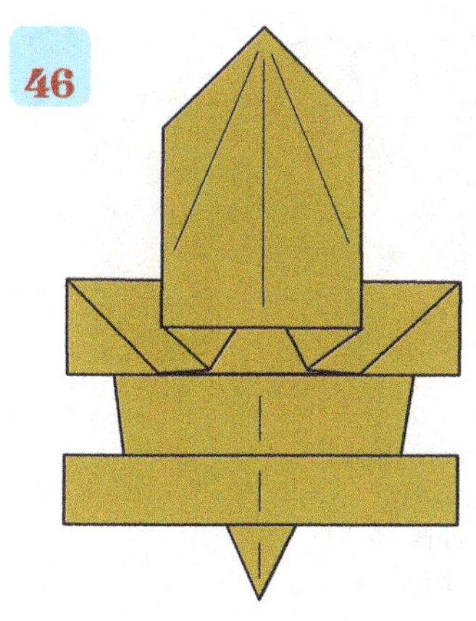

46

Rotate 90°.

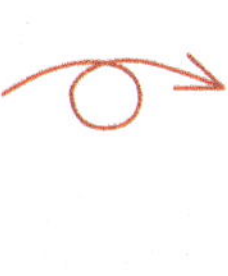

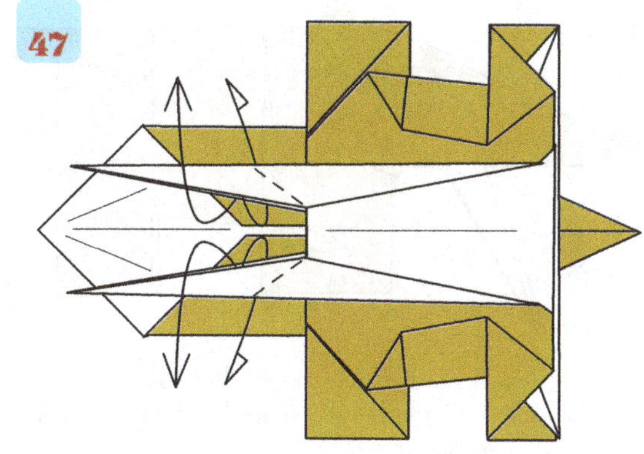

47

Outside-reverse folds.

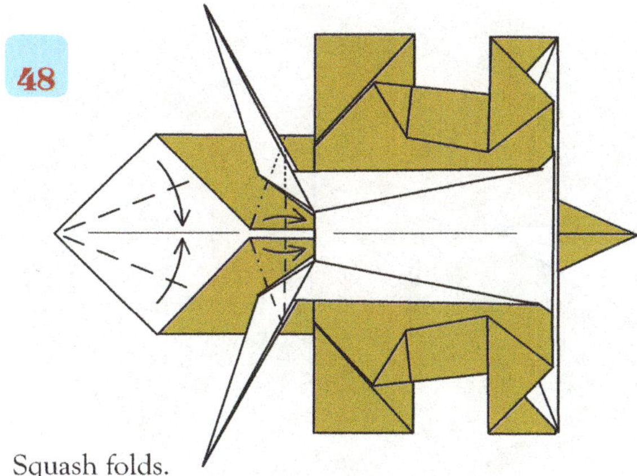

48

Squash folds.

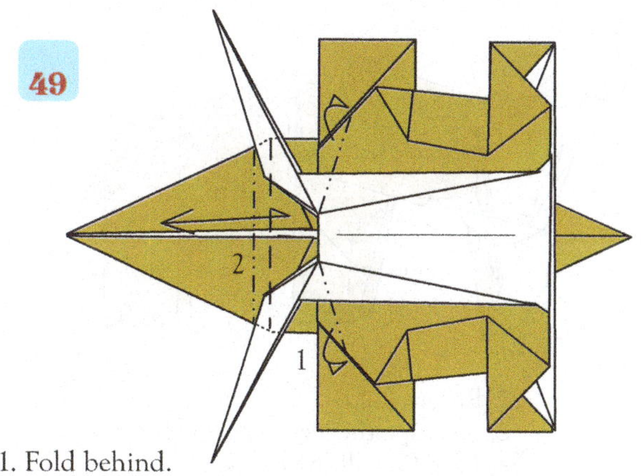

49

1. Fold behind.
2. Make a thin
   pleat fold.

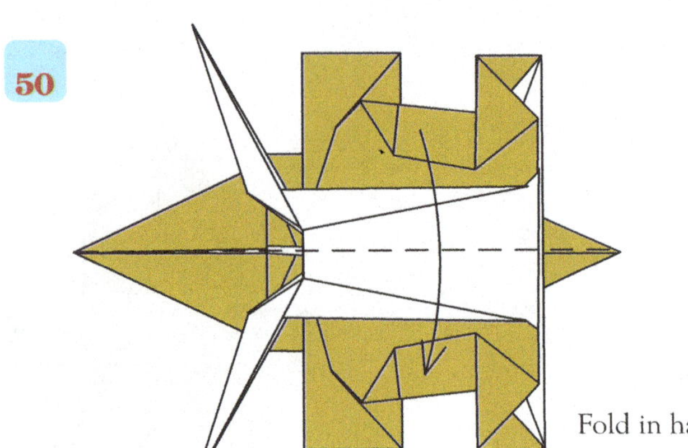

Fold in half.

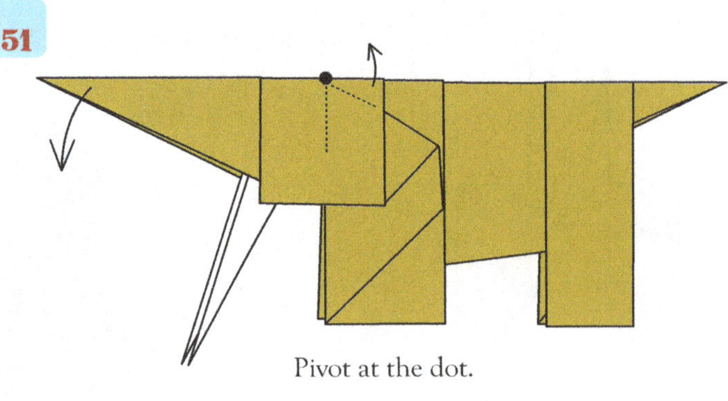

Pivot at the dot.

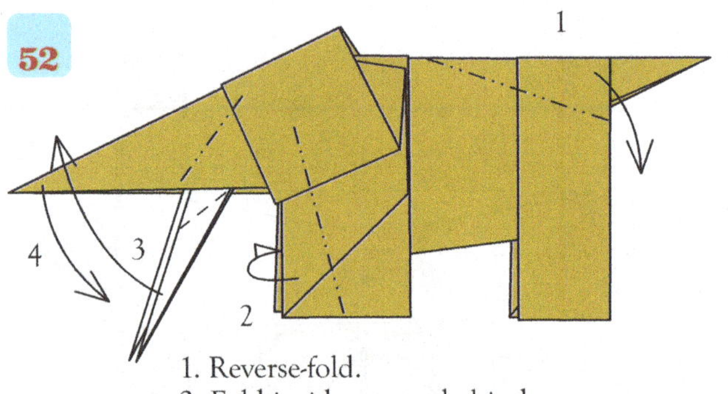

1. Reverse-fold.
2. Fold inside, repeat behind.
3. Outside-reverse-fold, repeat behind.
4. Reverse-fold.

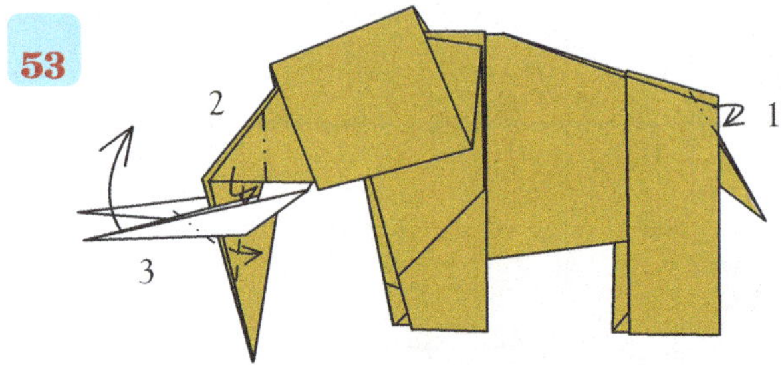

1. Reverse-fold.
2. Thin the trunk.
3. Reverse-fold.
Repeat behind.

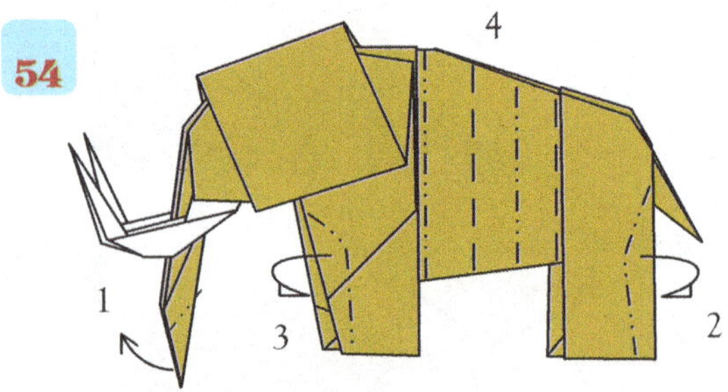

1. Reverse-fold.
2, 3. Shape the legs, repeat behind.
4. Pleat-fold all the layers.

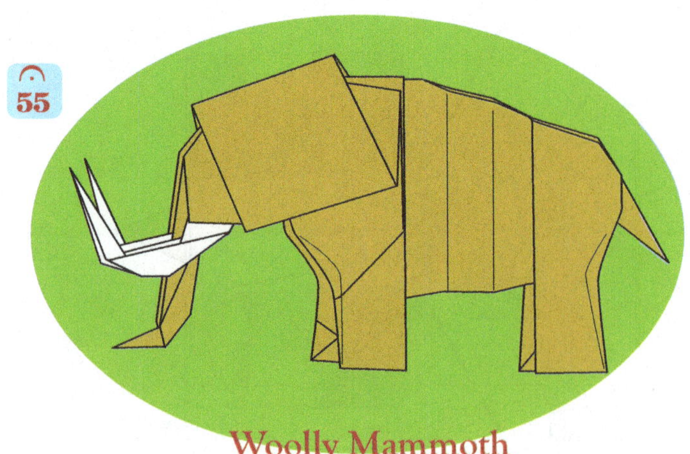

Woolly Mammoth

Made in the USA
Monee, IL
07 July 2026

56553287R00072